RADICAL
ISLAM
IN
EGYPT AND
JORDAN

RADICAL
ISLAM
IN
EGYPT AND
JORDAN

NACHMAN TAL

sussex
ACADEMIC
PRESS

BRIGHTON • PORTLAND

JAFFEE CENTER FOR
STRATEGIC STUDIES

2 4 6 8 10 9 7 5 3 1

First published 2005 in Great Britain by
SUSSEX ACADEMIC PRESS
PO Box 2950
Brighton BN2 5SP

and in the United States of America by
SUSSEX ACADEMIC PRESS
920 NE 58th Ave   Suite 300
Portland, Oregon 97213–3786

British Library Cataloguing in Publication Data
A CIP catalogue record for this book is available from the British Library.

Library of Congress Cataloging-in-Publication Data
Radical Islam in Egypt and Jordan / Nachman Tal.
    p. cm.
Includes bibliographical references and index.
ISBN 1-84519-052-1 (hardcover : alk. paper) —
ISBN 1-84519-098-X (pbk. : alk paper)
    1. Jam'åiyat al-Ikhwåan al-Muslimåin (Egypt) 2. Islamic fundamentalism—Egypt. 3. Terrorism—Government policy—Egypt. 4. Jamåa'at al-Ikhwåan al-Muslimåin (Jordan) 5. Islamic fundamentalism—Jordan. 6. Terrorism—Government policy—Jordan. I. Title.
BP10.J383R33 2005
962.05'5—dc22

                                                    2004020673
                                                    CIP

Typeset and designed by G&G Editorial, Brighton
Printed by MPG Books, Ltd, Bodmin, Cornwall
This book is printed on acid-free paper.

CONTENTS

List of Tables and Figures   vii
Preface   ix

Introduction   1
   The Essence of Fundamentalism   2
   The Crisis of the Faithful   5
   The Threat of Fundamentalism to Current Regimes   7

PART I   RADICAL ISLAM IN EGYPT

1 Egypt and Islamic Fundamentalism   13
   Socio-Economic Background   13
   The Muslim Brotherhood   16
   The Islamic Terrorist Organizations   25

2 Egypt's Struggle against the Muslim Brotherhood   35
   An Unbridgeable Divide   35
   The Confrontation under Nasser and Sadat   37
   Mubarak's Policy of Containment   39
   From Containment to All-Out Confrontation   58
   Suppression of the Muslim Brotherhood, 1998–99   74

3 Islamic Terrorism in Egypt   80
   The Surge of the 1990s   80
   Funding and Armament   88
   The Inclusive Range of Targets   93

4 Egypt Battles Islamic Terrorism   112
    Early Intelligence and Operational Efforts   112
    The Evolution of an Anti-Terrorism Strategy   119
    The Legislature and the Courts   132
    Propaganda and Psychological Warfare   135
    The Inter-Arab and International Arenas   137

5 Egyptian Resistance to Fundamentalism   153

PART II   RADICAL ISLAM IN JORDAN

6 Jordan's Struggle with Subversion and Terrorism   167
    The Hashemite Regime vs. Non-Fundamentalist Opposition   168
    The Rise and Suppression of Islamic Organizations in   171
      the 1990s
    The Regime vs. Palestinian Islamic Jihad Factions   182

7 The Muslim Brotherhood in Jordan   187
    The Movement's Establishment, Goals, and Activity   187
    The Muslim Brotherhood and the Political System   189
    The Palestinian Element within the Muslim Brotherhood   198
    The Challenge of the Peace Process with Israel   199

8 Jordan against the Muslim Brotherhood   203
    From Ally to Opponent   203
    Forming the Response   205
    The Regime's Containment Policy   209
    Deterrent and Stabilizing Factors   227

9 Jordanian Resistance to Fundamentalism   234

Radical Islam in Egypt and Jordan: An Integrative   238
    Conclusion

Notes   246
Bibliography   266
Index   270

TABLES AND FIGURES

Tables

1.1	Islamic Terrorist Organizations by Trend	26
2.1	People's Assembly Election Results, 1984	51
2.2	People's Assembly Election Results, 1987	52
3.1	Tension, Terrorism, and Regime Responses, 1952–93	81
3.2	Terrorism Casualties in Egypt, 1992	83
3.3	Terrorism Casualties in Egypt, 1993	84
3.4	Socio-Economic Profile of Egyptian Islamic Militants, 1970s–1990s	86
3.5	Islamic Violence and Terrorism by Geographic Location, 1970 onward	90
3.6	Foreign Tourist Fatalities, 1992–99	104
3.7	Copts Killed by Terrorists, 1992–99	104
4.1	Terrorism in Egypt – Casualties and Arrests in 1995	123
4.2	Terrorism in Egypt – Casualties and Arrests in 1996	126
4.3	Terrorism Casualties in Egypt, 1997	129
4.4	Terrorism Casualties in Egypt, 1998	130
4.5	Death Sentences in Egypt, 1993	134
4.6	Methods by the Regime to Combat Terrorist Organizations, 1990–99	149
5.1	Breakdown of Terrorism Fatalities, 1990–99	154
5.2	Comparison of the Muslim Brotherhood and Terrorist Organizations in Egypt	162
	The Muslim Brotherhood in Egypt and Jordan	239
	Islamic Violence and Terrorism in Egypt and Jordan	241

Figures

1.1	Structure of the Muslim Brotherhood in Egypt	18
2.1	Islamic and Secular Seats in the Major Trade Unions, 1993	56
4.1	Summary of Terrorism Casualties, 1994	122
5.1	Terrorism Casualties, 1990–99	155
7.1	Structure of the Muslim Brotherhood in Jordan	190

PREFACE

The heavy wave of Islamic fundamentalism that swept through the Middle East beginning in the late 1970s traveled across Egypt and Jordan as well. The Islamic fundamentalist movement operated in these states through two different channels – violent terrorist groups and non-violent organizations, mainly the Muslim Brotherhood. Despite their different modes of operation, both channels sought to topple the host regimes and replace them with Islamic theocratic regimes. This study will examine the ways that the Egyptian and Jordanian regimes met the challenge of Islamic fundamentalism. It will also evaluate the results of the confrontation and suggest a prognosis for the coming years.

The phenomenon of terrorism was not new to Egypt, where it surfaced periodically throughout the twentieth century, but the surge in terrorism that erupted in Egypt in 1992 was more violent and protracted than in the past. In addition, the fanatics of the 1990s differed from their predecessors in their socio-economic and educational backgrounds and their motivation. In Jordan, a country that has witnessed considerable attempts at subversion and political assassinations, radical Islam operated in its two forms but under different and more moderate circumstances.

The research presented here concentrates primarily on the 1990s – the main years of confrontation by the regimes – which lends it greater urgency for the present. I deviate from this time framework for the sake of historical context, particularly with events of the 1980s that led up to this critical period. Overall, however, the research focuses on developments of the last decade of the twentieth century.

My inclination notwithstanding, I have not explored the feelings and self-image of the Islamic radicals from their vantage point because I met with very few of them. To compensate partially for this lapse, I have expanded the descriptions of the radicals' lifestyles, their modus operandi, and their environment: for example, in the Islamic lawyers' struggle with the Egyptian regime (chapter 2); and the Cairo neighborhood of Imbaba (chapter 4). These descriptions may appear overly detailed, but I believe they reflect an accurate picture of the situation in Egypt. The Imbaba slum is only one of hundreds of such areas controlled by Islamic fanatics.

Since the following research concentrates on the challenge of grappling with Islamic fundamentalism, I chose not to include a detailed analysis of the various Islamic groups and their ideologies, particularly as many excellent works already exist on this subject. Egypt and Jordan, Israel's only Arab neighbors that have signed a peace treaty with Israel, were selected for this study. I was able to travel to those countries, obtain information more easily than elsewhere, gain first-hand impressions in research institutes and in meetings with Arab colleagues, and collect vital material on the regimes' methods of confronting the Islamic challenge. As a member of the Israeli delegation to the peace talks with Jordan, I held many discussions with Jordanian government and military figures, talks that added to my understanding of the relations between the Islamic movement and the Hashemite regime. Reference to the Islamic movement's activities in other countries will be made only within the context of Egypt or Jordan. The book's data has been gleaned from various sources, but for statistics on Egypt, I preferred the Ibn Khaldoun Center for Development Studies in Cairo, because I judged its data more reliable than that of other institutes. A number of Arab academics whom I interviewed wished to remain anonymous. In these cases I have only noted the dates of the discussions, while the names of those interviewed and transcripts of the conversations remain in my safekeeping.

The Introduction offers a general discussion of Islamic fundamentalism and the threat it poses to secular Arab regimes. Parts I and II, respectively, treat Egypt's and Jordan's different struggles with Islamic fundamentalism. The first chapter of each part presents background information relating to the growth of the Islamic movement in the respective countries. The chapters that follow discuss the strategies each regime adopted in its struggle with the Muslim Brotherhood and the related struggle with Islamic terrorism. The last chapter of each part contains an assessment of how the regimes confronted the threat they faced from fundamentalist Islam.

The final chapter of the study forms an integrated conclusion. Despite inherent difficulties, I attempt to compare radical Islam in Egypt with its Jordanian counterpart, examine the manner in which the two regimes have dealt with the threat, evaluate the results of the struggle and conditions at the end of the 1990s, and offer a prediction for the coming years.

The following text is based on a book that was first published in Hebrew in 1999. The text has been modified and updated to reflect additional developments. In general I have employed the standard spelling in academic publications for the transliteration of Arabic names and terms, but to facilitate reading I have at times deviated from these rules by using more commonly accepted spelling. Thus, for example, names such as Abdullah and Ali, which are familiar to English readers, are spelled without the prefatory apostrophe; other proper nouns follow suit and omit the prefatory apostrophe. The terrorist organizations al-Jihad and al-Jama'a al-Islamiyya and other select terms have been spelled throughout the book according to their standard transliteration, although in their Egyptian context they would otherwide be spelled differently.

Finally I would like to express my gratitude to the staff at the Jaffee Center for Strategic Studies who helped me in collecting the material and preparing the book. Thanks are also due Moshe Tlamim, principal translator of this work, and Judith Rosen, who edited the English version of the text.

Nachman Tal
July 2004

INTRODUCTION

A wave of Islamic fanaticism erupted in the late 1970s in the Middle East, and was bolstered by subsequent formative events. The Islamic Revolution in Iran in 1979, under the leadership of Ayatollah Ruhallah Khomeini, was a significant catalyst to the spread of Islamic fundamentalism. Related manifestations of Islamic fundamentalism in the 1980s and 1990s included the assassination of Egyptian president Anwar Sadat by Islamic extremists; the Islamic revolt in Hama, ruthlessly suppressed by the Syrian regime; the establishment of Hizbollah in Lebanon; the growth of Hamas in Israel's occupied territories; the military coup in Sudan by the Muslim Brotherhood under the leadership of Hassan Tourabi, which saw Sudan become the first Arab country to turn into an Islamic theocracy; the Islamic movement's victories in two parliamentary elections in Jordan (1989 and 1993); the brutal terrorism that began in Egypt in 1992; the movement's triumph in Algerian elections in 1992 (though the victory was quashed by military intervention); and the Islamic Welfare Party's claim to 22 percent of the vote in Turkey's 1995 parliamentary elections, which brought an Islamic prime minister to power for the first time in the seventy-three year history of the Turkish republic.

A seminal, decisive event that accelerated the rise of radical Islam in the 1990s was the victory of Islamic mujahidin over the Soviet army in Afghanistan. The Muslim volunteers, subsequently known as the "Afghan alumni," perceived the Soviet defeat not only as a battlefield achievement but also as a moral victory for Islam that restored the religion to its former glory. Fortified by this faith, hundreds of war veterans returned to Egypt, Jordan, Algeria, and other Middle East states where they enlisted in Islamic terrorist organizations and boosted the violent struggle against the secular Arab regimes. Other Afghan alumni, led by Osama Bin Laden, founded the al-Qaeda organization, which carried out major international terrorism attacks, including the September 11, 2001 strike against the United States. This event forced the free world to confront with greater urgency the strategic threat of Islamic terrorism and its core ingredient, Islamic fundamentalism.

The Essence of Fundamentalism

The term "fundamentalism" appears in literature, academic research, and the media, yet by definition has no connection to Islam. In fact, the term is rooted in Christian theology and relates to the cardinal principle of an unquestioning acceptance of scripture for the redemption of the soul.[1] When applied to Islam, it expresses the desire to return to original, ancient Islam in order to rectify the ills of contemporary Islamic society.

A semantic difficulty, however, exists in using "fundamentalism" within the context of the Islamic world. Some Islamic activists define their movement as *usuliya*, which means fundamental, original, first, and advocating the principles of Islamic law; it signifies the longing to return to the roots of Islam.[2] The West refers to this phenomenon as "Islamic extremism," "radical Islam," "fanatical Islam," and other terms, but all of these expressions fail to convey the true meaning of the concept. The closest term to *usuliya* thus appears to be fundamentalism. At the same time, however, various fundamentalist organizations shun any imposed label, *usuliya* included. Hamas leader Sheikh Ahmed Yassin claimed, "We Islamists believe in Allah and his Prophet, and live and conduct ourselves according to *shari'a* (Islamic law, based on the Qur'an)."[3] In general, Islamic activists perceive their way as the true path of Islam, and thus have adopted the name "the Islamic movement," rather than Islamic fundamentalism, a foreign term that smacks of Western connotations.

The developments that began in the 1970s established Islamic fundamentalism as an ideological movement that uses political means for obtaining its goals, the main one being the founding of a grand Islamic theocracy that governs a state based entirely on *shari'a*.

The exploitation of Islam for political objectives is not new. In effect, it began after Mohammad's death (632 CE) when his loyalists competed with one another under the cover of the battle for his true legacy. Over the centuries the aegis of Islam for political aims became an ongoing phenomenon, in which representatives of the civil government would ask the religious authority for assistance in establishing their legitimacy. Beginning in the 1970s Islam often assumed the character of a fundamentalist political ideology, albeit one that has not yet been realized institutionally, with the notable exceptions of Sudan, Iran, and Afghanistan.

The Islamic movement's non-participation in government affairs in Arab and Muslim countries has served it a great advantage by absolving it of responsibility for state mismanagement. Concomitantly, in recent times the masses have witnessed the successive failures and demise of dominant ideologies: the Ba'ath ideology is a symbol of injustice and savagery, and pan-Arabism and Arab socialism came to represent the large, corrupt state companies. The defeat on the Middle East battlefield, especially in 1967, also added to the general despondency among the Arabs.[4]

Against the backdrop of disappointment, bitterness, and gloom, fundamentalism became a ray of light and hope for the masses, growing in the 1970s and strengthened by the 1979 revolution in Iran. While the Arabs did not wish to duplicate Khomeini's Islamic-Shiite model, its successful implementation of change in Iran encouraged them to pursue similar goals in Arab states. After the 1970s Islamic fundamentalism began to symbolize popular protest against the official religious establishment in the Arab states. Through the work of local activists, the Islamic movement initiated counseling and assistance in religious, public welfare, and educational services in cities and villages. In this way the movement rallied popular support against the injustices of officials in the Ministry of Religious Endowments and government bureaucracy, thus detracting from the credibility of establishment Islam.[5]

The fundamentalist movement could not ignore the nationalist and patriotic sentiments in the states where it originated and continued to operate. Islamic leaders realized the strength of patriotic fervor among the people and enlisted this feeling for the benefit of the movement. The merging of nationalism and Islam was necessary for the evolution of the Islamic revolution. Hamas writings refer to the state as paving the way for a grand Islamic state, with Palestine serving as a springboard for this goal, just as the Muslim Brotherhood in Egypt sees its country in this role.

Hassan al-Banna, the leading Islamic thinker in the Arab world who founded the Muslim Brotherhood movement in 1929, understood the overriding importance of patriotism and nationalism in building an independent state. However, while the Egyptian nationalist movement saw statehood as the final goal, according to the model of European nation states, Banna regarded statehood as only the first step toward the principal goal – the renewal of the Islamic caliphate. According to Banna, "We agree with the most radical patriots, but let me clarify, their mission will end once the motherland is liberated and its glory reinstated. For the Muslim Brotherhood [statehood] is only one step on a long path."[6] The first objective is thus to assume control of the modern national state in order to transform it into a foundation for a great Islamic state. In practical terms, the Islamic movement in Egypt aims to replace the regime of the infidel with an Islamic religious state as the basis for a grand Islamic theocracy. Hamas' goal, both in the occupied territories and in Israel, is to bring about the Islamization of Palestine as an intermediary stage toward the great caliphate. This is the same goal of the Muslim Brotherhood in Jordan and the Islamic movement in all countries where it is active.[7] Since the modern state that organizes the life of the individual and society according to Western patterns is perceived as the main threat to Islamic fundamentalism, the movement's first goal is the destruction of this state.

The Muslim Brotherhood might thus define Islamic fundamentalism as a popular ideological movement that emphasizes the imperative of implementing patterns of Islam as a way of life. It differs from Sufism [an Islamic mystical movement], where proximity and a personal approach to God are stressed, and from Islamic theology and philosophy, which emphasize thought and the manner of thinking as opposed to the manner of living. The Muslim Brotherhood is primarily committed to applying *shari'a* to all areas in the life of the individual and general society. The movement channels national patriotic sentiment to service to Islam so that no conflict appears between nationalism and Islam. Nor is there a contradiction between Islamic universalism and nationalist particularism. Every branch of the fundamentalist movement is responsible for implementing Islamization in its area. In this way local nationalism becomes the ground floor in the construction of the universal Islamic edifice and in the framework of the Islamic theocracy.

Islamic ideology derives its authority from a divine source and rejects every ideology or alternative proposed by man. As such, "Islam is the solution" is not only a slogan of the Muslim Brotherhood, but also furnishes a remedy for all the maladies of Muslim society (economic, social, and cultural) in the form of an Islamic theocracy that will institute an Islamic way of life. The fundamentalist movement sees this framework as the only solution.

Most believers in Islam are neither extremists nor radicals. They do not support revolutionary means nor do they act personally to advance the Islamic goal. Radical activists make up only a small percentage of the population, while the majority reject their activity and even fear it. The radical fundamentalists as well do not form a monolithic group. While they agree on the definition of their goal – the establishment of a theocratic state – they differ over the methods for attaining it; likewise there are differences from state to state.

Three principal trends dominate the Islamic movement. The first trend consists of those devoted to Islam that call for dissociation with infidel society and the transformation of the state into a religious "counterculture" of sorts. Their mentor is the radical thinker Sayyid Qutb. The Egyptian government termed this group *al-takfir wal-hijra* (meaning, the group that views society as heretical and calls for separation from it). The second trend does not demand separation from society but urges a jihad (holy war) for obtaining the goal of a religious state. The Islamic Jihad and al-Jama'a al-Islamiyya (the Islamic Group) in Egypt reflect this approach. The third trend, pragmatic and relatively moderate, believes that the goal can be attained gradually through education and preaching (*da'wa*). The Muslim Brotherhood movement represents this trend. Each trend has developed its modus operandi according to the degree of urgency it considers necessary for correcting the wrongs in Islam and society.[8] The first two trends, it should be noted, operate as sects, while the Muslim Brotherhood is a popular movement that strives to win hearts and minds and derives its strength from public support.

The Crisis of the Faithful

Thinkers and leaders of the fundamentalist movement who describe conditions of contemporary Islam illustrate the disappointment and frustration felt by the Muslim faithful and the yearning for change. Indeed, theirs is a dark picture of Islamic society on the brink of an abyss. Islamic thinkers have meticulously analyzed the reasons for Islam's decline and the difficulty of altering the demoralizing situation. They repeatedly exhorted the followers of Islam to enlist in the final battle for returning Islam to its former glory.

Dr. Mohammad al-Bahi, a leading Egyptian theologian closely linked to the Muslim Brotherhood, studied the waning of Islam. According to Bahi, when the caliphate was abolished in 1924, Muslim states such as Turkey, Afghanistan, Yemen, and others became marginal forces, and Muslim minorities were cruelly persecuted in Cyprus, the Philippines, Burma, China, and Ethiopia. The ruling elites grew increasingly secular and undermined the Islamic foundation. Nationalism in all its manifestations weakened religious ties and even usurped them. Under these circumstances the Islamic establishment stood impotent because of its traditional surrender to rulers motivated by self-interest. Islam was further enervated when it lost its economic basis – the holy properties (*waqf*) that were entrusted to the government authority. Materialism and individualism pervaded the Islamic world.[9]

Rashid al-Ghanoushi, leader of the Tunisian Islamic movement, argued that the decline of Islam began at the end of the Golden Age of Mohammad and during the reign of the first four caliphs. Islamic culture continued to develop theologically until the penetration by foreign elements of Western culture led to Islam's loss of originality, the distortion of its worldview, and paralysis of those who renew and fight the jihad. This situation bred tyrannical and heretical regimes in Islam that imitated Western culture, shattered the Muslim believer's sense of self-respect, and relegated Islam to the quagmire of ignorance and impoverishment. Aberrant forms of faith based on mysticism, such as the Sufi movement, entered Islamic society, hindered development, and implanted the view that all past and present events were the result of the will of God. Society grew despondent and fatalistic. Nonetheless, Ghanoushi's analysis of Islam's cultural decline closed on a hopeful note, recalling the eventual appearance of Islamic leaders like Abd al-Wahab, Jamal al-Din al-Afghani, Hassan al-Banna, Abul-Ala al-Mahdoudi, and Sayyid Qutb, who introduced reform, charted the correct path, and opened the way for Muslims to reacquaint themselves with Islamic truth and its sources.[10]

The spiritual leader of the Shiite sect in Lebanon, Sheikh Hussein Fadlallah, found similar patterns elsewhere in the Arab world. The imitation of Western culture, Fadlallah claimed, created heresies in Islamic culture and society, as well as at the political level. Muslims became divorced from the world; some surrendered to the situation created by contemporary reality in the belief that their leaders must be unquestioningly obeyed. Large groups of Muslims believed that submission to their rulers was an act of God, and as a result, Muslim masses dwelt in a state of subservience and demoralization. Although there was always a rebellious coterie in government that viewed secular rule as illegitimate from the Islamic point of view, it did not dare to attempt replacing it. This stemmed from deference to the concept of inaction until the end of days when the *mahdi* would arrive and redeem Islamic society.[11] A stagnant society developed that rejected change and took no initiative in improving conditions. In this way corrupt rulers perpetuated Islam's decline and reversal, while the Muslim world was split. Imperialism penetrated Arab countries and took control of the economy and other areas of life. Western culture shoved Islam into a corner; Muslim rulers began to speak of a separation between religion and state. Western concepts that were foreign to Islam – such as democracy, socialism, Communism, capitalism, dictatorship, and individualism – pervaded society. Imperialism dominated the state, and any attempt to resist it was at best temporarily successful.[12]

Islamic leaders and thinkers agreed that the main reason for the crisis, malaise, and despondency was the imposition of a foreign culture on the Islamic world, a lifestyle that stands in total opposition to the worldview and culture of the devout Muslim. Ghanoushi asserts that Western secular culture is limited and limiting, particularly in its elevation of the human being to the status of the divine. He accuses it of a materialism that worships man's achievements, and dominates and exploits the world for its own needs. Although Ghanoushi recognizes the West's great strides in science, industry, and technology, he also observes Western man's spiritual hollowness and dearth of values. The Muslim culture and worldview places God on the highest rung. While the world was created for man, there are also spiritual obligations that the belief in God and Islam furnish. With the rise of Western influence, Islamic culture sank into abject poverty, festered in ignorance and destitution, and saw its capabilities paralyzed.[13]

These views of Islamic leaders reveal only a fraction of what the larger group of the faithful feel in their hearts. The crisis is not only a cultural one but also a socio-economic one. Islamic fundamentalism has become the expression of a class struggle. It represents all classes of society – middle and lower class, rural and urban dwellers, the educated, and white-collar workers – that harbor feelings of frustration and alienation toward the regimes' ruling elite for failing to alleviate debilitating economic and social ills. Broad sectors of the public have been motivated to join the fundamentalist movement not only for cultural and religious reasons but also for socio-economic ones.

The Threat of Fundamentalism to Current Regimes

Arab rulers grew eminently aware of the threat of Islamic fundamentalism and identified its primary representative organization, the Muslim Brotherhood, as the major strategic danger to regime stability. Both the Arab governments and the Muslim Brotherhood realized that the organization's greatest asset was to win the hearts and minds of the Arab masses and present itself as the true path of Islam, rather than as an extremist or fringe organization.

Syrian president Hafez al-Assad conveyed this assessment in an interview with *Time* magazine on November 30, 1992. Assad was asked whether he shared the apprehensions of President Mubarak and King Hussein over the rise of Islamic fundamentalism. He answered that the secret of Islamic fundamentalism's attraction was the young generation's yearning to recover the lost respect of the Arab people. He also admitted:

I am worried [about the phenomenon of Islamic fundamentalism], but I understand the background. I can imagine that if I were younger and saw what has happened to the Arab homeland, I might find myself part of this movement. With the enthusiasm of youth, I would judge things hastily. I would see that the Arabs are downtrodden, that their land is occupied, that the Israelis appear victorious. Therefore young people have come to the conclusion that Islam is their salvation. The majority [of Arab leaders] are aware of this reality, but they don't talk about it.[14]

Above all, the secular regimes fear fundamentalism's influence on the army. This fear is based on the regimes' realistic awareness of their own vulnerability, the people's socio-economic misery, fundamentalism's powerful influence, and the army's underlying connection to the pulse of the nation. Despite the benefits that rulers lavish on the army, military personnel occasionally came under the sway of fundamentalism. In

January 1993 the Algerian government held a showcase execution of two officers guilty of membership in the fundamentalist underground. The greatest threat of fundamentalism is a successful forging of a link with military regimes, as took place in Sudan between General Bashir and Islamic leader Hassan Tourabi.[15] This merging of interests resulted in Sudan becoming the first Arab state to metamorphose into a Sunni theocracy.

Yet even if such a revolutionary scenario is not realized elsewhere, it should be kept in mind that radical Islam engages in educating the young generation in societies that are defined by their Islamic identification. The movement has gradually and patiently grown into a popular movement. It has shed the aura of elitism that shrouded it in the 1970s and has emerged as a strong mass movement. This is a dynamic development that threatens every Muslim regime, even if it continues to retain the loyalty of the security forces.

In addition, radical Islam seeks to achieve its goals by political means. Moreover, fundamentalists know how to compromise and act pragmatically, for example, regarding technological advances. While television was deemed a major culprit in the invasion of Western modernism into society, specifically the traditional bastion of the home, leaders understood the power of electronic communications to propagate the movement's message.[16] This stems from the awareness that reality often overpowers ideology. At the same time, fundamentalism will never compromise on the absolute sovereignty of God. In other words, rule must return to Allah, that is, to the embrace of Islam. Furthermore, fundamentalism aims for Islamic law to be sovereign and will never yield on the demand for society to abide by *shari'a*. *Shari'a* not only refers to a narrow code of laws but to a wider sphere, "the all-embracing way of living – values, customs, and social norms – that Allah determined for Muslims which, when taken together, can shape human life."[17]

The enormous gap between the worldviews of the fundamentalist organizations and the regimes' where they operate appears unbridgeable. Faithful to their principles, the radical organizations waged a struggle against the regimes in Egypt, Syria, Algeria, and Jordan in the 1980s and 1990s. Mubarak, Assad, and other Arab rulers were vilified as infidels to be deposed in order to pave the way for the foundation of a *shari'a*-based Islamic state. Lengthy confrontations had a great impact on the Islamic movement at both the violent and non-violent level. The regimes reacted by brutally suppressing and targeting Islamic extremists and from time to time succeeded in reducing the violence, but the recourse to force by the regime – even if quiet was temporarily restored – led to the next clash. Radical Islam was not deterred by killing and imprisonment since the very suppression nurtures the movement in a kind of vicious circle. Imprisonment has become an obligatory rite of passage for the maturation of many Muslim radicals. Extremist leader Sayyid Qutb developed his ideas during the nine years he spent in Egyptian prison (1955–64) and expressed them in his book *Milestones*, which became the guide for the generation of Islamic fanatics that followed.[18] Other Islamic leaders experienced a similar transformation.

By the late 1990s the secular Arab regimes of Egypt, Jordan, Algeria, and Syria had managed to block the spread of radical Islam with the help of the army and security and intelligence agencies. The story that follows of the experience of radical Islam in Egypt and Jordan illustrates the success of two Arab states in confronting, albeit in qualitatively different fashion, the existential threat that each regime faced in the guise of Islamic fundamentalism. Since then no new ideological movement has risen in Arab and Muslim countries, but neither have political reforms or basic socio-economic improvements taken place that could seriously counter and neutralize the challenge of Islamic fundamentalism. In the absence of these changes, the Muslim masses may well continue to believe that "Islam is the solution" to the maladies of society and the economy, and radical Islam will continue to pose a threat to secular Arab regimes. If so, then states like Egypt and Jordan are radical Islam's prime enemies, and the Islamic movement will do everything in its power to undermine and replace them.

PART I

RADICAL ISLAM IN EGYPT

1 EGYPT AND ISLAMIC FUNDAMENTALISM

Socio-Economic Background

Egypt spreads across more than one million square kilometers, of which only 2.5 percent can be agriculturally cultivated and is home to the overwhelming majority of the population. With its nearly seventy million inhabitants (1999), Egypt was one of the most densely populated countries in the world, and the hardship created by the country's already inadequate infrastructure was severely aggravated by the steady population increase. The government invested much energy in lowering the consistently high birth rate, but even an annual birthrate of 2 percent translates into an additional 1.5 million people a year, which if continued would double the population in twenty-five years. Ninety-three percent of the population was Muslim and 7 percent Coptic Christian.

Post-World War II Egypt was marked by an accelerated process of urbanization, primarily from two reasons: the diminishing amount of village land per family due to the increased population; and improved education in the villages, which drove young people to the cities in the search of jobs in commerce and industry and the hope for an improved standard of living. Rapid urbanization brought with it destructive consequences because the cities lacked the necessary infrastructure for absorbing the masses and providing basic services. Cairo was an outstanding example of unchecked population migration. Slums sprang up in the city's outlying districts, and thousands of people lived in the streets and cemeteries. Most of the urban homeless were unemployed, uneducated, and unskilled, and hence became a social time bomb and breeding ground for radical and terrorist elements.

Egypt took vigorous steps to develop domestic industry in an attempt to reduce unemployment and ease the country's dependency on imports. Yet investment in infrastructure and economic development was difficult, since a large portion of the state budget was allocated to food purchases. Economic aid from the United States was channeled to forestall mass starvation, which aside from a humanitarian disaster could lead to major social unrest. High rates of unemployment continued, and despite some improvement in the Egyptian economy, the standard of living of the masses, especially the lower classes, did not undergo a significant change. Thus at the end of the 1990s Egypt's chronic problems remained: according to official reports, unemployment came to 13 percent, while in 1999, 23 percent of the population subsisted below the poverty line. Egypt's technological capability continued to be low, and a wide gap still existed between the haves and have-nots. A particularly acute problem was unemployment among university graduates, who were expected to be the driving force behind the economy. The Egyptian press also regularly published stories of government corruption and economic mismanagement. Mubarak was aware that the economy had to be privatized but at the same time he understood that privatization could leave thousands of workers jobless. Therefore he proceeded with economic reform slowly and cautiously.[1]

From the regime's standpoint, the country's most volatile area was Upper Egypt (the entire Nile River valley from Cairo south to the Aswan High Dam). The development of radical Islam in Egypt and its violent nature cannot be understood without understanding the complexities of this region, which in 1999 was home to 30 percent of the population. Upper Egypt differed culturally, socially, historically, economically, and politically from Cairo and the Delta, and overall the south was poverty-stricken and backward in comparison to the north. It lacked a basic infrastructure: agriculture was underdeveloped, equipment was antiquated, and water was still drawn by primitive devices. The level of unemployment in the southern districts was twice as high (30 percent) as the national level, and reached 45 percent among the region's young people. The inhabitants of the south, known as *sa'id*, were cut off from the Egyptian-Arab society of Cairo and the north. Their social structure was tribal, a closed society still bound to traditions of blood revenge between families or tribes, or hostility toward the state's security forces.[2]

The *sa'id* population never shared in the country's political and historical experience. In contrast to the north, the south escaped colonial domination, and during British rule, bases were not set up in this part of the country. Thus the inhabitants of Upper Egypt took no part in the anti-colonial protest and struggle for national liberation that left its stamp on the Egyptian national movement. The *sa'id* had little interest in Nasser's pan-Arabism and the designs of other regimes. They had no access to the government-controlled media or independent media sources. Under these circumstances the people's main link of communication was the mosque where they received news, and where they grew especially receptive to the Islamic message "Islam is the solution."[3] In these circumstances Upper Egypt served as a hotbed for Islamic fanaticism and terror.

The Security and Intelligence Services

The security and intelligence services were the regime's main instruments for dealing with radical Islam. Responsibility for the country's domestic security lay with the minister of the interior, and the various security agencies, including the prison services, were subordinate to him. Unlike other countries, Egypt refrained from calling on the army to thwart Islamic terror.

One of the organizations in charge of internal security was Central Security (al-Amn al-Markazi), which in 1995 employed 300,000 people. Founded in 1977, by the start of Mubarak's presidency the force numbered 100,000 policemen,[4] and by early 1996 some estimated the force's size at 700,000. Central Security resembled a regular army, with its manpower divided into battalions and regiments deployed in different areas of the country. It also included specialized units, such as SWAT teams, a security unit for protecting individuals and foreign embassies, a surveillance unit, and other task-oriented and intelligence branches. Central Security collected information on Islamic organizations through a wide network of agents. Most of the force was engaged in operations: patrols, weapons searches, suspects tracking, and escort assignments. Since the 1992 terrorism wave began, Central Security received top quality officers into its ranks, posted there rather than in the regular army.[5]

Egypt had three intelligence agencies, two of which dealt with radical Islam. The main agency that handled counter-terror and counter-violence was called the Directorate of State Security Investigations and was subordinate to the minister of the interior. General Intelligence (al-Mukhabarat al-Aama), the leading intelligence body in Egypt, was run by a general[6] who was directly responsible to the president. The other agency was Military Intelligence,[7] which apparently limited its fundamentalist-related activity to uncovering radical Islamic activity within the army, and was responsible to the minister of defense.

General Intelligence, with headquarters in Cairo and offices in every district, was in charge of safeguarding the regime and countering terrorism, subversion, and espionage; a special unit protected senior officials and guarded vital facilities. The agency watched over the Muslim Brotherhood and Islamic terrorist groups and broke up their activity when necessary. General Intelligence observed radical organizations' conferences, meetings, and demonstrations, and kept watch over their general activity; surveillance was maintained via agents and informers who penetrated radical circles or were enlisted from their ranks. Not infrequently, office workers at public institutions and hotel staff were hired as agents and informers. The agency had branches abroad that dealt with Islamic activity in Arab states as well as in certain Western countries. Cooperation with foreign agencies included the exchange of intelligence information, particularly with states with which Egypt had signed extradition agreements. Supervision inside Egypt was carried out through border checks at airports and ports by a special unit of General Intelligence.

Like General Intelligence, the Directorate for Investigations was also dispersed throughout all of Egypt's districts and villages, and was comprised of various units. One unit (*magmua*) dealt with counter-terror and the activity of radical Islam; another unit conducted operations such as arrests and interrogations. Here too the agency gathered information from its vast array of agents and informers, as well as from electronic devices.[8] The Directorate's tasks included: thwarting acts of terrorism, subversion, and espionage; protecting individuals and facilities; and guarding foreign embassies and foreigners. It also combated criminal activity, such as corruption in the public sector. The Investigations Directorate differed from General Intelligence in dealing only with internal security, not overseas operations. It was the main operations branch in the domestic war against radical Islam, and routinely carried out arrests, searches, and interrogations. General Intelligence, on the other hand, performed only a small portion of these tasks.

The intelligence and security agencies were thus the regime's main bulwark against Islamic fundamentalism. Ongoing surveillance of the Muslim Brotherhood and Islamic terrorist organizations furnished the state's leaders with information and warning signals that allowed the preemption of terrorist activity and organizational assembly. The security agencies' success in suppressing radical Islam enabled the regime to avoid calling in the army, a move that could have propelled Egypt into a state of chaos.

The Muslim Brotherhood

The Muslim Brotherhood movement was founded in Ismailia in 1929 by Sheikh Hassan al-Banna as a reaction to the increasing penetration of Western culture, economics, and technology into Egypt. In addition, Egypt was in the throes of a deep economic crisis, a result of the global depression of 1928–29 and the sharp decline in the price of cotton, one of Egypt's leading exports. The global crisis created a high level of urban unemployment and severe shortages in the villages, which also triggered the rise of the Muslim Brotherhood.[9]

Hassan Ahmed Abdel Rahman al-Banna was born in Ismailia in 1906 to a devout Muslim family. In his childhood he studied at a religious school (*kutab*) and afterwards became a teacher of Islamic studies in Ismailia and in Cairo. Banna led a humble life, and was a charismatic speaker who could excite the masses. His speeches reflected great knowledge of the Qur'an and Muslim literature, and his messages were clear and to the point. Under his leadership the Muslim Brotherhood grew into a large, powerful, and influential movement in Egyptian society and politics. On February 12, 1949, Banna was assassinated in retaliation for the Muslim Brotherhood's murder of Mahmoud Fahmi al-Nuqrashi, the Egyptian prime minister. Since Banna's death the movement has lacked a leader of comparable stature.[10]

The Structure of the Movement

The Muslim Brotherhood's structure is designed according to by-laws written by its founder, which have evolved over time to reflect lessons gained from experience. It is a highly centralized movement that instills in its followers obedience to their leaders.

The Muslim Brotherhood's main institutions are the Office of General Guidance (*Maktab al-Irshad al-'Aam*), and the Shura Council, headed by the General Guide (figure 1.1).[11] The general guide (*al-murshid al-'aam*) is the official head of the movement and its practicing leader, with all of the branches and sub-departments subordinate to his authority. He determines the movement's general orientation and activity. The general guide is the movement's representative to the government and public on all important matters. He must be an older man who has proven his ability and his loyalty to the movement, and he works with one or two deputies.

The Office of General Guidance is the Muslim Brotherhood executive authority in Egypt, comprising between twelve and sixteen members, most of whom have been from Cairo, with a few from Upper Egypt and others from the Egyptian diaspora. Membership is for four years, while the general guide serves as the permanent chairman. The office designs and implements the general policy. It sets up and supervises the movement's branches and committees, and oversees preaching and the Islamic educational system (*da'wa*). It outlines the movement's operational agenda and submits it to the Shura Council for approval, and presents an annual report to the Council on the movement's activity and progress in the branches.

The Shura Council, convened by the general guide twice a year, functions as a legislative body. It is made up of seventy members who serve a four-year term. Like the Office of General Guidance, most of the delegates

…

have come from the Cairo area, with the rest from other districts and Egyptian communities abroad. To be elected to the Shura Council, a candidate has to be at least thirty years old and a member in the movement for over five years. The council elects the general guide and members of the Office of General Guidance.[12]

The Muslim Brotherhood has three systemic branches that deal with all

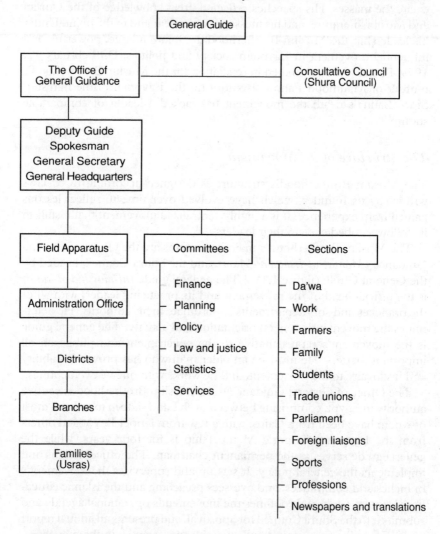

Figure 1.1 Structure of the Muslim Brotherhood in Egypt

Source: Richard P. Mitchell, *The Society of the Muslim Brothers* (London: Oxford University Press, 1969), pp. 164, 167; "Muslim Brotherhood Regulations," pp. 401–16.

the areas of the movement's activity. The first branch generally includes eleven sections, although the number is variable. The first and most important, the *da'wa*, disseminates Islamic religion; other sections deal with farmers, students, trade unions, foreign liaisons, and so forth. The second branch consists of the committees that deal with the daily management of the movement. The committees handle finances, planning, statistics, and services, and new committees are set up when necessary. The third branch directs and promotes Muslim Brotherhood activity throughout the country. The branch is headed by the Administration Office (*al-Maktab al-Idari*) that is responsible for activating local Shura councils (according to Muslim Brotherhood regulations, each district has its own Shura council), departments, and committees that deal with the same matters that the national leadership does.

The Administration Office supervises local branches in cities and villages. The local branch's basic framework is the *usra* ("family"). According to Muslim Brotherhood doctrine two types of *usra* operate: the open *usra* (*usra maftoucha*) and the closed *usra* (*usra mughliqa*). The latter is sworn to secrecy. The open *usra* generally meets in the mosque, and numbers up to ten members. The Qur'an and Islam are studied in the *usra*. Muslim Brotherhood activities, such as collecting donations, preaching, organizing demonstrations, and running programs beneficial to the community are planned. Members of proven dedication and loyalty to the movement sit in the closed *usra*, which meets either in private homes or mosques. Its activity parallels that of the open *usra*.

Hassan al-Banna also founded the Brotherhood's military organization, known as the "Special Organization," the "Military Branch," or – and most commonly – the "Secret Organization." The clandestine nature of the military organization testifies to the movement's intention to include violence if necessary to attain its goals. It also affirms belief in the primacy of the jihadic principle in the Islamic movement, whether it actively pursues its violent nature or not. The general guide has authority over the military organization.

Banna planned the secret organization as a strictly military group that answered to him directly. One section of the organization was made up of highly skilled people who remained outside of regular activity and shunned public appearance. They were activated in the event of an emergency or if the movement had to go underground. Some sections were on constant alert, and others were in charge of weapons and their concealment. There was also a special company comprising hundreds of suicide fighters, zealous fanatics who were sent on missions only in extreme cases. Likewise, according to Banna's instructions, reconnaissance units were set up inside the secret military organization, and weapons and equipment were acquired. The reconnaissance units consisted of five-man squads led by a commander (*amir*). Candidates for this elite group were meticulously selected by an intelligence committee, pending the general guide's final approval. Each company underwent basic military training, usually from former Egyptian army officers and NCOs. Members of the reconnaissance companies, generally students of higher education, were groomed for leadership positions in the movement.

The secret organization became operational in the late 1930s. In 1938 Banna ordered one day a week to be set aside for military training. The organization multiplied in size during World War II, and by 1945 numbered 45,000 members. On November 15, 1948 the Cairo police stopped a jeep transporting Muslim Brotherhood members who were carrying weapons and scores of documents indicating organizational terrorist activity. Indeed, the police attributed several acts of terrorism and assassination to the organization in this period, and in this context Hassan al-Banna was murdered in retaliation for terrorist activity. At times the secret organization has openly disputed with the leadership. For example, after the death of Banna, an altercation broke out when his successor, Hassan Ismail al-Houdeibi, chose a moderate policy that eschewed violence.

Because of the violence perpetrated by the secret organization, Nasser, Sadat, and Mubarak were wont to blame the entire Muslim Brotherhood for terrorist activity, and at times pursued it aggressively with arrests and interrogations. In the 1980s and 1990s the Muslim Brotherhood's leadership testified that no secret organization existed in its ranks and declared its opposition to violence as a means of attaining the movement's goal. But in February 1992 Egyptian security forces discovered a detailed plan of the Brotherhood's secret organization to stage a coup and take control of the government. This was enough to convince the regime that a secret military wing still flourished.

According to the movement's regulations, there is also a global Muslim Brotherhood; it directs and organizes all Muslim Brotherhood branches worldwide. Its headquarters are located in Cairo, unless it is forced to relocate. The general guide of the Egyptian branch, or his deputy, stands at the head of the world organization.[13]

Muslim Brotherhood Ideology and Implementation

The Muslim Brotherhood casts contemporary society in general and Egyptian society in particular as rife with decay and humiliation, caused by foreign conquerors who introduced alien values that in turn were adopted by the local rulers. In this spirit Hassan al-Banna wrote to King Farouk that Egypt was lying at a crossroads and had to choose one of two directions: the way of the West or the path of Islam. The Brotherhood sought a return to pure, original Islam, and not, as some observers claimed, only a reversion to ceremonial worship. Islam in this sense is more than belief and ritual. It encompasses the sense of nation (*watan*), nationalism, religion, creative spirit, the Holy Book, and the sword.

According to Banna, ideologies created in the East and West – nationalism, socialism, capitalism, and bolshevism – are worthless when compared to Islam, which rises above all foreign "isms" since it exists for the entire world. The Islamic revolution preceded the French Revolution by a thousand years in declaring the rights of man, liberty, and equality, and antedated the Russian Revolution by more than a thousand years in decreeing social justice. The Islamic revolution, in the Muslim Brotherhood's eyes, relates to these values not merely as philosophies, but as a binding code for man's conduct.

In light of Islam's ostensible benefits to mankind, the Brotherhood is convinced that Islam has the power to reawaken the slumbering nation and recoup its national honor and political and social independence. The goal is to create a great Islamic theocracy in Egypt and spread the rule of Islam throughout the world. The structure of the future theocracy is built on three principles:

1 The Qur'an is the basic constitution.
2 The government operates through internal consultation and deliberation (the Shura Council).
3 The ruler of the state must be subordinate to the teachings of Islam and the will of the people. There is no special importance to the terms for the head of state mentioned in the Qur'an – caliph, imam, king, ruler (*hakim*), and others – all are acceptable. What is important is that the ruler administers the state according to the commandments of Allah and Shura principles.

These principles guarantee a just and efficient government in conformity with social tradition and capable of providing for the general well-being. All state institutions will function according to these principles.

In the Muslim Brotherhood worldview this goal will be won by waging a vigorous struggle against Western influences that infected the Islamic countries and led to their decline. This struggle will eradicate imperialism, political parties, interest rates, foreign companies, licentiousness, and anarchy in education; it will end despair and stagnation. Abstinence from alcohol must be observed and women must behave modestly; offenders will be brought before religious courts. The Muslim Brotherhood will strive to liberate the entire great Islamic state from the sovereignty of non-Islamic governments. Islamic minorities throughout the world will be given the necessary assistance to merge into the framework of the unified Islamic nation. A great Islamic state will arise that painstakingly upholds the laws of Islam, propagates their teaching, and preaches their observance in the Islamic state itself and abroad.[14]

Muslim Brotherhood regulations call for the following measures in order to achieve the movement's goals:[15]

1 Preaching (al-da'wa) carried out via radio, television, books, journals, and newspapers, and by instructions to Muslim Brotherhood delegations in Egypt and abroad.
2 Education (al-tarbiyya) – emphasis on Islamic education for the younger generation. Western education will cease.
3 Observance (al-toujiyya) – an exemplary Islamic lifestyle will be observed in every social framework, including the economy, education, health, law, and army. It will be applied ubiquitously.
4 Implementation (al-'amal) – by setting up educational, economic, and social institutions, mosques, schools, clubs, and charity organizations.
5 Preparation for jihad – the nation will prepare a united front against the invaders, the enemies of God, as part of the realization of the Islamic state.

The Muslim Brotherhood's goal will be attained gradually by winning the hearts and minds of the masses in preparation for the establishment of an Islamic theocratic state. Hassan al-Banna stressed the importance of Muslim education for the young generation. He rejected the study of subjects antithetical to the spirit of Islam, and therefore called for the abolition of foreign education. Education would alter the face of society as a precondition for the takeover of government. Banna did not dismiss the Islamic people's patriotism (wataniya) and nationalism (qa'umiya), but he opposed the European interpretation of these concepts that translated into territorial-national states. This perspective remains a mainstay of the Muslim Brotherhood doctrine.

According to Banna, wataniya is the love of the Islamic homeland, which includes all countries where Muslims live, liberated from the yoke of the foreigners who usurped the homeland. Qa'umiya (nationalism) refers to walking the path of Islam's great founders and the willingness to wage jihad (holy war) when necessary. Therefore the Muslim Brotherhood emphasized its struggle against the British and demanded Britain's departure from Egypt. In 1944 Banna appealed to King Farouk to replace the political culture of Egypt with Islamic doctrines from the period of the first caliphs, annul all political parties, enact the laws of Islam, and prepare the army for jihad. He also pressed for strengthened ties with Muslim states as a step toward renewing the caliphate. The Brotherhood is simultaneously pan-Islamist and pan-Arabist, and thus the great theocracy's attitude toward minorities would be based on the superiority of Islam. The political reality in Egypt forced Banna to recognize, at least on paper, the civil rights of the Copts (although in practice the Muslim Brotherhood never abided by this rule), but the rest of the non-Muslims, including the Jews, were regarded as undesirables. Unquestionably, the cornerstone of Muslim Brotherhood ideology, then, is the preeminence of Islam and the progress toward the goal of founding a great Islamic, *shari'a*-based state.[16]

Milestones before the Free Officers Revolution

The division of Egypt into regions, districts, and branches under the centralized rule of the Muslim Brotherhood's general guide proved to be extremely efficient, especially in a state with a low socio-economic level.[17] Indeed, the Brotherhood's growth from a modest, popular Muslim association to a huge, aggressive political movement was nothing less than astounding. The failure of the liberals and other parties to deal with the complex economic and social problems in the 1930s may partially explain the meteoric rise of the movement. The Brotherhood's skillful organizational ability *vis-à-vis* the managerial incompetence of the establishment also contributed to the Islamic revival movement. The general atmosphere ushered in by the rise of Nazism familiarized the use of violence and force to the extent that brutality in the defense of Islam and Islamic culture became accepted and even respected behavior.[18]

Numerous terrorist acts were attributed to the Muslim Brotherhood in the late 1940s, such as the explosion in the Oriental Advertising Company building (November 1948) and the murder of the Cairo chief of police (December 1948). On December 8, 1948 Prime Minister Mahmoud al-Nuqrashi declared the Muslim Brotherhood an illegal organization; in revenge, the Brotherhood assassinated him. Two months later Hassan al-Banna was in turn murdered, apparently in retribution for Nuqrashi's death.

In 1948, Muslim Brotherhood units serving with the Egyptian army in the war against Israel attacked Jewish settlements in the Negev. The Wafd government showed a degree of compassion toward the Brotherhood that, at the time, remained a formidable political power in Egypt (between 100,000 to 1,000,000 people, which included a secret organization), and permitted it to renew its activity in the spring of 1951. In October Hassan Ismail al-Houdeibi was elected general guide and adopted a more moderate stance than his predecessor. He declared that the Muslim Brotherhood had no "liberation battalions" since its goal was the peaceful spread of Islamic doctrine and not the launching of a revolution. The movement took almost no part in the clashes with the British in the Canal

Zone in the early 1950s. Its moderate line caught Egypt's political circles off guard and rumors flew of a secret agreement with the king or the British.[19] The Brotherhood's new approach may be attributed to Islam's ability to adapt to fluctuating circumstances by temporarily lowering its profile.

In the early 1950s, on the eve of the 1952 Free Officers coup, the Muslim Brotherhood was a large, powerful political movement in Egypt, with strong prospects of continuous growth. The time was ripe for a fundamentalist movement in Egypt bearing religious and social messages to capitalize on a crisis to generate mass recruitment. Egypt's socio-economic plight and the dismal outlook for a solution to its problems ensured an ongoing crisis situation that could advance Muslim Brotherhood growth. Another major feature of Egypt's endemic crisis was its soaring population, without the accompanying expansion of cultivatable land. The recurrent political crises in the country also helped the Brotherhood propagate its message that Islam was the alternative to the teetering, unpopular regime.

The Brotherhood steadily expanded its activity into new areas of social involvement. It made impressive strides in education, preaching, and public relations because of its conviction that society's adoption of an Islamic way of life is the prerequisite for attaining the main goal of the Islamic theocracy. The movement's gains were accomplished through meetings, newspapers, books, and other publications. Its Office of Preaching was responsible for the large-scale information campaign. Tens of thousands of private mosques under the Brotherhood's auspices were assigned to carry out educational activities, study programs, and ideological indoctrination. The mosques also served as the headquarters for welfare agencies, health clinics, and employment bureaus – all Brotherhood-sponsored.

Over time the movement extended its activity into parliamentary areas and trade unions. In all these environments it proved itself a formidable challenge to the regime, and its organizational skills and powerful ideological motivation often overshadowed the government's efforts in social and welfare services. However, as an extra-parliamentary body, the Muslim Brotherhood did not gain its power from voter support but from political groups and parties that sought ties with it in order to block their rivals and gain popular legitimacy. In effect, then, every regime in Egypt has needed the support of the Muslim Brotherhood, especially in periods of crisis. Nevertheless, Egyptian rulers have been unwilling to co-opt the movement into government partnership and have struggled to prevent it from attaining state offices. Moreover, Egypt's difficulties were so extensive that even if the Muslim Brotherhood reached the helm of power, it would not have been able to solve the overwhelming problems.[20]

The Free Officers coup of July 1952 catapulted the Muslim Brotherhood, along with the rest of Egypt, into a new area and a new Egyptian political structure, fraught with its own set of challenges.

The Islamic Terrorist Organizations

Several Islamic terrorist organizations arose in the latter portion of the twentieth century. Like many of his colleagues, Dr. Ahmed Galal Ezzeddin, an expert on terrorism in Egypt, was convinced that all of the organizations are offshoots of the Muslim Brotherhood. He argued that notwithstanding the Brotherhood's essential rejection of violence and terror as a means of realizing its goal, it erred in 1942 when it established a secret faction that was in effect a paramilitary organization. Members of this group assassinated Judge Ahmed Khazindar and Prime Minister Nuqrashi in 1949. Afterwards, Nasser's assassination policy against the Muslim Brotherhood – to whom he attributed an attempt against his own life – spawned the Brotherhood's radical ideology. Sayyid Qutb put his radical doctrine into writing while he was in prison, in the years leading up to his execution. From the ranks of the Muslim Brotherhood emerged the al-Qutbian group that translated Sayyid Qutb's ideology into practice. In the 1970s veteran members of the organization who had adopted Qutb's doctrine formed the al-Jihad and Jama'at al-Takfir wal-Hijra offshoots. In this way the fundamentalist ideology, which continued to emerge from the crushing socio-economic reality, transformed into a manifesto for violence and terrorism.[21]

The Islamic terrorist organizations in Egypt fell into three principal categories: fundamentalist (*al-salafi*), jihad, and *al-takfir* (deeming the society as heretical). Over the years breakaway groups continued to operate along the lines of one of the main trends, and every group adhered to the fundamentalist doctrine whose prime objective was the replacement of the regime with an Islamic state. There were ideological and organizational differences among groups and sometimes operational disputes escalated to open clashes; there have also been personal conflicts among the leadership. Most groups had no qualms about resorting to terrorism, sometimes mercilessly, to achieve their goals.[22]

The ideological differences stemmed from multiple religious interpretations given to the modus operandi. For example, was it justifiable to injure people and property in a society guilty of heresy? Regarding operational modes, were clandestine operations and terrorism sufficient to advance political objectives or should open activity also be employed? The Jama'a al-Islamiyya organization, for example, employed both methods: open activity in the form of preaching, complemented by secret military activity. Finally, divisions occurred because of power struggles for movement hegemony. Moreover, while ongoing fragmentation pointed to the terrorist organizations' internal weakness, it was also harder for the government to obstruct them, since small groups operated secretly much more easily.[23]

The fundamentalist trend included the Muslim Brotherhood, the largest movement in Egypt, and groups of young people who were members in official legal associations such as al-Da'wa wal-Tablir, Ansar al-Suna, and al-Gamiy'a al-Shari'a. These associations utilized the Muslim Brotherhood's legitimate methods of activity to advance their own organizational goals.[24]

Two organizations – al-Jama'a al-Islamiyya and al-Jihad – were the main groups in the jihad trend and spearheaded terrorist activity against the regime. Differences between them blurred over time, but the main dividing line was the social and geographical environment from which they grew. While al-Jihad developed mainly in Cairo and Giza, al-Jama'a al-Islamiyya crystallized in Upper Egypt, Minya, and Assiut – poorer regions whose inhabitants, the sa'id, were alienated from the central government in Cairo. For a brief time, beginning a few months before Sadat's assassination, the two organizations coordinated their operations, aware of their common cause. They both came under the personal and fiercely religious leadership of the blind sheikh Omar Abdel Rahman.[25] Following sentencing of those convicted of Sadat's murder, however, the two groups parted ways. Abdel Rahman left al-Jihad with his retinue and became the spiritual leader of al-Jama'a al-Islamiyya only.[26]

The third trend was motivated to levy accusations of heresy and was represented by al-Takfir wal-Hijra and some small groups that adhered to the same ideology.

Table 1.1 charts the main terrorist organizations in Egypt according to the jihad and *takfir* trends.

Table 1.1 Islamic Terrorist Organizations by Trend

The *Jihad* Trend	The *Takfir* Trend
Al-Jihad	Al-Takfir wal-Hijra
Al-Jama'a al-Islamiyya	Al-Tawakuf wal-Tabyeen
Tala'ie al-Fath	(also called: Al-Nagoun min al-Nar)
	Al-Shawkiyoun
	(also called: Al-Jihad al-Jadid)
	Al-Samawiya

The Jihad (Holy War) Organization

Al-Jihad was established in 1979 by Mohammad Abdel Salam Farag. Farag adopted the views of Sayyid Qutb, detailed in his book *Milestones* (*Ma'alim Fi-al-Tariq*), according to which jihad should be waged against Muslim rulers who are deemed infidels for failing to abide by Islamic religious law. Farag crystallized his own ideas in his book *The Missing Tenet* (*Al-Farida al-Ghaeba*), in which he stressed the need to establish an Islamic theocratic state and place a caliph at its head. According to Farag, this goal will be attained only by waging a jihad against the secular regimes, which is today the neglected obligation. From its inception al-Jihad began attacking the Coptic community in order to undermine the regime, acts that received religious approval from Farag. Al-Jihad operated throughout Egypt but most of its members were recruited by Farag from the Cairo and Giza districts. The organization attracted followers of high status – white-collar professionals, students, and even senior military officers. When al-Jihad and al-Jama'a al-Islamiyya merged some months before Sadat's assassination, Farag offered the blind Sheikh Rahman the leadership in the united organization and the title *amir* (leader). Rahman refused, claiming that since he was handicapped he was unsuited for the office according to strict Islamic law. He remained the spiritual leader of al-Jihad and in this capacity granted his colleague in the organization, Khaled al-Islambouli, the legal ruling (*fatwa*) to murder Sadat. Farag plotted the October 6, 1981 assassination, which included a follow-up plan for al-Jihad to seize the reins of government, on the assumption that chaos would ensue after the murder.

After Sadat's murder, most of al-Jihad's leaders and members were arrested and some were executed, including Farag. Sheikh Rahman was charged with being the organization's *amir* and tried in a military court. After lengthy deliberations, the court acquitted him due to a technical error on the part of the prosecutor who alleged that Rahman had served as al-Jihad's *amir* while in fact he had rejected the role. As head of al-Jihad and al-Jama'a al-Islamiyya, Rahman continued inciting against the regime in his writing and speeches until July 1990 when he fled Egypt, fearing arrest. Eventually, he settled in New Jersey, attracted a following, and quickly organized a subversive Islamic network.[27]

Immediately after Sheikh Rahman's trial, the pact between al-Jihad and al-Jama'a al-Islamiyya dissolved. The split occurred over the question of leadership and disagreement over operational methods. While al-Jihad sought the continuation of secret operations and terrorism, al-Jama'a al-Islamiyya favored open, public activity. In the end, al-Jihad suffered from the split with al-Jama'a al-Islamiyya, and many members quit the organization and joined smaller jihad groupings. One group was later convicted of assassinating the chairman of the parliament in 1990, Rif'at Mahgoub.[28]

Yet although the organization was relentlessly pursued and almost completely liquidated after Sadat's assassination, in 1993 it successfully revived. Some observers referred to it as the New al-Jihad, but it is more commonly called Tala'ie al-Fath (Vanguard of Conquest). Smaller groups also broke with al-Jihad and continued their operations according to its methods. These groups include al-Harakiyoun, which tyrannized the Copts; the Disciples of Victory (al-Wathikoun min al-Naser); the Survivors of Hellfire (al-Nagoun min al-Nar); and al-Shawkiyoun. The latter two organizations adopted the modus operandi of the *takfir* trend.

Al-Jama'a al-Islamiyya (The Islamic Group)

Al-Jama'a al-Islamiyya was established in the 1970s and began operating in Egypt in the early 1980s, becoming the most active and strongest of the radical organizations. Its goals included:

1 The struggle against the "enemies of Allah," such as government officials, backers of the regime, the Copt minority, foreigners, and tourists.
2 Destruction of the present regime in Egypt and its replacement with an Islamic, *shari'a*-based state.

The most expedient path to attaining these goals was deemed terrorism. In the 1990s the organization carried out many attacks: attempts on the lives of public figures; the assassination of police and security officers; the murder of tourists, foreigners, and members of the Copt minority; and the sabotage of vital facilities. Among the more prominent attacks were three attempts on the life of the Egyptian minister of information, two attempts on the lives of the ministers of the interior, an attempted assassination of Boutrous-Ghali, secretary-general of the United Nations and Egypt's former minister of foreign affairs, and two attempts on the life of President Mubarak,[29] the last one being on June 26, 1995 in Addis Ababa. Al-Jama'a al-Islamiyya flourished mainly in Upper Egypt against the backdrop of economic destitution, high unemployment, especially among the youth, and the *sa'id* population's hatred of the central government. Perhaps predictably, most of the people involved in the assassination of President Sadat hailed from Upper Egypt. Lieutenant Khaled Islambouli, who shot the president on October 6, 1981, was born in the southern city of Minya.[30]

Al-Jama'a al-Islamiyya leaders sent many of the organization's young members to the mujahidin in Afghanistan to fight the Soviets. The young men first went to Saudi Arabia under the guise of laborers or pilgrims. Once in Saudi Arabia they stayed in safe houses until their documents were ready. They were then flown to Peshawar in Pakistan where the main mujahidin base was located. From there they crossed into Afghanistan and received military training and combat experience before returning to Egypt and other Middle East countries to carry out terrorist attacks. In 1993, after Benazir Bhutto's appointment as prime minister of Pakistan, many al-Jama'a al-Islamiyya operatives were apprehended and expelled from the country, including the organization's military commander, Mustafa Hamza. Many made their way to Sudan where they secured assistance from the government in the form of housing, documents, training, and staging areas. From their bases in Sudan, al-Jama'a al-Islamiyya terrorists smuggled weapons into Egypt for future operations.[31]

The relentless pressure of Egypt's security agencies forced most of the group's leaders to flee to Sudan, Pakistan, North Africa, and Europe. In April 1994 the security forces assassinated Tal'at Yassin Hamam, commander of the organization's military wing. The leaders who managed to escape traversed continents, traveling between Europe, Afghanistan, and North Africa, and setting up a framework called the "Diaspora Council." The council's leadership consisted of:

1 Mustafa Hamza – sentenced to death in absentia in Egypt for planning terrorist attacks. As the commander of the organization's military wing, Hamza was likely operating out of Sudan. He masterminded and led the assassination attempt on President Mubarak in Ethiopia.
2 Mohammad Shouki Islambouli – brother of Kahled Islambouli, who killed President Sadat, and was sentenced to death in Egypt in absentia.
3 Tal'at Fuad Qassem – jailed in Egypt during the 1980s, left for Europe on his release.
4 Sheikh Omar Abdel Rahman – former member of the Diaspora Council until his arrest in the United States. Rahman served as spiritual leader of al-Jama'a al-Islamiyya, and was the acknowledged authority of the diaspora leadership and local commanders in Egypt.
5 Rifa'i Taha – sentenced to death in absentia in Egypt for planning terrorist strikes, fled the country.[32]

Together with its military wing, al-Jama'a al-Islamiyya also operated a civilian branch that organized preaching in the mosques, propaganda meetings, and health and welfare services. Most of these activities took place in Upper Egypt, and the organization gained strongholds among university students in Assiut, Minya, and Qena.

The government's counterattack shattered the organization's centralized structure, which in turn allowed second-level, local commanders to assume authority over the terrorist teams.[33] Also in response, al-Jama'a al-

Islamiyya, in an effort to demonstrate its survivability, transferred some of its activity abroad, such as the 1995 assassination attempt on Mubarak in Addis Ababa, and the explosion of the Egyptian embassy in Pakistan that same year. In 1995 Egyptian security forces managed to drive al-Jama'a al-Islamiyya members from the Cairo region to the south of the country. The minister of the interior and other officials announced the successful elimination of the organization, but in reality, al-Jama'a al-Islamiyya activists who escaped to Upper Egypt landed in the arms of a sympathetic population, and many simply returned to their families. To prove the organization's existence, a terrorist team killed eighteen Greek tourists in front of the Hotel Europa near Cairo in April 1996; and on November 21, 1997 the organization launched an attack at the Hatshepsut Temple in Luxor, killing sixty-eight people, including fifty-eight foreign tourists. Security units struck hard at the organization, forcing it into a ceasefire with the government so that by the end of the 1990s, al-Jama'a al-Islamiyya, excluding rare incidents, no longer engaged in violent activity.

Tala'ie al-Fath (Vanguard of Conquest)

Responsibility for an assassination attempt in 1993 on the life of the Egyptian minister of the interior was claimed by Tala'ie al-Fath, the successor to al-Jihad after it was liquidated following Sadat's assassination. Tala'ie al-Fath, also known as the "New Jihad," drew its name from a newspaper published by al-Jihad during its heyday and was made up of religious groups from different places, especially Alexandria, al-Qalyubiya, and Port Said. It was unclear who headed the organization and constituted its leadership cadre, since when al-Jihad tried to reorganize following Sadat's assassination, differences of opinion were voiced over the selection of the leadership.

Abud Zumur, a jailed former senior commander in al-Jihad, announced his opposition to granting authority to Sheikh Rahman. The latter responded by declaring it forbidden for a prisoner to run the organization. At the same time, Dr. Ayman al-Zawahiri gained power as he tirelessly strove to reorganize the remnants of al-Jihad. In an attempt to offset a clash with Abud Zumur, Zawahiri renamed the organization Tala'ie al-Fath, and appointed al-Jihad activists in Egypt as its commanders. Born in 1948, Zawahiri was a surgeon and strong al-Jihad leader, and wrote several books on the principles of the Islamic movement. In 1985 he left Egypt after serving three years in prison for his part in President Sadat's assassination;[34] he subsequently moved to Switzerland. Years later he became a leader of al-Qaeda, second to Osama Bin Laden.

In 1993 a military court in Cairo heard witnesses present another version of the founding of Tala'ie al-Fath and its leadership. According to their testimony, the organization was headed by Omar Abdel Hamid Habalah, a medical student who went by four aliases: Samir, Marwan, Hassan, and Habalah. In his youth Habalah joined the Muslim Brotherhood and came under the influence of Sheikh Rahman. In 1987 he traveled to Peshawar and underwent training with the mujahidin in the use of weapons and explosives. Three months later he returned to Egypt and embraced the teaching of Abud Zumur. In 1989 he founded the Tala'ie al-Fath organization whose name was inspired by the Syrian Taliat al-Muqatelin (Warrior Pioneers) group. He recruited new members at mosques and universities in Cairo and its vicinity.

During his interrogation after his arrest it was revealed that Habalah was the sole amir of Tala'ie al-Fath in Egypt and abroad. He justified this status by contending it was inconceivable that the role would be held by a prisoner (Abud Zumur), a blind man (Sheikh Rahman), or someone outside the Egyptian arena, that is, from the Afghani group. Habalah admitted that the organization comprised al-Jihad survivors and remained loyal to Abud Zumur. The organization hoped to seize control of the state by launching guerilla units. The authorities uncovered in Habalah's possession a list of Egyptians targeted for assassination. On December 15, 1992 Tala'ie al-Fath failed in its attempt to seize an armory as part of its plan to overtake Cairo. The 1993 assassination attempt on the minister of the interior was meant as a signal to the Egyptian public that the organization still flourished despite the regime's drive to extinguish it.[35] By the end of the decade the regime's campaign against Islamic terror finally crushed Tala'ie al-Fath.

Jama'at al-Takfir wal Hijra

Jama'at al-Takfir wal Hijra (The Group that Sees Society as Heretical and Calls for Dissociation) was established in the early 1970s by a Muslim Brotherhood member, Shukri Ahmed Mustafa (born in the Assiut district), who bore the title "Amir of the Faithful" or "caliph." The group claimed that Egyptian society and the state institutions were steeped in ways of the infidel, and that the true believer in Islam had to withdraw from this culture and return to an ideal Islamic counter-society in order to realize the jihad.

The organization demanded that its members break off all contact and loyalties to society and even their families. The neophyte was required to renounce his family unless it too joined the organization. The organization was very hierarchical and cloistered, and divided into groups according to neighborhoods, quarters, and regions. Discipline was absolute and severe measures were taken against anyone who questioned the leader's authority. Each group was headed by an *amir* whom Mustafa appointed. Mustafa was also credited with role of *mahdi*, the Muslim messiah who will one day return to the world to establish the reign of Islam.

The group decided that a *hijra* (flight or emigration) should be carried out as in the days of Mohammad. The *hijra* would be to North Yemen where the group would organize itself along the lines of a new Islamic society. Afterwards, under Mustafa's leadership the group would embark upon a campaign of conquest in the Middle East and later the rest of the world until Islam dominated mankind. In practice, the group's plan did not get very far. Most of Jama'at al-Takfir wal Hijra members were educated; some came from established families, and a number of them were engineers and teachers, in addition to the workers and peasants (*fellahin*) in the group. According to members' confessions after their arrest, among the reasons for joining the organization was the charismatic personality of Shukri Mustafa and members' individual problems. The main motive for their affiliation with *al-takfir* was the overwhelming sense of ideological emptiness in their lives and the need to fill this vacuum with new religious and personal meaning.

On July 3, 1977 the group kidnapped the former Egyptian minister of religious endowments, Sheikh Hassan al-Dahabi, and demanded ransom and the release of imprisoned members. Two days later Dahabi was brutally murdered. In response the authorities arrested hundreds of the group's members. On November 20, 1977 five of the leaders were handed death sentences, among them Shukri Mustafa; twenty others were sentenced to long jail terms. For all practical purposes Jama'at al-Takfir wal Hijra was liquidated, but the organizational and theological school of branding society with the mark of apostasy spawned new groups that pursued a similar ideological path.[36] These spin-offs were responsible for a string of attacks beginning in 1993 in which scores of civilians were killed and injured.

Al-Tawakuf wal Tabyeen

Al-Tawakuf wal Tabyeen was founded in 1987 by Mohammad Hazem, Yousri Abdel Muneim, and others on the basis of condemning society for heresy. The media occasionally referred to the group as al-Nagoun min al-Nar (Survivors of Hellfire). It concentrated its activity in the Damietta and al-Qalyubiya districts. During the 1990s the group carried out a number of assassination attempts on leading figures in Egypt, such as the former ministers of the interior, Hassan Abu Basha and Nabawi Ismail, and the editor of *Al-Musawwar*, Makram Mohammad Ahmed.

At first the police encountered difficulty in dealing with the group because of its small size and veils of secrecy. But in a clash at the village of al-Khirkaniya on August 28, 1987, the group's leader, Mohammad

Hazem, was killed while hiding in the house of the village pharmacist, and Hazem's deputy, Yousri Abdel Muneim, was arrested. In September 1987 more members of the organization were apprehended in Alexandria and Cairo, and large quantities of fighting matériel captured. Thirty-three members of the group were brought to trial for participating in assassination attempts of senior state officials.[37]

Al-Shawkiyoun

Al-Sha'ukiyoun was another group that believed in the ideology of *takfir* and self-imposed retreat from the society of infidels. It was founded in 1989 in Fayoum by Shawki al-Sheikh (hence its name). The group is also called al-Jihad al-Jadid (The New Jihad). Shawki al-Sheikh's father was the local leader of the National Democratic Party. At one time Shawki al-Sheikh had been a pupil and friend of Sheikh Rahman, but he moved away upon adopting the *takfir* view. Sheikh built a strong organization, recruiting people of wealth to serve in the leadership, a step that helped finance the group's activity. The organization's rank and file was a mixture of lower-class farmers, fishermen, drivers, and day laborers. Sheikh trained al-Shawkiyoun members in the Fayoum desert until their activity was accidentally discovered by a surveyor. The group murdered the surveyor and hid in the village of Kahak.

In May 1990 Shawki al-Sheikh was killed along with several of his people in a shoot-out with the police, and almost the entire remnant of the organization was arrested. Those who managed to evade the authorities fled to Cairo's neighborhoods or remote desert villages, and began engaging in terrorism and robbery. After reorganizing, they murdered Ahmed al-Barawi, the officer of the Directorate of State Security Investigations in Fayoum. The police moved to crush the organization, but were hard pressed to do so because of its centralized nature and protective secrecy. During 1993 al-Shawkiyoun was accused of detonating an explosive device in Cairo. Its main arena of activity was Fayoum, but at times its members carried out operations in Cairo as well.[38]

Al-Samawiya

Al-Samawiya, a radical terrorist organization that ascribed to the *takfir* doctrine, was founded by Abdullah Ahmed al-Samawi and was called by his name. Samawi, a former member of al-Takfir wal Hijra served time in prison with Shukri Mustafa, and together they devised the *takfir* ideology. Upon his release in 1971, Samawi returned to his village in Upper Egypt and began establishing his group. With radical and violent fanaticism, Samawi railed against the government in his mosque speeches and often stated that obedience to him would guarantee entry into the Garden of Eden since he was the holder of the keys. The group's ideology was based on accusing the society and government of heresy. Samawi charged that President Mubarak's government was anti-Islamic, illegal, and unjust, and that only its replacement by an Islamic state would revive Egypt and bring an end to corruption. Samawi further declared that any form of government job – including employment in the school system and universities – was an act of heresy.

The group should not be considered an "organization" in the ordinary sense of the term since it lacked a hierarchy and compartmentalization; instead, it was built on the presence of the preacher before his congregation. This nontraditional structure helped Samawi and his group in 1992; when on trial for torching video clubs and Christian churches, he was able to refute any link to the crimes. Samawi also told the court that he accepted the path of Egypt's religious establishment, al-Azhar, and even wanted to see it have greater influence on the regime. In the end, Samawi preferred to employ tactics that would guarantee him, his followers, and their families freedom in the anti-Islamic state, and the avoidance of arrest, torture, and suffering.[39]

Additional rifts in Egypt's terrorist organizations gave rise to other small groups whose influence was marginal and for this reason have not been included in this survey.

2 EGYPT'S STRUGGLE AGAINST THE MUSLIM BROTHERHOOD

An Unbridgeable Divide

After the Free Officers revolution in Egypt in 1952, basic ideological differences between the Muslim Brotherhood and the regime dominated the relations between them. The Brotherhood sought to depose the secular government and replace it with an Islamic theocracy, while the government naturally had its own political interests at stake. Moreover, from the beginning of the twentieth century, every regime in Egypt has advocated a nation state based on a Western legal, bureaucratic system. For decades Egyptians have been exposed to a Western lifestyle, and during Mubarak's rule, Egypt's ties with the West, especially with the United States, were greatly strengthened, to the point of economic dependence and wide-scale military cooperation.

The gap between the outlook of the Muslim Brotherhood and the regime, therefore, is inherently unbridgeable. Starting in the early 1980s the Brotherhood adopted a long-range strategy aimed at a single goal: the establishment of a state based on *shari'a*. This strategy was based on three main elements:

1   The Islamic cultural tradition, rooted in the Egyptian people, enabled the Muslim Brotherhood to win the hearts and minds of many people to their cause. The Brotherhood advanced this goal in the mosques and through published material.
2   In light of Egypt's deplorable economic conditions, the Muslim Brotherhood set up welfare institutions that simultaneously served the public and propagated the Islamic message.
3   The Brotherhood exploited the weakness of Egypt's secular political parties by forming coalitions with other parties. In this way it over-

came the interdiction against it for organizing as an independent political party, and gained entry to the People's Assembly in 1984 and 1987. The Brotherhood placed political, social, and cultural issues on the public agenda, and forced the government's parliamentary representatives to respond to its proposals. The greatest difficulty facing the regime was the Muslim Brotherhood's outstanding organizational skill and the support of a large labor sector; the movement's coalition with the Labor Party also posed a formidable challenge.[1]

Following the escalation of terrorism in Egypt in the 1990s, a full-scale campaign against it became a national priority. At first the solution appeared simple: total war against the radical terrorist organizations. But in practice, dealing with a widespread, non-violent Islamic rival such as the Muslim Brotherhood movement proved to be an exceedingly complicated undertaking. The regime perceived the movement as a long-term threat to the country's political stability. Moreover, the Brotherhood's political and social successes did not lead to a reduction in Islamic terrorism. Despite the movement's achievement at the polls, the radical Islamic groups persisted in violence and terrorism and steered clear of the political process. Paradoxically, terrorist activity increased in almost direct proportion to the Muslim Brotherhood's political gains.[2] In turn, the 1990s witnessed an escalation in the regime's policy of containing the Brotherhood. The government enlisted the religious establishment to counteract the Islamic message by means of public debates, parliamentary frays, information distribution, intensified supervision in the mosques, and the promulgation of religious edicts decrying radical Islam. Yet the regime's power and resources notwithstanding, it failed to suppress the Islamic message, and at times was even forced to yield to the demands of fundamentalist circles.[3] After the regime's failure in the religious domain, it tried applying pressure in the political arena. This resulted in the Brotherhood's withdrawal from the People's Assembly and its decision to abstain from the 1990 and 1995 general elections. Subsequently the regime and Brotherhood clashed over the trade unions, where the movement had made impressive inroads. In June 1994 the regime further discredited the Muslim Brotherhood by excluding it from the government-sponsored national dialogue.

From mid-1994, and in the wake of its headway in the struggle against Islamic terrorist organizations, the regime embarked upon a rigorous anti-Muslim Brotherhood policy. Mubarak reiterated that since the Brotherhood posed a long-term strategic threat to Egypt, the government would implement a policy of "all-out confrontation."

The Confrontation under Nasser and Sadat

After the Free Officers revolution, a single-party regime was established under President Nasser's leadership. It was authoritarian, centralized, and opposed to political pluralism. Nasser's regime reflected grandiose hopes for pan-Arabism, was outwardly secular, and professed Arab socialism; in every way, its worldview was antithetical to that of the Muslim Brotherhood. Despite the gaping disparity between the two sides, however, they searched for common ground. The regime even suggested that the Brotherhood join the Free Officers government, but the general guide, Hassan al-Houdeibi – successor to the founder, Hassan al-Banna – rejected the offer. Indeed, the enormous divide between the basic positions of the Muslim Brotherhood and those of the revolutionary, secular Free Officers regime put the two sides on an inevitable collision course.

Intent on destroying the hotbeds of competing powers, including political parties, the government struck at the Muslim Brotherhood and sought to liquidate it by smashing its infrastructure. An assassination attempt on Nasser by Muslim Brotherhood members in October 1954 prompted the unleashing of a severe blow against the movement, and in December 1954 the Brotherhood was declared illegal. Hundreds of members were thrown into detention camps and jails; six of the leaders were executed. A decade later, on October 29, 1965, the senior figure in the movement, Sayyid Qutb, was hung. He had been arrested and put on trial a number of times during Nasser's reign. *Milestones*, which he wrote in prison, detailed the path of uncompromising warfare against the regime and would serve as an inspirational guide for numerous radical Islamic groups.[4] The president's sudden death in 1970 gave new momentum to the Brotherhood. Also, the nationalist socialist regime that hoisted the banner of pan-Arabism had failed to alleviate the ills of Egyptian society. Eventually this miscarriage benefited the Muslim Brotherhood, whose "Islam is the solution" slogan increasingly penetrated into society.

Some argue that Nasser's liquidation policy was an error; that he misjudged an ideological phenomenon impervious to physical destruction; and that a long-term, carefully planned policy should have been employed. From Nasser's policy emerged Qutb's militancy, which inspired the following generation of Islamic radicals.[5]

When Nasser's heir, Anwar Sadat, assumed the presidency, an atmosphere of reconciliation pervaded the government's relations with the Muslim Brotherhood. As part of Sadat's de-Nasserization policy, a central principle of his regime, Muslim Brotherhood political prisoners were gradually released from jail. The regime even permitted their activity in social and cultural areas. However, within a number of years the modus vivendi deteriorated, and friction led to clashes in the following areas:[6]

1 The Muslim Brotherhood opposed Sadat's open-door economic policy (*infitah*) and the adjustment of the Egyptian economy to a Western-style free market. It claimed that Western influence would increase in the country and lead to the exploitation of Egypt's resources.

2 Sadat vigorously rejected the establishment of a political party with religious or ethnic characteristics, despite the gradual renewal of political parties in 1978. The Brotherhood saw this as a blow against Islam's credo of unity between state and religion (*din wa'da'ula*).

3 Sadat rebuffed the Brotherhood's demands that *shari'a* serve as the exclusive legal source in Egypt, though he compromised by allowing it to be a main source of legislation. Nevertheless, the movement accused Sadat of reneging on his promise.

4 The signing of a peace treaty with Israel infuriated the Brotherhood, which claimed that the Arab–Israeli conflict was a religious struggle whose only solution was the liberation of Palestinian lands by means of jihad.

Sadat's Muslim Brotherhood policy failed to produce the desired results. On assuming the presidency in 1970, he strove to stabilize his rule against possible opposition from Nasserites, left-wing circles, and pan-Arab groups by negotiating with the Brotherhood's veteran members, some of whom were still serving jail sentences. Sadat reached an agreement with them based on the release of their colleagues in exchange for the guarantee of Brotherhood support against the regime's opponents and its forswearing of violence. In general, the Brotherhood kept its part of the bargain; Sadat, however, was unaware of the depth of the schism in the movement when he signed the deal. Radical leader Sayyid Qutb had been executed by Nasser in 1965, and his supporters, who were relatively young at the time, were unknown to Sadat and his advisors. According to the agreement these young men were freed from prison together with long-standing Muslim Brotherhood members. It took some time until the regime realized the degree of fanatical zeal in these young men, but by then it was too late and the regime learned its lesson the hard way, at a cost of much blood.[7]

As the Brotherhood's confrontation with the regime on the four points intensified, Sadat ordered a clampdown in September 1981 lest mounting criticism erode the regime's public support. The prisons were again filled with many Muslim Brotherhood members and the movement's infrastructure was once more severely damaged. On October 6, 1981, shortly after this assault, Sadat was assassinated by members of the al-Jihad organization. At their trial the perpetrators claimed that their main motive had been Sadat's failure to enact Islamic law. Like his predecessor, Sadat's presidency ended with many Muslim Brotherhood members languishing in prison. The challenge they presented now passed on to the Mubarak regime.

Mubarak's Policy of Containment

During his first years as president (1981–87), Husni Mubarak tried to buttress Egypt's democracy that had seriously weakened at the end of the Sadat decade. Mubarak worked to establish political parties and expand freedom of the press. He aspired to create a broad national consensus by integrating moderate forces and groups that were previously banned into the political and cultural mainstream. The regime's goal was not to wipe out the Islamic circles but to reduce political tension so as to create suitable conditions for implementing economic reforms. It realized that success depended on building up a relationship of credibility with the Islamic opposition since it still remained the most potent threat to the regime's legitimacy and survival. Thus, Mubarak's policy toward the Islamic opposition was two-pronged: first, to attain a degree of equilibrium between the religious and secular opposition forces; and second, to distinguish carefully between the two segments of the Islamic opposition competing for influence and control of resources, that is, between the moderates, represented by the Muslim Brotherhood, and the violent radical groups. He implemented the policy by setting up a coalition between the Muslim Brotherhood and the secular parties to run in the National Assembly elections, while at the same time the regime waged a determined war against the Islamic radicals.[8]

Mubarak proceeded cautiously with the problems he inherited from Sadat. Even as Sadat's deputy he had understood the latent danger in creating glaring Islamic symbols; once president he avoided transforming Sadat's assassins into martyrs by insisting that most of them receive relatively light sentences. At the same time, he adopted a policy of symbolic, cosmetic Islamization, such as levying heavy taxes on imported alcoholic beverages and broadening television censorship to include programs incompatible with the spirit of Islam. The government agreed to set up libraries stacked with political literature in the mosques, organize seminars on Islamic subjects, and publish religious books and pamphlets. The Muslim Brotherhood, however, was forbidden to print its own newspaper.[9]

The regime calculated that the Brotherhood and its leadership understood that they stood no chance of usurping the government's power. At the same time, the government encountered obstacles of its own in providing for the religious needs of the Egyptian public. The state's religious establishment – al-Azhar, Islam's most prestigious educational institution, and the Ministry of Religious Endowments – proved inadequate in supervising pulpit preaching (da'wa) because they had lost any vestige of credibility among many groups, especially supporters of Islamic circles. The state found itself in need of assistance from a strong force within political Islam, and the natural candidate was the Muslim Brotherhood. The government's limited ability to impact on the young population forced it to reach a tacit agreement: the Muslim Brotherhood would implement religious law without violence, and the regime would be under no obligation to grant the Brotherhood political legitimacy.[10] This truce enabled the Brotherhood to entrench its position in the religious life of the state, which consequently weakened the regime's stature in this area. In the long run the regime was forced to adopt a policy of containment against the Muslim Brotherhood in every field of activity where its influence was manifest. The challenge facing the Mubarak government on the religious level proved difficult and complex.

The Struggle on the Religious Level

The Brotherhood's strongest foothold in the struggle against the regime was unquestionably the religious front. Islam remained the main focus of identity in Egyptian society, which accounts for the attempts over many decades of all political institutions to obtain the backing of the religious circles and thus strengthen the regimes' credibility. Since the 1970s the empowerment of radical Islam made the need for religious legitimacy of the regime all the more necessary, but also transformed Islamic ideology into a popular form of protest. In response to the establishment's salaried clergy who carried out their work according to government interests, the Muslim Brotherhood installed its leaders and religious loyalists throughout the country. This move allowed Islamic activists and the masses of the faithful to choose their religious leaders without recourse to the appurtenances of the official religious establishment. The presence of fundamentalist leaders in cities and villages also bestowed Islam with a more open-minded ethos and allowed individual Muslims to consult with and seek assistance from any religious leader they chose. This phenomenon detracted from establishment Islam's credibility and threatened the government's absolutism over the interpretation and application of Islamic scripture.[11]

During the 1980s and early 1990s the government made several attempts to coordinate efforts with the Brotherhood in the realm of religion, thus differentiating between the movement's religious and political influence, particularly on the young generation. The Supreme Committee for Islamic Preaching was created on February 15, 1983, according to the prime minister's order and endorsement of the chief sheikh of al-Azhar. Committee members included the ministers of religion, education, and information. In 1987 the committee's budget was increased and stood at seven million Egyptian pounds, and more than three thousand preachers were hired. The following year Mubarak approved a sum of six million Egyptian pounds. Committee preachers and those from al-Azhar were assigned the task of reaching out to the younger generation and initiating a dialogue. In 1988 the Ministry of Religion held seventy-two meetings with the nation's youth.[12] In addition to the Supreme Committee for Islamic Preaching, the Higher Council for Islamic Affairs was renewed in 1988. This council had been set up by Nasser in 1960 to spread state ideology, and sponsored conferences and research on preaching. The Brotherhood was wary about integration into the council lest it be identified as partner to the regime – and therefore did not participate.

The regime tried competing in other areas with the Muslim Brotherhood to limit its influence in the religious sphere. The authorities confiscated millions of audio and video cassettes that the Brotherhood had distributed free of charge to its followers. The minister of education canceled radio and television programs that exploited the state's communications networks for disseminating messages with radical Islamic content. The government decided that only officials from al-Azhar University and the Ministry of Religious Endowments would appear in the media. Censorship was heightened, and the weekly *Al-Usra al-Arabiya* was temporarily shut down after the Muslim Brotherhood seized it and used it to attack Mubarak and his regime.[13]

In practice, all attempts at coordination and reconciliation between the Muslim Brotherhood and the regime in the 1980s and early 1990s were strained, as each side feared that the association would threaten its independence. The regime, in particular the Ministry of the Interior, perceived the Muslim Brotherhood as an illegal rival to the state, and therefore it doubted that the movement's activity would be constructive participation. Ministry officials were uneasy over the Muslim Brotherhood's appearance in public as a legitimate group, lest its strength soar at the expense of the state and the regime find itself in a trap. The interior minister regarded the Brotherhood's members as cunning, incorrigible, and prone to violence. During Zaki Bader's term as interior minister (1986–90), the Brotherhood was under heavy police surveillance, with young members often taken into custody, maltreated, and tortured in prison. The Ministry of the Interior lost no opportunity to denounce the Brotherhood and exhibit them as seekers of power and acclaim who defiled the spirit of true Islam. Ministry officials also tried to uncover conspiracies between the Muslim

Brotherhood and radical circles. The police confiscated the movement's publications and forbade it to hold public meetings.

Consternation in the Ministry of Religius Endowments was even greater. The growing need to recruit qualified, popular clergymen to counter radical Islam proved that al-Azhar sheikhs and officials of the state religious establishment were incapable of doing the job. For all practical purposes, they were caught in a bind: on the one hand, they represented the regime; on the other hand, they were liable to be seen as evangelizing messengers of Muslim Brotherhood.[14]

The government's repeated efforts at curtailing the young generation's identification with the radical Islamic movements were unsuccessful. In April 1993 a report published in the newspaper *al-Wafd* acknowledged that government-sponsored preaching delegations aimed at turning the youth away from extremism and terrorism had failed. The government had squandered millions of Egyptian pounds on sparsely-attended symposia organized by establishment preachers in various districts; most of the audience had to be corralled into attending in order to avoid totally discrediting the Ministry of Religious Endowments. A large proportion of the participants were, in fact, ministry officials and government proxies, while the youth, for whom the symposia had been arranged, were conspicuously absent. Young radicals who wanted to attend were hustled away so as not to disturb the organizers. In the end, no form of dialogue with the nation's youth took place in the symposia, and demagogic speeches against extremists widened the gap between the establishment and the young generation.[15] Despite this, the minister of religious endowments, Mohammad Ali Mahgoub, met with ministry directors and declared that the religious delegations would continue reaching out to young people to shield them from Islamic terror and fanaticism.[16]

A particularly vexing issue for the regime was the supervision over tens of thousands of mosques throughout the country. The mosque serves as the central pillar of every Islamic movement. It also functions as a focal point for prayer, social gatherings, preaching, the announcement of messages, recruitment of members for radical Islamic organizations, and as a safe house for secret meetings and fugitives. The mosque provides living quarters for the homeless, an alternative to welfare agencies, and social and cultural institutions that are practically nonexistent in certain districts, especially in southern Egypt. The fundamentalist movement, along with its ancillaries and particularly the Muslim Brotherhood, has made extensive use of the mosques. According to the Ministry of Religious Endowments, in 1993, 170,000 private, small mosques functioned in Egypt independent of government supervision, while 20,000–30,000 mosques were under state control. Senior officials in the ministry claim that the actual number of small, private mosques was much higher and approached 400,000. The majority of them (excluding those under ministry supervision) were havens for private preachers, members of the Muslim Brotherhood and other Islamic organizations, who stirred opposition to the regime. According to ministry reports, many mosques became hideouts where fanatics stashed bayonets, chains, propaganda fliers, and even guns. The situation was exceptionally precarious in Upper Egypt where private mosques were used as bases for incitement and violence against the regime. In one private mosque the preacher fulminated that the state rulers were infidels and a jihad should be waged against them. Young people attending the mosques regularly absorbed religious edicts from the leaders of radical groups.

Under these circumstances and as part of a comprehensive plan to counter the Muslim Brotherhood's religious operations, the regime launched the nationalization of the country's mosques. It drew up a plan to take over the private mosques and hinged the establishment of new mosques on the formal approval of state security agencies. Only state appointed preachers could serve in the nationalized mosques. The government plan for 1993, for example, was designed to subordinate 5,000 small private mosques to state supervision at a cost of half a billion Egyptian pounds.[17]

Forcing the private mosques under the control of the Ministry of Religious Endowments generated hostility and sparked great tension, especially in Upper Egypt. Islamic groups felt that since the government had exhausted its means of struggle in the schools, universities, and trade unions, it now turned to the Islamists' last stronghold – the mosques. In the southern city of Minya tension flared after the Directorate of State Security Investigations announced the nationalization of all private mosques, first and foremost the prestigious Omar Ibn al-Khatab Mosque. The mosque, administered by the Muslim Brotherhood, served as the Brotherhood headquarters in Upper Egypt for meetings, conferences, and regular public addresses. The Brotherhood adamantly refused to let the Ministry of Holy Endowments appropriate the mosque. The police were mobilized, entered the mosque's courtyard, and demolished a charity market for distributing textbooks and writing supplies that had been set up by the Brotherhood as the school year approached. The police then stormed into the mosque, stopped the local preacher in the midst of his sermon, and substituted another preacher who was employed by the Ministry of Religious Endowments. The takeover of the Omar Ibn al-Khatab Mosque triggered massive unrest among the worshippers and in the local branch of the Muslim Brotherhood.

Elsewhere, the regime replaced clergymen affiliated with the Brotherhood and radical groups in the nationalized mosques with imams and preachers who were al-Azhar graduates. But in 1992, for example, although 40,000 imams were needed, only 3,000 imams from al-Azhar were accepted by the Ministry of Religious Endowments. On the other hand, the mosques that stayed under Muslim Brotherhood control enjoyed financial backing from private contributors and charity funds.[18]

Despite these obstacles the regime continued to pressure private mosques to submit to government control, but the pace of implementation was slow, especially in a state as vast and densely populated as Egypt. The remoteness of thousands of villages from the country's hub and the absence of communication links hindered the smooth flow of instructions from the Ministry of Religious Endowments and even led to their being ignored. The regime realized that a more vigorous and effective strategy was needed in the battle for the mosques. On December 7, 1996 the People's Assembly passed Law 238 on organized pulpit preaching, which placed mosque preachers in Egypt under the authority of the Ministry of Religious Endowments. The law obligated preachers outside the framework of the ministry to obtain permission for delivering sermons in the mosques. Violators of the law could expect a fine of up to one hundred Egyptian pounds, instead of the previous five pounds, or imprisonment of up to one month.

This new criminal law generated a dispute among the Egyptian religious leaders and aroused keen interest in other Arab states. The minister of religious endowments launched a vigorous information campaign and stressed that the law was a continuation and improvement of existing laws dating from 1960 and 1964 that had also emphasized the subordination of Egyptian mosques to the Ministry of Religious Endowments but that had not been stringent enough. He further stated that the new law on organized preaching was based on a religious and legal standing, that is, on the Abu Khanifa approach, in use in Egypt for centuries, which holds that Friday prayer is to be conducted only in the presence of the sultan or his deputy. According to the minister, the representative of the sultan's deputy is now the Ministry of Religious Endowments, and therefore all mosques must acquiesce to the supervision of the ministry with no one allowed to preach from the pulpit (manbar) without legal permission. The minister vowed that monitors would be dispatched for surprise inspections; they would listen to the sermons and report their findings. Within the framework of the new law 23,000 preachers would receive certificates, and 6,500 imams would be appointed for duty in the mosques, all al-Azhar graduates.

As expected, the new law proved highly controversial. Religious sages (ulama) divided into two camps. The holders of state jobs, such as the mufti Dr. Nasser Farid Wasel, who headed al-Azhar, supported the law, while the al-Azhar Front of Religious Sages rigorously opposed it. The minister of religious endowments, Dr. Mohammad Hamdi Zakzuk, clashed with this group, accusing it of acting as a social union, independent of al-Azhar. The minister reiterated that he neither nationalized the mosques, nor boycotted them or dictated the sermons' contents. Nevertheless, he acknowledged that 7,000 mosques had come under the jurisdiction of the Ministry of Religious Endowments in 1996, and that this step was taken in response to specific requests by the owners of the mosques. In his testimony before the People's Assembly, Minster Zakzuk made it clear, "There is no room among us for preachers who deviate from the true path of Islam."[19]

By the end of the decade, comprehensive nationalization of the private mosques had not succeeded, and many that were nationalized remained vacant. The transfer of private mosques to government control was extremely costly. The director of the mosque division in the Ministry of Religious Endowments disclosed that the cost of 5000 additional mosques to his bureau came to thirty million Egyptian pounds – for salaries, maintenance, and furniture – but the regime lacked the necessary funding. Another problem was the shortage of imams and preachers. Nonetheless, the Ministry of Religious Endowments continued to demand that private mosques accede to its supervision, even though according to government statistics, approximately 25,000 private mosques were still functioning in February 1997. Since then, new private mosques were erected legally, provided that the construction site was not under litigation. These mosques were often built for reasons of prestige, family status, or in reaction to the construction of a church. The Ministry of Religious Endowments ensured that preachers would avoid political issues or certain foreign and domestic matters, and sometimes instructed the clergymen to elaborate on current social issues such as population growth or water conservation.[20]

The regime's containment policy in the religion arena did not yield decisive results, and the balance of power at this level leaned mainly toward the Brotherhood. The regime did not manage to counter the Brotherhood's eagerly absorbed Islamic message because of the deep poverty in daily life, the Brotherhood's organizational skills, the spirit of volunteerism among its followers, and the warm embrace it extended to the general public, especially young people. The regime also lacked the requisite human and financial resources to bear the responsibility for so colossal a clerical system. Nevertheless, the law on organized preaching had great significance in relegating private mosques to state authority, and it testified to the regime's determination to persevere in this process. The law assisted the government in the campaign against the phenomenon of preachers summoning thousands of worshippers to prayer in the middle of the streets without state authorization – not to mention the many Islamic preachers who exploited their prodigious influence and exhorted their audience to acts of violence against the government. The need for permission also enabled the state to supervise Friday's money collection, ostensibly for charity, but frequently channeled to the coffers of Islamic political organizations.[21] The battle of the mosques was likely to continue, as long as thousands of mosques, imams, and preachers remained outside the regime's control.

The Challenge of Social Islam

One of the difficult challenges the Mubarak regime confronted in the Muslim Brotherhood was social Islam, meaning, a vast, efficient network of public aid and welfare services established by the Muslim Brotherhood. It was based on thousands of private, voluntary organizations set up in the 1980s whose number increased substantially in the 1990s. The welfare services intended to fill the vacuum created by the regime's inability to answer the public's burgeoning needs. For all practical purposes it was the Islamists who fulfilled promises made to the public by successive national regimes, and the Islamists who provided concrete solutions for genuine problems. Islamic activists fanned out into cities and villages and set up boarding schools, day schools, clinics, and medical services – all at prices the public could afford. These social services were generally annexed to local mosques. The benefit to the population far exceeded what the government or even the private sector offered.

In the early 1980s the Muslim Brotherhood also founded Islamic investment companies that were run strictly according to the spirit of Islam. They offered their customers and investors a higher yield rate than that of commercial banks, with the yield defined as profit distribution and not as interest, since interest is prohibited according to religious law. The Islamic companies acted through contracts with clients on the principle of partnership in profit and loss. Since the companies were independent of the central bank's control they were not obliged to publish financial statements. Tens of thousands of workers found employment in Muslim Brotherhood companies and projects. The firms succeeded in enlisting huge amounts of capital that they in turn passed on to the Muslim Brotherhood. Little information was available on their activity, but there was talk in social and economic circles of company transactions amounting to billions of Egyptian pounds. At the same time, word subsequently leaked out that a number of Islamic companies folded due to faulty management, and in some cases were bailed out by the government in order to stave off heavy financial losses among the investors.[22]

With its earnings the Brotherhood acquired already existing schools, and established new elementary and secondary ones. This investment was carried out according to the Brotherhood's policy of assigning priority to education, so that the Islamic message was inculcated in the young generation. And thus, by May 1993, a senior figure in the Education

Directorate's Security Division announced that the Muslim Brotherhood and Islamic radicals had infiltrated the entire education system, including schools in Cairo. According to the same source, the Ministry of the Interior had proved incapable of blocking this penetration due to the shortage of teachers. Acceptance into the Brotherhood's institutions required the pupil's mother to wear a veil and recite certain chapters from the Qur'an by heart.[23]

The Muslim Brotherhood channeled its social benefits mainly to the poor neighborhoods and slums of Cairo. In the impoverished Imbaba neighborhood in the early 1990s, for example, only four government schools were functioning for half a million residents. Parents lacked the money to pay for private teachers. The Muslim Brotherhood filled this gap by opening schools in the mosques and kindergartens on the ground floor of tenement buildings. These educational institutions were outside of state supervision, and tuition amounted to a token five to ten Egyptian pounds per month.[24]

Dozens of Brotherhood-owned Islamic investment companies complicated matters, since they functioned as the movement's economic tool, enabling it to operate in areas where the regime had failed. The private, voluntary Islamic organizations were especially effective during periods of crisis and economic depression. In October 1992 a devastating earthquake hit Egypt, leaving thousands homeless. The Brotherhood mobilized volunteers from its private organizations and the trade unions under its control, and supplied swifter, more efficient emergency assistance than the government and secular organizations.[25]

The regime acted on three levels for overseeing the private civilian associations. The first was through legislation. In 1964, Law Number 32 was issued, defining the associations' (Islamic and other) spheres of activity, such as social assistance, care of infants, the elderly and handicapped, cultural programs, and so forth. The law granted the authorities the right to disband or merge associations if they judged that the services of a particular association no longer corresponded with public needs, or for security reasons, or because of a liability, such as a danger to public health. The authorities also had the right, according to Law Number 32, to dissolve an association that replaced a previously disbanded one. The second level was through financial supervision regarding the amount of monetary assistance granted to each association. Although this level of control infringed upon the associations' independence, subordinating them – indirectly at any rate – to state control, for all practical purposes it barely touched the Islamic associations inasmuch as they were independent of state money, receiving their funding from Islamic financial sources, such as religious alms, private donations, and profits from the Islamic companies. The third level on which the regime acted was through issuing privileges to associations that operated in areas where the state had an interest, or to associations whose activity complemented that of the government agencies.

A turning point in the regime's struggle with social-economic Islam was the passing of Law Number 146 in 1988. The law proved fatal for Islamic investment companies and voluntary associations. It allowed the authorities to harass Islamic projects by carrying out searches, inspections, arrests, and investigations on the pretext of security exigencies. In the first stage of the law's implementation, social Islam was forced to curtail its activity and the Islamic companies suffered a setback. However, the law's impact on the Islamic associations soon waned. This was due in large part to the fact that Law Number 32 – which defined the activity of private associations – placed the same limitations on all the associations, whether Islamic or secular. Moreover, many associations did not even fall under the jurisdiction of Law Number 32. The Islamic associations operated according to the ruling of Law 384 of 1956 that permitted them to function in social and welfare spheres, not only in religious affairs. Even in the 1960s the Muslim Brotherhood had taken advantage of this breach and expanded their work in health and education. By the 1980s and 1990s, therefore, the Brotherhood was actively involved in kindergartens, schools, and housing for Egyptian and foreign students. The Islamic associations opened professional training courses that attracted many unemployed young people. These projects not only helped the Islamic associations legally surmount the regime's attempt to undermine their credibility, but they also increased association activity.

The regime was caught in a dilemma in its campaign against social-economic Islam, and this may explain why it failed to exhibit the same boldness as in other areas of struggle against Muslim Brotherhood operations. The government had to accept the fact that the Islamic investment companies and the voluntary associations that marketed products to the people at low prices and supplied food and services to the destitute appeared as oxygen to the suffocating masses because of the country's dire poverty level and the government's inability to relieve economic conditions. Indeed, in the latter part of the twentieth century, while economic misery deepened because of the oil crisis, the dependency of the unemployed, homeless, and poor on the aid and welfare services of the Islamic associations rose. Along with the voluntary associations, Islamic banks were set up to provide loans for the needy. Given Egypt's economic reality, the regime was powerless to counter social Islam's activity or bring it under its wing. Although political Islam made the daily headlines, it was social Islam that had a far greater influence over people's lives, and this in turn enhanced public sympathy for the Muslim Brotherhood.[26]

A final word: contrary to what is common in the West, voluntary associations are not an everyday occurrence in the Arab world; ironically, it was the fundamentalist movement that introduced this modern, Western phenomenon into Arab-Muslim society. In this light, the Brotherhood's achievements in establishing its social-economic project were even more remarkable.

The Struggle in the Parliamentary Arena

The Muslim Brotherhood's integration into the political system was not a simple matter since it involved two diametrically opposed approaches. For Islam, the source of absolute authority, truth, and sovereignty is God; according to democratic principles, the source, at least in political terms, is human. Islam is rooted in the consciousness of the masses and deeply embedded in Egyptian culture. Democracy, on the other hand, which is linked to the West and has a history of failures that have wrought the Arabs grave disappointments and obliterated cherished Arab values, is generally perceived as a force striving for cultural, political, and economic hegemony in the Arab-Muslim world. Compromise, therefore, did not come easily for the Islamic movement. Its willingness to participate in the democratic system implied a renunciation, at the pragmatic level, of the option of seizing control of the government. At the theoretical level, the willingness to participate in the system might suggest a surrender of the traditional non-compromising Islamic outlook, whereby the entire Muslim community must exist in a single political framework. Granting legitimacy to other systems would signify a division of the Islamic nation and is therefore inconceivable.

However, the tactical pragmatism that evolved in the Muslim Brotherhood enabled it to modify its attitude toward political pluralism. The Brotherhood of the 1980s recalled the precedents and arguments espoused by Hassan al-Banna that an advantage could be gained by integration into the pluralistic system since the goal of *da'wa* – preaching for the Islamization of society – was not only to reach out to the masses (the Brotherhood had accomplished this), but also to gain entry into the official level, and the closest path to this led through People's Assembly. Banna stated that it was forbidden to abandon the stage of the People's Assembly to the monopoly of other parties since this theater should also reverberate with the voice of the Islamic movement. Banna claimed that Islam embodies religion and state therefore there must be unity between the religious and political spheres in the life of the nation. The Muslim Brotherhood's participation within the official framework would demonstrate this principle to the public.

Fifty years after Banna delivered these principles, the deputy general guide, Mustafa Mashour (who was appointed general guide in 1996) reaffirmed Banna's vision, and supported seizing the opportunity to use the current system for the Brotherhood's needs. The movement's participation in the People's Assembly did not imply that it agreed with the justice of human legislation; the main goal of its parliamentary activity was to implement the laws of *shari'a*. Its participation in the elections would advance the dissemination of religious information, while the forum of the People's Assembly would serve as an effective conduit for purging people's hearts and minds of Western concepts.[27] From the Brotherhood's point of view, the path to the People's Assembly during the tenure of President Mubarak was legitimate.

Mubarak's attempts in his first years as president to progress toward a more democratic government included the participation of the Muslim Brotherhood in the 1984 general elections for the People's Assembly. The Brotherhood was allowed to take part in the elections, though it was prohibited from running as an independent political party since it was still officially illegal (based on Nasser's 1954 interdiction). In practical terms, the regime's policy called for the merger of the Muslim Brotherhood with a secular party – the Wafd – in a political alliance to form the principal opposition bloc in the People's Assembly. This coalition won fifty-eight out of 448 seats (approximately 13%) in the People's Assembly (table 2.1).[28]

As the 1987 general elections approached, the Muslim Brotherhood aligned with the Labor Party (al-Amal) and the Liberal Party (al-Ahrar) in a coalition referred to as "the three-way alliance" or "the Islamic alliance." Each partner had its reasons for joining. The Muslim Brotherhood needed to enter a legitimate alliance since it was still considered an illegal party. Like the Brotherhood, al-Amal was also interested in establishing an Islamic state (though by legitimate means), and the small al-Ahrar party had no prospect of getting elected to the People's Assembly if it ran independently. The results of the 1987 elections produced the largest opposition bloc, whose strength in the Assembly, led by the Muslim Brotherhood, rose from seven delegates to thirty-four (table 2.2).[29]

By deciding to take part in the democratic process the Muslim Brotherhood enjoyed the best of both worlds. It retained its two key principles: one, that *shari'a* would serve as the main source for legislation (as stipulated in the coalition platform); two, the movement's entry into the People's Assembly would be legal, legitimate, and acceptable to the regime.

The Brotherhood acted with great energy and initiative in the People's Assembly, pressuring the government to realize its objectives. The permanent issue on its agenda was to have *shari'a* as the exclusive system in the state. Between 1987 and 1990 the Brotherhood submitted numerous queries to the minister of the interior during Assembly debates, demanding answers for actions that it regarded as violations of individual rights, such

Table 2.1 People's Assembly Election Results, 1984

Number of seats in the elections	Number of seats (appointed)	The National Democratic Party (NDP)	The Wafd-Muslim Brotherhood Alliance	Labor (al-Amal) (appointed)	Liberal (al-Ahrar)	Progressive National Unity Party (al-Tajamu)
448	10	390	58 51 (Wafd) 7 (Muslim Brotherhood)	4	—	—

Note: The consitution authorized the president to appoint ten representatives to the People's Assembly in addition to the 448 elected delegates. This number includes the al-Amal representatives.

Source: Mustafa, *The Political Regime and the Islamic Opposition in Egypt,* pp. 315–16.

Table 2.2 People's Assembly Election Results, 1987

Number of seats in the elections	Number of seats (appointed)	The National Democratic Party (NDP)	The Wafd	The Islamic Alliance (al-Amal, the Muslim Brotherhood, al-Ahrar)	Progressive National Unity Party (al-Tajamu)	Independents
*448	10	348	35	**60	1 (appointed)	5

* Four hundred representatives were elected from the lists, 48 as independents.
** The Muslim Brotherhood – 34, al-Amal – 22, al-Ahrar – 4. In addition, 4 independent Islamists were elected.

Source: Mustafa, *The Political Regime and the Islamic Opposition in Egypt*, p. 317.

as torture under interrogation and unlawful imprisonment. It insisted on ending the country's state of emergency and prosecution of citizens in military tribunals.[30]

The regime's reaction to the Islamic offensive in the People's Assembly was twofold: first, it rejected the bulk of the opposition's legislative proposals through the overwhelming majority of the government party; and second, it put forward alternative proposals through government ministers in the Assembly. Parallel to these moves, the regime made a number of concessions of a moral and social nature, such as prohibiting alcoholic beverages on Egyptian airlines, but this had little impact on the Brotherhood, which exerted greater pressure in the People's Assembly to institute the primacy of Islamic law in the state. The Brotherhood attempted to capitalize on the powerful religious emotions, latent or at the forefront, among the Egyptian public.[31]

The integration of the Muslim Brotherhood in the People's Assembly had been planned not only to promote democracy in Egypt, but also to diminish the strength of the Islamic opposition that denied the regime's legitimacy. The government had tried to achieve this goal by splitting the Brotherhood's ranks. In the first years of Mubarak's presidency this policy succeeded in reducing the Islamic opposition to a certain degree, but after some time three indications of the policy's drawbacks emerged. The first indication was the alliance formed between the Muslim Brotherhood and the Wafd party in the 1984 elections to the People's Assembly, which augmented the Islamic trend rather than foiled it. Wafd's strength weakened, and as the 1987 elections approached, the Muslim Brotherhood, together with the liberal and labor parties, established the tripartite alliance and scored an impressive victory at the polls. The second indication in the late 1980s was the escalation of terrorist acts executed by radical Islamic organizations. The third indication was the Brotherhood's success in linking itself not only to political parties but also to various institutions and associations, such as the students union, and in expanding its social-economic projects at the grassroots level.

The main reason for the government's failure was the difficulty in using one party (al-Amal) for creating a split in the Muslim Brotherhood, especially when both parties had a common political goal: the founding of an Islamic religious state by political means. Although al-Amal was not an Islamic party, it supported the Muslim Brotherhood's demand to establish an Islamic theocratic state. The third partner in the alliance – al-Ahrar – was too weak to be of use to the government in dividing the Brotherhood. In effect, all of Egypt's political parties had been sapped of power beyond recovery from the time they were disbanded by Nasser's revolutionary regime. Against this backdrop, the Muslim Brotherhood was conspicuous in its organizational ability and discipline, and the dedication of its members. The movement's credibility remained firmly intact despite the government's expectations. The authorities had forced the Brotherhood to join a coalition with legitimate parties, but this had not deterred it from spreading the Islamic message directly to the public by addressing its innermost religious feelings. Concomitantly, the Brotherhood took full advantage of the forum in the People's Assembly. Overall, therefore, its strength and influence burgeoned in the 1980s while on the ground the radical organizations' terrorist operations showed no sign of a letup. The regime found itself unremittingly engaged in countering terrorist groups that threatened to paralyze life in the country, but it was incapable of solving the social-economic problems that were the breeding ground of Islamic militancy.[32]

The rising wave of terrorism in the late 1980s, the Brotherhood's vigorous activity in the People's Assembly, and the government's failure in the area of religion led to changes in the regime's policy against the Muslim Brotherhood. The entire state network, especially the legal establishment, went into action on two levels: it intended to quash the Brotherhood on the political–parliamentary level and in the trade unions. President Mubarak published an edict, Law Number 206, concerning the forthcoming 1990 elections to the People's Assembly that instituted changes in the electoral system and the gerrymandering of voting districts. The opposition, led by the Islamic alliance (with 17 percent of the seats in the Assembly), vehemently criticized the law and charged that it was designed in part to add towns to voting districts where the government party was weak in order to bolster its position. In the final analysis, the new law that was passed in order to redistribute the balance of power between the tripartite alliance and other political forces drove the Muslim Brotherhood out of the People's Assembly and forced it to boycott the April 1990 elections. The Wafd party joined with the Muslim Brotherhood, abandoned the People's Assembly in protest, and also boycotted the elections. The regime was relieved of the Islamic and liberal political opposition that had been weighing heavily on it, but its policy for curbing Islamic influence fell short of the mark.[33]

Both the regime and the Brotherhood learned a lesson from their six-year, democratic–parliamentary experiment. The regime's lesson was never to make a similar political overture toward the Muslim Brotherhood. For its part, the Brotherhood searched for a new channel to advance its goals, and chose the trade unions.

The Battle in the Trade Unions

From the mid-1980s the Muslim Brotherhood dominated most of the executive boards in the Egyptian trade unions as a result of its electorial achievements on the national and local levels. During the tenures of General Guides Omar Talmasani (died 1986) and Mohammad Hamad Abu Nasser (died 1996), the Brotherhood adopted a vigorous policy to gain influence and control in the trade unions. Between 1987 and 1990 it won a majority of seats on many union boards. In elections to the engineers union in 1987, the movement captured fifty-four out of sixty-one seats; in 1988 it won all twelve seats in the doctors union; in 1990 it took the entire management council of the professors at the University of Cairo; and in the same year it took ten out of twelve seats in the pharmacists union's executive board.

Because of the ban against the Brotherhood's movement as an independent party, the trade unions served the Muslim Brotherhood as an alternative arena for political activity once banned from the People's Assembly. Thus, the regime's attempt to neutralize Muslim Brotherhood opposition inadvertently pushed the Brotherhood toward the trade unions, which then became the political stage for confrontation. Following its ouster from the People's Assembly, the movement invested profuse energy in gaining control of the unions. By means of an enticing Islamic message and superb organizational skill, it succeeded in obtaining public support that proved invaluable in the elections to many of the unions. In September 1992 it scored an impressive victory by gaining control of the most important of all unions – the lawyers union.[34]

As the regime anxiously observed the Brotherhood's takeover of the trade unions, it was forced to devise a response. It tried to handle the threat legislatively, publishing Law Number 100 in 1993 that dealt with elections to trade unions. The law was intended to obstruct the Muslim Brotherhood and its operations in the unions by stating that the elections would be binding only with a minimum of 50 percent voter participation. It further stipulated that the court would monitor union elections, and in this way the regime planned to influence the election results. Law Number 100 was severely criticized, especially in the unions led by the Muslim Brotherhood, and it proved ineffective in reducing the Brotherhood's influence. In 1993 the movement gained control of a large number of trade unions,[35] as illustrated in figure 2.1.

An attempt was made in March 1994, apparently with regime support, to set up alternative trade unions comprised of opponents of the Muslim Brotherhood. These unions were called the "National Committee of Egyptian Tradesmen." The initiators of the alternative unions claimed that the Brotherhood, instead of providing equal services to all union members, had shown partiality toward its own followers.[36] The plan for alternative unions, however, never came to fruition, and the regime considered more drastic measures and began to arrest and interrogate senior Brotherhood activists.

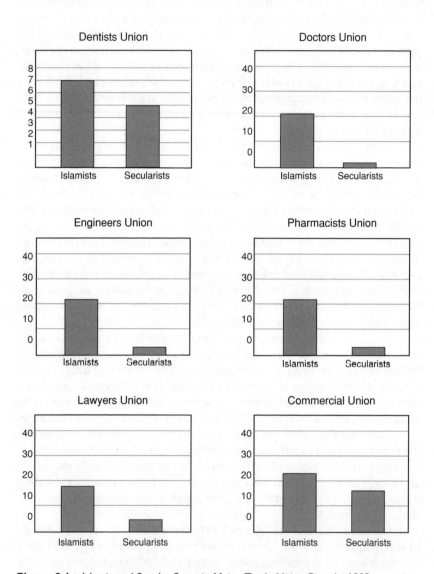

Figure 2.1   Islamic and Secular Seats in Major Trade Union Boards, 1993

Source: Saad Eddin Ibrahim, "Arab Modernity and the Challenge of Islam: The Case of Egypt's Islamic Activism" (Cairo: Ibn Khaldoun Center for Development Studies, 1994), p. 8.

Relations between the government and the Brotherhood deteriorated steadily following the death during police questioning of Abdel Kharit Madani, a lawyer and important figure in the movement. Madani (born in 1962) was arrested on April 26, 1994 in his Cairo office, brought to his home with hands tied while a house search was carried out, and was then taken for questioning. A week later he died in prison. On May 5 the police summoned his family to retrieve the body. The corpse was placed in a casket, but the authorities refused the family's request for an autopsy. According to the official police statement, Madani died of natural causes, but the Muslim Brotherhood insisted that he died under torture. Madani's death sparked an outburst of anger and demonstrations. The lawyers union organized protest rallies, which were dominated by the Muslim Brotherhood. On May 17, one thousand lawyers attended a mass protest that met in the union's Cairo headquarters; thousands marched in the streets carrying placards accusing the government of interrogating Madani under torture and employing electric shocks that had caused his death. The police clashed with the demonstrators and tried to herd them into the union's headquarters with tear gas and plastic bullets.

A number of demonstrators were injured and thirty-nine were taken into custody, thirty-seven of whom were lawyers. The incident smoldered on the public agenda, and the minister of the interior, Hassan al-Alfi, in charge of internal security, was called on to furnish explanations. In an interview on May 21 with the semi-official daily *Akhbar al-Yawm*, Alfi denied that Madani had been tortured by the police and claimed he had a severe asthma attack – an illness he was known to suffer from. Alfi contended that when Madani was brought to a second home that he owned for a house search, he suffered an asthma attack, collapsed, and lost consciousness. He was rushed to the prison hospital and as a result of his illness died on the evening of April 27. Alfi asserted that Madani never even arrived at the building of the Directorate of State Security Investigations, and he further stated that he was in possession of a document certifying on the basis of an autopsy that no signs of violence were found on Madani's body. The authorities wanted Madani alive in order to glean vital information from him, and as Madani had been one of ninety-eight people arrested, any accusations would have to account for why he was the only person in custody tortured.

Alfi reiterated the suspicions against Madani of complicity in relaying instructions from terrorist commanders in prison to their cohorts on the outside. According to Alfi, the documents discovered in Madani's home testified to his role in financing terrorist cells and transferring money to the commander of the military wing of al-Jihad, who had recently been shot by the police. Finally, Alfi mentioned that the lengthy delay in producing an official explanation for Madani's death was due to security needs for maintaining media silence in order to ensure the success of the investigation and avoid leaks. Alfi failed to convince Muslim Brotherhood circles of the government's innocence in Madani's death, and the demonstrations continued for a long time afterwards. The affair was eventually consigned to the realm of unsolved political mysteries.[37]

Against the background of rising tension in government–Muslim Brotherhood relations and after the authorities gained the initiative in the campaign against terrorist organizations, the regime decided the moment had come to clash with its moderate Islamic rival, the Muslim Brotherhood.[38]

From Containment to All-Out Confrontation

In mid-1994 the regime launched an aggressive, tenacious campaign against the Muslim Brotherhood. While political scientists, research analysts, and the Egyptian media are generally in agreement about this, and the regime's spokesmen have confirmed this assessment, various explanations have been offered regarding the regime's reasons for escalating the struggle at this particular time, and the style and substance of the confrontation.

On February 5, 1992 security forces in Heliopolis raided a building housing the offices of the Salsabil computer company. The search uncovered evidence of a plot by the Muslim Brotherhood in Egypt for toppling the regime and seizing power. The plans, outlined in fourteen documents, detailed the structure and methods of the Muslim Brotherhood, its worldwide organization, and the names of activists. The clinching piece was the *al-Tamkin* (capability) document that outlined in detail the scheme for overthrowing the regime, including "preparations for carrying out future tasks and acquiring administrative skills for managing state affairs." The document stated that the keystone of the plan was the Muslim Brotherhood's entry into public sectors and takeover of certain groups: students, workers, free tradesmen, businessmen, and the lower classes. The document also specifically referred to the army and police as targets for seizure by the Brotherhood in its master plan to expand its control in powerful institutions, first and foremost the media. The instruction manual (*dalil*) appended to the blueprint delineated the stages of the coup and a precise timetable for its execution.[39]

Tensions increased following the Muslim Brotherhood gains in the lawyers union in September 1992. Lawyers who were Brotherhood members found themselves in military tribunals in the High Court for State Security on trial for abetting the violent operations of extremist Islamic groups and for acting as intermediaries between Islamic leaders in prison and leaders on the outside. The violent activity referred to attacks on tourists, the murder of the writer Farag Foda, and attempted assassination of the Nobel Prize-winning author Naguib Mahfouz.[40]

Still, in early 1994 the regime was unable to focus on the Muslim Brotherhood because it was involved in a bitter struggle against radical extremists who had perpetrated serious terrorist attacks. The Brotherhood continued unfurling its banner "Islam is the solution," a slogan that attracted a huge number of adherents because of the sorrowful reality of Egyptian life. The Brotherhood condemned violence and terrorism, but never concealed its intention of replacing the secular regime with an Islamic theocracy. It exploited the relatively liberal atmosphere in the country in order to secure control of the trade unions. The regime – in addition to combating the terrorist organizations – still deliberated over the question of how to neutralize the long-term Islamic threat without directly confronting it, since a head-on clash could be viewed negatively by the public and there was no guarantee that the regime would emerge the victor.

By the middle of the year, against the background of several factors – escalating friction with the Muslim Brotherhood, Madani's death in police custody, and the government's upper hand in the battle against terrorists – the regime decided to wage an all-out confrontation against the Muslim Brotherhood. In an interview with *Der Spiegel* published on May 16, 1994, Mubarak termed the Muslim Brotherhood "an illegal organization, standing behind most of the fanatical religious activity." But, mindful of the heavy price of a total war against the movement, the regime defined its objective: redrawing the red lines within which the Muslim Brotherhood would be allowed to operate.[41]

According to an approach put forth at the Al-Ahram Center for Political and Strategic Studies, the regime's change in strategy from containment to all-out confrontation was a function of two major factors:

1 The regime realized that the Muslim Brotherhood had made only a limited contribution to preventing or even reducing terror.
2 Evidence of the Brotherhood's clandestine activity and its links to radical Islamic groups (for example, the Salsabil case).

Dr. Gehad Auda of the Al-Ahram Center argues that government strategy gradually crystallized parallel to events unfolding on the ground. According to Auda, in the early days of Mubarak's rule, a mutual under-standing was reached between the regime and the Brotherhood regarding each side's limitations to overpower the other and unilaterally impose its terms. Both rivals realized that political coexistence, within a framework of recognized areas and limitations, would serve their mutual interests. Thus, a degree of normalization of regime–Brotherhood relations was achieved in the 1980s, with a particular understanding regarding religion. The regime permitted the Muslim Brotherhood to propagate its religious message publicly, allocated it money, and placed the state's religious establishment at its disposal. The government's motive was to gain quiet and stability so that it could channel its efforts to promoting economic reforms. Mubarak even reconciled himself to the Muslim Brotherhood's growing influence in the People's Assembly, perhaps because he realized that for all practical purposes Islamic representation in this body had no influence on the decision-making process.

However, in the early 1990s it became clear that the normalization process had failed. Before the outbreak of the wave of terrorism in mid-1992, the government adopted a strategy of "selective containment," meaning that on occasion it took countermeasures to block the Muslim Brotherhood. Yet more and more the Egyptian bureaucracy, especially the internal security agencies, could not tolerate the Muslim Brotherhood as a legitimate entity; from their point of view it was nothing short of an illegal organization that was restrained regularly on suspicion of links to violent groups, and as such, the security officials concluded, it should be relentlessly pursued. Another factor that shattered the chances of normalization with the Muslim Brotherhood was the radical Islamic groups. These organizations defied the rules of the game that the state had drawn up in its Muslim Brotherhood policy, and when the terrorist acts intensified in mid-1992, the tacit understanding between the regime and the Brotherhood dissolved. At this point the government launched a campaign to extirpate terrorism in Egypt, and the Muslim Brotherhood lost much of its credibility. After the assassination attempt on Mubarak in June 1995, the regime implemented the strategy of exclusion and non-recognition of the movement's existence (*istib'ad*).[42]

In 1996, Professor Saad Eddin Ibrahim, director of the Ibn Khaldoun Center in Cairo, described Mubarak's first nine years in government as quiet years that were not utilized properly to advance an understanding with the Muslim Brotherhood. Instead, radical Islamic organizations gained influence and prestige and the situation deteriorated. Quietly and confidently the moderate Brotherhood continued to improve its standing in the trade unions, including the most important union, the lawyers union. Meanwhile, the radical al-Jihad and al-Jama'a al-Islamiyya organizations intensified their terrorist activities, murdering government and security officials, tourists, and members of the Copt minority. The wave of terrorism reached its climax in 1993 with well over one thousand victims (killed and wounded). The regime had been caught off guard and feared the disruption of life and onset of instability in the country; therefore at the end of the year it decided to implement an aggressive policy against the Islamic organizations. As in the past, the iron fist was directed against the

Muslim Brotherhood. The government estimated that the Brotherhood posed a greater danger to the regime in the long run because of its size, organizational strength, its populist Islamic message, and its influence on the public.

Two different approaches toward internal security policy were at work in the regime. The first, drafted by the former minister of the interior Hassan Abu Basha, claimed that radical Islam should be countered not only by the state's anti-terrorism unit but also through the integration of political measures and social-economic reforms. In other words, the suppression of Islamic radicalism required the implementation of a comprehensive medium-range policy rather than police action alone designed to defuse short-term emergencies. The second school was the concept of Fu'ad Allam, who for over a decade served as the head of the Directorate of State Security Investigations. Allam believed that all the Islamic organizations, including the Muslim Brotherhood and terrorist groups, were of one ilk, so that even the most extensive economic, political, or social reforms would have no effect in dissuading the Islamic groups to abandon their dream of replacing the government. Faced with this reality the state had no choice but to deal decisively with them. The Abu Basha policy was implemented from 1982 to 1992. From 1993, the Allam school was adopted by the minister of the interior Hassan al-Alfi, who brought members of the Muslim Brotherhood and terror activists alike before military tribunals.[43]

Notwithstanding reservations regarding specific analyses of academics and the media, top government sources have acknowledged that since the latter half of 1994, after the containment strategy proved ineffective, the regime applied a relentless policy of "all-out confrontation" against the Brotherhood. The regime's basic premise was that the Muslim Brotherhood harbored a radical al-Qutbian branch, which was determined to destroy any democratic elements in Egypt and supplant them with Islamic theocratic rule. Since they were illegal they adopted a cover to camouflage their activity.

Furthermore, in 1995 several government agencies assessed that the Muslim Brotherhood in Egypt received instructions from its world organization whose headquarters were in Geneva, with branches in London and other European cities – thereby signifying an even larger threat. In addition, many leaders of terrorist groups had their roots in the Muslim Brotherhood, and many younger Brotherhood members, especially the most militant, eventually joined the terrorist organizations. The situation estimate thus viewed the Muslim Brotherhood as a longer-range strategic threat to the regime than all the other operational, fanatical terrorist organizations. To deal with this threat the following measures were instituted:

> The erasure of all signs of the Muslim Brotherhood's legitimacy, and the closure of its main headquarters in Cairo by security forces.
> A strike at the key components of the Brotherhood's strength: the trade unions, university students, and economic companies.
> The prevention of its participation in the November 1995 elections to the People's Assembly.
> The disclosure of the Muslim Brotherhood's links to the world organization and its branches.
> The liquidation of the al-Qutbian radical section of the Muslim Brotherhood.
> The exposure of secret activity under the guise of the Muslim Brotherhood.
> Arrests, investigations, and trials before military tribunals in order to paralyze the movement.[44]

Tightening the Pressure on the Muslim Brotherhood

The strategy of all-out confrontation with the Muslim Brotherhood and Islamic militants was based on three main elements:

1 The transition from defense to offense, with the objective of destroying the organizational infrastructures and minimizing the Islamic threat.
2 Broadening the restrictions on the Brotherhood's activity, especially limiting its ability to infiltrate social and cultural institutions and trade unions.
3 Enlisting the support of all legitimate political parties to form a united front against terrorism and totalitarianism.[45]

Following the lines of its new offensive, the government intensified the struggle against the Brotherhood's domination in the lawyers union and strove to increase secular influence there and in other unions. To that end, government circles divided the executive board of the lawyers union into two groups. One included Muslim Brotherhood sympathizers, and the other, under the leadership of the union's chairman, was comprised of members with alternative political views. Sharp tensions arose between the two groups after several lawyers demanded an investigation of financial misdealing in the union's executive board.[46] The authorities reacted swiftly, and in January 1995 examination proceedings commenced on charges of money mismanagement in the lawyers union as well as in the Brotherhood-controlled doctors and engineers unions. The government was intent on humiliating these three leading unions and subordinating

them to the regime's supervision and control. One member of the engineers union, Abu Ala Mahdi, rejected the charges of financial misconduct
and denied that the Muslim Brotherhood had converted the unions into
forums for political activity. Mahdi contended that political activity was
extremely limited and that 95 percent of the union activity was professional. He added that the engineers union had increased its income since
the Muslim Brotherhood took control of it in 1988, and repeated that the
charges of monetary mismanagement were totally unsubstantiated.[47] Also
in January 1995 Dr. Essam al-Arian, the deputy secretary-general of the
doctors union, was arrested with six of his colleagues. All seven,
Brotherhood members, were charged with attempting to rebuild the movement's underground infrastructure and engaging in acts designed to
institute an Islamic theocracy in Egypt.[48]

The government passed a series of laws as part of its strategy of all-out
confrontation against the Muslim Brotherhood. In late May 1994 a law
was enacted that rescinded the right of university professors to elect the
deans of their institutions, and transferred this prerogative to the government-appointed university presidents. Two months later another law
canceled the popular election of village heads and their deputies, and
granted the minister of the interior the right to appoint them.[49] The regime
also resorted to interrogations and police detention to damage the
Brotherhood's organizational infrastructure. On May 23, 1994 the general
guide, eighty-two year old Sheikh Hamad Abu Nasser, was brought in for
questioning. The charge: illegal documents bearing his signature. Several
days later the pro-government weekly *Al-Musawwar* – whose editor,
Makram Mohammad Ahmed, was a close friend of President Mubarak –
began publishing a series of Brotherhood-related documents confiscated
at the Salsabil computer company on the plan for overthrowing the regime.
Over the two weeks that the series appeared the police rounded up scores
of Muslim Brotherhood members.[50]

In addition, the judicial system joined the effort to limit the activities of
the Muslim Brotherhood in the People's Assembly and the professional
unions, acting to maintain the status of the organization as an illegal body.
The judiciary thus enabled President Mubarak to issue orders whereby
activists in the Muslim Brotherhood could also be tried in the military
courts.

The National Dialogue

June 1994 marked an important step taken by the regime designed to
degrade and stifle the Muslim Brotherhood. That month a national
dialogue was convened in the form of a symposium between the regime,
the ruling party (the National Democratic Party), and all other legal

parties. As part of the strategy of all-out confrontation, the regime tried to garner the support of all the legal political parties in its anti-terrorism campaign, and at the same time prevent them from establishing a pact with the Muslim Brotherhood. Prior to the dialogue, Mubarak was asked why the Muslim Brotherhood had not been invited. His reply was curt: to his knowledge, there was no such group by this name. The opening session of the symposium was postponed several times because of squabbles between the ruling party and opposition parties. The latter demanded that the discussion focus on political reform, political rights, and economic liberalization, while the government party preferred to emphasize the parties' support in the campaign against Islamic organizations.

The dialogue opened on June 25, 1994 and was attended by 276 delegates from nine political parties, the People's Assembly, the governmental Shura Council, trade unions, academia, the media, the business community, and intellectual circles. President Mubarak hosted the symposium and announced that his main concern was Islamic extremism. He appealed for a national consensus in the war on terrorism for the sake of stability in the homeland. A number of decisions were made, including an amendment of the law for political rights, and the commitment to hold proportional elections under the inspection of jurists. A resolution was also drafted to accelerate the campaign against extremists. The decisions expressed a partial acquiescence to the opposition parties' demands, thus satisfying them to a degree, but overall the public displayed profound apathy to the proceedings.[51]

The Arrest of Intellectuals

The arrests and interrogations continued, and the regime attacked the Brotherhood's enclaves outside the trade unions. Mindful that police detention and cross-examination were the most effective means for destroying the Muslim Brotherhood's organizational infrastructure, the regime harbored no qualms over the arrest of prominent public figures linked to the movement.

Adel Hussein, a left-wing journalist who was secretary-general of the Egyptian Labor Party, was arrested in Cairo on December 24, 1994. The party had ties to the Brotherhood and its newspaper *Al-Sha'ab* functioned as the mouthpiece of the Muslim Brotherhood, which was prohibited from publishing its own paper. Hussein's articles proclaimed *shari'a* as the highest authoritative norm in Egypt, and this had angered the government. Arrested on his return from a trip to France, Hussein was taken into custody, brought to the Tora prison, and placed in solitary confinement. All contact with him was severed. Unlike many other arrests, Hussein's triggered an angry reaction in wide circles of the public because of his prestige as a journalist, politician, and opposition leader. The lawyers union launched a campaign for his release, and the journalists staged a sit-in at their union's headquarters in Cairo. The police were called in to break up the demonstrations. In the Cairo suburb of Ein Shams, scores of al-Amal party activists were arrested, and arrests also occurred in the village of al-Dawar after the local residents, in support of Hussein, had plastered their homes with pictures of the imprisoned leader.

On December 31, one week after Hussein's arrest, the Ministry of the Interior revealed the reason for placing him in custody. Under Hussein's seat on the plane, a packet was found containing leaflets pertaining to al-Jama'a al-Islamiyya with Hussein's handwriting on them. Ministry spokesmen claimed that these fliers were proof of his ties to a terrorist group, and warned against Hussein's arrest being used for political agitation. At the interrogation and in the presence of his lawyers, Hussein denied that the envelope was his. Hussein, who suffered from chronic heart disease, appeared extremely weak. During a visit to the international writers fair in Cairo in January 1995, journalists pleaded with Mubarak to release Hussein, but the president stammered that he knew about the arrest only from the media. Mubarak's evasive answer only added to the general consternation.

On January 18, 1995, twenty-five days after his arrest, Hussein was suddenly set free. The release was explained as President Mubarak's positive response to the request of the head of the journalists union, Ibrahim Nafa, who was also the editor of *Al-Ahram*. The opposition considered the release a great victory, but the entire incident had put the heads of state into an awkward predicament, forcing them to decide how to handle intellectuals like Hussein who supported, directly or indirectly, various trends in political Islam. Observers in Egypt pointed to another aspect of Hussein's arrest. At the end of the year, general elections to the People's Assembly would take place. The government had not forgotten the success of the Islamic tripartite alliance (the Muslim Brotherhood, al-Amal, and al-Ahrar) in the 1987 elections, and as a countermeasure this time it launched an intimidation campaign against the small al-Amal party in order to dissolve its partnership with the Muslim Brotherhood. The regime hoped to neutralize the Islamic coalition, keep the Brotherhood out of the elections, and eliminate al-Amal altogether from the political map.[52]

At the same time, the Egyptian judicial system contributed to the regime's confrontation. Eighty-two Brotherhood activists went on trial before a military tribunal in a desert base east of Cairo. On November 23, 1995, fifty-four received prison sentences of three to five years and others were sentenced to forced labor, while twenty-eight were exonerated. Among the fifty-four were academics and leading professional figures, such as Dr. Essam al-Arian, deputy secretary-general of Egypt's doctors union; Mohammad Habib, a science lecturer at the University of Assiut; Sa'id Mahmoud Ezzat, professor of medicine at Delta University; and Abdel Moneim Abu al-Fatah Abdel Hadi, deputy secretary-general of the federation of Arab doctors. All of the accused were convicted of holding unauthorized meetings and organizing an illegal group that planned to undermine the constitution. The verdict was handed down just prior to the November 29 elections to the People's Assembly. As elections drew near, the Muslim Brotherhood announced 160 candidates in an alliance with al-Amal. The Brotherhood charged that the aim of the trial had been to block the suspects from participating in the elections. Government spokesmen responded by claiming that the accused were linked to violent Islamic groups engaged in a struggle against the state's security forces. Amnesty International defined the accused as conscientious prisoners, and called on the authorities to release them and cease placing citizens before military tribunals.[53]

The 1995 Elections

On December 19, 1994 the Muslim Brotherhood spokesman announced that the movement had decided not to boycott the coming elections to the People's Assembly as it had done in 1990. The regime was caught off balance and faced a new challenge in its campaign against terrorist groups and only shortly after it had launched its full-fledged attack against the Brotherhood.[54] The Muslim Brotherhood spokesman, Ma'amoun al-Houdeibi, stated that the decision to participate in the 1995 elections had been made by the Brotherhood's Office of General Guidance. Nevertheless, the opposition parties along with the Brotherhood had decided to boycott elections to the Shura Council to be held in April 1995, when half of the council's members would be replaced. This decision stemmed from the assessment that the Shura Council was of no value in the decision-making process and therefore it was inadvisable to risk one's standing by participating in the elections. Houdeibi emphasized that the crisis over the trial of senior Brotherhood activists in a military court had nothing to do with the 1995 elections to the People's Assembly.[55] The decision to participate in elections to the People's Assembly ran counter to the regime's basic policy forbidding the Islamic party to utilize the political process for advancing the establishment of a theocratic state in Egypt.

The Mubarak government was determined to foil the Brotherhood's plans to run in the elections. On the night of July 17–18 security forces apprehended nineteen senior Brotherhood members and placed them in extended custody. Among those arrested was Sheikh Sa'id Askar, the director of the information department of al-Azhar, and Islamic activists who had served in the People's Assembly, the heads of trade unions, and teachers. The prosecutor claimed that they were held for participating in discussions on the Brotherhood's involvement in terrorism, associating with armed Islamic extremists, and affiliating with the Brotherhood and serving on the movement's Shura Council. Houdeibi denied all of the charges and claimed that the arrests were designed to prevent his colleagues from presenting their candidacies for election to the People's Assembly (which most of the nineteen certainly intended to do). The regime responded by carrying out a second wave of arrests on July 28, seizing another 180 Muslim Brotherhood members and charging them with complicity in terrorist activity.[56]

According to orders from the Office of General Guidance, leaders and members of the Muslim Brotherhood continued preparing for the elections. Fearing that legal measures would be used against them as part of the state's crackdown on the movement, many prospective candidates gave their attorneys authorization to present their names on the list. The candidates went to the police stations and security agencies to obtain documented proof that they had no criminal records, as required by law in national elections. Another reason for these steps was a report that Egyptian security agencies were tracking Brotherhood members who planned to participate in the elections.[57]

Since the Brotherhood was unable to gain legal participation in the elections as an independent party, it decided to unite with a legitimate party as it had done in the past. The Brotherhood and al-Amal announced they would run on a joint slate, without al-Ahrar, because it had violated the terms of the tripartite Islamic alliance by taking part in the 1990 elections to the People's Assembly, despite the boycott by its two coalition partners. Al-Ahrar was also guilty of participating in the elections to the Shura Council in April 1995 without consulting its two coalition partners.[58] Interestingly, as the elections approached, al-Amal chairman Ibrahim Shukri dispelled rumors of the tripartite alliance's demise by declaring that it was still binding. Shukri further stated that the authorities' suppression of the Muslim Brotherhood was motivated by fear of the movement's strength and influence on the election. Shukri disclosed that the government had taken similar steps against al-Amal, and he asserted that his party regarded Islam as more than religious ritual but as an all-embracing way of life. Accordingly, the alliance members would run in the elections in order to fulfill their commitment to place responsible people in the administration of state affairs.[59]

It became clear that the opposition party's 682 members, including the Muslim Brotherhood's 150 members, nominated themselves as candidates in the elections. At the same time, security forces continued to hunt down the Brotherhood, arresting its members on charges of links to terrorism.

The deputy general guide, Mustafa Mashour, defended his organization and in frequent interviews claimed that the arrests were designed to prevent his colleagues from participating in the elections. Mashour predicted that the government's measures would achieve the opposite results and public support for the Muslim Brotherhood would be expressed at the polls.[60]

In the last week before the elections the police broke up eleven Muslim Brotherhood political rallies and arrested over 400 supporters. Public demonstrations were illegal in Egypt, but the police turned a blind eye to those held by candidates of the government's National Democratic Party. Mustafa Mashour warned that these measures were just the start of meddling with election results.[61]

On November 29, 1995, the government party won an overwhelming victory, while the opposition and Muslim Brotherhood suffered a devastating defeat. The following week the minister of the interior announced the election results (after two rounds of voting – the first on November 29, the second on December 6): the ruling National Democratic Party had gained 317 seats out of a total of 444 in the People's Assembly; independent candidates won 114 seats (one hundred of them were expected to join the ranks of the ruling party); and the opposition gained only thirteen seats (Wafd – six, al-Tajamu – five, al-Ahrar – one, and the Nasserites – one).[62]

On the eve of the elections the Muslim Brotherhood leaders were confident that many of its 150 candidates competing in 222 election districts would gain access to seats on the People's Assembly. Brotherhood leaders who had believed that their people would enter as independent candidates were now frustrated by the obstacles that had been placed before them and by the fact that not one of their candidates attained a seat in the People's Assembly. At this point, charges of tampering with the election results grew louder.[63] The end result, however, was that the regime emerged victorious in parliament and achieved its objective of banishing the Brotherhood from the legitimate political arena.

The Brotherhood's Affiliation with the World Organization

In accordance with the regime's all-out confrontation strategy against the Muslim Brotherhood, in early 1995 Egypt's internal security forces launched a major operation that included the ties with the movement's world organization. Many Muslim Brotherhood leaders were arrested and accused of engaging in hostile activity according to instructions received from the world organization. At the same time, the relationship of the world organization to the Egyptian movement was scrutinized. Were the Islamic centers based in European cities part of the same organization, and to what degree was all international, subversive Islamic activity coordinated by a monolithic, centralized headquarters? Substantial evidence pointed to the presence of a viable, active world organization.

As with the Muslim Brotherhood in Egypt, the world organization is made up of three main bodies – the general guide, the Office of General Guidance, and the General Shura Council – and their functions parallel on a global level those of the Egyptian organization. Officially the world leadership is based in Cairo, and the title of general guide is given both to the international leader and the head of the Muslim Brotherhood in Egypt.

As part of the regime's crackdown on the Muslim Brotherhood's relations with the world organization, the weekly *Al-Musawwar* published an exposé in February 1995 entitled "Secrets of the Muslim Brotherhood's World Organization." The newspaper revealed that a document had been captured showing the existence of a strong world organization. The document was written and signed by Mustafa Mashour, the general guide of the Muslim Brotherhood's world organization, and his deputy in Egypt. Among its principal contents, the document bore witness to a Brotherhood plan, entitled "Capability and Hegemony," whose goal was the takeover of several Arab capital cities, starting with Cairo. According to the document, the world organization was founded on July 29, 1982 and held its sixth conference in Istanbul in 1991. The document stated that the organization had failed to teach the Ba'ath regime in Syria a lesson after the events in Hama in the early 1980s and had failed to persuade the Muslim Brotherhood in Sudan, headed by Hassan Tourabi, to adhere to the organization's instructions (which resulted in the transfer of its headquarters from Khartoum). The document also mentioned the need to set up offices and additional units to counter the Brotherhood's exclusive control in Cairo, the turf of eight of the thirteen representatives in the Office of General Guidance. According to the document, the time had come to prepare the Islamic nation for a jihad, as in Afghanistan. In other words, a Muslim Brotherhood government had to be created in an Arab country where it would serve as the basis for the Islamic movement's global expansion. Egypt was the preferred location. The objective of establishing an Islamic state and renewing the caliphate had not been realized yet because planning had been faulty in such countries as Algeria, Tunisia, and Sudan. The Arab nation should prepare itself more gradually and realistically for jihad.[64]

The Muslim Brotherhood's spokesman in Egypt, Ma'amoun al-Houdeibi, denied all charges of connections to the international organization, and claimed that the information published concerning the Brotherhood's international links was fabricated.[65] Senior government officials insisted that the Muslim Brotherhood's active world organization existed. Minister of the Interior Alfi repeated the accusation, stressing that the international organization along with the Islamic Front in Sudan and terrorist groups in Egypt and other Arab countries were conspiring to topple the legitimate regimes in those countries.[66] The minister's statements were refuted by Houdeibi the following day. He declared that the Muslim Brotherhood's relations with the Sudanese Islamic Front, led by Tourabi, amounted only to courtesy calls and had nothing to do with organizational links. Houdeibi admitted that his movement had attended the majority of Islamic conferences in the world and in this capacity had traveled to Khartoum in early 1995. But, he argued, his movement had always received prior permission from Egyptian security agencies. He repeatedly disavowed Muslim Brotherhood involvement in an international organization, and charged the minister of the interior with attempting to blacklist the Muslim Brotherhood as the general elections approached in November 1995.[67]

The Egyptian authorities were convinced that an active world organization not only existed but also oversaw the operations of scores of Islamic organizations in Arab countries, as well as in Asia, Africa, Europe, and even the United States, and that its headquarters were located in Geneva, with branches throughout Europe acting in the guise of "Islamic Centers." These centers focused on cultural and social affairs, as well as fundraising for subsidizing the Muslim Brotherhood in Arab countries where they operated ostensibly as charity organizations.[68]

Dr. Abdel Moneim Sa'id of the Al-Ahram Center was certain of the existence of an active world organization. In his estimation, the organization's head and leaders were Egyptians, and therefore the Sudanese were excluded from it. The members of the world leadership also sat on the General Shura Council. The organization's headquarters may be in Turkish Cyprus; its main centers were located in Geneva, Munich, and Bonn.[69]

Countering the Brotherhood's Foreign Connections

Based on information that the world organization was directing terrorist operations inside Egypt, the Egyptian security forces struck at what they termed the movement's "foreign links," beginning in the latter part of 1995. By the end of the year the Directorate of State Security Investigations uncovered a clandestine Brotherhood center operating in the city of Suez, where it provided a link between the movement in Egypt and leaders of the al-Jihad terrorist organization in London. The Directorate charged that a logistical headquarters had been set up in the offices of a Suez shipping agency whose owner, Abdel Wahab Sharf Eddin, was a Brotherhood member and the secretary-general of the engineers union in Suez. A police search uncovered cassettes, video tapes, computer disks, and faxes, including messages from the terrorist Yasir Taufik Ali Sari, an al-Jihad leader sentenced to death in Egypt for his role in an assassination attempt of the previous prime minister, Atef Sidki. Sari had found asylum in London, and in 1994 Sharf Eddin was ordered by the Shura Council to fly to London and make contact with him. Logistical arrangements were finalized at the meeting, whereby the Suez company would relay instructions to another al-Jihad figure in Egypt, Hilmi Issa Ibrahim al-Azzazi. The fax communiqué from London referred to attacks on security targets and key buildings in order to spread an atmosphere of panic in Egypt. Sharf Eddin and Hilmi al-Azzazi were arrested and brought to trial.[70]

Another large strike against the world organization took place in early April 1996. Twelve key Brotherhood leaders were arrested and charged with causing disorder, plotting to undermine the state, and spreading Islamic propaganda according to instructions received from the organization's foreign leadership, mainly in London. The suspects were seized during the raid on their clandestine cells in the Cairo vicinity and other parts of Egypt. Among those apprehended was Mohammad Mahdi Othman Akef, a member of the Office of General Guidance and Shura Council, and regarded as one of the most senior members of the Brotherhood's world organization. Akef was responsible for the West Europe section, using his position as head of the Munich Islamic Center as a cover. At one time he had been sentenced to death in Egypt, but was granted a pardon. Another detainee, Abdel Azzim Abdel Majid al-Mughrabi, was also a member of the Shura Council. The remaining people likewise held top positions in the Brotherhood's hierarchy. The bulk of the incriminating material discovered during the searches detailed the ties between senior figures in the Muslim Brotherhood in Egypt and their colleagues in Jordan; material was also found relating to the extent of activity in branches in the United States, Canada, and Europe. Other documents demonstrated the Muslim Brotherhood's links with al-Jama'a al-Islamiyya and al-Jihad, with the aim of expanding the Brotherhood's military wing in order to gain control in trade unions, municipal councils, and mosques. The files of the accused were handed over to the prosecutor for the remainder of the investigation.[71]

The Egyptian authorities also tried to deal with the world organization through cooperation with several Western countries in the war on terrorism. The Egyptian government called on Britain to extradite wanted terrorists, such as Sari. Egypt likewise requested the extradition of Kamel al-Halbawi, an Egyptian businessman and the Brotherhood's official spokesman in Western Europe. Britain rejected the Egyptian requests for legal and other reasons, and other countries in Europe replied in similar fashion.[72]

The Muslim Brotherhood Response to the Regime's Offensive

After two years of an all-out confrontation, the Muslim Brotherhood began to crack. The confrontation had come in the wake of the regime's initiative in combating terrorist groups and its decision to dissolve the Brotherhood, which it regarded as a long-term, strategic threat. The Brotherhood's Cairo headquarters in the Taufikiya market was shut down, and the movement's newssheet *Al-Da'wa* was suspended. Many leading figures as well as the rank and file were arrested and put on trial before military tribunals. Most of the indictments dealt with the movement's links to its overseas branches and terrorist organizations active on Egyptian soil. The charges were leveled primarily at the young cadre of leaders. The regime thwarted the Brotherhood's plans to participate in the November 1995 elections to the People's Assembly and tightened its surveillance on the movement in the trade unions.

The Muslim Brotherhood's reaction was limited, and many of its members capitulated under the security forces' relentless pressure. Some of the young members advocated taking to the streets and responding in force, but the older generation called for moderation and prudence. The argument highlighted the movement's generational rift. The young members had been reared in a quieter and freer atmosphere than their older cohorts, and had almost no experience with the need to operate clandestinely; on the other hand, the veterans had known periods of underground activity and persecution, which made them more cautious. Sources in the Brotherhood expressed concern that a violent crisis was brewing and feared it would be more destructive than the schisms in 1954 and 1966 during the Nasserite period when the movement was outlawed. The Brotherhood acknowledged that the internal conflict was related to the movement's modus operandi and its tentative response to the regime's offensive, whereas in the past it had known how to react effectively to government attacks.[73]

The government's offensive took place at a most inauspicious time for the movement's leadership. Hamad Abu Nasser, the aged general guide, lay ailing on his sickbed just when unity in the ranks and tough decisions were necessary regarding the potential response to government pressure.[74] On January 20, 1996 Abu Nasser died at the age of eighty-three. During the burial ceremony the movement's spokesman, Ma'amoun al-Houdeibi, announced that Mustafa Mashour, Abu Nasser's deputy, would be the new general guide. The mourners were shocked that such information was given during the burial, but in line with discipline common to centralized ideological movements, they were quick to swear allegiance to the new leader. Mashour had been directing the Muslim Brotherhood de facto for two years ever since Abu Nasser took ill. Previously he had served in the movement's military wing and spent nine years in prison for an assassination attempt on Nasser in 1954.

Mashour officially assumed his role at the height of the government assault and immediately had to mastermind the Brotherhood's response. As expected, the young members clamored for a vigorous reaction by leaders who displayed decisiveness and extremism. Mashour, however, had no intention of deviating from his predecessor's moderate, non-violent policy. What was needed at this stage, he avowed, was a dialogue with the government, definitely not collusion with extremist groups.[75] Within the Brotherhood the response was widespread dissatisfaction, not only over Mashour's leadership style but also his very appointment during Abu Hamed's funeral – a procedure, it was claimed, that flouted the movement's constitution. Young members charged that it reeked of a hijack and created a severe credibility crisis at a most inconvenient period.[76]

In an interview with the newspaper *Al-Ahali*, Mashour was asked whether contact had been made with the government: "We asked for a dialogue but they refused." Mashour also discussed the government's persecution of the movement and noted that in the past the Muslim Brotherhood had refrained from conflict with the regime. As an example, he recalled that when Yasir Arafat and the former prime minister of Sudan had visited the Brotherhood's headquarters in al-Taufikiya, it was undoubtedly with the authorities' knowledge. At present relations are amiss, he related, and the government has shut down the headquarters because it feared the Muslim Brotherhood.[77] The movement's leaders in Egypt and abroad implored the government to enter negotiations in order to resolve mutual differences. The heads of the doctors unions of Egypt and the Arab states protested the incarceration of fifteen Brotherhood members and said that in the past they had continuously appealed to the government to sit with the Brotherhood and work out their differences, but had been repeatedly rebuffed. Again they requested the start of a dialogue.[78]

The regime refused to comply and pressed forward with its offensive against the Muslim Brotherhood. The movement failed to come up with a fitting response acceptable to all its members, and in the ensuing delay, the young members exploited the consternation and internal conflict to launch a new party. In early 1996 the younger wing of the Brotherhood founded the Wasat party and a newspaper with the same name. According to the Law for Political Parties, the new party's leaders had to obtain permission from a special seven-man committee consisting of four ministers and three government-appointed members. When the judicial committee reviewed the party's platform, it flatly rejected the request. The security forces were convinced that the young people's request masked a Muslim Brotherhood stratagem to sidestep the interdiction against organizing the party in its original name. The authorities also charged that the Brotherhood had recruited Christian Copts and political leftists to the nascent party to add a non-ethnic, liberal luster to it while in truth the party was a ruse concocted by the Muslim Brotherhood. The thirteen people who submitted the request were arrested, interrogated, and tried in a military court.[79]

In confronting the issue of the new party, Mashour showed restraint in handling the crisis so as to avoid further tension with the regime and limit the aftershocks of the split in the Brotherhood. At the same time he made it clear that the young members, who would be allowed to remain Brotherhood members, had defied the movement's rules and regulations and had acted independently of the movement. Mashour also revealed that from the outset he knew their prospects of obtaining government permission were nil, and that when they went to the authorities for permission, they dissociated themselves from the Muslim Brotherhood to increase their chances of receiving government approval. Mashour announced that the young people could remain members of the movement.[80] This was one of the Muslim Brotherhood's most demoralizing hours.

Throughout 1996 the security forces continued to crack down on the organization. In the last week of the year, the police arrested two hundred people connected with the underground organization al-Qutbian that was conspiring to overthrow the government and replace it with an Islamic state. The government daily *Al-Ahram* claimed that the Muslim Brotherhood was financing al-Qutbian. A senior official in the High Court for State Security declared that the sole Muslim Brotherhood representative in the People's Assembly, Ali Sayyid Fath Elbab, "was responsible for the activities of the new underground organization." The prosecution, therefore, would revoke his immunity, interrogate him, and put him on trial. As in the previous wave of arrests, Houdeibi, the movement's spokesman, denied all the charges. He told the French News Agency that the detentions were intended to instill fear in the Brotherhood because of the approaching elections to regional councils, the same stratagem employed by the authorities just before the 1995 elections to the People's Assembly. Houdeibi also said that the Muslim Brotherhood had no intention of running in the local elections, though some members might participate as independents.[81]

Suppression of the Muslim Brotherhood, 1998–99

The regime continued to harass and debilitate the Brotherhood throughout 1998 and 1999. Its main tactic was to assure that the Muslim Brotherhood remained illegal and keep in prison members who held meetings or rallies associated with the movement. The determined implementation of this policy led to the Brotherhood's continued paralysis.

On March 21, 1998 nineteen members were arrested for membership in an illegal group. The prosecution in the High Court for State Security claimed that they had been caught with books, Islamic posters, and cassettes dealing with Brotherhood matters of instruction, meetings, and plans in their possession while ostensibly organizing a sports day in a city south of Cairo. In an interview with Radio Tehran, Houdeibi denied the accusations and asserted that some people were seized in their homes and others while playing soccer.[82]

On November 1 the Egyptian News Agency reported that the High Court for State Security ordered the prolonged custody of twenty-eight suspects charged with affiliation with the outlawed Muslim Brotherhood. The prosecutor alleged that the suspects had attempted to restore the Brotherhood's activity, propagate its ideas in schools and universities, and set up a special organizational structure. He also noted that the movement's meetings had taken place in the homes of the suspects. According to the plan, the movement was ready to incite young people and citizens to organize demonstrations against the regime. The suspects were accused of putting up posters announcing anti-government rallies.[83]

January 1999 saw the arrest of additional Brotherhood activists: five were apprehended in the city of Dasuk in the Kafr al-Sheikh district on charges of affiliation with an illegal movement. On January 15 security forces arrested in Cairo and Fayoum a group of twelve Brotherhood members, charged with attempting to found a new Brotherhood chapter. A search of the premises as well as in their homes uncovered political placards and documents connected with the suspects' activities.[84] Houdeibi termed the arrests "part of the security agencies' plan to hunt down the movement in every district."[85]

In mid-October 1999 the regime delivered one of its most decisive blows when twenty senior members of the Muslim Brotherhood were arrested. Sixteen were seized at a meeting in the office of the engineers union in the Cairene suburb of Ma'adi, and four were arrested in their homes. The most senior figure in the roundup was Mukhtar Nouh, a leading attorney who had defended the Muslim Brotherhood in court. Nouh was the finance manager of the lawyers union and a former representative in the Egyptian parliament. Among the others arrested were: Mohammad Ali Bisher, a member of the engineers union's council; Khaled Badawi, an attorney; and Sa'ad Zaghlul, the secretary-general of the doctors union in Cairo. They were all accused of membership in an illegal group, attending unlawful meetings, attempting to renew the Muslim Brotherhood movement, and infiltrating the trade unions in order to carry out anti-government activity.[86] The seizure of twenty senior members triggered a strong public reaction. The Egyptian Association of Human Rights and many trade unions demanded their release. They called the arrests a crude intervention by the authorities in trade union affairs in order gain control of them. Moreover, the Human Rights Association claimed that those arrested had merely been engaged in legitimate activity permitted by the Egyptian constitution and international treaties.[87]

Bitterness spread through the Islamic circles after the decision to bring the twenty detainees before a military tribunal. General Guide Mashour denounced the move, charging that the accused had met to discuss steps for ending the authorities' boycott of the lawyers union. Mashour also claimed that the meeting had taken place in an open, public area without a trace of secrecy. He averred that the Brotherhood had no wish for a confrontation with the government and would consider participation in the trade union elections only if it benefited the public.[88] The authorities were unimpressed by Mashour's repudiations, whereupon the military prosecutor changed the indictment against the twenty from "affiliation with the outlawed Muslim Brotherhood" to "participation in the founding and administering of the movement." If convicted on these new counts, they could expect much harsher sentences. The accused denied the charges and disclaimed any part in establishing a new movement. They declared that their meeting at the engineers union in Ma'adi had been to coordinate trade union matters and their participation in the approaching union elections – legitimate activity in every society that recognizes political parties and trade unions.[89]

During the trial the prosecutor called for the maximum punishment according to the law's 1990 amendment, known as the "anti-terrorism law," which imposed heavy penalties on anyone guilty of plotting against the regime.[90] A lengthy delay of several months passed until the verdict was delivered on November 19, 2000. The Brotherhood explained this as part of the government's intention to disrupt the movement's nomination of candidates to parliamentary elections.[91] Twelve of the accused were sentenced to prison terms of three years, three received terms of five years, and five were exonerated. During the sentencing, the president of the High Military Court stated that according to the captured documents the suspects had striven to re-establish the illegal Muslim Brotherhood movement and incite Egyptian citizens to act against the state through strikes and demonstrations. In order to attain their goals, the accused had recruited college and university students to the Muslim Brotherhood, who would join the trade unions after graduation in order to strengthen the Brotherhood's hegemony in them.

The trial received international coverage, especially from human rights groups whose representatives sat in the hearings and met with members of the court. Egyptian human rights activists and scores of journalist were also present at the trial,[92] but the regime was undeterred and relentlessly pursued the Brotherhood. Four journalists from *Al-Sha'ab*, an al-Amal associated paper, were accused of libel against the deputy prime minister and minister of agriculture and were convicted in Cairo on August 14, 1999. Three of them were sentenced to two years in jail and a fine of 20,000 Egyptian pounds, and the fourth, the secretary-general of the party, was also fined 20,000 Egyptian pounds. Claiming that the journalists were entitled to freedom of expression, the Egyptian human rights watchdog group protested the jail sentences and argued that what was due the accused was a fine at most. They also pointed out that the verdict intimidated journalists from fulfilling their professional obligation, which included criticism of the government.[93]

As a result of this offensive, the Brotherhood's general guide was unable to stabilize the organization. Two years after the al-Wasat crisis, the Brotherhood suffered another severe blow. Six of the nine members in the political office resigned over sharp differences with Mashour and Houdeibi, criticizing the leadership for failing to integrate the young generation into key positions and neglecting to investigate members connected with financial misconduct. The criticism reflected on the general deterioration in the movement.[94] In response, the Office of General Guidance set up a Committee for the Arbitration and Reconciliation of Conflicts and assigned it a three-fold task: to investigate internal complaints; to prevent the exacerbation of incidents within the movement; and to bar their leakage to the press. The committee failed to stave off the resignation of the six members who claimed that the political committee included only people close to the Office of General Instruction and lacked intelligent members from the rank and file. Observers concluded that the resignations together with the establishment of the new committee reflected a breach of discipline in the movement.[95]

The Muslim Brotherhood continued its efforts to introduce political reforms which would enable it to overcome the regime's offensive. Turning to President Mubarak via the London-based newspaper *Al-Hayat*, Houdeibi reiterated the opposition's demands to implement political reforms for the enhancement of democracy in Egypt. Simultaneously Houdeibi called for the revocation of Egypt's official "state of emergency" that had long paralyzed party activity and stifled freedom of speech. He also urged the cancellation of the military tribunals and release of all political prisoners.[96] As expected, the regime shunned a response and continued to pressure the Brotherhood.

In the meantime, the Muslim Brotherhood began to express its views of the next general election campaign (to be held in two voting sessions,

October and November 2000). It decided on its limited participation in the elections by presenting half the number of candidates that had run in 1995. This step was taken with the assumption that the government would try to block representatives of Islamic organizations from entering parliament. For the first time in the Brotherhood's history, women were allowed to appear on its list of candidates, although only one woman and one member of the Christian Copt community were actually named; the Egyptian government believed this was merely a tactical move rather than a veritable transformation in the Brotherhood's outlook.[97] Since the Brotherhood was still officially banned, its candidates ran in the elections as independent candidates and won seventeen seats in parliament. Like other political observers, the Brotherhood regarded this as a great success because of the difficult circumstances surrounding its participation in the elections. The gain of seventeen seats elevated the Brotherhood into the position of being the second largest parliamentary force, after the government party. Sa'if al-Banna, the son of the Muslim Brotherhood's founder, Hassan al-Banna, noted that the results were proof of the Brotherhood's popular support, and while it received less than it deserved, the achievement was still great. Banna expressed hope that the government would recognize the new reality and normalize relations with the movement.[98]

Summary

The Mubarak regime's policy against the Muslim Brotherhood evolved over time. Like his two predecessors, Muburak ushered in his rule with a policy of rapprochement. The Brotherhood exploited this conciliatory gesture by expanding its influence among the public, thus leading the regime later in the 1980s to revert to a policy of containment. The regime sought to counter the Brotherhood in all areas where it had gained influence. The struggle raged at the religious level over the transfer of control of tens of thousands of Muslim Brotherhood mosques to the government; in the realm of social Islam, the regime failed to make any significant headway in reducing the Brotherhood's widespread activity in education, health, and economics. In early 1990 the government managed to oust the Brotherhood from the People's Assembly and preclude its participation in the 1995 general elections. In the general elections of 2000, however, the Brotherhood competed under the guise of independent candidates, and won seventeen seats in the parliament, an impressive achievement in light of the difficult conditions it had to overcome.

The regime waged a determined struggle with the Brotherhood over hegemony in the trade unions. The authorities forced the unions that were under Muslim Brotherhood control to submit to government supervision and to restrict their activity. In mid-1994, emboldened by its victories in the war against terror groups, the regime decided to intensify its anti-Muslim Brotherhood policy and embark upon an all-out confrontation. It employed massive force in its operations. Many members of the Brotherhood, including senior leaders, were apprehended and brought before military tribunals, and the movement's main headquarters were shut down. The Brotherhood found itself besieged on all fronts. The policy of all-out confrontation also caused a severe internal crisis in the movement, which had failed to consolidate a commensurate response. The Brotherhood's leader was insistent on applying the movement's secret weapon – patience and endurance (*sabr*), which had proven itself effective in restoring its activity on two occasions in the past, after its near liquidation in the Nasserite period, and after its persecution under President Sadat. Nonetheless, the regime's view of the Muslim Brotherhood as a long-term strategic threat promised to continue to besiege and hamper the organization.

3   ISLAMIC TERRORISM IN EGYPT

The Surge of the 1990s

The terrorism at the end of the twentieth century was not a new phenomenon to Egypt. Over the century it had surfaced in waves, with every new wave more severe and cruel than the preceding one. There were three waves of terrorism during the twentieth century, each featuring the murder of the head of state. In 1910, Prime Minister Boutrous Ghali was assassinated. During the second wave, in the middle of the century, two prime ministers were assassinated: Ahmed Maher in 1944 and Mahmoud al-Nuqrashi in 1949. In 1981, during the third wave, which started in the 1970s and continued, with intermittent breaks, through the rest of the century, President Anwar Sadat was assassinated. The third wave – the most protracted, cruelest, and most violent – penetrated the depths of Egyptian society, presenting an unprecedented internal threat to the public, the governing regime, the modern state, and society.

The third wave commenced on April 18, 1974, when a group of military cadets, assisted by civilians, took control of the Military Technological Academy in the Abasiya quarter of Cairo and prepared to march on the headquarters of the Socialist Arab Union, where President Sadat and his senior aides were visiting. The rebels intended to kill or imprison the Egyptian political elite, take control of the state radio and television, and declare the establishment of the Islamic Republic of Egypt. Their plan failed, and in the exchange of fire with the defense forces, some were killed and others were injured; those who were captured were sentenced to death or long terms of imprisonment. This band of conspirators, dubbed the Military Technological Academy Group, was the forerunner of the al-Jihad organization, members of which ultimately assassinated President Sadat.

Politically motivated violence has been carried out not only by Islamic fundamentalists. In Egypt's modern history, there were other political groups that operated in this manner. Nonetheless, Islamic fundamentalists have perpetrated the lion's share of violence, starting long before the intense wave of Islamic extremism in the Middle East that began in the late 1970s. Table 3.1 presents selected data relating to the social and political tensions and terrorism in Egypt from 1952 to 1993. Some of the occasions of unrest since 1952 were spontaneous, such as riots by workers or students seeking to achieve their respective interests. But many of the events were initiated by Islamic activists seeking to undermine the regimes of Nasser, Sadat, and Mubarak.

Table 3.1 Tension, Terrorism, and Regime Responses, by Presidential Periods, 1952–93

Action	1952–1970 Nasser		1971–1981 Sadat		1982–1993 Mubarak	
	#	%	#	%	#	%
Demonstrations	10	16	16	26	36	58
Strikes	2	7	13	42	16	51
Riots	3	5	6	9	55	86
Coup attempts	2	50	2	50	0	0
Assassination attempts	2	12.5	2	12.5	12	75
Assassinations	0	0	2	11	16	89
Arrests (arrest warrants)	14,000	24	19,000	33	25,000	43
Sentenced to hard labor	42	26	69	42	53	32
Death sentences	27	36.5	20	27	27	36.5
Casualties (killed and wounded)	49	3	205	11	1,557	86

Source: Ibrahim, "Arab Modernity and the Challenge of Islam," p. 7.

Table 3.1 shows there was extensive growth in terrorism over the years. In direct proportion to the growth of Egypt's population (from 22 million in 1952 to 60 million in 1994), the average annual number of violent incidents multiplied during the Sadat period over the previous era, and spiraled further under Mubarak. Of the total number of casualties, 1,557 (86 percent) occurred under Mubarak.[1] Even more dramatic is that during the first four years of Mubarak's presidency (1982–85), there were only thirty-three incidents of violence, while the first four years of the 1990s were the bloodiest of the entire century in Egypt. During this period, 1,164 suffered injuries from terrorism and violence (an average of 291 annually).

Thus, 92 percent of all casualties from acts of terrorism and violence occurred during this period. When the number of casualties from the years 1994–99 is added, the total for the years 1952–99 reaches 3,698.[2]

On July 23, 1992, Egypt celebrated its national holiday marking the fortieth anniversary of the Free Officers Revolt, which, at the time, reflected and inspired many hopes for a better future for the country. However, over the years, these hopes were disappointed. The socio-economic conditions worsened, and tension and violence increased. In mid-1992, there was a severe escalation in terrorism, with a series of attacks beginning with the murder of the liberal writer Farag Foda. Terrorist attacks against prominent members of the establishment and military followed, inevitably impacting negatively on the Egyptian economy; all were carried out for the purpose of harming the governing regime and undermining its stability.

As in similar previous situations, the regime responded with heavy and uncompromising force. The security forces killed terrorists, conducted mass arrests, and placed large numbers on trial. Toward the end of 1992, President Mubarak declared: "We have crushed them. The terrorist organization has been destroyed,"[3] but it soon emerged that his assessment was premature. Overall, during the years 1990–99, 1,599 people were killed – and of these, the overwhelming majority were killed from 1993 onward – compared to the 275 who were killed during the waves of terror of the 1970s and 1980s.[4]

The year 1993 was marked by a particularly high level of terrorism, especially as the Islamic fundamentalists gained in armed confrontations with the security forces. Their actions reflected the experience they had earned while fighting with the mujahidin against the Soviets in Afghanistan. They demonstrated greater daring, initiated operations against the regime, and, on occasion, were victorious over the security forces. The militants expanded their targets to include the Copts, whom they regarded as Muslims not living in accordance with the spirit of Islam, and foreign tourists. Table 3.2 depicts the number of terrorism casualties in 1992: most of the casualties occurred from June, when the wave of terror escalated sharply. Table 3.3 charts casualties for 1993, when more than three times as many people were killed and injured over the previous year. For the sake of comparison, the data for 1992 is included at the bottom of table 3.3.

The escalation that took place during the 1990s derived from a number of factors. In context of the Islamic fundamentalist wave that started to spread throughout the Middle East in the late 1970s, all of the elements of the radical Islamic movement accelerated and intensified their activities. The greater part of the movement in Egypt, which was not violent and was represented primarily by the Muslim Brotherhood, operated with much

Table 3.2 Terrorism Casualties in Egypt, 1992

Month	Security Forces			Terrorists			Civilians			Total
	Killed	Wounded	Total	Killed	Wounded	Total	Killed	Wounded	Total	Killed
January	—	—	—	—	2	2	2	—	2	2
February	—	—	—	—	8	8	—	4	4	—
March	1	—	1	—	—	—	3	11	14	4
April	1	—	1	6	5	11	—	2	2	7
May	—	—	—	—	5	5	—	2	2	—
June	6	4	10	4	18	22	8	12	20	18
July	3	7	10	1	—	1	1	8	9	5
August	1	9	10	14	37	51	5	—	5	20
September	6	6	12	1	4	5	1	1	2	8
October	2	9	11	2	2	4	10	30	40	14
November	1	1	2	3	2	5	1	30	31	5
December	2	1	3	8	—	8	1	7	8	38
Total	**23**	**38**	**61**	**39**	**83**	**122**	**32**	**107**	**139**	**94**

Source: Ibrahim, "Arab Modernity and the Challenge of Islam," p. 10.

Table 3.3 Terrorism Casualties in Egypt, 1993

Month	Security Forces			Terrorists			Civilians			Total Killed
	Killed	Wounded	Total	Killed	Wounded	Total	Killed	Wounded	Total	
January	6	4	10	4	—	4	12	16	28	22
February	1	1	2	5	2	7	8	28	36	14
March	20	41	61	49	2	51	4	66	70	73
April	23	4	27	2	3	5	4	1	5	29
May	5	7	12	1	3	4	10	30	40	16
June	8	10	18	1	—	1	11	40	51	20
July	1	10	11	7	2	9	4	17	21	12
August	11	7	18	6	88	94	11	54	65	28
September	8	30	38	—	72	72	4	45	49	12
October	10	36	46	10	57	67	7	12	19	27
November	7	12	19	4	15	19	2	1	3	13
December	20	19	39	22	8	30	24	31	55	66
Total 1993	120	181	301	111	252	363	101	341	442	332
Total 1992	23	38	61	39	83	122	32	107	139	94

Source: Ibrahim, "Arab Modernity and the Challenge of Islam," p. 11.

momentum among the Egyptian public in areas such as social welfare services via the broad infrastructure of thousands of volunteer organizations spread throughout the country. At the same time, extensive proselytizing was conducted from the pulpits of tens of thousands of mosques, and the Islamic message found its targets among those frustrated segments of society that were socially and economically disadvantaged. Society grew increasingly religious, giving rise to the political and social polarization between the religious and secular that led to steadily more intense confrontations between the two sectors. Such confrontations had their own dynamic, ultimately developing into violent actions and terrorism. In this framework, the hawkish elements designated more targets for attack, leading to greater numbers of casualties. In turn, every act of terrorism or civil disobedience triggered a harsher response from the regime. Together, the adversaries set the stage for further violence, which was intensified by the desire for revenge.

The contemporary terrorist groups arose in the 1990s, when they splintered off from the groups of the 1970s and 1980s. While they resembled their predecessors in one regard – their Islamic message – they were otherwise entirely different. The young extremists of the 1990s emerged from the recurring failures on the part of both political leaders and ideology, which could not be concealed from the public in the age of television. These young people were greatly influenced by the Islamic revolution in Iran and the mujahidin victory in Afghanistan.[5] Their distinguishing characteristic lay in the socio-economic profile, as depicted in table 3.4. In comparison to their predecessors of the previous two decades, the extremists of the 1990s were younger and less educated, with most coming from villages, small provincial towns, and impoverished neighborhoods. The average age of Islamic extremists sentenced to prison for terrorist acts and violence dropped from twenty-seven during the 1970s to twenty-one in the 1990s. For example, of the seven extremists who from a group of thirty were sentenced to death in December 1993 for an attack on tourists, three were between the ages of sixteen and nineteen.

The 1990s saw a sharp rise in the percentage of terrorists from rural and less developed areas, and in the wake of the 1990s wave of terrorism, for the first time Egyptians heard the names of small towns such as Sanbo and Salamon in the Assiut district of Upper Egypt, when confrontations took place between fundamentalists and security forces in those small villages. There was also a sharp decline in the level of education among Islamic extremists serving sentences for violent activities. Apparently, the alienation and disappointment trickled down to the younger and less-educated strata of Egypt, and hence the extremism of the terrorist actions that characterized the terrorism surge of the 1990s.[6]

Table 3.4 Socio-Economic Profile of Egyptian Islamic Militants, 1970s–1990s (in percentages)

	1970s	1980s	1990s
Age Range			
Up to 20	5	11	23
20–25	28	31	48
25–30	61	53	24
30+	6	5	5
Formal Education			
Less than high school	2	5	9
High school	8	12	29
Junior college	11	24	42
College students and graduates	79	59	20
Professionals (e.g., doctors, engineers)	51	27	11
Residence			
Villages	—	7	18
Shantytowns	8	16	36
Towns	37	43	31
Large cities	55	34	15

Source: Ibrahim, "Arab Modernity and the Challenge of Islam," p. 13.

During the early stages of the 1990s terrorism, the Islamic movement and its new momentum benefited from the fact that the security forces did not have an efficient strategy for countering Islamic fundamentalism. Concomitantly, the strategies and tactics of the extremist camp changed. Whereas in the past they had been given to attacking only government targets, which they characterized as "enemies of Islam," by the 1990s the extremists had broadened their range and began attacking any targets that could embarrass the regime and undermine its credibility. They thus began attacking foreign tourists, banks, and the Coptic minority. This resulted in greater numbers of casualties among civilians than during the 1970s and 1980s. In addition, the terrorists received great reinforcement when hundreds of Islamic fighters arrived in Egypt from Afghanistan.[7] They arrived highly trained, greatly experienced in warfare, and filled with motivation following the victory over the Soviets.

Thus, most of the members of the terrorist organizations were from Upper Egypt, in large measure due to the harsh socio-economic conditions prevailing in the south. Many young people in the south believed that terrorism provided the only way for improving the conditions in which they lived. Against this backdrop, the largest and most active Egyptian terrorist organization, al-Jama'a al-Islamiyya, was established at the University of

Assiut in Upper Egypt in the 1970s. The organization emphasized domestic injustice within Egypt, calling for a war against corruption, poverty, and economic distress. The organization had branches throughout the south, and most of the commanders came from there. The extensive involvement in terrorism by southern Egyptians was reflected in the assassination of President Sadat on October 6, 1981. Of the 280 members of al-Jama'a al-Islamiyya connected with the president's murder, 183 were from the south, and seventy-three had migrated from there and were living in the densely populated, impoverished neighborhoods of Cairo, while only twenty-four were from Lower Egypt. The person who actually shot the president was Lt. Khaled Islambouli, born in Minya, in the south.[8] Between the Sadat assassination and the April 1993 attempt against the minister of information, Safwat al-Sharif, 82 percent of those accused of terrorism were residents of Upper Egypt.[9]

Table 3.5 (p. 90) shows that between 1990 and 1997, 1,198 terrorist attacks were carried out in Egypt, 918 of these in Upper Egypt, and 280 in Lower Egypt. Of the latter, the majority (221) were in Cairo.

The large number of terrorist incidents in Upper Egypt was also connected to the tradition for vendetta among the *sa'id* (southerners) in the region. After any operation by an army unit in which a *sa'id* member of al-Jama'a al-Islamiyya was killed, the man's family would seek the officer responsible for the death of its son and kill him. This created an endless cycle of death–revenge–death, to an extent that it became no longer possible to distinguish between revenge killings and terrorist attacks.[10] The *sa'id* population took revenge not only on security forces, but also on Coptic Christians, whose primary enclaves were in Upper Egypt. To the *sa'id*s, the Copts symbolized the hated regime in Cairo. The authorities found it extremely difficult to break this cycle of retaliation in the south, since tribal and family discipline demanded that no one report crimes and attacks to outsiders or the authorities.[11]

One of the explanations for the immense growth in the volume of terrorism in Cairo (from nineteen attacks during the 1970s to 221 during the 1990s) relates to the growth in the number of impoverished neighborhoods around the capital. These neighborhoods, dubbed by the Egyptian media *manatek ashwa'iya* (poverty-stricken illegal neighborhoods that sprang up without planning) – *ashwa'ayiat*, for short – contained some six million residents in 1990, a number equivalent to the total in all other sections of Cairo. The *ashwa'ayiat* in the Cairo area and some 600 neighborhoods in other parts of Egypt were the primary reservoirs from which the Islamic fundamentalists drew recruits during the 1990s. In 1992 some twelve million individuals lived in these slum areas, representing 20 percent of the total Egyptian population.[12]

The data regarding Islamic violence and terrorism (cited in table 3.5) thus highlights a clear connection between terrorism and socio-economic distress. The situation was particularly severe in Upper Egypt, explaining why the success the Egyptian security forces enjoyed in striking at the terrorist organizations around Cairo and in the Nile Delta was not matched in Upper Egypt. The militants who fled there from the northern part of the country found support among an admiring populace, with many of them simply returning to the arms of their own families. In such conditions, it wasn't difficult to recruit new blood into the ranks of the terrorist organizations.

Funding and Armament

The Islamic terrorist organizations operating in Egypt enjoyed funding from a variety of sources. Iran financed the al Jama'a al-Islamiyya and al-Jihad organizations, according to information obtained by Egyptian intelligence via investigations and trials of Islamic fundamentalists. The terrorist organizations also obtained financing via contributions collected in the United States, as well as in various Asian and European countries. Contributions were solicited in the name of Muslims in Bosnia, with large sums raised among Arab and Egyptian individuals and families living outside of Egypt. The minister of the interior and intelligence sources frequently warned that such monies ultimately flowed to the terrorist organizations.[13] Large sums of money also reached the fundamentalist organizations from millionaires, including members of the Muslim Brotherhood who left Egypt during the 1960s and made fortunes in Saudi Arabia, Germany, the US, and elsewhere. One major source of funding was Osama Bin Laden, one of the primary underwriters and masterminds of the fundamentalist organizations in several Arab countries.[14]

One substantial source of funding for terrorism within Egypt was generated by members of organized groups throughout the country – on the streets, at the entrances to theaters and cinemas, on trains and buses – who collected money under the cover of contributions for building mosques. These collectors carried receipts stamped by the Ministry of Social Affairs, but no one tracked what happened to this money, and some terrorists admitted that they used these contributions to finance terrorist actions. There was also extensive commercial activity at the entrances to mosques, where Islamic volunteers sold religious books, ritual objects, clothes, and video cassettes. This yielded extensive profits, part of which reached the terrorist organizations.[15]

Those organizations also received monies from financial institutions connected with the Muslim Brotherhood, such as Islamic banks, investment companies, and Islamic commerce firms. In 1988, an Islamic bank,

Bank al-Taqwa, was established in the Bahamas, becoming the largest source of financing for the Muslim Brotherhood. Its board was controlled by Egyptian citizens connected to the Muslim Brotherhood and radical organizations. The bank, which had a branch in Switzerland, supported various Islamic groups, evidently under the cover of contributions to charitable organizations. Egyptian authorities were aware that bank monies reached the militant organizations conducting terrorism in the country, and from time to time administrative officials and the media tackled the bank over its funding of violent activities.[16]

Drug smuggling also served the terrorist organizations as a source of income. In 1993, Egyptian citizens who had been engaged in growing hashish in Pakistan to help finance the war of the Afghani fundamentalists established connections with the leaders of the terrorist organizations in Egypt, and introduced them to the hashish fields and drug production laboratories in Afghanistan. As a result, Egyptian militants started receiving monies from the profits on drugs smuggled into Egypt from Afghanistan via Sudan. Under interrogation, one drug dealer related that he revealed his drug connection to members of a terrorist organization while serving in a Cairo prison for drug smuggling. The head of the drug-enforcement department of the State Security Investigations administration in Cairo, Akid Abdullah al-Watidi, averred that many prisoners convicted of drug smuggling had admitted that they and the fundamentalists had received religious dispensations to engage in selling drugs for the sake of financing the terrorist organizations.[17]

As for weaponry, the terrorist organizations had no difficulty obtaining arms from various sources within and outside Egypt. The weapons acquired domestically were either produced locally or smuggled into the country. According to Ministry of Interior data of 1993, about 2.5 million weapons were held by criminals and members of terrorist organizations, with only 244,350 licensed for possession.[18] According to data of the security services, there were 184 shops in Egypt that were licensed to sell weapons. Of the 250,000 licensed weapons owned by 243,000 Egyptians, only 489 were ever reported to the authorities as lost. In parallel, during a sixteen month period in 1992–93, security authorities seized some 70,000 weapons that had been held without license. According to estimates, these represented only a small fraction of the total number of weapons in Egypt. Illegal gun sales were conducted primarily by Islamic fundamentalists and drug dealers who were also the main users of such weapons.

The sale of illegal weapons flourished primarily in Upper Egypt. Over the course of 1993, the security forces uncovered an illegal factory in Assiut for the manufacture of automatic weapons based on Russian designs. The factory sold its output to fundamentalists and drug dealers for 500 Egyptian pounds per handgun. The main weapons market, at Mount al-

Table 3.5 Islamic Violence and Terrorism by Geographic Location, 1970 onward

District	Number of Islamic Terror Attacks				Socio-Economic Data		
	1970s	1980s	1990s	Percent increase from 1970s to 1990s	Infant mortality rate (per 1000)	Natural growth rate	Percentage of illiterate women
Urban							
Cairo	19	24	221	1063.2			
Alexandria	11	7	27	145.5			
Port Sa'id	—	—	13	—			
Suez	4	7	5	1.3			
Total/Average	34	38	266	682.4	43	2.8	26.4
Lower Egypt							
Damietta	—	—	—	—			
Daqahleya	—	3	3	0			
Sharqeya	—	3	6	100			
Qalyubeya	—	—	—	—			
Kafr al-Sheikh	—	—	—	—			
Gharbeya	—	5	5	0			
Monofeya	—	—	—	—			
Beheira	—	—	—	—			
Ismailia	—	—	—	—			
Total/Average	—	11	14	27.3	61	3.2	43.5

Upper Egypt							
Giza	9	19	82	911.1			
Beni Suef	2	12	34	1700			
Fayoum	13	19	67	515.4			
Minya	9	17	191	2122.2			
Assiut	11	21	302	2745.5			
Suhag	—	11	71	—			
Qana	8	20	98	1225			
Aswan	—	7	73	—			
Total/Average	52	126	918	896.2	98	4.7	53.3
Border Areas							
Red Sea	—	—	7	—			
New Valley	—	—	—	—			
Marsa Matrouh	—	—	10	—			
Northern Sinai	—	—	—	—			
Southern Sinai	—	2	3	—			
Total/Average	—	2	20	1000	54	4	40.9
Egypt	86	177	1218	951.2	73	3.6	43.7

Sources: Egypt Human Development Report 1995, Cairo Institute of National Planning; *Egypt Demographic and Health Survey* (Cairo: National Population Council, September 1996).

Matarid in Assiut, was an automatic weapons exchange of sorts that operated on the principle of supply and demand. Because of the tradition of revenge killings among the *sa'id* residents of Upper Egypt, every family kept weapons both for self-defense and revenge purposes. The growth that took place in the volume of weapons sold contributed to the success of the local industry, which operated without a license. As a result, blacksmiths converted their forges into small factories for producing semi-automatic weapons, which sold for 50–100 Egyptian pounds each. Expert smiths were successful in refurbishing old German guns, selling them for 200 Egyptian pounds each.

The weapons smuggled into Egypt arrived primarily via Sudan from members of al-Jama'a al-Islamiyya living on bases in Sudan. The difficult economic conditions in Sudan motivated those Sudanese with access to military arsenals to sell army weapons to Egyptian merchants, who in turn sold them to terrorist groups; in 1993, Kalashnikov rifles sold for about $100 each. From Chad, Sudanese merchants purchased arms that had remained in the possession of the militias after the Libya–Chad war and then sold them for low prices in Sudan and Egypt. Some of these weapons made their way to the weapons market at Mount al-Matarid. Small-scale arms smuggling was uncovered on the Libya–Egypt border.

Large stores of arms and explosives remained in the Sinai Desert following the hasty retreat by the Egyptian army during the 1967 Six Day War, augmented by arms caches left by Israeli forces six years later during the Yom Kippur War. Bedouin merchants in southern Sinai collected the weapons and mines they discovered in the desert and transferred them into Egypt proper, where they found their way to the terrorist organizations in Cairo, Giza, and other cities.[19]

The terrorist organizations acquired explosives for preparing varieties of bombs primarily from privately owned mines and quarries, such as the quarries of Tara and Hilwan, the quarries of Upper Egypt (for example, Deirut and Beni Suef), and the phosphate mines of Aswan. Explosives were also produced from chemicals that could be purchased in local shops. One expert found that 140 types of chemicals from which bombs and incendiary devices could be assembled were sold without supervision in Egypt. Part of the explosives used by the fundamentalists came from military industry plants, which invites the question how it was possible to bypass the army's controls and smuggle dangerous materials to the terrorist organizations.[20] The head of the Egyptian Geological Survey and Mining Authority, Atef al-Dardiri, denied the involvement of the quarry owners in the smuggling of explosives to the terrorists, insisting likewise that the mines had no connection with the terrorists. Al-Dardiri further stressed that it was impossible for the terrorists to obtain explosives from the military industries. He said that the main source serving them for the manufacture of bombs was the chemical materials that were easily obtained in the markets.[21]

The head of the explosives department in the Directorate of State Security Investigations in Cairo, Colonel Adel Hussein Saad, reported that over the years the terrorists had gradually advanced in the field of explosives production. Initially, the fundamentalists used to empty simple materials used in children's games into plastic containers, add nails, and drop these devices from high places, without causing much damage. Later, they used Molotov cocktails, bottles filled with a mixture of gunpowder, benzene, kerosene, and paint thinner. Finally, the terrorists developed the ability to make booby traps out of everyday items, such as pens, transistor radios, tape recorders, and children's games. Bent rusty nails were added to heighten the damage the devices would cause. Many devices of this nature were used in attacks of 1993, including the lethal attacks on the Cairene coffee house Wadi al-Nil, on Shubra Street in Cairo, and in the "medinat al-Nasser" zone.[22] Captured terrorists were caught with a handbook on the preparation of explosive devices.[23]

The Inclusive Range of Targets

Terrorism against Government Officials and Public Figures

The murder of liberal writer Farag Foda marked an important shift in terrorist activity, as it sparked a trend of more frequent and more intense violence than Egypt had experienced previously. In the months and years following, there were more attacks, more casualties, including many more fatalities, and new types of terrorist operations, including attacks against tourists. Nonetheless, the whole story of Islamic terrorism in Egypt began earlier and took shape around different types of targets, including government officials, security personnel, intellectuals, ethnic groups, and eventually foreign tourists as well.

Political assassination was attempted more frequently following the murder of Egyptian President Anwar Sadat by the al-Jihad organization. Harming public figures and senior members of the security apparatus became a particularly important objective of the radical Islamic groups. To them, attacking the security forces, which were their official adversary, was an imperative. The confrontations with the police, especially when the radicals were successful, enhanced the admiration among the public for the fundamentalists. Attacks against individuals in the government or the security establishment undermined the stability of the regime and its ability to maintain law and order. In addition to these practical explanations, radical Islam also assigned a religious context for attacking rulers who did not fulfill Islamic religious law. Twenty reasons were given to justify the 1981 assassination of President Sadat: of these, seventeen concerned his failure to adhere to Islamic law, while the peace treaty with Israel was cited only at the end.[24] A religious imprimatur was also given to the units of al-Jama'a al-Islamiyya, which attacked President Mubarak in June 1995.

Of the many attempts to attack government and security figures, ministers of interior were favored for assassination, since they were responsible for the security forces fighting terrorism. On May 5, 1987 an attempt was made against the former minister of the interior Hassan Abu Basha as he got out of his car near his home in Cairo; he was seriously injured. The terrorist group al-Nagoun min al-Nar (Survivors of Hellfire) claimed responsibility for the attack.[25] On August 13, 1987, an attempt was made against the life of another former minister of the interior, Ismail Nabawi, who preceded Hassan Abu Basha in office and, as head of the security services under Sadat, had supervised wide-ranging arrests among the radical groups. The attackers waited in ambush for Nabawi for two days, and unsuccessfully shot at him when he went out on the terrace of his home. The same group claimed responsibility for this incident.[26] More than two years later, on December 16, 1989, there was an attempt against then Minister of the Interior Zaki Bader, when a booby-trapped truck exploded thirty meters from his car in the center of Cairo. Bader had become known as the person who had initiated the iron-fist policy against the Islamic militants, pursuing them and other adversaries of the government relentlessly. Responsibility for this attack, in which no one was injured, was assigned to al-Jihad, but it is likely that it too was carried out by al-Nagoun min al-Nar.[27]

On August 8, 1993, an attempt was made against the life of General Hassan al-Alfi, who, as minister of the interior, was responsible for the domestic security systems in the country. The attack, which injured Alfi, took place during the morning hours when the minister's convoy was passing in front of the American University in Cairo, near Liberation Square, the busiest intersection in the city. The attackers set off an explosive charge near the minister's car, then opened fire on it. The minister was hit by bullets in his arm and chest, and a number of bodyguards and passers-by were killed or injured.[28] The minister of the interior had employed certain safety measures: he changed his route daily, while an identical car to his preceded him, as a decoy to would-be attackers. Nonetheless, the attackers exploited the one weak point – the entry to the minister's office building. While previous interior ministers had always instructed that the road be closed at least a quarter hour prior to their arrival, Alfi felt this caused resentment and he therefore objected to the closure. The radicals identified this security lapse and took advantage of it, while also managing to override other security measures.[29] This attack differed from previous ones in that explosives were used, whereas prior incidents had involved only close-range fire from automatic weapons. Investigation revealed that the perpetrators had planned to escape on the motorcycle to which they had tied the explosives, but they had not correctly assessed how forceful the blast would be. Apparently, the planners of the attack had intended that those sent to carry it out would themselves be killed, in order to prevent revealing the identities of the planners. The entire action was evidence of an escalation in terrorism and reinforced the assumption that the terrorist groups sought to target specifically the interior minister as the one responsible for the security measures being leveled against them.[30]

During the 1990s, there was extensive escalation in the number of attempted and successful murders of other political figures, beginning with the assassination of the chairman of parliament, Dr. Rif'at Mahgoub, by al-Jama'a al-Islamiyya on October 12, 1990 in Cairo. The attackers opened fire after ambushing Mahgoub's car. Mahgoub, his driver, three bodyguards, and a police officer who chased after the assassins were killed.[31] The Egyptian minister of information, Safwat al-Sharif, escaped an attempt on his life on April 20, 1993. Islamic underground members opened fire on his armored car shortly after he left his home in Heliopolis. He was injured lightly by glass fragments, while his bodyguard was mortally wounded. Four of the five attackers escaped, and the fifth was captured. The leader of al-Jama'a al-Islamiyya in Assiut, Sheikh Mohammad Sayyid Salim, announced in a phone call to foreign journalists in Cairo that his fighters had carried out the attack. He promised to continue the war until the downfall of the secular government in the country and the establishment of an Egyptian Islamic republic.[32] A few months later, on November 25, 1993, Egyptian Prime Minister Atef Sidki survived an attempt on his life. As Sidki was leaving his Heliopolis home, a booby-trapped car exploded. With no one in his convoy having been injured, it continued on its way, although a ten year-old girl was killed by the explosion, eleven others – mostly schoolchildren – injured, and many other children went into shock. This attack, which took place near a school, caused angry reactions among the Cairo public. An anonymous caller who contacted a local news agency said that the New Islamic Jihad had carried out the attack.[33]

Attacks against security forces were mounted frequently, particularly during the 1990s and especially in 1993. In all, 469 members of the security forces, including soldiers and police, were killed in the 1990s. Among the noteworthy attacks: Brigadier General Mohammad al-Shiami, deputy commander of general security in the Assiut district, was killed on April 11, 1993, when his car was fired upon from an ambush in Abu Tig in Upper Egypt. His assistant and driver were also killed. On August 7, 1993, a police general, Mohammad Abdel Hammid Gebara, commander of the

North-Qena District, and two policemen who were with him were killed when their vehicle stopped at a railroad crossing near the town of Nagi Hamadi in Upper Egypt. Al-Jama'a al-Islamiyya claimed responsibility for these murders. According to police investigations, the terrorists carried out the murders in response to the execution of fifteen Islamic fundamentalists during the preceding months.[34]

In 1994, the terrorist attacks against members of the police all took place in Upper Egypt. In January, a police colonel was murdered in Assiut, shortly after which the deputy commander of the General Security Service was killed while visiting there. A police officer was also killed in Aswan. In early April 1994, General Ra'uf Khirat, the deputy head of the Directorate of State Security Investigations, was murdered: he was well-known for his intensive experience in the struggle against the Islamic extremists in Egypt. The murder shocked the public, since Khirat became the most senior security person to be murdered by the Islamic radicals. The murder took place in Giza, near Cairo, when two motorcyclists drew near the officer's car and opened fire.[35]

The year 1995 also opened with a serious terrorist act against the police. On January 2, two Islamic fundamentalists murdered eight policemen and three civilians. In four separate incidents, the Islamic extremists, disguised as police, stopped buses on the main highway near the town of Malawi on the shores of the Nile, about 260 kilometers south of Cairo. They ordered the passengers to leave the bus, detaining five policemen, whom they killed at the roadside. In other incidents in the south, the attackers boarded three mini-buses and, after checking the identity cards of the passengers, killed three policemen and three civilians. The total number of killings was one of the highest in one day since the beginning of the surge of attacks in 1992.[36]

Other serious terrorist acts against government and establishment officials punctuated these years. There were attempts against members of the judicial establishment, most of which failed. In particular, al-Jihad issued a *fatwa* calling for the assassination of eight military judges who had been involved in serving terrorists with death sentences. Extremists, primarily from al-Jama'a al-Islamiyya, also attacked Egyptian intellectuals who disagreed with the fundamentalist concepts. Though the majority of the attacks failed, they damaged the government's image, both within Egypt and abroad, and shook its foundations. The editor of the widely distributed weekly *Al-Musawwar*, Makram Mohammad Ahmed, escaped an attempt on his life on June 5, 1987, without injury. Gunfire erupted from a car that had been following Ahmed's car through Cairo. In spite of the fact that twenty-five shots were fired, he was injured only lightly. The attempt on his life occurred after Ahmed published a series of articles in which he criticized the Islamic extremists.[37]

On June 8, 1992, in a subsequent attack against men of letters, Farag Foda, an author and journalist, was killed in broad daylight by two motorcyclists while walking to his car near his home in the Cairo suburb of Heliopolis. Foda, an outspoken liberal, was one of the foremost critics of the religious extremists. He sought to establish a political party comprising Muslims and Copts to fight the Islamic radicalization. One of the apprehended attackers confessed that he had been sent by al-Jama'a al-Islamiyya to murder Foda because of his anti-Islamic views. Evidence from other sources revealed that Foda was murdered on orders of Sheikh Omar Abdel Rahman and that he figured on a list of people marked for elimination, among them politicians, writers, actors, and liberal intellectuals. The murder shocked the educated classes of Egypt. Foda's funeral turned into a demonstration in which participants chanted "no to terrorism," and his death triggered a public dispute over the phenomenon of Islamic radicalism and ways of combating it. At the same time, Foda's murder was a harbinger of increased terrorism in Egypt during the ensuing years, especially in the south of the country. Significantly, it also marked the point the regime adopted a new approach for coping with Islamic fundamentalism.[38]

One particularly chilling terrorist attack was the October 14, 1994 attempt against Naguib Mahfouz, the Egyptian Nobel Laureate for Literature, who was then eighty-three years old. Mahfouz had been decried as a heretic by al-Jama'a al-Islamiyya for having described God in a distorted manner in one of his books. The author was stabbed and seriously injured in the arm by an Islamic extremist and had to be hospitalized for seven weeks. Indeed, the stabbing was so severe that his very survival was impressive, while it seriously impeded his subsequent use of his arm. The attackers were caught and two of them sentenced to death; two others who had assisted as lookouts and in the ambush were sentenced to life imprisonment. The attack echoed throughout the Egyptian and world media given Mahfouz's national stature, and much of the public denounced the attack against a defenseless elderly man as an act of cowardice.[39]

Largely as a result of the fact that the security forces had taken initiatives for the war against terrorism into their hands, no attacks were attempted in Egypt against government figures in 1995, and President Mubarak stated in a newspaper interview that Egypt had succeeded in gaining control over terrorism. Although Mubarak's statement reflected the security reality, within a year an attempt was made on his own life. On November 29, 1996, Egyptian security thwarted a daring plan to kill him in his Alexandria palace. The French news agency in Cairo, which reported the news, depicted the detailed plan that included taking control of the presidential palace in Alexandria and executing the president. According to the report, twenty members of a terrorist unit, armed with extensive automatic weapons, bombs, grenades, and RPG launchers, were arrested before they could set out on the operation. The unit evidently belonged to al-Jama'a al-Islamiyya, though a different report assigned them to al-Jihad. Egyptian authorities denied that an attempt had been made on the president's life, and a spokesman of the Ministry of the Interior stated that the news reports were without foundation. In contrast, the Cairo reporter for Radio Monte Carlo cited the name of the commander of the group, Ahmed Ismail al-Sheikh, who in the past had been charged with and cleared of attacks on tourists. Radio Monte Carlo added that among those arrested on suspicion of planning the attack was Mustafa Mahmoud, an attorney charged with being the liaison between the group and imprisoned leaders of al-Jama'a al-Islamiyya.[40]

Terrorism Against Tourists and Foreigners

With the outbreak of the surge of terrorism in Egypt in mid-1992, tourists were considered prime targets for attack. The terrorist organizations, especially al-Jama'a al-Islamiyya, defined this kind of soft target as part of an objective to harm the Egyptian economy, since tourism was one of the three leading sources of revenue. Terrorism against tourists also damaged Egypt's image around the world as a strong and stable country in the Middle East.[41]

The first of a rash of attacks against tourists in this period was in Luxor, on June 24, 1992, when two bombs exploded near the temple at Karnak, one of the main tourist sites in the region.[42] On July 15, 1992, a homemade bomb was thrown at tourists, again in Luxor. Although up until this point no one was injured, damage to the tourism industry was already evident. On October 2, 1992, four gunmen opened fire on a Nile cruise ship in Upper Egypt carrying German tourists. Three Egyptian crew members were lightly injured. Four days later, a bomb exploded on a train crossing Deirut on the Assiut-Minya line, killing four and injuring nine. On October 21, a tourist bus was attacked near Deirut, killing a British woman and injuring two other British tourists. On November 2, shots were fired at a bus carrying Coptic tourists near Minya, injuring ten passengers, and ten days later, eight people were injured, five of them German tourists, in an attack on a tourist bus near Qena.[43] In all, attacks against tourism targets in 1992 resulted in five dead and forty-eight injured.[44]

The international and Egyptian media gave broad coverage to the attacks against tourists, emphasizing the extensive damage to the industry and to foreign investments in Egypt. The Islamic leaders understood well that they were harming a primary national asset. To justify their activities, they published a fatwa issued in the US by Sheikh Omar Abdel Rahman, averring that certain tourist activities, such as the interacting of men and women in leisure activities, were contrary to the spirit of Islam and there-fore forbidden [*haram* – banned]. This ruling was spread by the Islamic extremists via recordings, which also included sermons by the sheikh.[45]

Al-Jama'a al-Islamiyya warned that it would attack foreigners and foreign embassies if the Egyptian security forces didn't withdraw,[46] and indeed by 1993 tourists in Cairo were also targeted. In May 1993 a bomb was detonated in a Cairo cafe frequented by tourists, killing four. At the same time, another bomb was detonated on an adjacent street, killing seven and injuring fifteen. In early June, a bomb was set off near four empty tourist buses parked in Cairo's Liberation Square, near the Egyptian Museum, the busiest area in the city. While it caused only property damage, the shock and further decline to tourism were substantial. Hotel occupancy decreased substantially, by 60–80 percent, from the levels of October 1992.[47] Al-Jama'a al-Islamiyya, which carried out most of the attacks against tourists, called on other Arab countries to follow the example of Great Britain and the US and instruct their citizens to leave Egypt as a precaution. Business people were also urged to cancel their investments in Egypt.[48] Other violence included the January 5, 1993 attack on a bus carrying Japanese tourists in Deirut.[49] For the first time in the confrontations between the Islamic extremists and the Egyptian regime, a bomb was detonated in one of the pyramids in Giza on March 30, 1993. This incident took place in a burial chamber of the second-largest pyramid at Giza. No one in the group of Russian tourists visiting the site was injured.[50]

The year 1993 included a record number of attacks against tourists, and in all, two tourism seasons – 1992 and 1993 – were severely disrupted, with damages of $3–4 billion to Egypt.[51] From January through March, 1993, there was a 50 percent decline in the average number of tourists visiting Egypt, with 3.5 million room reservations recorded, versus six million during the parallel period in 1992. Canceled reservations totaled some 7.5 billion Egyptian pounds (about $1 billion). Tourism companies had to reduce employee salaries by 50 percent. Occupancy was lowest in the resort villages, and room occupancy of the luxury hotels in Cairo dropped from the 80 percent average of previous years to 50 percent. Some 600,000 workers employed in factories supplying goods to places such as the famous outdoor Cairo market, Khan el-Khalili, consequently found them-selves jobless. According to the airports authority, there was a 90 percent drop in charter flights to the tourism sites in Luxor, Aswan, al-Gardaka on the Red Sea, and Cairo during the period of October 1992 to April 1993. The total passenger traffic through Egyptian airports dropped 50 percent from 1992, when 15,596 flights by fifty-one scheduled carriers had ferried four million passengers to the country.[52]

The Egyptian public and media began speaking out against this terrorism, analyzing its negative ramifications. The harm to tourists and foreigners and the large number of security forces engaged in protecting them generated frustration and anger within Egyptian society. An editorial in *Al-Wafd* stated:

> At the same time that we are opposed to the terrorists' objective to harm tourists and that we condemn both the plan and those who carry it out, we also object to having the vehicles used to transport tourists being escorted by police armed with machine guns. While we have an obligation to protect the tourist visiting our country, we object to a tourist being vulnerable to the threat of terror and immersed in an atmosphere of excessive police protection. On the streets of Cairo and the resort cities, convoys of vehicles escorting tourists have started to be seen, with police motorcycles and cars, sirens blaring, leading them, and another string of motorcycles and cars following from behind.[53]

Annis Mansour, in his column in the daily *Al-Ahram*, pointed out the problem in the resort villages of al-Gardaka and Sharm el-Sheikh, where "the number of waiters is greater than the number of guests." Against this backdrop, Mansour condemned the terrorism that had "driven the tourists from Egypt," emphasizing that "there is no religion or religious system which demands in the name of the religion that we sacrifice the country in which we live, expel tens of thousands, and cut off the source of income of hundreds of thousands."[54]

Egypt's security authorities adopted a tough stance against the terrorists, conducting arrests and placing many on trial. These trials resulted in stiff sentences, including capital punishment. As a result, there was a brief lull in attacks against tourists during the second half of 1993. During December of that year, however, despite the efforts of the government, the attacks resumed and President Mubarak was forced to admit that "no country in the world can guarantee the safety of its visitors at all times."[55] On December 27, 1993, a bus carrying eighteen tourists was fired upon near the Omar Abul Aas Mosque in the old city of Cairo. Eight Austrian tourists were injured, three of them seriously. Again, al-Jama'a al-Islamiyya claimed responsibility for the attack. In another attack the same month, a group of tourists was fired upon at the entrance to the luxurious Cairo hotel Semiramis, killing two Americans, one Frenchman, and one Italian.[56]

On February 19, 1994, Islamic extremists attacked a train on the Cairo–Luxor line, injuring a Polish architect, a Taiwanese student, and two Egyptians. The attack took place not far from Assiut, an al-Jama'a al-Islamiyya stronghold.[57] A bomb explosion in a railway car in Upper Egypt on February 23, 1994 injured five tourists (a German, two Australians, and two New Zealanders) and five Egyptians.[58] In August 1994, al-Jama'a al-Islamiyya attacked a tourist bus in Upper Egypt, killing a Spanish tourist. The organization exploited this attack to warn tourists not attend the

International Population Conference scheduled for September in Cairo.[59] The following month, three men armed with automatic machine guns attacked a bus with tourists near Nakadah, a city about 500 kilometers south of Cairo.[60] In early November 1995, within two days, terrorists attacked two passenger trains in the Qena district. Scores of Egyptians were injured in the first attack, while a French and a Dutch tourist were among the injured in the second. Once again, al-Jama'a al-Islamiyya, which claimed responsibility for the attacks, issued a call for tourists to leave Egypt immediately, since the organization planned to continue its attacks against them, citing its state of war with the Egyptian authorities.[61]

Once Egypt's security forces took the initiative to battle terrorism in mid-1994, however, there was a decline in attacks on tourists and foreigners. No foreign tourist was killed during 1995. The tourism branch began to revive, and the number of tourists steadily increased. Senior government officials trumpeted with pride their success in returning security to the cities and villages of Egypt, as well as the security of foreign tourists.

The period of quiet, however, turned out to be more of a respite than a permanent situation. On April 18, 1996, three armed men opened fire on a group of tourists about to board a bus at the entrance to the Europa Hotel, not far from the pyramids. Eighteen Greek tourists were killed in this attack. Al-Jama'a al-Islamiyya took responsibility, but claimed it had intended to attack Israeli tourists in revenge for the slaughter of Lebanese citizens by Israeli artillery during the course of Operation Grapes of Wrath.[62] In broad daylight on September 18, 1997, four men attacked a tourist bus with gunfire and Molotov cocktails in Cairo's Liberation Square. Ten people were killed, nine of them German tourists. Commentators connected the attack to the court conviction three days earlier of seventy-two terrorists, four of whom had been sentenced to death and eight to life imprisonment. Others connected the attack to the government's rejection in May and August 1997 of calls for a ceasefire by six fundamentalist leaders serving time in Egyptian prisons. Although no organization claimed responsibility for the attack, it was generally ascribed to al-Jama'a al-Islamiyya or al-Jihad. A few hours after the attack, an Islamic organization based in London and close to the Egyptian al-Jihad urged foreign tourists to stop visiting Egypt until the government stopped its acts of violence against the Egyptian people. In the aftermath, the Egyptian police announced the capture of three terrorists.[63]

The two severe attacks against the Greek and German tourists in Cairo did not damage the continuing tourism to the wondrous sites at Luxor. Many tourists tended to fly there from Cairo, both because of the distance (about 400 kilometers south of the capital) and to avoid the danger involved in traveling southward by train or bus, targeted more than once by Islamic terrorists. On October 12, 1997, President Mubarak officiated at the Luxor opening of a showcase production of Verdi's *Aida*, speaking before a large audience of foreign tourists. This seeming idyll was shattered, however, on November 17, 1997, with the most murderous terrorist attack in Egypt's history. At ten o'clock in the morning, several gunmen dressed in police uniforms attacked tourist buses near the Temple of Hatshepsut, killing its occupants. The terrorists also burst into the courtyard of the temple, shooting indiscriminately at the tourists waiting to enter the site. A Swiss woman who survived related that the terrorists walked among the bodies, shooting at any which still moved. Sixty-eight people were killed, including fifty-eight tourists, and twenty-four were injured. Among the victims were thirty-six Swiss tourists, eight Japanese, five Germans, four British, and other nationalities, plus six terrorists and two Egyptian policemen. Al-Jama'a al-Islamiyya claimed responsibility for the attack via leaflets left at the temple. In its announcement, the organization called upon the United States to release Sheikh Rahman, who had been sentenced to life imprisonment. The attack in Luxor dealt a heavy blow to Egypt's tourism branch, as masses of tourists quickly left the country. Waves of cancellations flowed in from Europe, the US, and Japan, and the foreign offices of various countries advised their citizens not to visit Egypt.

The massacre at Luxor took place during the height of a tourism promotion campaign that had been undertaken after the attack against German tourists in the heart of Cairo. The minister of tourism, Dr. Mamdouh al-Biltagi, participated in the campaign, and at the time of the Luxor attack, was in London for an international tourism exhibition. Biltagi, who described the massacre as a horrid tragedy, expressed concerns over serious harm to Egyptian tourism. Indeed, the graphic pictures, the shocking accounts by the injured, and the warnings from experts about the danger from Islamic fundamentalists in Egypt would not quickly be forgotten. The fact that the attack took place at one of the most frequented tourism sites, in spite of the tight security, also was likely to amplify reluctance to visit Egypt. The Temple of Hatshepsut, the 3400–year old palace of the ancient queen, and the hundreds of ancient tombs at Luxor, including that of King Tutenkhamen and Queen Nefertiti, were famous sites that drew some two million visitors to Luxor annually. Following the massacre, it was assumed tourists would avoid Egypt for a long time, preferring more secure destinations.

Many international leaders condemned the attack, including President Clinton, Israeli officials, and other Western leaders, among them the pope. The sheikh of the religious Islamic university, al-Azhar, Mohammad Sayyid Tantawi, considered the highest authority for the Sunni Muslims, condemned the massacre, characterizing it as a criminal act contradicting the tenets of Islam. A furious President Mubarak flew to Luxor to assess security measures and to attempt to contain the damage to tourism. He described the security measures in the area as embarrassingly inadequate, expressing severe criticism of the minister of the interior, who was responsible for the police and domestic security forces. The minister, Alfi, was forced to resign, and was replaced by General Habib al-Adli, who had been commander of the Directorate of State Security Investigations (the Egyptian parallel to the Israeli General Security Services or the FBI in the US).[64] Adli became the seventh person to serve as minister of the interior under Mubarak.

The three new severe attacks – on the Greek tourists in Giza, the German tourists in Liberation Square in Cairo, and the massacre in Luxor – proved again how exposed tourists and foreigners in Egypt were to terrorist attacks, even after the government had undertaken initiatives against Islamic terrorism. Tourists were Egypt's vulnerable target, and thus Islamic extremists continued to impress the government with their willingness to embarrass it and cause damage to the national economy. Table 3.6 shows that in the wave of terror of the 1990s, ninety-seven tourists were killed in Egypt. In 1998–99, tourists were not killed in terrorist activity, and the tourism industry continued its recovery.

Ethnically Motivated Terrorism

Aggression by Islamic fundamentalist organizations against minorities was a familiar phenomenon and by no means unique to Egypt. Christians were persecuted in Sudan and, along with the Baha'i faithful, in Iran. The Muslim animosity toward the Christian minority in Gaza, Jerusalem, and the West Bank was well known. After the Palestinian Authority (PA) received control of Bethlehem and preparations commenced for the general elections, the idea arose to establish a Christian political party there, the city of Jesus' birth. However, Elias Freij, the city's Christian mayor, opposed the idea, to avoid friction with the Muslim majority.

In Egypt, the radical Islamic organizations marked the Copts and their property as targets for terrorism. The Copts, who in the 1990s comprised approximately 7 percent of the Egyptian population of 68 million, were regarded, from standpoints of religion, ethnic group, and social status as a foreign element. They generally endured the attacks against them without responding, although at times they took revenge on their Islamic enemies, thus bringing upon themselves the next calamity and a cycle of mutual retribution. Ethnically motivated terrorism – sometimes labeled "social violence" by various researchers and experts – existed primarily in Upper Egypt, but was also found in Cairo and the Nile Delta. Envy of the Copts' economic success also fueled terrorist acts. In Imbaba – a crowded, dense suburb of Cairo with one million people, most of them unemployed – the

Table 3.6 Foreign Tourist Fatalities, 1992–99

1992	1993	1994	1995	1996	1997	1998	1999	Total
1	6	4	0	19	67	0	0	97

Table 3.7 Copts Killed by Terrorists, 1992–99

1992	1993	1994	1995	1996	1997	1998	1999	Total
22	19	8	29	30	28	3	20	159

Note: The numbers include Copts killed in hate crimes by Muslims, and not only Copts killed by members of terrorist organizations.

Copts were attacked for representing a higher social level. Similarly, their property was attacked, their shops burned, and they were prevented from hanging Christian icons in the windows of their shops or homes.[65]

Attacks against Copts were ongoing, rather than functions of the periodic waves of terrorism, and occurred before the 1992 surge commenced. On August 28, 1988, a homemade explosive device was planted at a wedding in a Coptic church in the Shubra quarter of Cairo. Fifteen people were injured by the explosion. Egyptian authorities attributed the attack to al-Jihad, theorizing it was meant to exacerbate inter-communal tensions in the neighborhood heavily populated by Copts.[66] On September 2, 1988 some sixty Islamic extremists destroyed the house of a Coptic family in Dir Muas following a rumor of plans to convert the house to a Coptic church. They opened fire on the police who were called to the site, and in the ensuing gunfire two people were killed and more than twenty-five injured.[67]

In March 1992, the attacks grew against Coptic churches and property, with a particularly large number of attacks in Deirut. Against this backdrop, the general guide of the Muslim Brotherhood attempted to conduct negotiations with Coptic leaders to reach an agreement but the talks failed because the Muslim Brotherhood was unwilling to change its slogan, "the Copts are under our protection." The Copts characterized the stance of the Muslim Brotherhood as being an attempt "to cut our throats."[68] On May 4, 1992 there were clashes between Copts and Muslims in the village of Sanabu, home to 20,000 people. Fourteen were killed, including some Copts who were brutally murdered. Extensive police forces arrived to separate the two factions. The following month, on June 21, 1992, riots again broke out in Sanabu and in Deirut, when Muslims set fire to Copt shops and houses. At least six people were killed.[69]

The British *Sunday Express* revealed additional shocking facts about the Islamic extremists in Egypt, including kidnapping and raping young Coptic women in an effort to force them to convert to Islam. Once raped, the women were ostracized by the society in which they grew up and there were even occasions where the victims were murdered by family members because they had allegedly sullied the family's good name. Jubilee, a British human-rights organization, expressed concern that the Egyptian authorities were not doing enough to assist these young women. The organization claimed that some courts did not regard the rape of a non-Muslim woman as a crime.[70]

In early 1996 there were additional attacks against Copts in the Nile Delta region. On February 24, 1996, Islamic extremists murdered eight Copts in Upper Egypt. Two days later, severe ethnic riots broke out in the Sharqeya district of the Delta, further belying the assumption that ethnic violence was limited to Upper Egypt. The riots erupted in the wake of a rumor that a Coptic priest in one of the villages of the Sharqeya region was planning to enlarge his church. Thousands of angry Muslims surrounded the church and tried to set it on fire. Forty-one houses belonging to Christians were torched, and many people were beaten. The Ministry of the Interior announced that eighty of the attackers were arrested. In all, thirty people, most of them Copts, were murdered in the Assiut area during the second half of February 1996.[71]

The beginning of 1997 was similarly difficult for the Copts. On the evening of February 12, a group of Coptic youth gathered for a weekly lesson in the Mary Georges Church in the city of Abu Kurkas in the Minya district, about 250 kilometers south of Cairo. The youths sat facing the altar, their backs to the church entrance, when masked men burst in and opened fire, killing ten. Two days later, the bodies of three young Copts were found near Abu Kurkas. A number of different "reasons" for their murder were offered: refusal by the Copts to pay protection money to the Islamic extremists, their being agents of the Egyptian police, and their having visited Israel. Responsibility for the attacks was claimed by al-Jama'a al-Islamiyya. The defense authorities carried out numerous arrests in response to these events, also seizing weapons. A number of Egyptian newspapers reported that the unit which committed the church murders had been arrested. At the same time, the Copts reported that the police unit called to the church didn't arrive for at least an hour, while the injured lay bleeding on the floor for a half hour before medical assistance arrived.

On March 3, 1997, a unit of al-Jama'a al-Islamiyya carried out another attack in southern Egypt, in the village of Izbat Kamel in the Qena district, 580 kilometers south of Cairo. Members of the unit, dressed in army uniforms and armed with automatic weapons, opened fire on the villagers, killing thirteen and wounding six. This attack was among the attacks with the most casualties among the Copts in five years. In general, the Copts were easy prey, particularly when Islamic extremists sought exposure and publicity. Table 3.7 shows the number killed from 1992 to 1999.[72]

The Egyptian authorities were embarrassed and troubled by the continuing attacks against the Copts. The regime understood the world's sensitivity to ethnic violence and was concerned it would be accused of not doing enough to defend the Coptic minority. Consequently, in addition to sending the security forces into action after an attack, the government mobilized the state information and religious institutions to condemn the anti-ethnic terror and emphasize that the Islamic extremists were seeking to harm not just the Christians, but the unity of all of Egypt. After the murders in the church, there was also a large gathering in Abu Kurkas at which Tantawi, the sheikh of al-Azhar University, condemned the attack. The imams across the country received instructions to condemn the massacre in their Friday sermons, and the Egyptian media were also recruited for this purpose. At the same time, as standard procedure, government ministries denied there was a Coptic problem in Egypt, citing the example of the previous UN secretary-general, Boutrous Boutrous-Ghali, a Copt who represented the country with honor.

Terrorism Abroad

During 1995, terrorist activities also commenced against Egyptian targets abroad. Commentators and researchers believe that the success of the security forces in striking at the terrorist groups within Egypt, particularly in the Cairo area and the Delta, led the fundamentalists to act against Egyptian targets abroad, far from the purview of Egyptian intelligence. The terrorist organizations – particularly the largest of them, al-Jama'a al-Islamiyya – had personnel and logistics infrastructures in or near those places they chose to attack Egyptian targets. Two notable attacks carried out abroad were the attempted assassination of President Mubarak in June 1995 in Ethiopia, and the bomb at the Egyptian embassy in Pakistan in November of that year; 1995 also marked serious terrorist activity by Egyptian Islamic militants and others in the West, primarily in France and the US.

On November 19, 1995, a suicide bomber drove a pickup truck loaded with hundreds of kilograms of explosives into the courtyard of the Egyptian embassy in Islamabad, Pakistan and detonated it, causing at least fifteen deaths and injuring about sixty people. Three Islamic organizations claimed responsibility for the attack: al-Jama'a al-Islamiyya, al-Jihad, and the Group for International Justice. Among those killed in the explosion were the second secretary of the Egyptian embassy and three Egyptian security guards. The other fatalities were Pakistani security guards, local embassy staff, and passersby; the Egyptian ambassador was not injured. This was the most serious attack in recent years against an Egyptian target outside of Egypt. It was one link in a chain of attacks that commenced with the attempted attack on President Mubarak in Ethiopia and continued with the detonation of a car bomb in Croatia and the murder of an Egyptian diplomat in Geneva a few days before the attack in Pakistan. The Islamic groups were assisted in these attacks by an infrastructure built by expatriate Egyptian terrorists in countries like Iran, Sudan, and Pakistan who had left Egypt to assist the Afghani rebels in their war against the Soviets. Upon the conclusion of the war in Afghanistan, many of them joined the struggle of the Islamic fundamentalists against the various Arab regimes. Some of them returned to Egypt to advance the struggle there; others remained abroad. Hence the support behind the bombing at the Egyptian embassy in Islamabad.[73]

On December 21, 1995, a car bomb exploded on a busy street in Peshawar in northwest Pakistan. At least thirty people were killed and several were injured. The explosion took place in a crowded market adjacent to a department store. Al-Jihad, which claimed responsibility for the attack, had warned the Pakistani government a week earlier against extraditing Islamic militants to Egypt according to an extradition agreement with the Egyptian government signed in July 1994,[74] and in an announcement made by al-Jihad in Cairo, the organization announced it was prepared to take action against the Pakistani government.

A branch of Egyptian terrorism was also active in the United States. Sheikh Abdel Rahman, spiritual leader of al-Jama'a al-Islamiyya, led a network comprising sixteen Islamic terrorists. Even while living in the US, the sheikh issued instructions and religious rulings to units within his organization. He issued the religious imprimatur for attacking foreign tourists in Egypt and assassinating President Mubarak. The group carried out two terrorist acts: the murder of Rabbi Meir Kahane in 1990 and the bombing at the World Trade Center in February 1993. The group had planned large-scale attacks, intending to target the George Washington Bridge and the Lincoln and Holland Tunnels connecting Manhattan and New Jersey, the United Nations, and the FBI headquarters in Manhattan, as well as President Mubarak himself on his visit to New York, UN Secretary-General Boutrous Boutrous-Ghali, and other individuals. The sheikh and nine of his cohorts were convicted in a trial that lasted almost a year and were sentenced to life imprisonment.[75] The arrest and trial sent shockwaves through the American public as it began to experience the dangers of Islamic fundamentalism.

There were also branches of Egyptian terrorist groups in European cities, including Geneva, Munich, Bonn, Copenhagen, Milan, and others. The Italian police issued an announcement that Islamic fundamentalists were planning an attempt on Mubarak's life during an official visit to Rome in November 1994. The announcement emphasized that as a result of the information received by the police, Mubarak's schedule would be changed; in the end, his three-day visit took place without incident. At a news conference, the commander of the Milan police stated that an investigation that had opened two years earlier had led to seventy-two people suspected of having links with al-Jama'a al-Islamiyya and al-Jihad, along with other terrorist organizations in Egypt, Algeria, the United States, Afghanistan, Germany, and Austria. The Italian police made arrests at the Islamic Culture Institute in Milan and Anwar Sha'aban, the imam who managed the institute, fled. The Italians had gathered information about him via electronic surveillance to prove his connections with Rahman in New York and his involvement with attacks in Egypt and Denmark. Sha'aban was also thought to have given logistical support to terrorists passing through Italy on their way to Bosnia.[76]

Further indication of the activities of Egyptian terrorists in Europe came with the arrest of three Egyptians living in Denmark who belonged to al-Jama'a al-Islamiyya, believed to have planned terrorist actions in train stations and against Jewish targets. They were arrested in November 1993 on suspicion of arson in Aarhaus, the second largest Danish city, but they were released for lack of evidence. Among their possessions, the Danish police found telephone numbers and addresses of people connected with the bombing of the World Trade Center in New York.[77]

The Attempt on Mubarak in Addis Ababa

On Monday morning June 26, 1995, as President Husni Mubarak was proceeding from the Addis Ababa airport to the Conference for African Unity, his motorcade was fired upon from a car that appeared suddenly and blocked the way. In the ensuing exchange of fire, two terrorists and two Ethiopian policemen were killed. Mubarak's armored limousine, which was third in the motorcade, was about seventy meters from the point where the road was blocked by the terrorists' car. Because of the relatively large distance from the attackers' vehicle, the bullets failed to penetrate the president's armored limousine, and the assassination attempt failed.[78] Following orders from the security personnel, the limousine turned around and rushed back to the airport, from where the president immediately flew to Cairo. Upon arriving in Egypt, Mubarak blamed Sudan for serving as a base for the attackers. He also charged that Sudan maintained training camps and offered both refuge and ongoing assistance to Islamic terrorists. Al-Jama'a al-Islamiyya took responsibility for the attempted assassination.[79]

In the wake of the incident, Ethiopian authorities uncovered the hiding places and caches of weapons belonging to the attackers. Three terrorists were caught by the Ethiopians, and three others were killed when Ethiopian forces broke into a safe house in Addis Ababa. The attempt was condemned by the Egyptian public and by part of the Arab world. Syrian President Hafez al-Assad condemned the assassination attempt and in a telephone conversation with Mubarak said that it also harmed Arab interests. The Muslim Brotherhood vigorously denounced the attack, describing it as a "low effort that contradicts every religious, human, and moral value and which expresses the desperation of the terrorists."[80] Iraq spoke in praise of the attack, while Iran denied any connection to it.[81]

In January 1995, the French monthly *Issues* claimed that three attempts had been made against Mubarak's life during the first three weeks of

January, but that they had been successfully kept from the public by Egyptian authorities. Immediately upon learning of the attempt in Ethiopia, Prisma, an Italian news service, reported that an attempt to assassinate Mubarak when visiting Rome in November 1994 had been foiled.[82]

The attempted assassination in Ethiopia took place after Egyptian security forces had succeeded in dealing a hard blow to the terrorist organization, particularly in the Cairo district and the Delta area. Further analysis of the attempt hypothesized that al-Jama'a al-Islamiyya had moved its arena of action outside of Egypt, because it was unable to attack the president within the country. The Islamic terrorists, their backs against the wall, saw an urgent need for a bold action, in order to relieve pressure on themselves and lift the morale of their people.[83]

Over the two months following the assassination attempt, the Egyptian daily *Al-Ahram* published new evidence affirming the involvement of the Sudanese regime. The newspaper published the names and photographs of eight members of al-Jama'a al-Islamiyya who had taken part in the action. The terrorists arrested following the attack identified the pictures of those who had perpetrated the crime and furnished details about Sudan's part in the incident. They related that Mustafa Hamza, commander of the military arm of al-Jama'a al-Islamiyya, had planned the action and trained the Addis Ababa unit, along with supplying the members with documents and funds. Hamza, who twice had been sentenced to death in Egypt, enjoyed special treatment from the Sudanese authorities, infiltrating Egypt as needed for his operations. The detainees also identified the picture of another Egyptian fundamentalist, Abdel Karim Nadi, nicknamed Yassin. The unit trained in Khartoum, rehearsing the plan during the morning hours – the time planned for the attack. *Al-Ahram* learned that Mohammad Shouki Islambouli, a terrorist who had fled Egypt after being sentenced to death, was living with his family in Khartoum, and that the Sudanese authorities had issued him a diplomatic passport and enabled him to make the *hajj* pilgrimage to Mecca in 1994.[84] Mohammad Sarag, another terrorist, succeeded in escaping from Ethiopia on a Sudanese passport after the failed attack.[85]

The failed assassination attempt notwithstanding, operational abilities had clearly reached new levels. An action of this nature required several months of precise planning, including the establishment of an operations infrastructure in Addis Ababa that secured safe houses, weapons, and vehicles. Escape routes were planned and equipment, communications, documents, and certificates prepared. At the second stage, the participants and their equipment were transferred from Sudan to Ethiopia. The intelligence-gathering, planning, preparations, and the daring of the implementation testified to the high level and determination of al-Jama'a al-Islamiyya. It can also be assumed with a high degree of certainty that Egyptian intelligence did not have advance information of the planned attempt, despite the fact that the complex planning of the terrorists had been ongoing for a protracted period. Had the Egyptian authorities known of the intentions in advance, it is hard to believe they would have allowed Mubarak to attend the conference in Ethiopia.

The surge in acts of terrorism that erupted in Egypt in the middle of 1992 was difficult, cruel, and the most costly in human lives in a country that had already experienced much terrorism and violence. The Islamic fundamentalists of the 1990s, operating on the basis of the combined motives of religious mission and socio-economic distress, disrupted life in Egypt and brought it to the threshold of domestic instability. Egypt invested great efforts in preventing severe deterioration. Terrorist attacks declined extensively in the Cairo area and Lower Egypt from 1994, and to a lesser extent in Upper Egypt, where attacks continued and with foreign tourists and members of the Coptic minority the main targets of terrorist attacks during 1996 and 1997.

4 EGYPT BATTLES ISLAMIC TERRORISM

Early Intelligence and Operational Efforts

The surge in terrorism that erupted in Egypt in 1992 surprised the regime in its scope and its power. Understanding that terrorism is both a disruptive influence in the country and a threat to stability, the government was forced to restore terrorism to the top of its agenda. However, the security services lacked the tools as well as a comprehensive cohesive strategy for mounting an appropriate response to the attacks they confronted. Intelligence information was lacking, and much of what was obtained was of dubious quality or reliability. Under such circumstances, the government responded – as have many others in similar situations – with a massive show of force. This attempt to use brute force to quash terrorism did not yield the necessary results: radical groups went underground, dividing up into autonomous cells scattered across the country. Each cell was an independent fighting unit, financing its activities with foreign contributions and stolen money. Weapons were smuggled from Sudan, and the cells developed independent bomb-making capabilities. Given their great distance from Cairo, infiltrating these cells with intelligence agents was well-nigh impossible. The regime was also hindered by an almost total lack of cooperation from the general population, primarily in the south of the country, but also in certain economically depressed quarters of Cairo, such as the densely populated Imbaba neighborhood, where anti-government animosity was rife.[1]

The massive force that the security services used took its toll on the population as a whole. Innocent civilians were arrested, imprisoned, or even killed on a broad scale, and the relatives of those killed, motivated by revenge, were sucked into the cycle of fighting. Government successes were often temporary – when the regime succeeded in quelling violence in a given area, it would recur there later. Over the course of 1993, terrorist attacks took place on a daily basis, and Egyptian citizens were in a state of constant danger.[2] Prisons quickly filled to capacity. Rather than serving as a deterrent, they turned into breeding grounds and schools for terrorism, and many inmates absorbed the radical Islamic message within prison walls. Many of those arrested without cause left the prisons as recruits of the terrorist organizations and seeking revenge against the government.[3]

Herein lay the vicious cycle, where the authorities would repress violent outbreaks or impose collective punishments in the wake of terrorist attacks, to which the terrorists would respond, and so it went. The security services were largely responsible for the loss of control over the situation. In spite of the ongoing calls among the public and in the media regarding the need to establish a national strategy to combat terrorism, efforts made in this direction were few and short-lived. No targets were defined, no master plans drawn up, and neither priorities for missions nor stages for carrying them out were decided on. Efforts were uncoordinated, and the phenomenon was not studied in depth to better assess its nature. From 1991 through late 1993, the security forces had no overarching strategy whatsoever. In most cases, the police were taken by surprise, and each event was dealt with on a separate basis, without any attempt to arrive at a comprehensive outlook.[4]

The regime's Achilles' heel was its dearth of intelligence resources. The Central Security forces (*al-Amn al-Markazi*), which along with responsibility for domestic security also dealt with gathering intelligence, responded by mobilizing vast numbers of agents. Many of them were recruited from among cab drivers and waiters. Extensive use was also made of telephone wiretaps and eavesdropping devices. However, this system of information gathering was more appropriate for uncovering political subversion than for exposing terrorist activity. As a result, Central Security was fairly unsuccessful in penetrating the inner circles of terrorist cells. Its successes were largely fortuitous, the products of information gathered from police investigations and a policy of imposing closures on entire neighborhoods. House-to-house searches and mass arrests, as in the Imbaba section of Cairo in December 1992, followed such closures.[5]

In the face of mounting violence, and with no workable plan or intelligence infrastructure in place, searches and mass arrests became regime policy. The security services imposed closures and curfews in order to facilitate unimpeded searches and arrests. These steps, augmented by arduous interrogations, punitive measures, and preemptive arrests, particularly following successful terrorist attacks, proved effective during the early stages of the wave of terrorism.[6] However, over the course of 1993, as terrorist organizations broadened their range of activity, the heavy-handed measures instituted by the regime proved unable to keep pace.

The operation mounted by the security services in Imbaba ultimately became an emblem of the regime's response to Islamic terrorism in Egypt. Imbaba, an impoverished quarter of northern Cairo, was home to over a million people, most of them unemployed and living in dire poverty. The neighborhood lacked a requisite infrastructure, public services, and suitable drinking water, and mountains of refuse were scattered through the streets, with the stench of sewage everywhere.

It was not always thus. In the 1920s, Imbaba was home to the Egyptian intellectual elite, with a total population of about 10,000 people. Several decades later, then President Nasser turned it into an industrial area, which attracted thousands of migrants from rural villages. The quarter quickly mushroomed into an ugly urban monster, lacking the infrastructure and municipal services of Cairo. During the 1970s, Communist activities flourished, with the residents believing that Communism was the solution to their abandonment by the regime to poverty and ignorance. Imbaba residents were the first to take to the streets during the food riots of early 1977.

During the late 1970s and early 1980s, the residents of Imbaba were also among the first to adopt the Islamist slogan "Islam is the solution," having despaired of the government and hinging their social goals on the Qur'an. Hundreds of mosques were built in the quarter, and the militant al-Jama'a al-Islamiyya established its base there. Islamic radicals made Tuesdays a weekly holiday, during which thousands would gather to hear sermons denouncing the authorities. The preachers pressured the residents to disavow the regime and its leadership, with the minister of the interior receiving an especially large share of the criticism. Youths aged thirteen to seventeen served as informants and collaborators for the extremists, reporting on the movements of the security forces. These youths did not attend school, since the nearest ones were located some four to five kilometers away. The activists terrorized residents who did not behave in accordance with the spirit of Islam, and Coptic residents had to pay "taxes" to Islamic organizations. At the end of 1992, radicals living in the quarter declared the establishment of the Islamic Republic of Imbaba. Riots, which included gunfire and arson, increased.

The extremists ultimately overplayed their hand, and President Mubarak ordered a comprehensive operation against them. On December 8, 1992, 15,000 Central Security forces descended on the quarter. After placing the entire quarter under closure, a weeklong curfew was imposed. House-to-house searches were conducted and some 700 people arrested, based on lists prepared in advance. Among those arrested were approximately seventy people described as leaders in al-Jama'a al-Islamiyya, including the organization's local commander, Gaber Ahmed Ali. Large·

caches of weapons were seized. On December 16, at the close of the operation, Mubarak announced that the regime had taken tough measures, that about 90 percent of the terrorists had been arrested, and that the organization had been liquidated.[7]

This announcement was highly premature; many more years of terrorism were to follow, and the regime would ultimately repeat similar operations time and again, in other quarters of Cairo, in Assiut, Qena, and Deirut in the south. The security services also returned periodically to Imbaba to uproot new radical organizations that would implant themselves there. One morning in early March 1993, the security forces descended in eight simultaneous operations on a number of impoverished neighborhoods in Cairo, among them Imbaba and Shubra, conducting a coordinated search for wanted terrorists. Twenty people were killed and scores injured in a tumult of street battles between hundreds of police and security personnel and Islamic extremists in the poor neighborhoods of Cairo and the southern city of Aswan. Among the fatalities were fourteen members of al-Jama'a al-Islamiyya and four policemen, including a ranking officer – the largest number of fatalities in a single day since the surge in terrorism began in mid-1992. By all indications, the Islamic extremists, who had entrenched themselves in the densely populated slums of Cairo, were expecting the attack, and they opened fire on police and intelligence personnel the moment they entered the neighborhoods. In Aswan, the security forces opened fire on hundreds of demonstrators, killing seven.[8]

At the same early hour of the morning, hundreds of security personnel, backed by armored vehicles and helicopters, imposed a siege on Assiut, considered a radical stronghold. Intense battles between security forces and Islamic extremists raged in the city. Twenty extremists and two security personnel were killed, and twenty-one people were wounded. Two hundred and fifty extremists turned themselves in, handing over their weapons. Among those killed was the leader of al-Jama'a al-Islamiyya in Assiut, Ahmed Zaki, who had issued a *fatwa* calling for the killing of foreigners in Egypt. During the operation, the security forces, with the assistance of helicopters and speedboats, took control of a group of islands in the middle of the Nile River to which some of the Islamic extremists had fled.[9]

In the course of the war on terrorism, the security forces also resorted to collective punishments: houses were demolished, relatives of wanted terrorists were held hostage, protracted curfews were imposed on cities and towns, mass arrests were made, and agricultural property was damaged, such as burning sugar cane fields. Senior figures in the regime, frequently questioned on the subject, would emphasize that they were engaged in a protracted and painful struggle, and therefore occasionally the innocent would have to suffer. Many of the collective punishments were imposed in Upper Egypt because of the concentration of terrorist factions there. In addition, the tribal structure in the area was such that even minimal cooperation with the authorities did not exist. Collective punishments were also imposed more in rural areas than urban ones, where security forces were unable to duplicate their urban successes. Fugitive terrorists would flee the cities for rural areas, where they found sanctuary and support. Whenever the security forces uncovered terrorists or weapons in a village, they would respond with collective punishment measures against the villagers.[10]

Following an incident where shots were fired at a bus of German tourists, General Hassan al-Alfi, then serving as the governor of Assiut, asserted that "violence has to be put down with violence." Accordingly, numerous arrests were made in the village from which the attackers had come; among those arrested were the mother and grandmother of one of the suspects. The detainees were held under harsh conditions, and the homes of five suspects were bulldozed. By the end of November 1992, some 7,000 arrests had been carried out, primarily in the south. According to Islamic sources, 1,600 were arrested in the Assiut district alone.[11]

The many closures imposed on the slums of Cairo and the cities of Upper Egypt, along with the house-to-house searches, mass arrests, and collective punishments, were expressions of the regime's tougher policy against Islamic terrorism. The terrorist attacks against foreign tourists, and the accompanying harm to the Egyptian economy and the country's image as a law-abiding society, prompted the government to use massive force against the offenders, including live fire, in order to strike at the core of the terrorist groups.[12]

Prisons as Schools for Terrorism

The mass arrests quickly filled the Egyptian prisons beyond capacity, creating a difficult problem for the regime. By mid-1993, thirty-one prisons housed some 40,000 criminal convicts and political prisoners. These prisons were over 100 years old, and no new ones had been built. The assistant to the minister of the interior responsible for administering the prisons, Gen. Nabil Siyam, admitted there was chaos in the prisons because of overcrowding and a shortage of personnel. The crowding made it difficult to separate political prisoners from the criminal population. The Abu Za'abal prison, for example, was designed to hold 800 prisoners but by the middle of 1993 housed more than 1,500.[13] Tora Prison, more than 150 years old, housed some 7,000 prisoners in 1992, far beyond its capacity.[14]

Over the years, radical leaders gained control of the prison populations. Every new prisoner was interrogated by the radicals, to determine his suitability for recruitment and operations. At the direction of the leaders, punishments were meted out to inmates who refused to join the Islamic organizations by appointed *amirs*. In one case, an *amir* put five prisoners "on trial" in his cell in the Abu Za'abal Prison, sentencing them to death. Consequently, the prison became a slaughterhouse of sorts, when three inmates were killed and seventy-eight injured in riots that lasted for six hours. In a different incident, extremists at Abu Za'abal succeeded in taking two guards hostage, one of them an officer, and threatened to kill them unless their demands were met. The hostages were released only after the prison administration promised not to punish the hostage-takers. The extremists also sparked inter-ethnic friction by causing fights with Christian prisoners. Many inmates held on criminal offenses were forced to grow beards and demonstrate loyalty to the radicals, and many ultimately joined their ranks.

The terrorist organizations al-Jihad, al-Jama'a al-Islamiyya, and others were all represented among the radicals in the prisons. The inmates included well-known, charismatic leaders, and numerous terrorist actions were planned from inside prison walls, such as the murder of liberal writer Farag Foda. There were also escape attempts, some successful. In early 1993, the *amir* of al-Jama'a al-Islamiyya, Ibrahim Mohammad Sayyid Ahmed, attempted to escape by disguising himself as a woman, using clothes that had been smuggled into the prison by visiting relatives. He was shot and killed outside the prison.[15]

By the end of 1993, six new prisons were constructed, enabling some separation between the criminal and political inmates.[16] Nonetheless, mass arrests caused ever-worsening overcrowding, greatly hampering orderly administration. Furthermore, little occurred to wrest the control of the inmates from radical leaders. Al-Jama'a al-Islamiyya continued to control the Abu Za'abal prison, and when a new inmate from another organization or one who belonged to no organization arrived, pressure – generally successful – was immediately exerted upon him to join the group. Prisons intended to punish, rehabilitate, and deter criminal activity thus became schools for religious extremism and terrorism.[17]

The mass arrest policy did not alter the situation in favor of the Central Security forces. The closures, curfews, and other measures in Imbaba and similar impoverished neighborhoods did not depend on specific intelligence, and the extremists there functioned largely out in the open. While security forces operations did result in the death of some extremists, the arrest of many others, and the seizure of large quantities of weapons, the ability of the organizations to recruit new members into their service was not impaired. Not enough leaders were restrained, and their channels of communication and finance were not harmed. Doing so would have required more reliable, precise, and comprehensive intelligence information, along with more efficient use of security forces resources. None of these existed at this stage, so the authorities were forced to examine additional untested modes of action in their war against terrorist organizations.

Negotiations with Terrorist Leaders

In light of the ongoing terrorism, the regime decided in 1993 to attempt a dialogue with the extremists, a departure from its traditional "no negotiations" stance on terrorism. This experiment was advanced by then Minister of the Interior Abdel Halim Mussa. In February 1993, Mussa held a five-hour meeting in his office with Abud Zumur, a senior commander in al-Jama'a al-Islamiyya, signaling a "green light" for negotiations. A mediation committee was formed, which included twenty Islamic scholars and which undertook numerous efforts to arrive at an agreement between the government and al-Jama'a al-Islamiyya. The agreement proposed that, in exchange for the release of 60 percent of those imprisoned under emergency orders and not suspected of any connections with terrorist actions and the transfer of the trials of those connected with terrorist actions from military to civil courts, al-Jama'a al-Islamiyya would cease violent activities. It was widely held among the organization's leadership that a deal should be struck. Members of the organization outside of Egypt also agreed to the negotiations, assuming they would reap benefits from the agreement and that the dialogue also signified government recognition of the organization as a strong and effective force. At the same time, the organization took pains to make it clear to the regime that it would not give up its strategic goal of establishing the supremacy of *shari'a* in the country.[18]

The negotiations ultimately failed, primarily because of the fundamental lack of trust between the two sides. In view of the public criticism which developed, senior government officials, among them Prime Minister Atef Sidki, denied that negotiations had even taken place. Minister of the Interior Mussa was dismissed. Against a backdrop of rising terrorism, on the one hand, and the absence of a strategy of response on the other, his replacement acted fairly conservatively and did not surprise either the public or those close to security affairs. It is possible that Mussa had not consulted with the president or the prime minister, moving forward instead with negotiations at his own initiative.[19] There were, however, newspapers that noted that it was improbable that Mussa would take such action on his own authority. It is more likely that the negotiations served as a pretext for firing him, the real reason being that Mubarak was dissatisfied with his overall handling of the fight against terrorism.[20]

Abdel Halim Mussa was the fifth minister of the interior to serve during the Mubarak regime. The high turnover rate in this critical post was at least in part because of its responsibility for internal and public security. Mussa's replacement was General Hassan al-Alfi, who as governor of the southern region of Assiut had earned much experience in dealing with terrorism. Appearing frequently in the media, Alfi adopted a tough stance in the fight against terrorism, and he unequivocally rejected the possibility of negotiating with radicals, noting that there was no point in talking to "groups of criminals and murderers who committed acts of terror against civilians and tourists."[21]

The Evolution of an Anti-Terrorism Strategy

During the second half of 1993, the regime finally adopted a comprehensive security strategy for the war on terrorism, which included the following principal components:

➤ Improving intelligence gathering, with the goal of infiltrating Islamic organizations and recruiting agents among their ranks.
➤ Establishing a central computerized database to track extremist organizations, their membership, and their activities.
➤ Upgrading the level of professionalism among the security forces, including training in up-to-date weaponry.
➤ Killing commanders and leaders of terrorist organizations, in an attempt to paralyze the organizations. This decision was made in light of conclusions drawn from past experience that killing rank-and-file cadres was ineffective, since the organizations could quickly find new recruits to take their places.
➤ Undertaking to study and monitor the infrastructure of terrorism abroad, in order to find and exploit vulnerabilities in it. To that end, cooperation was to be sought with other states for the exchange of information and the extradition of wanted terrorists.

The new strategy began to bear fruit as early as the first quarter of 1994. A central database was established that coordinated information on terrorist organizations, and talented commanders were attached to the internal security forces.[22] The new minister of the interior initiated a reorganization of his ministry and the police and dismissed police, security officials, and district governors whose loyalties were in question.[23] Thanks to these efforts, intelligence units were able to plant agents in terrorist cells, and recruit new agents from among their ranks. This pointed to a success on the part of the security services in overcoming the compartmentalization and extreme secrecy that characterized the organizations. A network was created of informers and agents who lived among the terrorists in various parts of the country, studying them and supplying the internal security services with vital information.

The decision to upgrade the operational level of officers and troops in the domestic security forces, as defined in the new security strategy, was also implemented. The forces, including new recruits, underwent training in the operation of up-to-date weaponry and special equipment. Police were instructed in maintaining special vigilance with regard to terrorists, and were taught to recognize their modes of action. A specialized intelligence effort was undertaken in order to take the fight directly to terrorist leaders, in an effort to paralyze their respective organizations. On the basis of information from investigations in Egypt and abroad, detailed maps and organizational charts were prepared to assist in identifying and locating members and leaders of Islamic organizations. Likewise, efforts were made to determine who among them was engaged in recruitment, financing, arms acquisition, and operations planning, and who was providing them with advance information about the security forces operations or sheltering wanted terrorists. At the same time, terrorist commanders living abroad were also placed under surveillance, and international cooperation was broadened to facilitate intelligence sharing. Agreements were signed with other countries for the extradition and deportation of terrorists.[24]

To stem the flow of weapons, the security forces tightened controls on the borders with Sudan and Libya. The same was done with regard to quarries and mines, primarily in the south, from which terrorists had acquired explosives. Throughout the country, supervision was also imposed on businesses and shops selling chemical agents from which bombs could be manufactured. In the Sinai Desert, steps were taken to prevent Bedouin traders from transferring landmines and other weapons that had been left in the area after the 1967 and 1973 wars to terrorist organizations within Egypt proper. This was done by alternately pressuring or recruiting Bedouin dealing in weapons, and as a result, the trade in weapons between the Sinai and Egypt proper was greatly reduced. Bedouin traders transferred other arms to the security forces in exchange for payment.

In the framework of organizing the internal security services and improving their effectiveness, rapid response units were established, for which high quality individuals were recruited. After undergoing special training for fighting terrorism, they were put into action in the ongoing struggle against terrorist organizations, as well as in special operations.[25] The rapid response units succeeded in penetrating far from Cairo deep into agricultural areas, and closing in on the terrorists' hideouts. These areas, primarily in the south of the country, had heretofore been outside the sphere of the security services. The units deployed along the fertile plains of the Nile – some eleven kilometers wide and thick with vegetation

– where the terrorists were found hiding. The new strategy placed great pressure on the extremists, forcing them to abandon these areas and flee to the desert, where there was neither food and water, nor a supportive populace, aside from scattered groups of Bedouin.[26]

As part of this new strategy, Interior Minister Alfi announced an award of $30,000 for anyone conveying information leading to the arrest of wanted extremists. In his announcement, the minister addressed the importance of cooperation between the public and the police. He expressed regret that such cooperation did not exist in Upper Egypt in contrast to Cairo, where residents largely cooperated with arrest operations.[27]

The adoption of the strategy for the war against terrorism changed the concept of how the domestic forces were used in the struggle against the Islamic extremists. Instead of merely responding to terrorist strikes, the government began to initiate actions of its own based on intelligence information that drew on the element of surprise to keep the radical groups off balance. As a result, there were direct confrontations between the two sides, with hundreds of terrorists, security personnel, and civilians killed or injured – in part because the security services adopted a shoot-to-kill policy.[28] And indeed, from the time the security forces took this initiative in April 1994, a special effort was made to kill as many terrorists as possible, especially from the command echelons. A senior commander, Adel Siyam, was killed in April 1994, followed shortly by Tal'at Yassin Hamam, commander of the military arm of al-Jama'a al-Islamiyya, who was killed in Assiut, along with four associates. Tal'at had been a charismatic leader with much influence over his men, having battled the regime for two years and bearing responsibility for planning and executing numerous terrorist actions. The extremists were dealt an additional blow in November 1994 with the death of Ahmed Hassan Abdel Galil, the new military commander of al-Jama'a al-Islamiyya, who was killed during a confrontation with the security forces at a hideout in the Nubian Desert near Aswan. Abdel Galil, a veteran fighter in Afghanistan, slipped into Egypt via Sudan to take command of the organization's military arm following Hamam's death. During the course of 1994, between 130 and 150 terrorists were killed. In the wake of the initiative, and, particularly because of the liquidation of prominent leaders, the terrorist organizations withdrew from the Cairo area and the cities of the Nile Delta, moving to Upper Egypt. In addition, the defense forces succeeded in thwarting planned terrorist actions during the course of 1994.[29]

Figure 4.1 depicts the first fruits of the new defense strategy employed against the terrorist groups. As can be seen, the number of casualties reached a record level in October 1994 (about 130 dead and injured on all sides), as a result of direct confrontations between the security forces and the Islamic extremists, most of them initiated by the former. During the following two months (November and December), there was a drastic drop in the number of casualties.

It is thus clear that the actions of the security forces, operating in accordance with the strategic plan decided upon in 1994, brought about a reduction in terrorist activities and curtailed the threat of terrorist attacks from the large cities. Forced to reduce attacks on cities and populated areas, terrorist organizations resorted to less significant targets, if only to prove they were still around.[30]

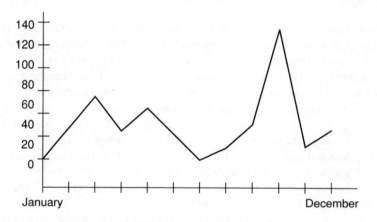

Figure 4.1   Summary of Terrorism Casualties, 1994

Source: Civil Society, April 1995, p. 23.

Throughout 1995, the security forces continued the pressure by means of anti-terror strikes taken at their own initiative. The situation remained extremely difficult at the beginning of the year, and in January the number of casualties among the security forces, civilians, and the terrorists themselves reached the highest monthly level since mid-1992. In January 1995, eighty-four people were killed – twenty-four policemen, fifty-one Islamic radicals, and nine civilians – and over the course of the year, 217 extremists and 108 police were killed, compared to 1993, with 120 police and 111 extremists fatalities. The ratio of 217 fatalities to only fifteen wounded among the extremists during 1995 demonstrates the implementation of the shoot-to-kill policy among the security forces, as charted by table 4.1.[31]

The security forces continued imposing collective punishments even after taking the initiative in the war against terrorism. In response to the murder of the eight policemen by members of al-Jama'a al-Islamiyya on January 2, 1995, large numbers of police, accompanied by an armored vehicle, entered Maris, a village adjacent to where the incident had taken

Table 4.1 Terrorism in Egypt – Casualties and Arrests in 1995

Month	Killed			Wounded			Arrests	
	Security Forces	Islamic Terrorists	Civilians	Security Forces	Islamic Terrorists	Civilians	Civilians	Islamic Terrorists
January	24	51	9	16	—	9	—	427
February	9	19	3	9	1	4	—	184
March	6	28	7	1	1	3	—	190
April	5	11	6	2	7	6	—	211
May	4	14	4	3	—	5	—	230
June	20	35	20	9	—	11	2	551
July	9	19	2	4	—	10	225	396
August	3	14	8	8	—	4	60	209
September	2	3	16	7	—	3	18	291
October	13	15	6	22	4	18	27	369
November	13	4	1	5	2	16	62	291
December	—	4	8	9	—	6	95	281
Total	**108**	**217**	**90**	**95**	**15**	**95**	**489**	**3,630**

Sources: Nemat Guenena and Saad Eddin Ibrahim, *The Changing Face of Egypt's Islamic Activism*, 2nd Draft (Cairo: Ibn Khaldoun Center for Development Studies, 1997), p. 62; and conversation with Saad Eddin Ibrahim, January 16, 1996.

place. Maris is approximately 260 kilometers south of Cairo in the Minya district of Upper Egypt, a district where at least sixty police and security personnel were killed in 1994. A curfew was imposed on the village and hundreds were arrested. A number of houses, whose owners or their relatives were suspected of giving shelter to extremists, were demolished. In addition, security forces arrested hundreds of civilians in Minya and held them, without charge, in open-air detention camps. The security forces set fire to sugar cane fields in which extremists were hiding or from which there had been shootings on passenger trains and vehicles. By order of the minister of the interior, it became forbidden to grow sugar cane within twenty meters from highways and roads in order to prevent ambushes. The villagers complied, reducing the country's annual yield of sugar cane by a third. The phrase "sugar cane war" became a well-known watchword in the Minya area. The collective punishments in the southern region intensified the enmity that had already existed there *vis-à-vis* the central government in Cairo. The farmers of Maris protested that the punishments were outright acts of misplaced revenge on the part of the authorities; injury was inflicted on people having absolutely no connection with terrorism.[32]

The regime took additional steps to achieve its goals. A report by Human Rights Watch/Middle East stated that the Egyptian security forces systematically took relatives hostage in an attempt to pressure Islamic radicals to surrender. According to the report, innocent members of the families of Islamic radicals, including women and men of all ages, were regularly arrested. Some were held blindfolded in secret detention areas, while others were tortured. Predictably, these arrests were carried out primarily in Upper Egypt, the stronghold of the Islamic radicals, but also in Cairo; they were systematic and had the approval of the authorities.[33]

In the framework of collective punishments, the authorities were given to imposing curfews for extended periods. In March 1996, Minister of the Interior Alfi announced the lifting of the curfew on the city of Malawi, bordering the Minya district in Upper Egypt. The curfew, which had caused great suffering to the residents and had harmed the local economy, had been imposed more than two years earlier. In announcing its end, Alfi stated that he had acceded to requests from the residents in view of the stability that had been brought to the city because of the successes of the security forces in fighting terror.[34]

The security forces succeeded in thwarting planned terrorist actions during the course of 1995, primarily in the Cairo and Delta areas. This was made possible by virtue of intelligence obtained by running agents and telephone monitoring, and from information gleaned from interrogations of arrested extremists. The success of the security forces compelled the terrorists to distance themselves from the Cairo and Delta areas and retreat to Upper Egypt and mount their attacks in other countries. The crowning achievements of the terrorists in 1995 were the attempt on the life of President Mubarak in Ethiopia in June, and a car bomb explosion in front of the Egyptian embassy in Pakistan at the end of the year. No foreign tourists were killed in Egypt during 1995, nor were there any attempts on the lives of senior government officials inside the country.

Table 4.2 charts the marked decline in violence and terrorism in Egypt during 1996, when there were 187 fatalities, compared to 415 in 1995.

The Proposed Ceasefire: Signs of Distress among the Extremists

In 1997, al-Jama'a al-Islamiyya, the largest terrorist organization in Egypt, proposed a ceasefire (*hudna*) of limited duration. The suggestion arose several times – in May, July, August, September, and November 1997 – causing much media stir and arguments within the terrorist groups. The concept of a ceasefire is anchored in Islamic tradition with the religious dispensation permitting a ceasefire with heretics and enemies based on the Hudaibiya Agreement arranged between the Prophet Mohammad and the people of Mecca in 628. At the foundation of the agreement was Mohammad's undertaking to desist from war for ten years. After two years, however, when his forces had increased, he attacked Mecca with his army, conquering the city and imposing Islam on its inhabitants. Since then, the Hudaibiya Agreement has become a concept of religious law which accords permission to Islamic military commanders and leaders to sign temporary ceasefire agreements with their enemies. Ceasefire proposals are usually put forward following severe attacks – because of fear of harsh reprisals by the authorities. Proposing a ceasefire does not imply abandoning the path of armed holy war. On the contrary, a ceasefire is only a temporary suspension of struggle intended to earn time, during which adjustments and appropriate preparations can be made for its future resumption. According to precedents, the Islamic side is also permitted to violate the agreement, as was done by the Prophet.

One of the surprising proposals for a ceasefire came on July 5, 1997, during the trial of ninety-eight members of al-Jama'a al-Islamiyya accused of terrorist activities. During the trial, which took place in a military camp near Cairo, one of the defendants, Mohammad Amin Abdel Halim, made a dramatic call to members of the organization both in Egypt and abroad to suspend all violent activities. Repeating his request several times, Halim said he was speaking in the name of six senior leaders of al-Jama'a al-Islamiyya and al-Jihad who at that point had been imprisoned in the Tora prison for sixteen years, serving life sentences at hard labor for their roles in the assassination of President Sadat in 1981. Halim explained that unlike

Table 4.2 Terrorism in Egypt – Casualties and Arrests in 1996

Month	Killed			Wounded			Arrests	
	Security Forces	Islamic Terrorists	Civilians	Security Forces	Islamic Terrorists	Civilians	Civilians	Islamic Terrorists
January	—	6	—	—	—	—	—	17
February	4	8	3	2	1	2	—	165
March	1	13	9	5	—	—	41	286
April	3	4	19	6	3	15	21	393
May	5	6	2	4	3	3	31	748
June	4	8	1	3	—	—	11	335
July	3	6	2	2	1	—	9	332
August	7	4	10	1	—	3	4	294
September	5	6	8	3	—	—	3	378
October	4	7	8	3	3	2	2	295
November	3	4	3	2	—	—	3	350
December	4	5	2	4	—	—	—	340
Total	**43**	**77**	**67**	**35**	**13**	**30**	**126**	**3,933**

Source: Ibn Khaldoun Files of Islamic Activism Project, Cairo, 1997.

previous calls for a ceasefire, the present proposal carried no preconditions.

When Halim was asked why he was making such a call at this particular time, he said that it was in the interest of Islam and the Muslims, since they no longer saw a purpose in continued bloodshed. He emphasized that the six leaders were also opposed to attacks upon Copts. In his statement, he praised the release from prison of Abassi Madani, the Algerian Islamic leader, and called upon other Arab countries to follow this example. The ceasefire idea of the six leaders sparked disagreements within the terrorist groups and between Islamic radicals in prison and those outside. The imprisoned leaders of the al-Jihad and al-Nagoun min al-Nar (Survivors of Hellfire) accepted the proposal, while the leaders of the Tala'ie al-Fath (Vanguard of Conquest) organization, a segment of al-Jihad, rejected it. The expatriate leaders of the terrorist organizations also rejected the proposition. On August 9, 1997, the argument between those supporting and opposing the idea was settled when Sheikh Omar Abdel Rahman sent out the message from the federal penitentiary in Missouri that he supported the proposal.

The lawyers of the Islamic extremists, along with various Islamic moderates, tried to persuade the government to accept the ceasefire proposal. Minister of the Interior Hassan al-Alfi, however, released a statement on August 11 in which he rejected the idea, casting it as an exercise geared at relieving the heavy pressure that security forces were exerting on the terrorists. The terrorists, Alfi believed, were seeking a respite so they could reorganize.

On August 19, 1997, five policemen and a civilian were shot and killed in an ambush in the city of Manfalut, in the Assiut district of Upper Egypt. The timing of this attack was not incidental, the backdrop having been the call by the six imprisoned extremist leaders for an unconditional cessation of terrorism. The six condemned this attack on police in a statement issued on August 21, calling for the perpetrators to demonstrate restraint. In contrast, al-Jama'a al-Islamiyya issued a statement the following day in which it stated that the attack was aimed at demonstrating its determination to pursue the struggle for as long as the regime continued in its unjustified policy against the organization. Addressing the ceasefire proposal of the six senior members of the organization, the statement established conditions for ending the conflict: release of all Islamic prisoners; cessation of repressive activities by the regime; cessation of civilian trials in military courts; the return to Egypt of the group's spiritual leader, Sheikh Rahman, from prison in the US; and the suspension of diplomatic ties with Israel.

On November 20, 1997, three days after the massacre of the tourists in Luxor, al-Jama'a al-Islamiyya published another call for a ceasefire, with conditions similar to those issued after the Manfalut attack. In proposing a temporary ceasefire, the Egyptian radicals also sought to improve their image among the Egyptian public, in the wake of the slaughter of tourists. Moreover, they knew that the organization, which had incurred harsh blows in recent years and was under heavy pressure from the government, needed a time-out to preserve its infrastructure and refresh its ranks for a future renewal of armed struggle. The proposal for a cessation of violence after six years of terrorism – which the government rejected out of hand – was theologically justified, but more important, derived from necessity and distress.

Terrorist activity continued in Upper Egypt. Islamic extremists murdered defenseless Copts and residents suspected of cooperating with the authorities. Because the internal security forces had transferred their activities to the south in 1996–97, the terrorists were forced to find more sophisticated hideouts and started digging networks of underground bunkers and tunnels in various parts of Upper Egypt. The police succeeded in uncovering this method, and in 1997 captured one of the leaders of al-Jama'a al-Islamiyya, Aziz Sha'aban Hassan, who had been living in a bunker under his house for about a year and a half. Until his capture, the police had believed that he had escaped to another country.[35]

Yet despite continued terrorism, the decline in activity continued in 1997, when 162 people were killed, compared to 187 the previous year – though the massacre at Luxor somewhat curtailed this downward trend. Most of the events took place in Upper Egypt. Table 4.3 depicts the numbers killed and injured during this year.

The murderous attack carried out by al-Jama'a al-Islamiyya against foreign tourists in Luxor in November 1997 was a turning point for both sides. The radicals understood that killing fifty-eight foreign tourists on top of the Egyptian security personnel casualties put them beyond the pale, further alienating their organization from the public at large. At the same time, the government became more confident in its initial judgment that efforts to eliminate active terrorist cells should be intensified. Thus in 1998, the Egyptian security forces continued to battle the Islamic terrorists, particularly the members of al-Jama'a al-Islamiyya. Most of the clashes took place in the Minya district in Upper Egypt, causing many radicals to flee to other districts, among them the Delta area. Forty-one people were killed as a result of terrorist actions – security personnel, Islamic radicals, and civilians, as depicted in table 4.4. This was the lowest number of fatalities since 1992.

The successes of the security forces brought about a process of moderation within al-Jama'a al-Islamiyya, this time bringing about a suspension of violence without a written agreement between the organization and the authorities. Leaders of al-Jama'a al-Islamiyya heeded the call of Sheikh Rahman, issued from his prison cell in the US, which called for the

Table 4.3 Terrorism Casualties in Egypt, 1997

Month	Police		Terrorists		Civilians	
	Killed	Wounded	Killed	Wounded	Killed	Wounded
January	1	—	3	—	—	—
February	—	—	1	—	15	6
March	1	5	—	—	14	7
April	3	14	—	—	—	—
May	—	—	3	—	—	—
June	1	6	—	1	1	1
July	1	4	—	—	—	—
August	3	—	1	—	4	4
September	1	—	1	—	15	9
October	10	6	—	—	5	—
November	8	—	8	—	60*	23
December	—	—	2	—	—	2
Total	**29**	**35**	**19**	**1**	**114**	**52**

*58 of whom were tourists murdered at Luxor.

Source: *The Arab Strategic Report 1997* (Cairo: Al-Ahram Center for Political and Strategic Studies, 1998), p. 310 [Arabic].

Table 4.4 Terrorism Casualties in Egypt, 1998

Month	Police Killed	Police Wounded	Terrorists Killed	Terrorists Wounded	Civilians Killed	Civilians Wounded
January	—	—	—	—	—	—
February	—	—	—	—	—	13
March	6	11	9	1	—	—
April	1	4	4	—	2	—
May	—	4	—	—	1	1
June	1	—	2	—	—	—
July	—	1	2	—	—	—
August	—	—	—	—	13	9
September	—	—	2	—	—	—
October	—	—	—	—	—	—
November	—	—	—	—	—	—
December	—	—	—	—	—	—
Total	8	20	17	1	16	23

Source: *The Arab Strategic Report 1998* (Cairo: Al-Ahram Center for Political and Strategic Studies, 1999), p. 343 [Arabic].

members to stop terrorist activities and create a "peace front." One of the leaders of the organization abroad called upon its members not to kill civilians and foreign tourists, while one leader who had demanded that terrorist activities be continued, Rifa'i Taha, was dismissed from the leadership.[36] At the same time, the success of the security forces in suppressing terrorism moderated the policy of mass arrests. Under the new minister of the interior, General Habib al-Adli, the authorities now freed many who met the following criteria: those not proven to be involved in terrorism; the elderly; the ill; anyone whose period of administrative detention had expired and was not renewed; and anyone who declared a commitment to shun terrorism. The *Arab Strategic Report* of 1998 estimated that between 15,000–30,000 people were freed, and a source from al-Jama'a al-Islamiyya claimed about 3,000 of its members alone had been released.[37]

Following extensive discussions, al-Jama'a al-Islamiyya formally announced a suspension of armed violence on March 25, 1999. This announcement caused a strong reaction within al-Jihad, which issued an announcement six days later that vehemently rejected the al-Jama'a al-Islamiyya initiative. Yet the new reality of a ceasefire gathered some momentum, and voices supporting the cessation of attacks could also be heard from within al-Jihad.

The year 1999 was the first in a decade during which no civilians were killed as a result of terrorism. This was a product both of the Egyptian government's success in coping with the terrorist organizations and the ceasefire declared by al-Jama'a al-Islamiyya. The *Arab Strategic Report* for 1999 described the new condition by noting that "the curtain has fallen on religious violence." Only isolated terrorist attacks took place during the year, and in April, the commander of al-Jama'a al-Islamiyya in Minya surrendered to the authorities. In July, an attack by a police patrol resulted in two killed and two injured. In September, a lone individual attacked and lightly injured President Mubarak after he concluded a campaign speech in Port Said. It is unclear whether this attack could be attributed to terrorism. In any event, the fact that an individual could get so close to the president as to injure him cast this incident primarily as a security failure. An additional incident, also in September, involved a successful raid by security forces on an apartment in Cairo, during which Farid Kadamani, the operational commander of al-Jama'a al-Islamiyya, was killed, together with three associates. In all, six people were killed during 1999 (two security personnel and four radicals), and two were injured.

While the security forces continued in their efforts to hunt down terrorists, the authorities responded to the announcement of the ceasefire with positive gestures. Over 2,000 prisoners belonging to al-Jama'a al-Islamiyya were released during the year, notwithstanding the government's proclamation that it would not conduct negotiations with the organization.

Similarly, lighter sentences were served in trials of members of the organization, and, for the first time since 1992, no death sentences were issued against members of al-Jama'a al-Islamiyya accused of terrorism. In contrast, the authorities continued to deal harshly with members of the al-Jihad organization, which was not a party to the ceasefire, and some of its members were even sentenced to death. Ayman al-Zawahiri, the commander of al-Jihad, abandoned his position and moved to Afghanistan, to serve as the deputy of Osama Bin Laden in the al-Qaeda organization. A new commander of al-Jihad was appointed in his place.

Egypt's leading terrorist organizations (al-Jama'a al-Islamiyya, al-Jihad, and Tala'ie al-Fath) had been hit hard and were greatly weakened. In addition to the force used by the Egyptian authorities, closer operational and intelligence cooperation with other countries also hurt the organizations, which led to the extradition of wanted Egyptian terrorists from Kuwait, Pakistan, and other countries.[38]

The Legislature and the Courts

When terrorist activities spiraled in 1992, the government enlisted the legal system to its ranks. A judicial commission was convened to draft legislation against terrorism, and it prepared more effective legal tools for the regime than those provided by existing emergency powers legislation. On July 8, 1992, the cabinet approved the anti-terrorism law, and after a stormy debate in which the opposition claimed the law was unconstitutional and would endanger the liberty of the country's citizens, it was passed by the People's Assembly on July15. Prime Minister Atef Sidki deflected the opposition, saying that the measure was the very least the government could do against terrorism.[39] The new law gave the president the authority to transfer the trials of civilians involved in terrorism to military courts from the civil courts, where the judicial process was slow and the punishments meted out were relatively light. The law empowered the government to sentence anyone who took part in terrorist activities to death and to carry out preemptive administrative detentions, and it gave the regime a host of additional options.[40] President Mubarak issued various executive orders on the basis of the powers granted to him by this legislation, when requested by the security forces or the judicial system, or based on his own judgment. Among these, the president signed orders enabling bringing those suspected of involvement in terrorism to be tried before military courts in accelerated proceedings. The president signed several such orders in 1994, including Order No. 233, published in August, which ratified the treaty for extraditing Egyptian radicals from Pakistan to Egypt. Similar orders facilitated closer cooperation with other countries in the war against terrorism.[41]

On April 11, 1994, the People's Assembly ratified a three-year extension of the State of Emergency Act, in effect in Egypt since the assassination of President Sadat in October 1981, which intended to facilitate the struggles against terrorism and drug smuggling. Similarly, the approval process for laws relating to the war against terrorism occurred in the People's Assembly in one day, with no time allotted for debate or protest by the opposition. Only twelve members of the People's Assembly, all from the opposition parties, objected to the extension of the Emergency Powers Act, claiming that in spite of its protracted existence, terrorism had increased. Another suggestion called for implementing the law only in areas where there was a high level of tension. Administration spokesmen deflected these claims, stating that had the state of emergency not been in effect, terrorism would have been more widespread. They also stressed that the state had not exploited the law to limit freedom of expression. The authorities had even approved the establishment of new political parties during the period of the state of emergency.[42]

The regime, and President Mubarak in particular, was frequently attacked in the media and the People's Assembly for trying civilians in military courts. The Islamic opposition appealed this to the Supreme Court, which ruled in the president's favor.[43] The president himself defended the procedure in his speeches to the People's Assembly and in other public appearances. He emphasized that terrorism had become a threat to the lives of the residents of Egypt and to stability in the country; that it was thus necessary to bring efficiency to the war on terrorism by swiftly putting those involved in terrorism on trial, and that this was possible only via the military courts. "We must prevent another Iran in the region," stated Mubarak to his critics.[44] As Egyptian general elections of November 1995 approached, attacks also grew in the media. The *Al-Wafd* newspaper complained that trying civilians in military courts made a mockery of democracy. It claimed that this was particularly dangerous prior to the elections, posing a threat to the free election of representatives to the People's Assembly.[45]

Use of the military courts did indeed speed up the judicial process. The punishments meted out were more severe, and scores of defendants charged with terrorism were sentenced to death. Some were tried in absentia. Over the course of 1993, there was a rise in the number of death sentences, with nearly sixty issued (table 4.5). Of these, more than fifty were carried out, mostly against members of al-Jama'a al-Islamiyya and al-Jihad. These were the most executions for a one-year period in the history of twentieth-century Egypt, and the first since the 1983 executions of those involved in Sadat's assassination. Among the executed were radicals involved in the attempted assassinations of Prime Minister Atef Sidki and Minister of the Interior Hassan al-Alfi. As is the practice in Egypt, the executions were authorized by the chief mufti of the Republic, Sheikh Mohammad Tantawi, and by President Mubarak.[46]

The executions continued throughout 1994–96. During the first eight months of 1994, forty-four leaders and activists of al-Jihad and al-Jama'a al-Islamiyya were executed by hanging.[47] On June 2, 1996, six extremists were hung at a prison in Cairo for smuggling weapons from Sudan, with the intention of using them to assassinate senior Egyptian officials.[48]

Table 4.5 Death Sentences in Egypt, 1993

Subject/Incident	Court	Number Sentenced	Date Announced	Date of Execution
Al-Jihad and returnees from Afghanistan	Supreme Military Court in Alexandria	8	Feb. 3	1993
Attacks on tourists	Supreme Military Court	7	May 11	July 8
Murder of Lt. Col. Muqaddam, of State Security Administration	Emergency Court in Fayoum	1	May 26	July 20
The Group of 14	Supreme Military	6	May 27	June 17
Murder of Gohargi	Giza Criminal Court	6	June 6	No details released
Armed attacks on jewelry shops in Alcubra – Cairo	No details released	4	No details released	Aug. 22
Zinham Incident	Supreme Military Court	2	Sept. 15	Nov. 17
Tala'ie al-Fath 3	Supreme Military Court	3	Oct. 14	Dec. 16
Tala'ie al-Fath 3	Supreme Military Court	10	Oct. 23	Dec. 20
Incident of the 19	Supreme Military Court	11	Nov. 19	Dec. 19
Murder of Farag Foda	Supreme Court of State Security	1	Dec. 30	No details released
Total		**59**		**52 executions carried out; details of 7 additional pending executions not publicized.**

Source: *1993 Misr al-Mahroussa Report* (Cairo: Al-Mahroussa Center for Distribution, Press Services and Information, Cairo, 1995), p. 409.

In all, about 180 people were executed in Egypt during the years 1990–99, additional proof of the regime's determination to contain Islamic terrorism. The deterrence value of these executions was short-lived, however, and did not greatly reduce terrorism. In a country as large as Egypt, with a population in excess of 60 million, the news of the executions did not reach every part of the country, and public impact was limited in any event. Many of those executed were from the south, where there was strong identification with those facing execution. In spite of this, the regime was convinced that it needed to continue the use of capital punishment, believing that this was the appropriate punishment for those who murder government and security officials or innocent civilians.[49] The law against terrorism also changed the regulations regarding the use of deadly force during engagements with terrorists. The security forces were trained according to these new rules, which emphasized a shoot-to-kill policy in the field.

Propaganda and Psychological Warfare

In the framework of coping with the Islamic extremists, the authorities also employed psychological warfare, seeking to sully the reputations of terrorist leaders by presenting them as criminals who had deviated from the true Islam, and who were committing atrocities in its name. Government officials frequently impugned extremists by a variety of epithets. For his part, President Mubarak always took pains in his speeches to clearly differentiate between "Islam" and "terrorism," stating that in his opinion, the perpetrators of terrorism were not Muslims, but criminals.[50] The former minister of the interior, Zaki Bader, said: "It is a serious mistake to deal with these people through dialogue [...] I regard them as stupid dogs and my apologies to the dogs." When referring to the terrorists, Bader's speech contained unambiguous words and phrases such as "death," "amputation," and "live fire."[51]

Upon assuming office as minister of the interior, General Hassan al-Alfi also used harsh language with reference to the terrorists. For the purposes of the anti-terrorist propaganda effort, the regime recruited educators, clergy, intellectuals, journalists, and others. In the framework of professional psychological warfare, an effort was made to find those extremists among the imprisoned who would be willing to appear on television to express regret for what they had done and appeal to others to forsake the path of terrorism. The regime succeeded in finding only a handful of prisoners who agreed to do this. Because of the fear of reprisals from their fellow radicals and the great animosity against the regime, there was almost no chance of this approach being effective.

Another method of psychological warfare directly targeted leaders of the radical organizations in an effort to undermine their public standing. This was done by mocking them or by portraying their behavior as inappropriate, given the devoted Muslims they professed themselves to be. Among other rumors, it was publicized that the terrorist leaders led impure marital lives. It was alleged, for example, that a certain terrorist leader had married an already-married woman who had not received a divorce; another was said to be lusting after a young Christian woman, and had arranged for her kidnapping so that she could be brought to him. This psychological warfare was sometimes conducted on the basis of events that had actually taken place. Such information would be conveyed by the press, the electronic media, and in background briefings by members of government. At the same time, extremist leaders would be accused of adopting the Shiite practice of *mutha*, temporary marriage, a practice condemned by Sunni Islam. This accusation was meant particularly to blacken the extremist leaders and portray them as heretics. The use of the *mutha* accusation was quite limited; it was so extreme that there were concerns that the public would never believe it.[52]

The central battlefield for the psychological war was television, where there was continual emphasis on the cruelty of the Islamic extremists. For example, there was extensive coverage of an incident where an elderly shop owner was murdered after he refused to give assistance to the radicals. Another much publicized incident featured a policeman who was murdered for his gun. In addition, wide coverage was given to the attempted murder of the elderly and revered writer, Naguib Mahfouz, and to the attack against the Egyptian embassy in Pakistan, which resulted in numerous casualties.

Aside from publicizing the ongoing terrorist incidents, state television and radio also prepared a comprehensive plan as part of the struggle against terrorism. The Minister of Information, Safwat al-Sharif – who had himself survived an attempt on his life – personally supervised the planning and implementation of the plan, which included films, dramas, and animated programs. Terrorists were depicted as criminals who masqueraded as warriors for Islam. The films emphasized the economic and social devastation that terrorism had wrought. The television programs also included interviews with people involved in the war on terrorism. The information effort on television proved itself extremely effective from the viewpoint of the establishment, generating considerable public loathing for the terrorists. With that, attempts made to blacken the names of specific terrorist leaders seem to have been less effective.[53]

The Inter-Arab and International Arenas

The current of Islamic radicalism that swept through the Middle East and the Muslim world over the past several decades gave birth to an infrastructure for Islamic terrorism in a number of states both within the region and without. These centers were reservoirs of human resources for terrorist organizations in Egypt, supplying them with leaders, trained personnel, funding, and weaponry. Upon conclusion of the war in Afghanistan, for example, hundreds of Egyptian volunteers returned home and many of them joined terrorist organizations. Hundreds of others remained in training camps operated by senior commanders of al-Jihad and al-Jama'a al-Islamiyya in Afghanistan and Pakistan, which provided Egyptian terrorists with a strategic reserve.

Additional centers of terrorist activity outside of Egypt included Sudan and Iran, each governed by Islamic regimes hostile to Egypt. Both of these countries supported Egyptian radicals by providing training and financing, and encouraging terrorist attacks. During the 1980s and 1990s, Egyptian radicals found sanctuary in other Arab countries, where they operated against the Egyptian regime. Infrastructures for Islamic radicals were established in Europe and the United States, some by Afghan alumni and some by wanted terrorists who had escaped from Egypt. This infrastructure in the West also provided support to terrorist organizations within Egypt.

Thus, with the surge in terrorism in mid-1992, Egypt had to cope with organizations that had a firm external base. The most efficient and effective means for dealing with this was establishing operational and intelligence cooperation agreements with those states in which terrorist organizations were operating. To that end, Egypt sought cooperation agreements with Pakistan and Afghanistan. An agreement for inter-Arab cooperation was needed for dealing with the terrorist infrastructure in other Arab and Muslim countries as well – especially Sudan and Iran – and an international agreement was needed to deal with wanted terrorists who had found refuge in the West.

The Afghan Alumni

The term "Afghan alumni," alternatively known as "Arab Afghanis," refers to the thousands of Arab volunteers who fought against the Soviet occupation of Afghanistan in the 1980s. Many returned to their homelands and upon coming home, these veterans – so called "Egyptian Afghanis" and "Jordanian Afghanis" – injected new life into local Islamic terrorist groups battling the respective regimes. At its peak, the "Arab Brigade" that fought alongside the mujahidin comprised some 10,000 volunteers from throughout the Middle East, including Egyptians, Yemenis, Algerians, Syrians, and Palestinians.[54] The majority of volunteers were members of terrorist organizations in their countries of origin. They regarded ejecting the Soviet army from Afghanistan not only as a fulfillment of the obligation of jihad in its own right, but also as a rare opportunity to gain valuable military experience far from the tight controls of the regimes in their respective homelands.

There was no small number of ironies involved in the establishment of the "Arab Brigade." President Sadat had supported its formation, believing it was preferable to let the Muslim Brotherhood busy itself with conflicts far from home. He would eventually, however, die at their hands: some of those who carried out his assassination were Afghan alumni. At the beginning of his term of office, Mubarak also allowed hundreds of Egyptian volunteers to leave for Afghanistan via Saudi Arabia. As with Sadat, this decision would carry a personal price – the returning "Afghanis" galvanized terrorism in Egypt, and were behind the attempt on his life in 1995 and the attack on the Egyptian embassy in Islamabad.

The US Central Intelligence Agency (CIA), which had assisted in the training, arming, and transfer of Arab volunteers to Peshawar, Pakistan, also grew to suspect that their former protégés had come back to haunt them. The Americans believed that the explosive devices in the mid-1995 attack on the American military base in Riyadh and the attack in Daharan, Saudi Arabia on June 25, 1996, which killed nineteen Americans, were by Arab volunteers who had fought in Afghanistan. Saudi Arabia had subsidized the travel expenses of Arab volunteers flying via its airports under the cover of Islamic charitable organizations operating in the country with government approval. Saudi Arabia also assisted in the transfer of hundreds of Arab Afghanis to Bosnia, to assist the Muslims in their fight against the Serbs. Upon the conclusion of the war in Bosnia, many returned to the Middle East. Prime Minister Rafiq Hariri of Lebanon complained that the Iranians were introducing members of the Afghan alumni who had fought in Bosnia into his country.[55]

In the city of Peshawar, a camp was established for the absorption, training, and arming of the Egyptians and other volunteers. After the mujahidin conquered Kabul in April 1992, Peshawar became a base for radicals on their way to and from Egypt and other Arab countries. Al-Jihad and al-Jama'a al-Islamiyya established a training base in Peshawar, which included a print shop for preparing identity documents, leaflets, and instructions for activities in Egypt. Testimony to the broad freedom of activity which Egyptian terrorists enjoyed in Pakistan can be seen in the reports that their commanders regularly gave about terrorist activities in Egypt to the local press. The radicals in Peshawar even published their own newspaper, not hesitating to publicize the name of the editor. The number of Egyptian radicals in Peshawar totaled about 360, in addition to others who were involved in the welfare and assistance work of various organizations there. Egypt cast a worried eye on what was taking place in Peshawar, especially in view of the fact that the radicals who were there had been responsible for serious attacks within Egypt. It was estimated that some 150–250 Egyptian volunteers also stayed in Afghanistan, after the defeat of the Soviets. They received training under the command of the Afghani leader Golbodin Hekmatyar, and were equipped with weapons for carrying out terrorist attacks abroad.[56]

Cooperation with Pakistan

During the first year of heightened terrorism, and in the absence of formal cooperation agreements, the Egyptian security services turned to various countries through Interpol, requesting they keep a watch on escaped terrorists from Egypt who had been sentenced to death or to long prison terms. Egypt also requested that member countries in Interpol find and extradite these terrorists. One of the lists that Egypt submitted included eleven senior Islamic activists assumed to be in Afghanistan, Iran, Sudan, and Lebanon; among them, seven had been sentenced to death. Egypt also requested of Interpol that it work to extradite wanted terrorists from countries with which it did not have formal extradition agreements.[57] These requests did not yield results, forcing Egypt to invest great efforts in reaching agreements with Pakistani authorities regarding Egyptian radicals in Peshawar.

Initially, under the regime of Nawaz Sharif, these efforts did not bear fruit, and the Sharif government tolerated the presence of terrorists in Pakistan. Yet over the course of 1993, the Egyptian government was battling severe terrorist activity, directed by Afghan alumni who continued to receive guidance from Islamic commanders in Peshawar. In the absence of an agreement or understanding with the Pakistani regime, the Egyptian security forces cut telephone connections with Pakistan to prevent the transmission of instructions from Peshawar to the radicals in Egypt. Similar action was taken vis-à-vis Iran and Sudan.

Benazir Bhutto's rise to power in Pakistan brought about a policy change toward the Arab Afghanis. Speaking in the name of Prime Minister Bhutto, the Pakistani ambassador in Cairo announced that "Pakistan will not serve as a bridge to those plotting against the security and stability of Egypt." Immediately thereafter, a delegation of Egyptian officers left for Peshawar to discuss with the Pakistani government the issue of expatriate Egyptians who were wanted by the authorities in Cairo. The government of Pakistan then issued an order calling for the expulsion of the Arab

Afghanis from the country, which prompted the Islamic commanders to leave Peshawar for Egypt and elsewhere in the Middle East. Furthermore, following mutual consultations with Pakistan and the United States, Egypt received a list which included the names of 275 members of al-Jihad and other Islamic organizations who had fought in Afghanistan and then crossed into Pakistan. At the end of 1993, negotiations commenced between the governments of Egypt and Pakistan, which led to the signing of extradition agreements and to the exchange of intelligence information in the framework of the war on terrorism.[58] The cooperation with Pakistan continued throughout Benazir Bhutto's rule. Egypt was frequently handed Islamic radicals on its wanted list, and the two countries exchanged intelligence assessments and information.[59]

Attempts to Reach Agreement with Afghanistan

The complex situation in Afghanistan posed difficulties for the Egyptian government to deal with wanted expatriates. The ongoing civil war in Afghanistan had led to anarchy, and there was no central authority with which to conclude clear-cut agreements. Although the president of Afghanistan, Burhanuddin Rabbani, demonstrated goodwill when he visited Egypt in 1993, he did not have control over the entire country, and an effective agreement could not be concluded.[60] Egypt even tried to achieve an agreement with the Islamic leader Golbodin Hekmatyar when he was appointed head of a transition government, but apparently without success. Along with the issue of wanted Egyptian terrorists was the issue of training camps in Afghanistan for activating roadside bombs to would-be terrorists from Algeria, Sudan, Egypt, Iran, Saudi Arabia, and Pakistan: instructors were from Egypt, Saudi Arabia, and Yemen.[61] The agreement Egypt sought with Afghanistan was meant to help prevent and thwart all forms of terrorism, including the training carried out there.

Afghanistan's internal situation continued to deteriorate. On September 27, 1996, the Afghani Taliban militia took control of the capital. The former president Najibullah and his brother were hung in a public square. President Burhanuddin Rabbani, Prime Minister Golbodin Hekmatyar, and the army chief of staff fled the capital. The Taliban fighters declared Afghanistan an Islamic *shari'a*-based state. Death penalties were instituted for those who committed adultery or drank alcohol, and women were ordered to stay in their homes and dress modestly when appearing in public. After years of war, however, Kabul lay in ruins, with little likelihood that Egypt could have reached an agreement with the Afghani regime. The power vacuum there created favorable conditions for armed terrorist groups from around the world.[62]

Sudan and Iran: State Sponsors of Terrorism

Since the escalation in terrorism in mid-1992, senior Egyptian officials stressed that the radicals in Egypt were receiving extensive support from other countries, with Sudan and Iran leading the list. Minister of the Interior Alfi repeatedly claimed that training exercises and preparation for terrorist attacks in Egypt were taking place in various states, including three Muslim ones. The minister stressed that although these countries denied the charges, Egypt had clear proof of their activities. There was little doubt that Alfi was referring to Sudan, Iran, and Pakistan.[63]

President Mubarak and his advisor Osama al-Baz spoke often of the Arab Afghani coming from camps in Peshawar to Iran and Sudan for training, and then crossing the border into Egypt. Iran's involvement in assisting Islamic terrorism in Egypt commenced even as it was involved in its war with Iraq. At that time, Iran established special camps for Egyptian prisoners of war who had been fighting on the Iraqi side. Among these were leaders and activists of al-Jama'a al-Islamiyya and al-Jihad who had fled Egypt and joined the Iraqi army. From among these Egyptian POWs, Iran formed the first nucleus of terrorists who, along with volunteers from other Arab countries, underwent training in Peshawar. Hundreds of Egyptian radicals later arrived at these camps, after which they joined the mujahidin in Afghanistan. After the Soviets withdrew from Afghanistan, the radicals returned to Peshawar to refresh their training, then continued to Egypt via Sudan, in order to integrate into local terrorist activities. Iran provided material assistance to the Afghan alumni, among them Egyptians, for this movement.[64]

The pact between the Iranians and the camp of Hassan al-Tourabi, the leader of the Islamic movement in Sudan, helped facilitate this activity. In Sudan, those returning from Afghanistan were received in camps which the Iranian Revolutionary Guards (IRG) had established there. These camps also absorbed radicals who had fled Egypt, Algeria, and Tunisia. Over time, ten training camps were established in the Sudan, including on the Red Sea coast, in Kadolfi, al-Garif, Shambat, Badna, Karda, and Bahra. Turabi personally supervised the establishment of the camps, while training, arms, and exercises were handled by Iran though the Revolutionary Guards, who came to Khartoum under the cover of military experts assisting in the reorganization of the Sudanese army. Agents of Iran's intelligence services supervised all IRG activity. At the end of the training periods, which lasted about two months, the terrorists were issued Sudanese passports and sent on missions in Egypt. Radicals who were captured in Egypt confirmed these details and contributed additional information about the training camps in Sudan and the assistance which

Sudan and Iran provided to the terrorist groups.[65] In addition, Sudan hosted terrorist leaders, particularly of al-Jama'a al-Islamiyya, giving them places to live and Sudanese identity documents. A prominent example is Mustafa Hamza, a senior commander in al-Jama'a al-Islamiyya, who had been sentenced to death in Egypt. Hamza organized the passage of members of his organization from Peshawar to Sudan and from there into Egypt.[66]

Since the outbreak of the heightened violence in Egypt in 1992, Sudan's stance was to deny the presence of Egyptian extremists in its territory. In early 1996, confirmed information reached Egyptian intelligence services that three people who had been convicted of attempting to assassinate Mubarak in 1995 were still in Khartoum. This report, which had been sent by an organization connected with the former president of Sudan, Ja'afar al-Numeiri, emphasized that it was difficult to follow the trail of these wanted men, noting that they had likely changed their names and received new passports. This report also revealed that there were thirteen active terrorist organizations in Khartoum, among them the Egyptian al-Jihad and al-Jama'a al-Islamiyya.[67] During the Arab summit that took place in Cairo in June 1996, Mubarak met with the Sudanese ruler, Omar Bashir, and demanded that he either extradite or expel the wanted Egyptians from Sudan. Bashir replied that he knew nothing of them. According to Sudanese claims, the Egyptian extremists had left the country for destinations unknown.[68]

In Iran, the authorities established five camps to train Arab radicals who had fought with the mujahidin in Afghanistan, in al-Ahwaz, al-Mahmara, Abadan, Bakhtran, and Sarsabil. More than 900 Arab extremists received training in these camps, which were supervised by Iranian intelligence. The collective Iranian–Sudanese effort was geared at toppling the governments of Arab countries, particularly Egypt, Algeria, and Tunisia.[69]

Over the course of 1996, numerous reports were published of Iran's increased involvement in international terrorism. The British *Sunday Telegraph* reported on the establishment of at least eleven camps in Iran for training terrorists to execute attacks around the world. According to estimates, some 5,000 people were trained in these camps annually. Of these, 500 underwent special training connected with terrorism.[70] In Tehran and Qom, Egyptian radicals and those from other parts of the Middle East underwent training until 1996. The Egyptian authorities were convinced that the Iranian authorities, like the Sudanese, knew about the activities of the various terrorist groups and assisted them as much as possible. In view of this, Egypt made special efforts toward international and inter-Arab cooperation against the activities of Sudan and Iran.[71]

Inter-Arab Cooperation

From the onset of the escalation, Egypt acted to promote inter-Arab cooperation for the war on Islamic terrorism. In their speeches, Mubarak and the Egyptian leadership emphasized the importance of the matter *vis-à-vis* the stability of Arab countries and of the region as a whole. The central problem that troubled Egypt was the issue of Sudan and Iran as state supporters of the terrorism leveled against it. Sudan, the first Arab country in which a radical Islamic movement had assumed power, was Egypt's southern neighbor, and as a base of operations for Islamic radicals, posed a direct threat to Egypt's security. Iran was hostile to the Egyptian regime, and favored the effort to topple it in the spirit of Khomeini's Islamic revolution. Accordingly, one of Egypt's goals in achieving cooperation with Arab countries was to contain Sudan and Iran's support for terrorism. Egypt also strove to achieve agreements and understanding with Arab countries that harbored Islamic radicals connected with terrorism in Egypt, as well as with those Arab countries that, like Egypt, were struggling with Islamic terrorism.

Among the first agreements for coordination and cooperation were those between Egypt, Yemen, and the Persian Gulf states. Yemen served as a transit corridor for Egyptian terrorists returning from Pakistan and Afghanistan to Egypt and Sudan. Over the course of 1993, Egyptian radicals lived deep inside Yemen, far from the supervision of the authorities in Sana'a, receiving material support from the Yemeni al-Jihad organization. Yemeni instructors and others also trained the Egyptian radicals in Peshawar and other places. From the radicals' base in Yemen, the cell which carried out the assassination attempt on the life of Egyptian Prime Minister Atef Sidki received an operational plan, documents, and funds for purchasing arms. After the attempted assassination took place, the radicals issued a fax from Sana'a and publicized their responsibility in planning and executing the attack.[72]

Egypt and Yemen signed a pact for coordination and cooperation in 1993. Yemen committed itself to assist in resolving Egyptian security problems connected with organizations acting from within its territory. On the basis of this agreement, Yemeni authorities closed the al-Jihad office in Sana'a, and exchanges of intelligence between the two countries were increased extensively.[73] In early 1996, Yemen also extradited wanted Egyptian terrorists who had been living in its territory.

In addition, Egypt exerted special efforts to reach understandings with Saudi Arabia and the Persian Gulf states. Several Egyptian radicals had sought asylum in the Gulf area, while Egyptian radicals received large sums of money from sources in Saudi Arabia and the Gulf states. In May 1993 President Mubarak made an eight-day visit to the area, persuading officials to cooperate against Iran and terrorism.[74] On the basis of the under-standing reached between Egyptian and Gulf leaders, the Gulf states extradited twenty-five radicals to Egypt in 1993, among them members of al-Jihad and al-Jama'a al-Islamiyya. The Egyptian effort to block sources of funding from the Persian Gulf was ongoing, though it is doubtful that this was entirely successful.[75]

Additional cooperation, both in intelligence and in operations, was achieved between Egypt and Algeria, where it was agreed to take action against Iranian support of terrorism. Delegations from the two countries held several meetings, the most important of which took place in June 1993. In addition, a joint Egyptian–Tunisian committee was established for expanding security cooperation, with an emphasis on the exchange of intelligence information. The committee brought about the signing of a security pact between the two countries that became a model for other countries, including Eritrea and Ethiopia, which asked to be parties to the agreement in order to thwart subversive Sudanese activities directed against them, but it is unclear if this ever occurred.[76]

There was close intelligence and operational cooperation between Egypt and Jordan, both of which faced an ongoing threat from radical Islamic terrorism and subversion. In April 1996, Minister of the Interior Alfi announced that contacts were underway between Egypt and Jordan for extraditing fifty-seven wanted members of terrorist organizations who were trying to resurrect the moribund Jama'at al-Takfir wal-Hijra organization.[77] Similarly, a summit conference convened in Cairo in May 1996, which included King Hussein, President Mubarak, and Yasir Arafat. Also present were the chiefs of their respective internal security services: the head of Egyptian General Intelligence, Omar Suleiman; the head of Jordanian General Intelligence Directorate, Samih al-Batihi; and the head of Palestinian Preventive Security Agency, Mohammad Dahlan, from Gaza. They discussed coping with Islamic extremism and Hamas.[78]

In addition to efforts invested in achieving bilateral agreements with Arab countries, Egypt was active in promoting inter-Arab cooperation against terrorism. In a speech before police commanders from Arab League member states, Mubarak called for the urgent signing of an honorary covenant calling for battling and uprooting terrorism. Mubarak stated that talk was not sufficient; immediate action had to be taken in the war on terrorism.[79] At the same time, in January 1995, the first conference of Arab ministers of the interior took place in Tunis. The ministers sought to create a framework for cooperation against Islamic terrorism. Although the conference participants issued a joint call against terrorism, which they claimed damaged the good name of Islam, and commitments were made to further cooperation, each minister ultimately returned to his respective country to cope with the problem on his own. Mutual suspicions and political frictions among the Arab countries prevented establishing a foundation for true cooperation against terrorism.[80]

In late July 1996 in Cairo, the ministers of the interior of sixteen Arab countries convened again to discuss ways of increasing cooperation in the struggle against terrorism. As expected, the Egyptian minister of the interior called upon his counterparts to escalate their fight against the religious radicals and terrorism, which he characterized as a criminal phenomenon. The minister stressed that "security is a mutual responsibility, and its weakening in one Arab country will harm all the others." The states nonetheless found it difficult even to reach agreement on a definition of terrorism. Iraq, Syria, Sudan, and Libya insisted that the definition not include "national struggle," such as was being waged against the Israeli presence in the occupied territories and in southern Lebanon. Arab states, especially those that faced a large Islamic underground, repeatedly blamed the West for giving refuge to radicals responsible for acts of violence. The Arab ministers of interior had already ratified the draft of an agreement for fighting terrorism in January 1996, which included not giving refuge to terrorists, exchanges of intelligence information, and extradition of wanted individuals. But the extradition issue also proved problematic, as a number of Arab countries were concerned that requests for extradition would conflict with their respective sanctuary laws.[81]

In January 1997, the Council of Arab Ministers of the Interior met in Tunis to discuss Islamic terrorism. The summary document, drafted by a committee of experts over the course of a full year, expressed the participants' unity of opinion. A decision was taken to adopt a shared strategy for the struggle against terrorism and the establishment of a mechanism for this purpose (the details of which were not given). The main clauses of the document were: avoiding measures that would aid or abet terrorism; precluding sanctuary and the provision of weapons to terrorist groups; and exchange of information among Arab countries regarding radical organizations. The ministers of interior who were particularly active in this conference were those from Algeria, Egypt, Syria, and Libya – the four countries whose regimes were threatened by Islamic terrorism. The Syrian minister of the interior said that "the Arab nation is currently exposed to a threat from within on the part of terrorist influences, which have sold their souls to the devil," and the Jordanian minister of the interior demanded that cooperation against terrorism be increased.[82]

In practice, decisions taken at inter-Arab conferences tended to be primarily symbolic, with most never being implemented operationally. By contrast, there was real value in the bilateral cooperation between Egypt and each of the other Arab states. In this framework, which largely occurred clandestinely, Egypt exchanged important intelligence information about terrorism with others, while the height of bilateral cooperation was the extradition of wanted Islamic terrorists to Egypt.

At the same time, the ongoing struggle was conducted alone by each country in its own territory and in its own way, as it had always been. The Assad regime in Syria adopted a policy of liquidating Islamic radicals, reaching a peak with the 1982 slaughter by the security forces of Syrian Islamic radicals in the city of Hama. In doing so, Assad removed the threat of Islamic terrorism from his country for at least an extended period. The rulers of Iraq and Libya adopted policies of liquidation as well. Mubarak could not have adopted such policies, however, because of Egypt's special relations with the West, particularly the United States. The Egyptian regime had to fight terrorism in its own way.

Cooperation with Western Countries

After the Egyptians signed agreements with other Arab states on cooperation against terrorism, the radicals started to escape the pressure and sought political refuge in Europe and the US. Senior Egyptian officials, including Mubarak, frequently spoke of the problem and called for international cooperation to prevent giving sanctuary to terrorists. Rather, Egypt wanted to see such terrorists extradited, either to serve the sentences passed upon them in absentia or to face trial. In early 1995, Alfi expressed great satisfaction with the level of inter-Arab cooperation that had been attained. In spite of this, however, he stressed that senior terrorists involved in planning, financing, training, and operations in Egypt had been given political refuge in a number of Western countries, in the name of democratic freedom. Alfi noted that while Egypt had reached cooperation agreements with a number of Western countries, these were only for the exchange of information and mutual consultation, and not for extradition. Alfi added that Egypt had indisputable evidence of close contact between terrorists within Egypt and Egyptian al-Jihad and al-Jama'a al-Islamiyya terrorist leaders abroad, among them Sheik Omar Abdel Rahman in the United States.[83]

Egypt also turned to the United Nations, requesting active involvement aimed toward creating a system for the exchange of intelligence between the defense apparatuses of different countries. At the same time, Egypt started tracking wanted terrorists and accumulating evidence to form a legal basis for their extradition petitions. At issue were terrorists living in Denmark, Switzerland, France, Kenya, and Bulgaria. Egypt scored some temporary successes in this area. Thanks to diplomatic contacts, Switzerland agreed to Egypt's request that it not give political refuge to Ayman al-Zawahiri, the al-Jihad leader. Denmark responded to Egyptian pressure and arrested fugitive al-Jama'a al-Islamiyya leader Tal'at Fuad

Qassem, who had been sentenced to death in absentia in Egypt and living in Denmark since 1992. The Egyptian request for extradition was denied, and eventually both radicals were released. Similarly, Egypt's request that the United States extradite Sheikh Rahman was rejected because of legal problems associated with extradition.[84] Egypt, for its part, extradited an Egyptian citizen, Mohammad Abu Halima, to the US, where he was suspected of having been involved in the 1993 bombing of the World Trade Center.[85]

In the effort to pressure Western countries to extradite terrorists, delegations from the Egyptian security services visited a number of European capitals, particularly when there was solid information that wanted terrorists were living there. At every stop, the Egyptian delegations presented intelligence information and cautioned the countries of Western Europe as to the danger in providing sanctuary to and sheltering terrorist elements.[86] In January 1995, a delegation of Egyptian intelligence officers visited Germany; they were equipped with video presentations on terrorism, pictures of terrorists, copies of bank accounts through which the organizations had received funds, and personal dossiers on wanted terrorists. They tried to persuade their German counterparts to permit them to act on German soil in an effort to apprehend the wanted individuals living there. The Germans examined the material and supplied information at their disposal to the Egyptians, but they refused their main request: to allow Egyptian agents to operate on German soil.[87]

Egypt turned to Great Britain in 1996, requesting that it extradite the wanted terrorist Yasir Ali Sari, who had been sentenced to death in Egypt. The British declined for the following reasons: they would not, in principle, extradite anyone who had been sentenced to death in his homeland; they would not extradite someone who was set to be tried by a military court; and they would not extradite anyone without a prior commitment that he or she would not be sentenced more harshly than would be expected under the laws prevailing in Great Britain. In view of this stance, the chances were slim that Great Britain and other European countries with similar positions would extradite wanted individuals to Egypt, as many of those wanted had already been sentenced to death in absentia or were facing severe sentences. Indeed, this position was common to all the European governments that Egypt approached, and wanted terrorist leaders continued to enjoy freedom in much of Europe.

Following these apparent failures, British journalist Robert Fisk, a correspondent with Britain's newspaper *Independent*, reported in early 1996 that Mubarak had sent about 100 Egyptian intelligence and security operatives to London to establish a base for intercepting terrorists throughout Europe. This move in effect launched a secret war between the Egyptian intelligence services and radical Islamic groups that swore to bring down the Mubarak regime. This war, Fisk noted, was being fought all over the world, but was especially fierce in Europe, where many of the leaders of terrorist organizations were located. According to Fisk, a reliable military source in Cairo related that the goal of the Egyptian intelligence personnel sent to London was to liquidate the wanted Egyptian terrorists in Europe.

In November 1995, the Egyptian commercial consul to Switzerland, A'ala Eddin Nazmi, was killed in the underground parking garage of his home in Geneva. An unknown Islamic organization, the Group for International Justice, claimed responsibility for the killing, saying that the Egyptian consul had been involved in tracking down Egyptian Islamic activists under the cover of his diplomatic position. A few months earlier, Tal'at Fuad Qassem disappeared from Zaghreb, the capital of Croatia. Activists in his organization claimed that Qassem had been kidnapped and transferred via the Croatian port of Rijeka to the intelligence headquarters in Egypt. Two weeks after Qassem's disappearance, a car bomb exploded in Rijeka, killing a Croatian policeman.

According to Fisk, in kidnapping Qassem, Minister of the Interior Alfi achieved the first goal he had set for himself. Alfi had reportedly told Mubarak that if three particular Afghan alumni could be liquidated, the entire network of Islamic terrorism against Egypt would collapse. The other two leaders in the crosshairs were Ayman al-Zawahiri of al-Jihad, living in Switzerland, and Mohammad al-Islambouli, the brother of Sadat's assassin, who had been seen in different places around the world, including Afghanistan.

In 1996, the imam Anwar Sha'aban disappeared in Bosnia; according to rumors, he had been killed. Sha'aban had been forced to flee Milan after the Italian authorities had closed the Islamic cultural center that he had run there. The Egyptians attributed involvement in anti-Egypt terrorist activities to him.[88] Later that year, general awareness of the threat of Islamic terrorism and the need to organize against it increased among the governments of the West, spurred by a string of serious terrorist attacks that awakened international opinion. The suicide bombings of buses in Jerusalem and Dizengoff Center in Tel Aviv during February–March 1996 led to the convening of the International Anti-Terrorism Conference in Sharm el-Sheikh at the initiative of President Clinton. A serious attack against a US base in Daharan, Saudi Arabia, which killed nineteen US servicemen on June 25, further galvanized the US. Responding to this attack, the seven industrialized nations (the G-7), meeting in Lyons, issued a statement that terrorism had become a challenge to the entire Western world, and that it was thus necessary to fight against it. At the end of July 1996, the G-7 and Russia met in Paris. They stated that "terrorism is an international virus" and decided on a long list of actions for intensifying the struggle against it.[89]

Table 4.6 Methods by the Regime to Combat Terrorist Organizations, 1990–99

Confrontation Areas	Description	Result
Intelligence and Operations		
Mass actions: curfews, searches mass arrests, massive force	Force widely used at the beginning of the surge in terror, in the absence of specific intelligence information. Drawbacks: Prisons filled beyond capacity, becoming schools for terrorism; did not allow focused attacks on terrorists.	Limited effective- ness
Dialogue and negotiations with terrorists leaders	One-time attempt to reach agreement with terrorist organizations in 1993.	Failure
Localized collective punishments: protracted curfews, destruction of houses, uprooting groves and orchards, burning sugar cane fields, arresting and holding hostage family members of terrorists, mass arrests	Collective punishment as response to attacks or finding weapons caches; caused increased hostility toward the regime. Deterrent effect was limited.	Limited effective- ness
Intelligence: intellignece-gathering using live sources, technical means, and based on information gleaned from interrogations, thwart future operations	Limited at first. From early 1994, regime succeeded in establishing a large array of agents with the terrorist organizations, which provided important information.	Highly effective
Central computerized database	Became operational in 1994.	Highly effective
Rewards for providing information about terrorists	Insofar as can be determined, public response was insufficient.	Ineffect- ive
Blocking weapons supplies to terrorist organizations	Tighter controls instituted on Sudan-ese border from 1994 reduced weapons smuggling into Egypt.	Highly effective
Blocking financing from abroad	Despite government efforts to block funds, radicals able to obtain funds from within organizations and through acts of theft.	Limited effective- ness
Shoot-to-kill orders/targeting commanders	Lower ratio of wounded to killed among radicals, especially since 1994. Most of those targeted were killed, including large number of commanders.	Highly effective
Activation of elite units, such as the rapid-response force	Succeeded in infiltrating terrorist hideouts, and hitting terrorists.	Highly effective

Legislation and the Courts		
Anti-terrorism legislation (July 1992)	Gave president authority to try civilians in military courts.	Effective
State-of-emergency law	Law has been in effect since Sadat assassination, with regular parliamentary extensions. Law gave government authority to issue orders for the war on terrorism.	Effective
Death penalty	Capital punishment not effective deterrent in a country as large as Egypt. In the south, there was solidarity with those sentenced to death.	Limited effectiveness
Propaganda and Psychological Warfare		
Propaganda and information campaign conducted by the establishment; geared at isolating radicals	Publicizing particularly shocking terrorist acts on television and disseminating information on its negative economic consequences; created loathing for and opposition to terrorism among the public.	Effective
Sullying the reputations of commanders and leaders of the terrorist organizations by depicting them as violating Islamic values	A few attempts, which did not yield the desired results. Approach was abandoned.	Ineffective
Inter-Arab and International Spheres		
Cooperation with Arab states and Pakistan in spheres of intelligence and operations	Egypt acquired information on terrorist organizations, and terrorists were extradited.	Effective
Intelligence cooperation with the US and European countries	Intelligence information was exchanged but Western states refused to extradite on human rights grounds.	Limited effectiveness
Annual Arab League conferences on terrorism for Ministers of the Interior	Conferences provided joint statements that were seldom implemented.	Ineffective
Kidnapping and liquidation of terrorists commanders abroad	Egyptian intelligence operatives were active in Europe during the course of 1995–1996, killing or kidnapping wanted terrorists.	Highly effective

The changed international atmosphere regarding the threat of terrorism led the British government to cancel the rally for Islamic revival that was scheduled to take place in London on September 9, 1996. Initially, the rally had been planned as a massive international event, with some 7,000 Islamic activists from around the world, organized by the Immigrants Group under the leadership of Omar Bakri. On the program's agenda were videotaped speeches by Osama Bin Laden and Sheikh Omar Abdel Rahman. Egypt exerted heavy pressure on Great Britain to cancel the rally, claiming it was a terrorist convention in the fullest sense of the term. Ultimately, the British government placed security demands on the organizers that were so costly and extensive that the organizers could not possibly meet them, and the rally was subsequently canceled. Mubarak expressed his satisfaction over the cancellation, at the same time calling for the establishment of a mechanism to fight terrorism under the auspices of the UN.[90]

Despite the increased awareness in the West for the need to battle terrorism, leaders of secular Arab states continued to repeat their warnings to the West that closing their eyes to the Islamic presence in their countries would eventually harm not only the countries of the Middle East, but also their own. They argued that it was difficult to come to terms with the ambivalent attitude that the countries of the West displayed toward Islamic terrorism, calling for a war on terrorism on the one hand, and encouraging terrorism by giving refuge to its leaders on the other.[91] Ultimately, once Egypt finally despaired of repatriating wanted terrorists from the West through formal extradition proceedings, Egyptian intelligence operatives undertook liquidating the terrorism activists in various places through Europe. A military source in Cairo also stated that Mubarak had ordered sending 100 intelligence operatives to Pakistan, to hunt down and kill Egyptian extremists who had remained in Afghanistan after the end of the war with the Soviets.[92]

Summary

The initial Egyptian efforts at combating Islamic terrorism, including a failed attempt in early 1993 when the Egyptian government tried to reach a negotiated agreement with the terrorist organizations, were insufficient and not sufficiently directed. Soon after the surge in terrorism began, however, upon realizing the demand for qualitatively different efforts, Egypt adopted a clear, unified strategy, which it employed since. That is, the fight against terrorism constituted a war, and it must therefore be regarded as such when considering what means to use against it, including deadly force. To implement the strategy, the domestic security forces pursued a set of aggressive measures. Table 4.6 charts the government's methods and reviews their effectiveness in the struggle against terrorism.

Table 4.6 highlights the value of intelligence information, based primarily on agents operating within terrorist organizations. The agents and the information they provided enabled the targeting and killing of terrorists, and even their commanders. These capabilities came into being once the regime adopted a security strategy in the war on terror.

By the end of 1997 the regime had succeeded in preventing disruptions to daily life, in contrast to the chaotic situation that existed in 1993. Terrorists were pushed out of the Cairo region and from the north of the country to Upper Egypt. The infrastructure of terrorism in the south was not sufficiently harmed, however, enabling al-Jama'a al-Islamiyya to continue mounting terrorist actions in Cairo and the south. During 1996–97, the organization focused its attacks on foreign tourists and the Coptic minority, both of which represented the regime's "soft underbelly." These attacks caused much loss of life and embarrassment to the regime, both domestically and internationally. Nonetheless, in 1997 the radicals turned to the government several times for a ceasefire, testifying to distress among their ranks.

In 1998–99, the regime maintained its pressure on what remained of the country's terrorist cells. In March 1999, al-Jama'a al-Islamiyya published an official statement calling for an end to all armed activities. By the end of the decade, and on the threshold of a new millennium, the government had succeeded in putting down a wave of terror that had lasted some eight years.

5   EGYPTIAN RESISTANCE TO FUNDAMENTALISM

Already by 1994 the surge of Islamic fundamentalism in Egypt had been checked and its operations reduced, and by the end of the decade the intense outbreak of terrorism of the early nineties was successfully quashed. The Muslim Brotherhood as well suffered a related devastating blow in the regime's full-scale campaign, and it failed to organize an effective response for weathering the crisis.

At the end of the twentieth century, the major questions were: Had terror in fact been suppressed, or was the lull merely an intermediary stage? What would the future hold? To evaluate these questions as they presented then, it is necessary to analyze the regime's campaign against terrorism according to the following criteria: numbers of victims; an evaluation of the public's sense of personal security; and the terrorist organizations' abilities to continue their operations.

From 1990 to 1999, 3,457 people (including security forces, terrorists, and civilians) in Egypt were victims of terrorism. Of these, 1599 were killed, and the rest were wounded. Figure 5.1 illustrates that in the first two years, the casualties were relatively few, but in 1992 the figures multiplied (with 322 casualties) as Egypt began to experience the most brutal period of terrorism in its history. The number of casualties in 1993 soared to a high figure of 1,106. In 1994, the year the security forces began to take the initiative, 659 people were killed or injured. In 1995, the number dropped slightly to 620; in 1996 it fell to 265, and in 1997, 250 people were the victims of terror-related incidents. Further drastic reductions took place in 1998 (eighty-five casualties) and 1999 (eight casualties).

The pattern of terrorism fatalities charted in table 5.1 is somewhat different. The total number of fatalities for 1995 was the decade's highest because of the frequency of direct clashes between the terrorists and the security forces, primarily at the latter's initiative. That year, the year following the start of the security forces' initiative, for the first time the number of Islamic militants killed was double that of security force victims. In the course of 1995, terrorists failed in three assassination attempts on government figures, including an attack on President Mubarak in Ethiopia, but very few assassinations were attempted against the police or security forces, nor were any foreign tourists injured. Although in April 1996 a terrorist gang murdered eighteen Greek tourists outside the Hotel Europe in Giza, overall 1996 marked the start of a significant decline in the total number of fatalities (187) and a reduction in the number of terrorist acts (especially in the Cairo district). This should be attributed to the internal security forces' success in ousting Islamic fanatics from the Cairo region and the north of the country and forcing them to Upper Egypt.

Table 5.1   Breakdown of Terrorism Fatalities, 1990–1999

Year	Security Forces	Terrorists	Civilians	Total
1990	12	4	2	18
1991	14	16	4	34
1992	23	39	32	94
1993	120	111	101	332
1994	110	140	60	310
1995	108	217	90	415
1996	43	77	67	187
1997	29	19	114	162
1998	8	17	16	41
1999	2	4	—	6
Total	**469**	**644**	**486**	**1,599**

Sources for table 5.1 and figure 5.1: Guenena and Ibrahim, *The Changing Face of Egypt's Islamic Activism*, pp. 58–59; *The Arab Strategic Report 1997*, p. 410; *The Arab Strategic Report 1998*, p. 343; and *The Arab Strategic Report 1998*, pp. 324–25.

Most of the terror activity between 1996 and 1997 occurred in the south, and many attacks were directed against defenseless Christian Copts, a fact that points to the substantial weakening of the Muslim extremists.[1] In addition, nine German tourists were killed in September 1997 by terrorists at Cairo's Liberation Square; and November witnessed the Luxor attack, which resulted in sixty-eight people, including fifty-eight foreign tourists, killed. The Luxor massacre signaled a turning point in the anti-terrorism campaign. The authorities escalated their counterattacks, striking persistently at the extremist organizations. This produced a sharp decline in the volume of terrorism in 1998 and 1999 (figure 5.1 and table 5.1). Al-Jama'a al-Islamiyya, the leading terrorist organization, even declared a ceasefire and ordered its members to halt operations.

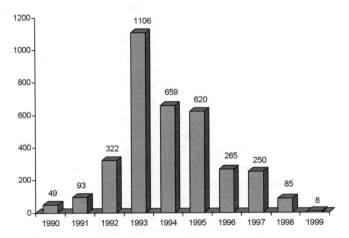

Figure 5.1 Terrorism Casualties, 1990–1999

The second criterion for examining the government's success in combating terrorism is public opinion, especially the degree of public anxiety over violence and terror. Dr. Ahmed Galal Ezzeddin, an international expert on terrorism, noted that the general feeling among Egyptian intellectuals and the Egyptian public alike was that terrorism began to ebb in 1994. In particular, public opinion changed markedly since the outbreak of the 1992 surge when Islamic extremists caught the government off guard, impelling it to respond with steps that often proved counterproductive. The regime then displayed massive force, deployed large numbers of troops in urban areas, and employed harsh suppressive measures, creating the impression both in Egypt and abroad that Islamic fanatics wielded enormous power and could be contained only by extensive use of government forces. Moreover, such drastic steps generally backfired since they aroused public opposition to the regime's harsh tactics and generated popular sympathy for the terrorists. But in 1994 the government adopted a different tactic, and the public no longer witnessed the massive deployment of security forces throughout the Cairo region. Security forces began to rely much more on intelligence and strategic planning, and television news reported regularly on the security forces eliminating terrorist groups. For their part, the terrorists sought to regain public sympathy, but their brutal acts of terror had the opposite effect. Popular support of the Islamic extremists soured, and the murder of innocent people, among them foreign tourists, was widely condemned.[2]

Dr. Abdel Moneim Sa'id, the head of the Al-Ahram Center for Political and Strategic Studies in Cairo, argued that increased public confidence corresponded with events on the ground. During 1994 and 1995, Egypt's security forces proved effective in counteracting terrorism, while the attacks carried out by the extremists incurred the loathing of the public. Images from the assassination attempt on Nobel laureate Naguib Mahfouz and the deadly explosion at the Egyptian embassy in Pakistan were aired repeatedly on television, which triggered revilement and wide-scale condemnation in Egyptian society. Terrorism was thus deemed on the wane, confirming the success of anti-terrorism tactics and casting doubts on any hope that Islamic terror groups might have of ultimate victory.[3] Continuing the trend, in 1996 Cairenes stated that their lives were much safer now that the terrorist gangs were driven out.[4]

To complete the assessment, the terrorist organizations' ability to continue operations should be viewed against the security forces' obstruction of their activities, based on the following criteria:

> The organizations' ability to recruit new members and increase in size

> The ability to replace commanders who were killed or arrested, and to install new, charismatic leaders capable of winning the absolute loyalty of subordinates

> The creation of a system of clandestine compartmentalization designed to protect the organization from betrayal or penetration by government agents, and severe punishment for deserters and traitors

> Training, financing, safe houses, and the uninterrupted supply of weapons

> International ties with similar ideological, multi-national organizations

> Enjoying substantial public support and sympathy

Ezzeddin contended that based on these criteria the potential for terrorism in Egypt at the end of the decade had declined. The government crackdown on terrorist organizations and the extremists' failure to propagate their violent ideological message limited the organizations' ability to enlist new members. Similarly, the elimination of many experienced leaders in government-initiated clashes, including the commanders of the militant wing of al-Jama'a al-Islamiyya, led to the paralysis of the groups they had headed. Furthermore, beginning in 1994, state security agencies managed to infiltrate the terrorist organizations, uncover members' identities and sources of foreign assistance, and obstruct pipelines of weapons and finances. Vast quantities of arms, explosives, and communications equipment were seized, and information led the police to the safe houses and hideouts of wanted terrorists. The heightened awareness of the terrorism threat at the regional and international level helped the Egyptians gain the cooperation of Arab and Muslim countries in intelligence gathering and operations (and to a lesser degree with Western countries). In this way Egypt succeeded in crippling the terrorist organizations' inter-Arab and international links, acquiring crucial intelligence data, and extraditing wanted terrorists based on bilateral agreements.[5]

Among the authorities, many grew optimistic and believed that the hard core of terrorist activity had been cracked. They too indicated mid-1994 as the turning point, as the result of a conjunction of factors. First, there was a marked improvement in effective intelligence gathering using a wide network of agents and wiretaps and gaining control of the Islamic extremists' communications links. Second, there was the extensive liquidation of terrorists, especially leaders, which seriously injured the morale of the radicals. In addition, inter-Arab cooperation was effective in intelligence gathering and extradition of terrorists. The last factor was the tightened surveillance on the Sudanese border, which allowed Egyptian security forces to thwart the smuggling of large numbers of arms shipments. Severing the extremists' financial sources proved more difficult, since they were self-financed or they obtained money by bank robbery and the plundering of gold merchants.[6]

The terrorist organizations failed to convince the Egyptian public that they offered a practical solution to Egypt's pitiful conditions, nor did they win popular support except in the south. Without popular backing, no terrorist organization could have a chance of succeeding. Furthermore, the structure of Egyptian society and its revulsion of violence benefited the regime in its campaign on terrorism. Hence the ceasefire proposal, made several times in 1997 by al-Jama'a al-Islamiyya leaders, which took effect in March 1999. Such an offer by hard-core Islamic extremists undoubtedly stemmed from their enervation.

Despite the authorities' success in suppressing the terrorism of the 1990s, however, some terrorist cells remained active, especially in the undeveloped, remote south. Terrorist leaders did not have control over all of these cells, thereby rendering the ceasefire with the government extremely fragile and unpredictable because of terrorist "rejectionists." Moreover, while the government proved itself able to protect the country's vital resources, such as energy and oil facilities along the Suez Canal, it was incapable of providing foolproof protection for the sensitive tourism sector. For this reason, tourists became a favorite target of the terrorists, which consequently damaged the national economy, upset the personal security of the citizens, undermined the national morale, and sullied Egypt's international prestige as the leading country in the Arab world. Thus, while the wave of terrorism of the nineties was checked, the phenomenon itself and its roots were not eradicated.

The campaign against Islamic terrorism was complex and yielded mixed results. Overall, the Egyptian internal security forces met the terrorism challenge successfully, even though the government refrained from sending its army against terrorist groups in the way that Jordan, Syria, and Iraq did. As with previous outbursts of terrorism, the regime triumphed over the gruesome period of terror of the early 1990s. By 1995 the regime succeeded in transforming a situation that in 1992 and 1993 had threatened to destabilize and disrupt public life into one under its control. In the following years, however, it became clear that although badly smitten, the terrorist groups had not been wiped out, and overall, the phenomenon of terrorism seemed unlikely to disappear completely, at least for the foreseeable future, since terrorism in Egypt was not a political phenomenon but also the product of a profound economic and social crisis that was very difficult to redress. Conditions of misery, poverty, and unemployment bred hatred of the government, and allowed the terrorist organizations to flourish even after long periods of subdued activity. However, the Islamic terrorist organizations no longer posed an existential threat to the regime. They might succeed in toppling a ruler, but establishing an Islamic government remained beyond their reach.[7]

The Muslim Brotherhood, the Islamic Movement's non-violent wing, posed a different challenge to the Egyptian government, and Egypt's three post-monarchy regimes (Nasser, Sadat, and Mubarak) shared in the struggle against the movement. At the outset of its rule, each regime sought understanding and cooperation with the Brotherhood even though it was aware of the deep ideological divide between them. Each regime hoped to secure quiet and stability so it could advance its political goals; each regime ended up disappointed by its conciliatory posture toward the Muslim Brotherhood, which often evolved into violence. The three regimes eventually contained the Muslim Brotherhood by pursuing determined action against it, while cognizant of the fact that a decisive victory was unattainable.

At the outset of its rule, Nasser's revolutionary regime tried to reach an understanding with the Muslim Brotherhood and even offered participation in the Free Officers government. The Brotherhood rejected the offer, and after it was involved in an assassination attempt on Nasser in October 1954, the Egyptian president attempted to liquidate the organization. In December 1954 the Brotherhood was declared illegal, many of its members were arrested, and several leaders were hung. Upon assuming office, President Sadat also attempted reconciliation with the Muslim Brotherhood, and within the framework of his de-Nasserization policy he ordered the release of Brotherhood prisoners from jail. In time, however, with the Brotherhood's vociferous criticism of the state's economic policy and the peace treaty with Israel, and with its persistent vigorous demands for *shari'a* as the exclusive legislation authority, Sadat changed direction and returned many Brotherhood activists to prison. Despite the bitter experiences of his two predecessors, Mubarak also hoped at the start of his administration to come to an understanding with the Muslim Brotherhood. The two sides tried the path of rapprochement even though both were aware that equal co-existence was unobtainable since the Brotherhood would have to conduct itself according to the regime's standards and interests. Mutual distrust coupled with the Brotherhood's successful activity soon darkened attempts at an understanding, and the regime initiated a policy of containment toward the movement. The main arenas of struggle between the Mubarak regime and the Brotherhood were the religious sphere, the parliament, the trade unions, and social Islam.

Against the backdrop of growing tension with the Muslim Brotherhood in mid-1994 and the adoption of a proactive anti-terrorism policy, the regime decided to move from containment to a strategy of all-out confrontation in its campaign against the Muslim Brotherhood. Reasserting that the Brotherhood posed a long-term strategic threat to the government, the regime successfully implemented a new, aggressive strategy, shutting down the Brotherhood's main headquarters in Cairo, and arresting and interrogating many senior leaders and activists. The regime used to its advantage the public's abhorrence of terrorist acts in order to attack the Muslim Brotherhood and discredit it by creating a link between the movement and Islamic terrorist organizations, charging that in effect the two formed a single entity. The regime also reminded the public that most of the terrorists had sprung from the Muslim Brotherhood – a fact that was historically true – and that Brotherhood members in custody were accused of ties with terrorist groups in Egypt and of having received instructions for subversive activity from the world organization of the Muslim Brotherhood abroad. The vigorous denials of Brotherhood members were of no avail, and military courts meted out stiff sentences.

In previous confrontations, the Brotherhood's leadership was conspicuous in its organizational strength and creative responses to urgent problems; this time, however, it was unable to supply a proper answer to the regime's assault. The confrontation shattered the movement's self-confidence and caused an internal rift. The general guide, Mustafa Mashour, rejected the pleas of young members for street protests and the adoption of belligerent anti-regime tactics. Fearing the outcome of a direct clash with authorities, he urged negotiations, but his advice was spurned. The young guard decided to break the deadlock by setting up a multi-ethnic party – al-Wasat. The authorities understood that this initiative was merely a ruse designed to found an illegal party, and the initiators were hauled in for questioning and put on trial. This affair aggravated the split in the Brotherhood and highlighted the generational gap. The movement managed to derive some encouragement from the results of the general election in 2000, winning seventeen seats in the People's Assembly.

In addition, the regime failed to puncture the widespread and efficient social Islam system that the Brotherhood had established, which included health, education, and welfare institutions, Islamic banks, and thousands of voluntary associations that formed the lifeblood of the Muslim Brotherhood movement. These institutions answered the needs of people suffering from unemployment, shortages of schools, and inadequate medical facilities in the poor neighborhoods. The huge population of indigent Egyptians felt gratitude toward the Muslim Brotherhood and absorbed the Islamic message. Nevertheless, since its ouster from the People's Assembly and its neutralization in the professional trade unions, the Brotherhood was incapable of translating the achievements of social Islam into political gains. Under these circumstances, therefore, social Islam posed no threat to the regime, even while it provided basic services to society.

Like any group, the Muslim Brotherhood also had its weak spots, and one was its leadership. Although the movement promoted the young generation, its leaders were older men who in the eyes of the younger members appeared unfit for the task of leadership. Mustafa Mashour revealed himself to be a weak and hesitant leader incapable of exerting his authority over the movement, particularly the younger generation. In addition, the Muslim Brotherhood in Egypt could not trumpet its cause by pointing to progress made by the Islamic movement in other countries. In Algeria, for example, the government succeeded in solidifying its power while the Islamic opposition remained floundering. The bloodbaths committed by Algerian militants generated hostility toward them in their own country and the Arab world. The Islamic regimes in Iran, Sudan, and Afghanistan were by no means seen as paradigms for emulation – on the contrary. Finally, the Muslim Brotherhood was forced to contend with the power of the Egyptian government, which enjoyed the loyalty of the army and was thus capable of defending the nation's vital resources, maintaining stability, and enforcing law and order. Moreover, while Egypt's international status restrained it from a liquidation policy against the Muslim Brotherhood, unlike the regimes of Assad, Saddam, and Qaddafi, the regime's strategy of all-out confrontation was sufficient to hurl the Brotherhood into one of its severest crises.

The regime may have succeeded in weakening the Muslim Brotherhood but it did not uproot it entirely. It was impossible to bar the Muslim Brotherhood from Egyptian society where Islam was and remained the main focus of public identity. Despite some economic progress in Egypt, substantial financial improvement for the population at large did not appear in the offing, especially not in Upper Egypt. The Muslim

Brotherhood, therefore, could be expected to offer a certain appeal to the impoverished, and was expected to continue broadcasting the Islamic message via the preaching system and voluntary Islamic associations.

The Brotherhood remained far from its goal of the Islamization of society through the establishment of a *shari'a*-based theocracy, but the movement was well aware that this goal demanded time and patience. In fact, the Brotherhood's strategic concept was anchored in the term *sabr*, meaning patience, restraint, and determination. Patience is one of the Brotherhood's key strong points that assist it in times of crisis.[8]

Table 5.2 compares the two major components of the Islamic fundamentalist movement: the violent wing (terrorist organizations) and the non-violent wing (the Muslim Brotherhood).

How the confrontation would continue to evolve in the twenty-first century remained a critical issue. Even if the regime chose to return the movement to the political–parliamentary arena under restrictions, distrust ran deep because of radical Islam's anti-democratic agenda and the fear that the Brotherhood might again exploit its integration into the political process. This concern pervaded government circles and the liberal and progressive public in Egypt that supported the transition to democracy.[9]

Some Egyptian intellectuals viewed the situation differently. They believed that the Muslim Brotherhood should be granted legal status and integrated into the democratic process. They claimed that "democracy is the solution" should counter the slogan "Islam is the solution." But President Mubarak, who met occasionally with intellectuals, rejected this approach. The government did not dare, and certainly did not succeed, in presenting an alternative ideology to that of the Muslim Brotherhood's. Government leaders never claimed that the Islamic ideological message was false; rather, they dealt with the Muslim Brotherhood and Islamic extremists as wayward sons who deviated from the true path of Islam.[10]

The regime repeatedly declared that the Muslim Brotherhood was the source of terrorism and terrorist leaders. The government establishment and the security and intelligence agencies despised the Brotherhood, were permanently wary of it, and linked it to conspiracies and deceit. Government officials were convinced that even in the Muslim Brotherhood's truncated and beaten condition it still retained numerous cells set up over the years, and maintained its organizational discipline and clandestine activity. The Brotherhood was also operational in other Arab states and European branches, and therefore the Egyptian leadership believed that the movement posed a long-term strategic threat to the stability of the regime. Prospects of the regime acceding to the Muslim Brotherhood's request to engage in dialogue did not appear auspicious. It was extremely doubtful that the regime would consider revoking the Brotherhood's outlawed status anytime soon or integrating the movement into the democratic process. The regime strove to hamper the Brotherhood's recovery, just as it maintained its policy of *à la guerre comme à la guerre* toward the terrorist organizations.

Table 5.2 Comparison of the Muslim Brotherhood and Terrorist Organizations in Egypt

	Muslim Brotherhood	Terrorist Organizations
Strategic goal	Establishment of an Islamic theocratic state	Establishment of an Islamic theocratic state
Intermediary goal	Control of society (Islamization of society)	Control of government
Direction	From bottom to top (from the infrastructure to the superstructure)	From top to bottom (from the superstructure to the infrastructure)
Strategy	New social order Constructive approach Building an alternative society	Undermining the social order Destructive approach Pushing toward an acute and immediate crisis
Image of the government	Muslim, secular, unrestrained, deviating from Islam	Heretical
Means	*Da'wa* (preaching, Islamization)	Terror (internal jihad)
Main arena	Wide-scale activity in different areas: on the religious level (mosques, literature, cassettes); on the socio-economic level (voluntary associations, investment companies, banks, educational and medical institutions); in the trade unions.	Concentrated effort exploiting the suffering and bitterness in society, the army, and the periphery. Attacking senior government figures and security forces; public figures and intellectuals who deviate from Islam; tourists; foreigners, the Coptic minority, and Egyptian targets abroad.
Social base	The entire Muslim public A popular movement	Revolutionary Islamic spear-heads Factional in urban centers Popular in the periphery and southern region.
Geographic base	Urban Concentrations: Cairo, Giza, Kalyubia, Alexandria, and the Delta and Canal districts. Numbers diminish in the south.	Agrarian Geographical presence the opposite of the Muslim Brotherhood's. Powerful strongholds in the south. Influence recedes north-wards.

Attitude toward modernization	Utilitarian Benefiting from the advantages of modernizing while negating its values.	Total negation
Time dimension	A gradual process Patience and restraint (*sabr*)	Immediate overturn of the government. Shortcuts and a sense of urgency.
Government strategy	Escalation in stages: The failed experiment with coexistence led to a policy of containment; containment gave way to the strategy of all-out confrontation (very intense but non-violent, concentrating on law enforcement).	*A la guerre comme à la guerre.*
Public opinion	Widespread credit The Islamic message has an influence on society where Islam is the main focus of identity. A positive image due to social Islam.	Sparse public support (except in the south).
Results of the confrontation	The Muslim Brotherhood in the throes of a deep crisis (1995–99). The regime attained its goal. The Brotherhood failed to achieve its stated goal of government seizure.	Initiative in the hands of terrorists (1992–93). Reversal, initiative passes to the regime (1994–95). Terrorist outrages against tourists (1996–97). Regime steps up its assault against terrorists (1998–99). Summary: terror wave of the 1990s crushed.

PART II

RADICAL ISLAM IN JORDAN

6 JORDAN'S STRUGGLE WITH SUBVERSION AND TERRORISM

Established in 1921 as a semi-independent emirate with the official name of Trans-Jordan, Jordan gained independence in 1946, and in 1948 was renamed the "Hashemite Kingdom of Jordan." Ruled as a constitutional monarchy by the Hashemite dynasty, believed to be direct descendants of the Prophet Mohammad, the country's executive, legislative, and judicial institutions are controlled by the king, as are the armed forces. In 1999, the population of Jordan approached five million, more than half of whom were Palestinians, refugees from the wars with Israel and the 1991 Gulf War, when Palestinians were expelled from Kuwait. An arid country that lacks extensive natural resources, Jordan has been beset by ongoing economic problems that have the potential to jeopardize the regime's stability. A high birthrate, rapid urbanization, and the lack of a correspondingly solid infrastructure have added to the potential volatility of the situation. High rates of unemployment, a large foreign debt, and rampant poverty have dominated every regime's agenda in the history of the country.

Hussein bin Talal inherited the throne in 1952 when he was still a minor, and following a brief regency rule assumed power at the age of eighteen in May 1953, reigning until his death in February 1999. His years as king, which encompassed most of the country's years of independence, were dominated by the attempt to modernize the country along Western ideas. They were also marked by attempted revolts and acts of subversion.

The security and intelligence agencies in Jordan consist of four units:

1 General Intelligence (*al-Mukhabarat al-Aama*)
2 Military Intelligence (*al-Istikhbarat al-Askariya*)
3 Military Security
4 General Security (*al-Amn al-Aam*) – the police

Of these, the largest and most influential is General Intelligence, which is responsible for internal security and attends to domestic and foreign threats to the regime. It maintains secret surveillance of opposition elements, especially Islamic groups and parties, terrorist organizations, and foreigners. Palestinian terrorist organizations were previously singled out for surveillance, but in the 1990s the emphasis shifted to Islamic groups. General Intelligence kept close watch over activity in the mosques, student organizations, the universities, and refugee camps, and the agency maintained ties with the intelligence services of Arab states and other countries. Thus, the fundamentalist threat was confronted primarily by General Intelligence. Military Security contributed little to this effort since fundamentalist activity was minimal in the army.

The Hashemite Regime vs. Non-Fundamentalist Opposition

Jordan has long suffered from terrorism. The country's first ruler, King Abdullah, was assassinated at Friday prayers on July 20, 1951, at the entrance to the al-Aqsa Mosque in Jerusalem. His grandson and successor, Hussein, was an eyewitness to the murder. Two of the ten assassins were Jordanians, while the rest were Palestinians, followers of the mufti of Jerusalem, Haj Amin al-Husseini. One of the Jordanians was Abdullah al-Tal, the former commander of the Arab Legion in Jerusalem and governor of Jerusalem from 1948 to 1949. Tal escaped to Cairo and disclosed publicly the details of King Abdullah's secret negotiations with Israel. The Jordanians sentenced him to death in absentia.

King Abdullah was ostensibly killed because he had annexed the West Bank to his kingdom and sought peace with Israel. These acts were anathema in the eyes of the Arab countries and Palestinians, and evoked vociferous protest in nationalist circles. The king's enemies viewed Jordan as an illegitimate brainchild of imperialism, an artificial entity that would be divided between Syria and Saudi Arabia after Abdullah's death. But they miscalculated, and the kingdom remained intact, due largely to the support of the country's elite – Bedouin tribes, the army, security agencies, and the large established families. The conspirators also did not take into account the role that foreign governments – Britain, the United States, and Israel – would play in stabilizing Jordan. Talal, the king's son, inherited the throne, but was forced to abdicate because of his mental illness. His son, Hussein, was crowned king in May 1953.

From the outset of his monarchy, Hussein faced a maelstrom of subversive and terrorist activity. The messianic pan-Arabism of Nasser and the revolutionary regimes in Syria and Iraq rejected Jordan's independent existence. They persisted in undermining it and threatening to overtake it. In April 1957 the king uncovered a Syrian–Iraqi plot to topple his regime. The kingdom's left-wing government – headed by Suleiman al-Nabulsi, a fervent admirer of Nasser – conspired with the Jordanian chief of staff, Ali Abu Nawar, to overthrow Hussein. Abu Nawar sought refuge in Syria. His replacement, Ali Khiari, was also disloyal and fled to Syria immediately after his promotion. While the young king worked with his military commanders to dispel the unrest in the kingdom and stabilize the throne, the American Sixth Fleet sailed into the eastern Mediterranean in demonstration of Washington's support of Hussein. The United States message was clear: it was ready to assist the king and back him with force if necessary, in accordance with the 1957 Eisenhower Doctrine.[1] This display of support was likewise a deterrent against subsequent enemies of the kingdom.

On August 29, 1960, after a few years of relative quiet, Jordan's pro-Western prime minister, Haza al-Majali, was killed by a time bomb placed under his table. Ten other people were also buried beneath the debris. The assassination was attributed to the United Arab Republic, i.e., the Egyptian–Syrian union, which hoped this act would trigger the overthrow of the regime. But the plan went awry as Bedouin troops rushed to Amman and immediately reestablished law and order. Four suspects were caught and sentenced to death by hanging.[2]

The Six Day War ended the violent, subversive threats of Nasserite pan-Arabism and other revolutionary regimes against Jordan, but increased the Palestinian threat. The war cost the Jordanians more than 6,000 soldiers killed or wounded; the West Bank, a fertile agricultural region; and East Jerusalem, an important tourist site. Some 224,000 refugees, mostly from the West Bank with some from the Gaza Strip, fled to Jordan, significantly adding to the Palestinian percentage of the population.

The Palestine Liberation Organization (PLO) had no role in the Six Day War, but following this latest in the series of defeats suffered by the Arab armies, the organization decided to open a guerilla struggle for the liberation of its lands. The various PLO organizations – Fatah; the Popular Front for the Liberation of Palestine (PFLP) under the leadership of George Habash; the Democratic Front for the Liberation of Palestine of Naif Hawatma; and other groups – transformed Jordanian territory into an operations base for attacks against Israel and the newly-conquered territories. At first Hussein tried to reach an understanding with the terrorist organizations, supplying them with training camps and other assistance. But between 1967 and 1971 the government and the terrorist organizations fought a bitter struggle over political control of the country. The terrorists, who were based mainly in refugee camps, managed to create a state within a state. They easily acquired financial aid and weapons from

Arab countries and the Soviet bloc, and flagrantly violated Jordanian sovereignty. Israel responded to every terrorist strike emanating from Jordan, and the pressure on the Hashemite regime increased.

The climax of the Palestinian threat against the Hashemite regime came in September 1970. The Palestinian organizations, which controlled several strategic points in the kingdom such as the oil refineries near Zarqa, instigated a full-scale civil uprising. On September 1 the king's motorcade was ambushed in Amman while passing through a neighborhood under control of the Democratic Front. Despite the terrorists' denials, the government was convinced they had tried to assassinate the king. Five days later, George Habash's Popular Front hijacked three civilian passenger planes to near Zarqa, hoping to disrupt regional peace talks between the UN envoy Gunnar Jarring and Egypt, Israel, and Jordan. Following this, the terrorists announced that the northern part of Jordan, adjacent to the Syrian border, was "liberated land." With his regime threatened, Hussein realized the need to take decisive action. On September 15 he met with a coterie of trusted civilians and loyal military officers in the Omar Palace north of Amman. The key figure in the group, Wasfi al-Tal, urged the king to crush the terrorists. The next day, Hussein formed a cabinet consisting of military figures. The king promoted loyal Bedouin leader Habes al-Majali to the rank of field marshal and appointed him commander of the armed forces and military governor of Jordan, and gave him free rein to extirpate the terrorists. Majali allowed the terrorists to lay down their arms and leave the cities, yet that same day Yasir Arafat assumed the role of commander-in-chief of the Palestinian Liberation Army (PLA), and a civil war erupted. For ten consecutive days PLO forces and the Jordanian army fought a vicious struggle until the terrorists were vanquished. Syria sent 200 tanks to assist the insurgents; Iraq hastily withdrew its troops from Zarqa; the United States dispatched part of the Sixth Fleet to the eastern Mediterranean; and Israel prepared its army to help Hussein if necessary. The Jordanians routed the Syrian forces, forcing their tank columns to retreat. On September 25 Hussein and Arafat signed a ceasefire agreement in Cairo that ordered the terrorists to leave the Jordanian cities. On October 13, 1970 both men signed another treaty binding the terrorists to recognize Jordanian sovereignty and the king's authority, and to refrain from carrying weapons outside the camps. In exchange, the Jordanians agreed to exonerate captured terrorists. The number of dead on both sides was estimated at 3,500, and many facilities in the kingdom had been severely damaged.

Even after the parties signed the ceasefire agreements, clashes with the terrorists continued in various parts of the kingdom. On September 28, 1970 the king appointed Tal, an implacable foe of the Palestinian terrorist groups, as prime minister and defense minister and ordered him to bring the situation under control. In June 1971, amidst rumors that the PLO was about to declare a "government in exile" in Jordan, the king ordered al-Tal to eliminate the terrorists, "who want to establish a separate Palestinian state and destroy the Jordanian-Palestine nation." On July 13, 1971 the Jordanian army assaulted and destroyed the terrorists' strongholds in Ajlun. Two thousand five hundred Palestinians were arrested, with many given the choice: leave for other Arab countries or promise to live peacefully in Jordan. Hussein had won a decisive victory, and his decision to enlist the army in September 1970 to crush the Palestinian revolt would later serve as a powerful deterrent against Islamic fundamentalism.

The king's triumph, however, left him isolated in the Arab world where he was accused of wielding an iron hand and killing many Arabs. On November 28, 1971 Wasfi al-Tal was assassinated in Cairo by the Black September group – a Fatah faction named to commemorate the September bloodbath – in revenge for the deaths of Arab Palestinians during the 1970 events. In December 1971 it failed in an attempt on the life of the Jordanian ambassador in London. In March 1973, seventeen Black September conspirators were put on trial in Jordan for the attempted kidnapping of the prime minister and cabinet members who were to be used as bargaining chips for the release of hundreds of Palestinian terrorists. Hussein commuted the death sentences to life imprisonment and eventually freed them in a general amnesty, a customary gesture on the king's birthday and in response to petitions from leaders in the Arab world.[3]

In the late 1970s, after Hussein joined the Arab states that opposed the Egyptian–Israeli peace treaty, hostility toward the Hashemite regime abated. The revolutionary Arab regimes that had sought to topple Jordan no longer existed. Still, in 1983 an assassination attempt was made against Prime Minister Mudar Badran. Jordanian security forces captured a hit team that had infiltrated from Syria. From the beginning of his reign until 1989, King Hussein himself survived at least nine assassination attempts.[4]

The Rise and Suppression of Islamic Organizations in the 1990s

The Islamic fundamentalist movement succeeded the Palestinian national movement in the 1980s as the Hashemite regime's main adversary. Alongside the veteran Muslim Brotherhood, Islamic groups and organizations engaged in insurrection and terrorism in Jordan in the 1990s. The groups can be divided into two categories:

(1) Those that sprang up in Jordan in the wave of Islamic fervor that first swept the Middle East in the late 1970s. Their goal was to completely eradicate the Hashemite regime. No Islamic radical organizations had

previously taken root in Jordan, such as al-Jama'a al-Islamiyya and al-Jihad had in Egypt. Scores of Jordanians returning from the anti-Soviet war in Afghanistan now formed the backbone of many of these groups. Throughout the 1990s, an average of one radical Islamic group a year was uncovered, including:

> The Army of Mohammad
> The Youth of the Islamic Trumpet
> The Islamic Liberation Party
> The Jordanian Afghanis
> The Movement of Islamic Renewal
> The Allegiance to the Imam Movement
> Al-Qaeda

(2) Syrian-based factions of the Palestinian Islamic Jihad that operated in Jordan and received military and financial support from Iran, which regarded the Hashemite regime as an American and Israeli ally that had to be uprooted and overthrown. The Islamic Jihad factions used Jordanian soil as an operations base for attacks against Israel. Syrian-based factions that operated in Jordan included:[5]

> The Islamic Jihad Movement in Palestinian – Shqaqi Faction (under the leadership of Ramadan Shalach)
> The Islamic Jihad Movement – Bayt al-Maqdas
> Hizbollah Palestine – Ahmed Hassan Muhana's organization
> The Islamic Army – Abdel Muati Abu Mualik group
> The Islamic Revolutionary Army – Sayyid Baraka

The Army of Mohammad (Jaysh Mohammad)

The Army of Mohammad was founded in 1988 by Dr. Samih Mohammad Zeidan, a fifty-year-old Jordanian physician who had been active in the Muslim Brotherhood. The new organization, also known as the Warriors for God, was established in the wake of the mujahidin victory over the Soviets in Afghanistan and the Islamic zeal that had infected thousands of volunteers, including those from Jordan. The idea behind the organization crystallized between Zeidan and Abdullah Azam when the two were serving in Afghanistan. Zeidan and Azam believed that founding an organization such as the Army of Mohammad and launching an armed struggle would be the first step in the region's liberation from Western tyranny.

Azam, a Palestinian Jordanian, was killed in combat in 1989 and became an Islamic legend. On his return to Jordan, Zeidan began recruiting Afghan alumni and setting up secret cells. The organization's goal was to replace the Hashemite government with an Islamic theocracy and renew the caliphate by means of a jihadic revolution. The group was structured on strict compartmentalization and by January 1991 twenty small cells were in operation. The Army of Mohammad had a military branch, a training branch, a religious branch, and a branch for foreign operations; three committees likewise functioned to deal with military affairs, financial matters, and the Western sector, that is, operations in Israel and the Israeli-occupied territories, and the enlistment of new members from the West Bank.

The Army of Mohammad devoted its first two years to training and procuring finances and arms. Money was collected from worshippers at mosques in Jordan under the guise of aid for fighters in Afghanistan. In early 1991 it launched a series of attacks inside the kingdom. Operatives tried to assassinate a Jordanian intelligence officer who had unmasked the organization: a booby trap in the officer's car exploded, severing his legs. Gang members also struck at banks in Amman, including the British Bank. The organization set fire to stores in Amman, Irbid, and Zarqa where alcohol was sold. The French Cultural Center and foreign diplomatic vehicles were torched. In contrast to other militant Islamic groups, the Army of Mohammad also targeted Christians living in Jordan. They fired a missile at a Greek-Orthodox priest. The Christian minority responded by demanding government protection. Jordanian intelligence believed the organization planned to kidnap one of King Hussein's sons at the start of the school year in late August 1991.

In mid-1991 the security forces began to clamp down on the organization. Police brought in two hundred suspects for questioning but released most of them by September. In October, eighteen went on trial in a state security court, presided over by three judges and headed by Colonel Yussef al-Fauri. The state charged the suspects with attempting to change the constitution, intending to reinstate the Islamic caliphate, possessing weapons, carrying out acts of terrorism, plotting murder, and belonging to an illegal organization. On November 25, 1991 the court sentenced eight of them to death, and the rest to prison terms of various lengths. One month later Hussein commuted the death sentences to life imprisonment.

During the counter-operation, the security forces netted a large quantity of fighting matériel: dozens of rifles, pistols with silencers, hand grenades, dynamite, and homemade explosive charges. In addition, the regime exploited the trial to convey a warning to the Muslim Brotherhood by emphasizing the former affiliation of Zeidan and other terrorists to the Brotherhood. Members of the Muslim Brotherhood, including those in parliament, vigorously denied their connection to the Army of Mohammad and denounced activity that violated the laws of the land.

The Jordanians were aggressive and determined against the Army of

Mohammad, which was successfully foiled through specific information obtained by Jordanian General Intelligence. In November 1992, the government released Zeidan and his fellow conspirators as part of the king's general amnesty. Thereafter, Zeidan avoided political affiliations, although the organization occasionally tried to revive its activity. Some Army of Mohammad members were involved in founding the Jordanian Afghanis in early 1994 and the Allegiance to the Imam Movement in 1995. Other attempts in 1995 to revive the organization were unsuccessful.[6]

The Youth of the Islamic Trumpet
(Shabab al-Nafir al-Islami)

On August 17, 1992, Jordanian security forces apprehended two merchants in Amman following the discovery in their store of a large weapons stash. During their interrogation they confessed that they were part of an Islamic terror group headed by two members of parliament, Laith Shbailat and Yaqub Karrash.[7] This information led to the uncovering of the Youth of the Islamic Trumpet group.

Shbailat was arrested at his home in Amman on August 31. According to the authorities, video tapes and other incriminating evidence linked him to the terrorist organization, and they claimed that he used his car, with its MP license plates, for transporting weapons to fellow conspirators. Shbailat was a Muslim fundamentalist, a dynamic parliamentarian, and a vociferous speaker known for his tirades against the government. He also headed the parliamentary investigating committee of corruption among government officials, including Prime Minister Zaid al-Rifa'i. While the public warmly supported him, the authorities viewed him icily and warily. Yaqub Karrash, another MP, was likewise apprehended in his Amman quarters, where documents and fighting matériel were found identifying him as a key figure in the Youth of the Islamic Trumpet. The forty-year-old Karrash, a Palestinian originally from Jerusalem, had been a Fatah activist. The Israeli General Security Service arrested him in 1979 and deported him to Jordan half a year later. A devout Muslim, he joined the pacifist mystic group known as the Path of the Qur'an.

The trial of the two parliamentarians, joined by the two merchants, opened in Amman on September 29, 1992. According to the indictment, Shbailat, the founder and leader of the organization, had taken part in an Iranian-sponsored terror symposium in Tehran in 1990. Together with Karrash, Shbailat planned to set up an Iranian-backed Islamic terror group, The Youth of the Islamic Trumpet, whose goal was to oust the Hashemite regime and replace it with an Islamic theocracy. On Shbailat's return to Jordan the organization began to procure weapons and recruit candidates for terrorism training. The prosecution charged the group's members with smuggling a vast array of weapons into Jordan from Iraq during the Gulf War when the refugee flow was as its peak and border control problematic. In addition, Karrash was indicted for heading another Islamic terror group, "The Islamic Liberation Front."[8]

The two merchants admitted their affiliation with an illegal organization, but denied their intent to overthrow the regime. For their part, Shbailat and Karrash likewise did not confess to all the details of the indictment. The trial dragged on. In the third week the MPs' lawyers resigned in protest over secret testimony presented to the court before they could review it or question the witness. The witness, who appeared under the alias of Yassin Ramadan, admitted to transferring 300,000 German marks to Shbailat in April 1992, a grant from the Iranian government. After the trial Ramdan acknowledged that his real name was Ali Shukri, that he was originally from Iraq, lived in Germany, and that the Jordanian authorities had forced him to testify against Shbailat. He disclosed that his entire testimony had been fabricated.

The court appointed a new lawyer on October 21, but the defendants refused to cooperate. At the same time a public campaign was underway to free the two MPs, especially Shbailat. Although the justice minister and state prosecutor published an official rejection of the public criticism, many observers were convinced that the trial was a message to the Islamists not to overstep the bounds of the law that allowed them to function as a political party. The Muslim Brotherhood petitioned the king to pardon Shbailat and Karrash; but on November 10, 1992 the court for state security sentenced the two men to twenty years and the merchants to ten years imprisonment with hard labor for affiliating with an illegal group and conspiring to overthrow the regime. Two days later Hussein announced a general amnesty in honor of his forthcoming birthday. The four newly-sentenced conspirators were included in the amnesty along with one hundred and forty security prisoners. The two MPs returned to their parliament seats.

Shbailat's popularity ultimately benefited the Muslim Brotherhood, although the Muslim Brotherhood faction in parliament, especially the speaker of the house, Abdel Latif Arabiyyat, rejected the insinuation that the Brotherhood was involved in the affair.[9] The trial had clearly been blown up out of proportion and designed to obtain a political objective – a warning to the Islamic forces in the kingdom not to deviate from the democratic lines set by the regime.[10] There was some speculation that the amnesty reflected the trial's fabrication.[11]

The Islamic Liberation Party (Hizb al-Tahrir al-Islami)

The Islamic Liberation Party was established in Jerusalem in 1952 by Sheikh Taki Eddin al-Nabahani, a former militant in the Muslim Brotherhood who moved to Lebanon in the mid-1950s following his expulsion from Jordan. As a fundamentalist organization, the Islamic Liberation Party aimed to transmit the Islamic message to the Jordanian public, win over the hearts of the people, and convert Jordan into a theocratic state and foundation for a great Islamic caliphate. The party regarded contemporary governments as transgressors of Islam that must be eliminated by armed revolution with the help of state officials and the military.

In contrast to the Muslim Brotherhood, the party lacked social, educational, and economic infrastructures and its membership was limited.[12] The Islamic Liberation Party was always illegal in Jordan and under tight surveillance by state intelligence services. Until the Six Day War, it was active in the West Bank; afterwards it transferred its main activity into Jordan. Despite its lack of legal status, the party had an official spokesman, Ata Abu Rishta, who occasionally expounded on the party's principles in public forums. According to Abu Rishta, the Islamic Liberation Party rejected the Western system of government, democracy, and political pluralism because it violated the code of Islam. The party saw the true government of the people as the rule of Islam. Abu Rishta insisted that the Palestinian problem was an Islamic one, and its only solution lay through jihad – the mobilization of all the Muslims into an Islamic army that would wage total war against the Jews. Negotiation and compromise were out of the question. Faithful to its principles, the Islamic Liberation Party refused to seek official sanction for its activity through the 1992 law of political parties, even though membership in an illegal party brought imprisonment of up to two years. Abu Rishta made it clear that while the state law obligated political parties to abide by the constitution and the Jordanian national convention, such law was antithetical to his party's worldview of the Qur'an and Sunna (the body of Islamic custom and practice based on Mohammad's words and deeds) as the only legitimate statutes.[13] Despite the prohibition on the Islamic Liberation Party, it engaged in political activity in Jordan, held meetings, and posted placards. It also published a journal, *Al-Wa'ee*, which appeared in Beirut.[14]

During the Gulf War, the Islamic Liberation Party declared its support for Iraq and urged Jordanian citizens to wage a jihad against the sacrilegious Arab regimes that backed the Western countries. The party bitterly condemned the Oslo Accords, at the same time that it opposed the PLO, because it saw the goal of establishing an independent Palestinian state as the negation of an Islamic theocratic state. The party denounced Arafat as a "traitor" once he entered the political process. The Israeli–Jordanian peace treaty was similarly described as a glaring betrayal of Islam, and the party's placards denounced King Hussein an "apostate."

The Islamic Liberation Party was also active in Egypt, Syria, Lebanon, Iraq, Tunisia, and Turkey, though outlawed and pursued in all these countries. In Egypt it was involved in an attack on the Military Technological Academy in Cairo in 1974. The party's Egyptian leader, Dr. Salah Siriya, a Palestinian, was executed for his part in the attack. In the wake of the growing pressure in the Middle East, the party set up branches in Europe and North America. The London branch of the Islamic Liberation Party published a journal called *The Caliphate*; one article entitled "3 March 1996 – 72 Years without a Caliphate" sums up the party's ideological outlook.[15]

Four times the party failed at overthrowing the Jordanian government – in 1974, 1977, 1993, and 1994. Each attempt included military officers who had been recruited into the party. The terrorist organization made a serious coup attempt in June 1993 with plans to assassinate the king during graduation ceremonies at Muta University, south of Karak. The thirty conspirators were all members of the Islamic Liberation Party and students at Muta's Faculty of Military Science. Jordanian intelligence learned of the plot in April, and was able to foil it well in advance. Another version of the event claimed that the uprising was fabricated by Jordanian intelligence in order to win greater support for itself in the kingdom. This version relies on the fact that when the plot was allegedly concocted, the party's leadership was in jail and therefore unable to coordinate the conspiracy. Furthermore, the accused conspirators were allegedly of limited operational ability.[16]

The conspirators, including junior officers and university students, were put on trial in September 1993. The prosecution accused the party of plotting to overthrow the regime, usurp the government by gaining control of the state's key institutions after the king's assassination, and terminate "the government of transgression."[17] The court handed out harsh sentences in January 1994: ten of the accused received the death penalty, the rest, long jail terms. The defense attorney appealed the verdict, and, surprisingly, all of the accused were exonerated in March 1995 for lack of proof and because the state security court had overstepped its authority in convicting them. Senior officials defined the conviction as an error of the prosecution.[18]

The party was hurt greatly by the government's campaign, though it was not eliminated. Its leaders were jailed and in 1997 its spokesman was sentenced to three years in prison for his tirades against the peace process with Israel, invective that was considered incitement. The party's young members continued to circulate posters critical of the peace process and advocating a new Islamic caliphate. One poster depicted the caliphate state that would be established in Amman. Other Islamic Liberation Party posters continue to denounce the Arab secular leaders as apostates and proclaim that the reinstatement of the caliphate was the only solution to the problems of the Arab and Islamic world.[19]

The Islamic Liberation Party's ideology sparked occasional debate in the Jordanian public regarding the threat it posed to the Hashemite regime. Since the organization conditioned the use of jihad on the establishment of the Islamic caliphate, then only a true Islamic government had the authority to order a jihad. This explains why the party aspired to replace the Jordanian government with an Islamic theocracy. But the party still had to answer the question of how to depose the government and reinstate the caliphate without the use of jihad.

This internal contradiction stripped the movement of its radical activism.[20] Nevertheless, the authorities still viewed the Islamic Liberation Party as a potential threat that was biding its time for the right moment to strike at the regime. Officials claimed that despite the attack the party suffered in Jordan and other Arab states, it continued to operate and preach ideological subversion. Jordanian officials note that in addition to its propaganda machine that expounded the Islamic gospel (*da'wa*), the party also maintained a military machine that infiltrated the army and recruited troops to overthrow the government. The regime viewed this activity as one of the most formidable dangers posed by the Islamic Liberation Party.

At the end of the 1990s, the party in Jordan numbered between 250 and 300 members of Jordanian and Palestinian background. Party activists were often brought in for questioning, and those caught circulating posters or inciting crowds were sent to prison. Since 1994, the party appears to have ceased terrorist activity.[21]

The Jordanian Afghanis

In early 1994 Jordanian security forces arrested dozens of suspects for attacks on movie theaters in Amman and Zarqa. Large quantities of explosives and weapons were discovered in the suspects' possession, most of whom were veterans of the war in Afghanistan and members of the 400-man Jordanian and Palestinian unit trained in Afghanistan. Some of the suspects came from the Army of Mohammad movement, and many were Palestinians. Saudi-born Osama Bin Laden financed this organization, as well as Egyptian and other Islamic terrorist groups, after Jordanian Afghan alumni contacted Mohammad Jamal Khalifa, Bin Laden's brother-in-law, for organizational and financial assistance. Khalifa had been taken into custody in the United States, extradited to Jordan, and put on trial, but the court released him due to a procedural error and lack of supporting evidence, at which point Khalifa left Jordan. The Jordanian Afghanis intended to torpedo the peace process by assassinating the Jordanian prime minister, Abdel Salam al-Majali, who headed the Jordanian delegation in the peace negotiations with Israel. They also planned to murder Yasir Arafat and two other members of the Palestinian delegation, Faisal al-Husseini and Hanan Ashrawi.

The trials of the Jordanian Afghanis took place in two sessions in 1994. Eleven suspects were found guilty and sentenced to death; the others received various prison terms. The death verdicts were commuted to life imprisonment. By 1997 there was no remaining trace of the organization.[22]

The Movement of Islamic Renewal (Harakat al-Tajdid al-Islami)

In March 1995 the Jordanian security forces confronted the radical Islamic organization the Movement of Islamic Renewal. The main feature of this organization was its Palestinian composition in contrast to most other Islamic organizations, whose members were primarily Jordanians. Sheikh Saber al-Mukbil, founder and leader of the movement, resided in Irbid. During the Gulf War he demanded that all the Islamic movements openly support Saddam Hussein, but when they hesitated he established the Movement of Islamic Renewal. The movement adopted a radical Islamic line, acquired weapons, and sought American and Israeli targets. The Islamic Jihad Battalions, a jihad organization linked to Fatah, helped in its initial organization. Fathi Shqaqi's organization the Islamic Jihad in Palestine provided the movement with money and matériel.

Members of the Movement of Islamic Renewal were under Jordanian intelligence surveillance and were arrested before they could carry out acts of terrorism. The security forces uncovered weapons and a wide assortment of fighting matériel. Three of the organization's militants went on trial in the state security court in March 1996 and were convicted of intent to commit terrorist acts and the possession of arms and explosives. During the trial it was also revealed that Mukbil planned on setting up an Islamic theocratic state in Jordan and other Arab countries. Each militant was sentenced to seven and a half years of imprisonment with hard labor.[23] The defense attorneys appealed the verdict, and the court of appeals acquitted Mukbil and two of his accessories and ordered their release. The court justified its decision by stating that the accused had concealed the explosives in order to dispose of them, not to use them.[24]

The Allegiance to the Imam Movement (Harakat Bay'at al-Imam)

Twenty-two members of the Allegiance to the Imam Movement, many of them Palestinians, were arrested by Jordanian intelligence toward the end of 1995. The authorities collected information on the group before it managed to act. This movement was considered one of the most dangerous terrorist groups uncovered in the 1990s. It adopted the ideology of the *al-takfir wal hijra* movement, which viewed all of society as a heretical violation of Islam. The true believer, ideology dictated, should dissociate from society and return only after it was purged and rectified in the spirit of Islam. The Allegiance to the Imam Movement was also tied to the Egyptian terrorist organization al-Jama'a al-Islamiyya through Zawahiri, one of the organization's senior commanders, who at the time was likely based in Switzerland.

At the head of the Allegiance to the Imam Movement stood Essam Mohammad Taher, alias Abu Mohammad al-Maqdasi, a Palestinian born in Jaffa in 1960 who was also linked to al-Qaeda. Taher had been a colonel in the Kuwaiti army, and obtained land mines and other fighting matériel in Kuwait. Upon interrogation the accused men acknowledged that their movement was set up in the early 1990s and that some of them had trained in Afghanistan. Among the founders were former members of the Army of Mohammad. The movement's funds were replenished by robberies. One of the detainees confessed to sending a booby-trapped envelope to the editor of *Al–Watan al-Arabi* in Paris in 1993 because of a poem published in the paper that offended the sacred name of the Prophet. The suspect had no knowledge if the editor ever received the envelope. Before their arrest, some of the terrorists had attacked a store where alcoholic beverages were sold.

Thirteen of the suspects were tried in the state security court and nine in a civil court. They refused to have anything to do with the court-appointed lawyers, whom they regarded as transgressors of Islam and whose laws had been written by human beings. Maqdasi, the leader of the organization, was sentenced to fifteen years with hard labor; the remainder also received lengthy prison terms.

In July 1997 Jordanian intelligence officers apprehended five Jordanian youths of Palestinian background (four of them born in Hebron) who planned to infiltrate Israel and murder Israelis and senior PA officials. They admitted belonging to the Allegiance to the Imam Movement and possessing weapons and explosives. The state security court sentenced them to prison terms of between ten and fifteen years.[25]

Al-Qaeda (the Foundation) – Osama Bin Laden's Organization

On the night of December 15, 1999, twenty-one months before al-Qaeda became a household term, Jordanian security forces raided a farmhouse in the suburbs of Amman where al-Qaeda-linked terrorists were hiding. Fifteen suspects were arrested in the raid: an Iraqi, Algerian, and thirteen Jordanians. Another thirteen terrorists managed to escape. The intelligence officers uncovered various types of fighting matériel, including explosives, chemicals, weapons, and ammunition. The network planned to attack local and foreign establishments in Amman, as well as Christians and Jews, during the millennium celebrations.

Preparations for the millennium attack had taken nearly two years. A group of Jordanian terrorists, not Bin Laden himself, apparently masterminded the attack. They had arrived in Amman with their ambitious goal and requested Bin Laden's help in training and financing. Bin Laden agreed since it appealed to his worldview; furthermore, he wanted to build an umbrella group broader than al-Qaeda for more terrorist groups, a new meta-group to be called "The Islamic Front for War against Jews and Crusaders." Bin Laden appointed Gazan-born and then twenty-six year old Mohammad Abu Zubeida to oversee the Jordanian group, who coordinated operations from Pakistan, directed the gangs' preparations, and opened a bank account in Islamabad for their activity. The Amman commander was Khader Abu Hoshar, an Afghani war veteran who had been in a Jordanian prison until 1993 for his membership in the Army of Mohammad. His assistant, Ra'id Hejazi, was a taxi driver from Boston who had American citizenship.

The American Central Intelligence Agency (CIA) and Federal Bureau of Investigation (FBI) obtained information on the network's plans and immediately brought it to the attention of the head of Jordanian General Intelligence, Samih al-Batihi. Four other Arab states also received the information. The dossiers contained the aliases of the terrorists who were about to return to Jordan from Bin Laden's training camps in Afghanistan. The Jordanian security troops waited patiently until December 15, 1999 for the raid.

The trial of those arrested opened in the state security court on March 27, 2000. The general prosecutor, Brigadier General Ma'amoun al-Qasawna, charged the twenty-eight members of the network (including thirteen still at large) with the following crimes:

➤ illegal possession of weapons and fighting matériel
➤ illegal manufacture of explosives
➤ intent to commit acts of terrorism
➤ damaging property and human life

> membership in an illegal organization
> forging official documents and using false passports

The indictment stated that the suspects had smuggled a large quantity of weapons into Jordan, including Lau missiles, and engaged in arms sales. It also charged the suspects with receiving financial aid from Bin Laden and additional money through robbery and kidnapping. The prosecution claimed that the suspects were planning a murderous attack at the millennium festivities in Jordan. One of the accused, Rami Khalawa, told the court that he had been recruited by Abu Hoshar and that the group's mission was to kill Jews and Christians during the celebrations. Khalawa's target was the Radisson Hotel in Amman, frequented by Jews.

The Jordanian weekly *Al-Hadeth* reported on January 17, 2000 that several radical Islamic organizations in the Middle East had joined Bin Laden's Afghanistan-based organization. According to the article, al-Qaeda carried out terrorist operations elsewhere in the Middle East, which led to closer security coordination to enable regional intelligence agencies to deal more effectively with the threat of radical Islam; for example, a high-level Palestinian–Syrian security meeting in Damascus attended by the Palestinian head of general intelligence, Amin al-Hindi, and his deputy, General Tawfiq Tirawi. A similar meeting took place later with senior Lebanese intelligence officers.

The verdicts for the twenty-eight members of Osama Bin Laden's Afghani network were handed down in Amman on September 18, 2000. Six of the accused were sentenced to death (four in absentia); six were exonerated, and the rest received jail sentences ranging from seven to fifteen years. Twelve remained at large. The accused were convicted of illegal possession of weapons and the intent to commit terrorist attacks in Jordan during the millennium celebrations.[26]

The Regime vs. Palestinian Islamic Jihad Factions

The Islamic Jihad Movement in Palestine – Shqaqi Faction (Harakat-al-Jihad al-Islami fi Filastin – Tanzim al-Shqaqi)

Dr. Fathi Shqaqi and Sheikh Abdel Aziz Uda lived in the Gaza Strip and established the Islamic Jihad Movement in Palestine in Gaza in the early 1980s. Both had been members of the Muslim Brotherhood but quit because they felt it was not radical enough. Shqaqi and Uda believed that the liberation of Palestine should precede Islamic preaching (*da'wa*), that is, the jihad should be launched directly, without any preliminary steps. Iran wielded more influence over the Islamic Jihad Movement in Palestine than over any other Islamic jihad group. It provided the movement with financial aid, weapons, and fighting matériel, and directed operations in the West Bank, Gaza Strip, Jordan, and Lebanon. The Islamic Jihad Movement in Palestine carried out suicide attacks in Israel, including the bombings at the Beit Lid Junction (1995) and Dizengoff Center (1996).

The Islamic Jihad Movement in Palestine was the largest Palestinian jihad faction. Syria provided it with a base and allowed it freedom of movement. The organization's offices were located outside Damascus, with training conducted in Syrian camps and Hizbollah and Iranian Revolutionary Guard camps in Lebanon. The organization would report its activities to Syrian intelligence officers who coordinated its deployment and military operations. Jordanian security forces thwarted attempts by the movement to establish bases in Jordan. Some members of the organization used forged papers to enter the kingdom from Syria, while others infiltrated across the border, but the Jordanian military was largely successful in countering illegal entry into the kingdom, laying ambushes along the Syrian border, and rooting out members of the group already inside the country. The Islamic Jihad Movement in Palestine used Jordan as a stage for activity against Israel. After the Israeli–Jordanian peace agreement, it planned attacks against Israeli tourists in Jordan, sabotage against various targets in the kingdom, and the assassination of King Hussein. Jordanian security forces foiled all of these operations.[27]

Gazan-born Dr. Ramadan Abdullah Shalach rose to head of the organization following the assassination of Dr. Fathi Shqaqi in Malta in October 1995. Shalach appeared to be a weaker leader than his predecessor, and was more involved in political affairs than in military operations. The Jordanians maintained a close watch on the movement, and in their estimate, the danger of the Islamic Jihad Movement in Palestine lay in its strong links to Iran.

The Islamic Jihad Movement – Bayt al-Maqdas (Harakat al-Jihad al-Islami Bayt al-Maqdas)

The Islamic Jihad Movement – Bayt al-Maqdas was a faction of the Palestinian Islamic Jihad. Its leader was Sheikh As'ad Bayud al-Tamimi, originally from Hebron, who lived in Amman following the Six Day War. In the 1970s he served as the deputy minister of holy places in Jordan. This faction was responsible for the attack on an Israeli tour bus near Ismailia on February 4, 1990, perpetrated by two militants, Ahmed Muhana and Abdel Muati Abu Mualik. In the early 1990s the Jordanian intelligence service pressured Tamimi to cease its sabotage activity inside Jordan and stop using Jordanian soil for its strikes against Israel and the territories. To convince him of their seriousness, intelligence officers arrested his two sons, and pulled Tamimi himself in for regular questioning. Relentless Jordanian pressure led to the ouster of Muhana and Abu Mualik from the Islamic Jihad Movement (Bayt al-Maqdas); they subsequently established their own jihad terrorist groups.

During the 1991 Gulf War, Sheikh Tamimi adopted a hard line position regarding the presence of foreign forces in the region and urged his followers to carry out suicide attacks against the Western powers. Iran furnished the faction with money and military aid, while Tamimi himself visited Libya frequently. Tight surveillance by Jordanian intelligence led to the faction's waning in recent years. In October 1996 Tamimi announced the termination of the organization's activity. He mentioned the possibility of establishing a political movement in PA areas but noted that Israel refused him entry into the territories.[28]

Hizbollah Palestine – Ahmed Hassan Muhana's Organization

Ahmed Hassan Muhana was born in the Gaza Strip in 1951. He began his career in the Islamic Jihad Movement in Palestine in 1989, but quit the movement and joined the Bayt al-Maqdas faction. In 1990 he left Tamimi's group as well and established Hizbollah Palestine. The organization's offices were located in Damascus, and most of its activists lived and trained in Syria. Muhana reported directly to Syrian intelligence, although Iran was the organization's main financial backer. The Muhana faction engaged in sabotage activity in Jordan against Jordanian and Western targets with the aim of undermining the kingdom's stability, in line with Iranian and Syrian policy. Hizbollah Palestine also planned attacks against the American embassy and American tourists, and Jordanian terrorists were supposed to take part in these operations. All of the schemes were intercepted in time.

Since its establishment until late 1993, Hizbollah Palestine planned many sabotage operations, including firing missiles into Israel from Jordanian territory; sabotage in the Aqaba–Eilat area, also against Jordanian targets; and attacks against the royal family and Jordanian military officers. As a result of efficient information gathering, Jordanian intelligence was able to block numerous attempts at smuggling fighting matériel into Jordan from Syria, especially between 1990 and 1993. Several Hizbollah Palestine members were killed in Jordanian army ambushes, and large amounts of fighting matériel were found in the terrorists' possession, including Katyusha rockets, hand grenades, and light weapons.

Since October 1993 the faction's activity diminished because of Iran's refusal to continue financial aid. Apparently the faction's repeated failures influenced the Iranians' decision.[29]

The Islamic Army – The Abdel Muati Abu Mualik Group

Abdel Muati Abdel Aziz Abu Mualik, alias Akrama, was born in the Gaza Strip in 1956, and later moved to Damascus. Following his expulsion from Tamimi's group in mid-1994 he led his own group, the Islamic Army. Based in Syria, the Islamic Army had ties with the Iranian Revolutionary Guards. The group regularly planned terrorist strikes against Israeli tourists in Jordan and Jordan-based attacks against Israel and the territories. Abu Mualik announced his intention to derail the Israeli–Jordanian peace agreement by shattering the stability of the kingdom and attacking Israeli and foreign tourists in the country. The group closely followed the movements of the king and crown prince in the vicinity of the royal palace and at tourist sites in order to booby-trap cars and set up ambushes. For the same reason the group collected information on the Israeli embassy in Amman. During 1995 huge stores of fighting matériel, which included missiles, light weapons, and explosives, were smuggled into Jordan from Syria. All of the terrorists who planned the attacks and arms smuggling were captured by the Jordanians.[30] Voice of Israel radio reported that the Syrians arrested Abu Mualik and other militants of the jihad group, at the request of King Hussein, because of their involvement in terrorist activity in Jordan.[31]

The *Washington Post* disclosed on August 18, 1996 that a month earlier Syria had apprehended a terrorist gang on its way to Jordan from the Lebanon Valley that apparently intended to attack Israeli tourists in Jordan. The paper stated that the terrorists had fought with the mujahidin in Afghanistan and had undergone training in the Syrian-controlled Lebanon Valley. According to official Jordanian sources, the capture was possible thanks to Jordanian intelligence passed on to Syria following improved relations between the two countries.[32]

The Islamic Revolutionary Army – Sayyid Baraka

In 1993 Sayyid Baraka and other terrorists established a small organization in Lebanon, the Islamic Revolutionary Army. The Revolutionary Guards supplied it with funds and Hizbollah provided it with training camps in Lebanon. Baraka's group smuggled fighting matériel into Jordan and planned to carry out terrorist acts within the kingdom and, apparently, against Israel via Jordan. Baraka coordinated his operations with Abu Mualik. The group did not carry out its plans,[33] and as of 1997 was not active in Jordan.

Summary

Subversion and terror against Jordan by Arab revolutionary regimes and the Palestinian national movement in the 1950s, '60s, and '70s seriously threatened the Hashemite Kingdom. The regime overcame these threats thanks to the political shrewdness of King Hussein, the loyalty and skill of the army and intelligence services, and the resolve of Jordan's elite to preserve the kingdom. In the 1990s, the threat of Islamic terrorism to Jordan, be it the fundamentalist fervor of the Middle East or the political fervor emanating out of Iran, did not pose an existential threat to the regime. Intelligence agents infiltrated the terrorist organizations, groups, and factions,[34] and were able to contain them without military intervention. For the most part, Jordanian intelligence officers managed to thwart the terrorist groups before they committed acts of sabotage.

The Syrian-based Palestinian Islamic Jihad factions that operated in Jordan carried out a number of military operations during the 1990s, but most of the planned operations were foiled by the Jordanian authorities. Excluding Ramadan Shalach's Islamic Jihad in Palestine, the other factions were not bona fide organizations. They came into being as a result of ideological splits and personal squabbles within the Palestinian Islamic Jihad; some quickly disbanded, and some gave rise to new factions. The main threat of the Islamic Jihad factions stemmed from their Iranian link. Iran financed them and determined their operations, since they served the state's interest. The leaders of the jihad factions were, essentially, the hired killers of the state – in this case Iran. They enjoyed freedom of activity in Syria, where the Palestinian organizations were seen as freedom fighters, not terrorist groups. During 1993 the Jordanian authorities realized that the Iranian embassy was engaged in fundamentalist Islamic subversion against the kingdom; the king therefore ordered twenty-one of the twenty-six member Iranian diplomatic staff in Amman to leave the country. The official reason for their ouster was the Jordanian government's aim to balance the number of diplomats in each country, as only two diplomats served in the Jordanian embassy in Tehran.[35]

7

THE MUSLIM BROTHERHOOD IN JORDAN

The Movement's Establishment, Goals, and Activity

The Muslim Brotherhood was the largest, oldest, and best organized Islamic group in Jordan. The goal of the movement, founded in 1945 under the sponsorship of King Abdullah, was to run charity, educational, and welfare institutions, and within this framework it established educational institutions and Islamic hospitals in Amman and Zarqa. When Jordan's political parties were dismantled in 1957, the authorities allowed the Muslim Brotherhood to continue its activity since they viewed it primarily as a "social and charity organization."[1] But there was an additional reason: it had originally been set up under the protection of the Hashemite government as a counterweight to elements hostile to the regime. In the 1950s and 1960s when Jordan faced the ideological challenge of Nasser's pan-Arabism, the regime and the Brotherhood fought as allies against Nasserite subversion.[2]

The goals of the Muslim Brotherhood in Jordan were identical to those of its Egyptian counterpart dictated by the movement's founding father, Hassan al-Banna: building a pure Islamic society and establishing an Islamic state based on *shari'a*. The movement's manifesto states that this goal should be attained gradually and in a controlled framework by educating the individual and society; preaching the value of an Islamic government; and systematically propagating the Islamic message in mosques, books, posters, newsletters, and the press. It holds that Brotherhood educational efforts will channel much attention to university students and staff, and it will also endeavor to organize charity funds for poverty-stricken families and students. The Muslim Brotherhood expended great energy on education, constructing an independent educational system that included kindergartens and elementary schools so that its target audience would imbibe the Islamic message from an early age. It also gained an important hold in higher education and for many years had control of the student unions, often attaining decisive victories in student union elections. The Brotherhood's influence was especially strong in universities with faculties for Islamic Studies, such as the state universities at Amman and Irbid and the private university in Zarqa. In 1995–96 the Islamic movement was the most powerful trend in Jordan's universities and student organizations. Students participated in Muslim Brotherhood-initiated demonstrations and protests throughout the kingdom.

In addition, the Brotherhood gained much influence within Jordan's trade unions. In the 1995 elections it obtained a strong position in the physicians, lawyers, and pharmacists unions, and except for the lawyers union, won control of them. The engineers union was also under Muslim Brotherhood control for several years. The Brotherhood's standing in the trade unions and academia reflected the Islamic trend's surge over the alliance of pan-Arabism and left-wing forces that had dominated the trade unions in the past. Observers note these gains were the result of the Muslim Brotherhood's organizational strength, from its careful delineation of priorities in comparison with other parties to its logistics, for example, transporting sympathizers to the polls on election day. Nevertheless, the single factor that contributed most heavily to its popularity was its involvement in social activity, that is, the education, health, and welfare services it provided, especially to the weak levels of society.[3]

Despite its success in the universities and trade unions, the Muslim Brotherhood and the Islamic Action Front (IAF – a political party founded by the Brotherhood) suffered a setback in local elections held on July 11, 1995. The Islamists won only 5 percent of the seats in the municipalities when, according to political observers, they were expected to win 20 percent. They lost their traditional control in Zarqa and Ruseifa, though they attained the mayoralties in eight cities, including Karak, Meidaba, and Irbid. Of 250 municipalities, thirteen were headed by the Islamists. Ishak al-Farchan, the secretary-general of the IAF, accused the government of rigging the elections and downplayed the defeat by claiming that the Islamists had not taken part in the elections in the majority of the municipalities.[4]

The Muslim Brotherhood's organizational structure in Jordan, similar to the one in Egypt, is based on the movement's general regulations, although the names of certain offices and functions are different (figure 7.1). Leading the Muslim Brotherhood in Jordan is the General Controller, who functions alongside the movement's two ranking institutions: the thirty-member Shura Council and the executive committee. The leadership and the representatives from all the districts and branches participate in the council and plan policies related to the movement's agenda. The council chooses the general controller every four years, while the movement's members elect the council once every four years. The seven-member executive committee functions as a kind of government within the movement and is responsible for Muslim Brotherhood administration throughout the kingdom. The committee has three sections:

1 Section for Preaching and Spreading the Islamic Message
2 Families (*usra*) Section
3 Institutions and Unions Section

The Muslim Brotherhood operates according to a four-year plan that determines the number of new members, the aims of the activities in different sectors, such as the trade union or university sectors, and other tasks. Though legal, the plan is classified and not accessible to every member.

Muslim Brotherhood branches are found in cities and towns throughout Jordan. The branch head (*nai'b al-shu'aba*) receives orders from the Operations Bureau, and is responsible for the operations of the *usras*: members of the *usra*, the Brotherhood's basic organizational cell, implement the movement's assignments. There are two kinds of *usra*: open *usra* (*maftoucha*) and closed *usra* (*mughliqa*). The open *usra* numbers from five to ten members and deals only with public activity, such as study of the Qur'an and religion, and political and organizational matters on the public agenda.

Meetings are held in mosques. The open *usra* absorbs new members into the Brotherhood and runs social projects and aid programs. It takes part in anti-government demonstrations and protests. The more exclusive closed *usra* has fewer members. Meetings are held in private homes. Members, identified only by name rather than by code name, engage in clandestine activity alongside religious studies and political and organizational affairs. Although it officially deals only in legal activity, the covert nature of the closed *usra* enables it to cross over to illegal operations if and when the movement decides. The leader of the closed *usra*, the *nakib al-usra*, oversees the cell's activities, receiving his assignments from the *rakib*, the official in charges of three or four closed *usras*. Above the *rakib* is the branch head.[5]

The Muslim Brotherhood and the Political System

The basic, pragmatic objective of the Muslim Brotherhood – the Islamization of Jordanian society – prompted the movement to participate

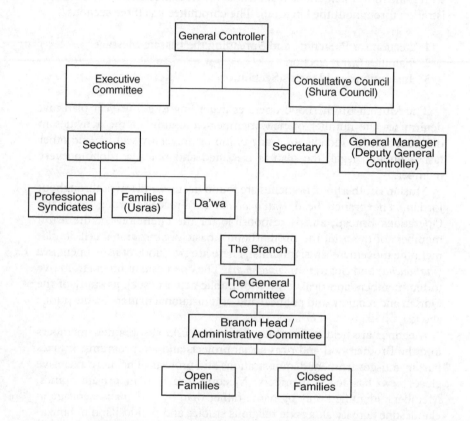

Figure 7.1 Structure of the Muslim Brotherhood in Jordan
Source: "Muslim Brotherhood Regulations," pp. 405–16.

in the political process as far as the regime permits. The Muslim Brotherhood's decision to embark upon this path was not easy. Before each election campaign it had to balance unqualified loyalty to Islamic ideology with the flexibility to succeed in Jordan's realpolitik. In other words, the Muslim Brotherhood demonstrated how to reconcile the incongruity between Islam and democracy. It participated in the elections of 1962, 1967, 1989, and 1993, but a bitter internal debate characterized each pre- and post-election period.

In the late 1980s and early 1990s two main ideological approaches dominated the movement: the pragmatic–dovish approach that espoused cooperation with the regime, participation in the political process, and negotiation toward the long-range strategic objective; and the hawkish approach that opposed any form of compromise. In late 1990 an argument between the proponents of the contrasting approaches raged over the question of joining the government. The pragmatics won the round and the Brotherhood entered the government and was awarded several ministry portfolios. Reflecting a similar spirit of compromise, Abdel Moneim Abu Zant, an MP and senior Islamic activist, said in November 1989 that as Islam was democratic in its outlook, it would accept the majority vote and not impose its opinion on an unwilling public. In contrast, his colleague Ahmed Nofal declared in November 1993 that if a choice had to be made between democracy and dictatorship the Islamists would prefer democracy, yet if the choice were between democracy and Islam, the latter is mandated. These declarations testify to the deliberations and trends among the hawks and doves of Jordan's Muslim Brotherhood. However, in a movement as centralized as the Brotherhood, the leader's opinion is all important. Discussing his organization's position on democracy and violence in August 1994, General Controller Abdel Majid Dunaybat stated:

> At this stage we condemn violence as a way of change. We are experienced in this. The Muslim Brotherhood in Syria tried it and ended up crushed by the regime. Violence was tried in other countries, and we learned a great lesson from these cases. . . . Therefore we are in favor of political pluralism, partnership in the government, and granting women the right to vote and be elected.[6]

This was a clear, fundamentally pragmatic expression of the position by the leader of the Brotherhood. It should be kept in mind, however, that the movement's strategic goal is to do whatever possible within the bounds of the law to gain political power because it believed that this would smooth the way to the ultimate end of establishing an Islamic theocratic state. Therefore, any political system, democratic or totalitarian, that could be instrumental in reaching this goal was acceptable.

When oil prices declined in the early 1980s, Jordan's revenues, coming mainly from the oil-producing states, gradually diminished. The country sank into a deep recession, and economic distress spread. To alleviate the crisis the regime adopted a more transparent, democratic approach to the political process. The hub of political life became the parliament, and concomitantly, the Muslim Brotherhood's position strengthened. In light of the country's economic woes the Brotherhood adopted the simple, catchy, slogan for the 1989 national elections – "Islam is the solution" – and won impressively at the polls, gaining twenty-two out of eighty seats in parliament. In all, the Islamic bloc won 40 percent of the total seats.

The main reason for the Brotherhood's achievement was its organizational monopoly. Since 1957, when all political activity in Jordan was declared illegal, the Muslim Brotherhood remained intact as an association, though functioning in effect, if not in name, as a political party. For thirty-two years it was essentially the only group allowed to continue operations in the domestic arena, and it amassed invaluable political experience and public support. It used the mosques throughout the kingdom as bases for distributing education and welfare services, as well as for transmitting the Islamic message to large audiences. Its strong internal solidarity contrasted sharply with the schisms in the secular and left-wing groups and also contributed significantly to the movement's support.[7]

In November 1990, the Brotherhood's spokesman, Abdel Latif Arabiyyat, was elected chairman of parliament, and shortly after that, for the first time in Jordan's history, the Muslim Brotherhood joined the Jordanian government, under the leadership of Mudar Badran. The period coincided with the mounting regional tension following Iraq's invasion of Kuwait. Relations between the Muslim Brotherhood and Iraq were weak, and the Brotherhood denounced Iraq for its secular rulers. Yet once Allied forces were stationed in Saudi Arabia – where Islam's holiest shrines are located – the Islamic movement in general and the Muslim Brotherhood in particular reversed their positions. The Islamists engineered anti-American demonstrations, exploiting the mosques as meeting places by inserting anti-American rhetoric into their Friday sermons, after which the incited worshippers stormed into the streets.

In light of the Brotherhood's successful enlistment of public support for Iraq, the regime formed a new cabinet on January 1, 1991, one that included seven ministers from the Muslim Brotherhood. This was the first time the movement had gained such political power, which included control of the Ministry of Education. This new partnership reflected the king's need of support from the strong Islamic movement, and the Brotherhood took full advantage of its new status in parliament and government. Arabiyyat, the Muslim Brotherhood speaker of the House, sent a telegram to France in protest over its participation in the anti-Iraq coalition. A Muslim Brotherhood delegation complained to the Turkish ambassador in Amman about Ankara's pro-Western position.

King Hussein came under great pressure to pledge his open support for Iraq in the war. On February 6, 1991 he delivered an unmistakably anti-American speech; in response the Americans cut back $113 million in aid to Jordan for 1991–92. The Brotherhood succeeded in rallying public support for Iraq and instilling the Islamic view of the war. Various Muslim Brotherhood spokesmen such as Abu Zant declared that the "battle is not between Iraq and the United States but between Islam and the Crusaders . . . not between Saddam and Bush but between the leaders of the trans-gressors and the Prophet of Islam."[8] The alliance of interests between the king and the Muslim Brotherhood also led to the torching of American, Israeli, British, and French flags in Jordanian streets, as the Brotherhood managed to stir the public into a frenzied response. This was the state of affairs until Saddam's crushing defeat.[9]

Iraq's defeat and the awakening from the disillusionment at the beginning of the crisis resulted in a steep drop in popular backing of the Muslim Brotherhood. The Brotherhood and those sections of the public that had been mobilized in support of Iraq's war against the apostate now returned to the gray reality of daily affairs. A few years later, when Iraqi forces assembled at the Kuwaiti border in October 1994, the Muslim Brotherhood berated the Iraqis for upsetting the region's security.[10]

In 1992, Jordan issued Law Number 32, the Political Parties Law, which stated that political groups could request government permission to establish a political party. Permission would be granted if the party pledged to act within the framework of the constitution, respect the supremacy of the law, and abide by the principle of political pluralism. The Muslim Brotherhood agreed to these conditions, received permission, and founded the Islamic Action Front. The main reason for this step was the movement's desire to transform its status from a religious association to a legal political party so that it could implement its policy legitimately and win greater influence in the Jordanian public. The IAF became the Muslim Brotherhood's political arm, even though the Brotherhood's secretary-general, Dr. Ishak al-Farchan, denied any connection with the party.[11]

The IAF and the Muslim Brotherhood had identical goals and principles: the gradual, peaceful Islamization of Jordanian society. The party would work to cancel laws that it believed violated Islam and would advance *shari'a*-based legislation, while seeking to implement "Islam is the solution" throughout the kingdom. In addition, the party would strive for the equality and freedom of all citizens. Regarding Israel, it declared that Palestine is Arab and Islamic, there would be no compromise on any iota of Palestinian land, and the coming generations must prepare for continuing the liberation struggle.[12]

As the 1993 elections approached, and against the backdrop of the Muslim Brotherhood's stunning victory at the polls in 1989, the regime decided to change the Voting Law. The government was based on proportional representation in parliament according to constituencies where the number of candidates (from two to nine) varied from district to district. In the previous system, voting proceeded according to the number of representatives in each district. If a constituency had five seats in parliament, the voter too had five votes. The Muslim Brotherhood took full advantage of its organizational strength and discipline to instruct its voters whom to select, and the results proved its influence and power. The amended law stated that the elections in November 1993 would be held on the basis of "one man, one vote." This was a far cry from 1989 when voters could choose as many candidates as they wanted.

Realizing it would be hurt by the new amendment, the IAF opposed it. Disagreement erupted between the doves and hawks in both the Muslim Brotherhood and the IAF. The issue was brought before the Shura Council, which decided by a majority of 85 percent to participate in the elections despite the amendment to the Voting Law. Thus once again the doves triumphed over the radicals as they had since the establishment of the association.[13] When the November 1993 elections approached, the IAF waged an efficiently organized election campaign, putting thirty-six candidates in seventeen voting districts. In absolute numbers the Brotherhood collected 92,525 votes (85.25 percent of all Islamic trend votes). Sixteen candidates were elected and became the largest bloc in parliament, though smaller than in 1989, and despite the setback Islamists controlled 20 percent of the seats.[14]

The Islamic leadership's perception of the 1993 election results as a defeat was instructive. Instead of attacking the government and demanding new elections, the Brotherhood reacted quietly and confidently. Ishak Farchan announced that the defeat would be investigated and conclusions drawn. Mohammad Abdel Rahman Khalifa, the General Controller, declared that the decline in parliament probably stemmed from campaign blunders. He also made it clear that, like his predecessor, the Brotherhood would draw the necessary conclusions so as not to repeat its errors, a position testifying to the movement's pragmatic policy. Nevertheless, the Muslim Brotherhood did not consequently change its ideology and objectives, and its mild reaction to the 1993 election results did not mean that it would act quietly and rationally if it gained power or was about to lose strength. Rather, the Muslim Brotherhood would do what best served its goal of the Islamization of Jordanian society.[15]

The internal debate between the doves and hawks in both the Muslim Brotherhood and the IAF heated up after the signing of the peace treaty with Israel in October 1994. The most disputed issue was whether or not to join the Kabriti government. The hawks claimed that participation in the government signified support for the peace treaty with Israel. On this occasion the hawks overcame the doves, and the Islamists remained in the opposition. But the fallout from the controversy precipitated a schism among the Islamists, and two MPs quit the faction. In advance of the November 1997 general elections, debate revolved around the question of participation. In July 1997 following a seven-hour meeting, the Brotherhood's Shura Council decided not to take part in the coming elections. The argument that clinched the decision was that the government in Jordan had become an autocracy since mid-1995 and denied the parliament of substance. The Muslim Brotherhood was also angry over the 1997 Publications Law that stipulated strict conditions for journalistic publication in Jordan. According to the new law, publishers had to supply capital in the sum of $450,000 – almost twenty times the previous amount. The government shut down thirteen dailies and weeklies that failed to meet these draconian conditions, most of which were connected, directly or indirectly, with the Islamic movement.

Furthermore, the Muslim Brotherhood was upset by the merging of eight centrist tribal parties into a single party, the National Constitutional Party, headed by Abdel Hadi Majali, brother of the prime minister, Abdel Salam Majali. Until the merger the parties had operated on a strong tribal basis, led by dynamic leaders from the Majali, Muashar, Arar, Khareisha, and Dawabda Kheir families, and others. Their awareness of the essential weakness of the political parties had led to the merger; but the unification was also linked to King Hussein's dramatic summons to raise the level of governmental efficiency and bureaucratic competency, and possibly testified to modern Jordan's realization of the limitations of tribalism as a form of public rule. Whatever the case, the Brotherhood interpreted the establishment of the new party – which was certain to nominate government-supported candidates – as a provocation and further step to weaken its strength.

General Controller Abdel Majid Dunaybat explained that the decision to boycott the elections stemmed from the Muslim Brotherhood's overriding doubt as to their honesty. All the signs indicated, he claimed, that government involvement in the elections would prove damaging to democracy. Since the Brotherhood was committed to acting according to the will of the people, it would not participate in the elections.[16]

This decision was not an easy one, as the Muslim Brotherhood had reaped political and propaganda gains as a power bloc in parliament. The decision to boycott the elections bears witness to the gravity of the internal debate over the image of the Islamic movement and its place in the Jordanian political system. The regime preferred that the opposition, including the Islamists, participate in the elections so as to keep up the semblance of a functioning democracy in Jordan. On October 25, 1997, the mufti of Jordan, Sa'id Khajawi, took an unprecedented step and issued a religious edict declaring participation in the elections a religious obligation. The Muslim Brotherhood leadership reacted furiously to the edict. However the regime did not labor to convince the Muslim Brotherhood to participate, and the two sides had become so polarized that common ground seemed to have eluded them.

Parliamentary elections were held on November 4, with 528 candidates, including seventeen women, competing for eighty seats. For the first time since 1989 when parliamentary life was restored to the kingdom, the Muslim Brotherhood and the IAF boycotted the elections at the behest of the Shura Council. Low voter turnout was attributed to the boycott – 54.62 percent compared to 68 percent in the 1993 elections. The king's supporters won sixty-two seats compared to forty-seven in the previous elections. Ten independent Islamists were voted in. Six candidates from the Muslim Brotherhood ignored the Shura Council decision and were immediately expelled from the movement, but two were elected to parliament. Not one woman earned a seat, although there had been one woman in the outgoing parliament. The election underscored loyalty, inherent in the Jordanian political system, to tribalism and the traditional extended families. This was manifested in the relatively high turnout (60 percent and higher) in areas under tribal control such as Jarash, Ajlun, Tufayla, and Karak, and in the number of votes for tribe-supported, independent candidates and the government-backed National Constitutional Party. This party went to the polls with twelve candidates from the parties united under its banner and with twenty-one additional candidates running as independents. It managed to collect ten seats in parliament. On the other hand, in Amman and Zarqa, Muslim Brotherhood strongholds, voter turnout was low (37 percent in Amman and 41 percent in Zarqa).[17]

The Brotherhood's success in distancing the voters reflected its power and influence over the public and embarrassed the regime. Although it wished to demonstrate that Jordan had a viable democratic process, one that included the opposition, the regime had not succeeded in convincing the Muslim Brotherhood to participate in the elections and had not been overly concerned if the Brotherhood was left outside the parliament. The traditional tribal-based parliament became a comfortable political environment for the regime, especially since the Muslim Brotherhood had willingly decamped into the political wilderness as an extra-parliamentary opposition with a lower status than it had during the previous eight years. For its part, the Muslim Brotherhood did not fare well by boycotting the national elections and consigning itself to the opposition. During 1998–99 its bargaining strength *vis-à-vis* the authorities waned and its influence in the kingdom declined.

The General Controller and his colleagues touted the movement's views and achievements to the media and in government meetings. In late August 1998 Dunaybat met with Crown Prince Hassan while Hussein was undergoing treatment for cancer in the United States. Dunaybat handed Hassan a paper detailing the Brotherhood's positions on political, economic, and social issues. The paper called for a freeze in the peace agreement and normalization process with Israel, and an amendment of the newspaper and election laws. It also demanded a renewal of the national dialogue between the regime and opposition, a request noted in the letter of appointment that the king delivered to the new prime minister Fa'iz Tarawnah.[18] In late November 1998 Dunaybat met King Hussein in the Jordanian embassy in Washington and wished him a speedy recovery in the name of the Muslim Brotherhood,[19] and when the king died on February 7, 1999, the Brotherhood sincerely mourned him. Dunaybat termed the Hussein's death an immeasurable loss to the kingdom.[20]

On March 18, 1999 Dunaybat met with King Abdullah, congratulated him on his coronation, and guaranteed the Brotherhood's trust in him and its continued support of the Hashemite leadership. Abdullah praised the Brotherhood's social and moral role and its stabilizing influence in the kingdom over the last decade. As a token of his appreciation, Abdullah ordered the release of sixteen members of the Brotherhood who had been arrested three months earlier for security crimes.[21]

The movement was still rent by hawk–dove tensions and differences. In June–July 1999 disagreement erupted over the handling of monetary and organizational matters. The doves were also embittered that the hawks had won the elections in the movement's Islamic Center Society. Despite the internal wrangling, the Brotherhood knew how to solve its problems: it convened the fifty-member Shura Council. At the end of three days of talks, an agreement was worked out whereby both sides would retract their grievances. Dunaybat, who also headed the Shura Council, informed the press that the movement had overcome its internal differences without having to expel any members. Everyone was prepared to assume responsibility for the movement and dispel the rumors picked up by the media.[22]

The Muslim Brotherhood succeeded in surmounting tension and discord thanks to its organizational strength and self-discipline. In the most important cases, excluding the boycott of the 1997 elections, the doves had emerged victorious. The boycott had been an unwise decision that many people in the movement came to regret, since at the end of the decade the Brotherhood was in the opposition outside of parliament, and found it difficult to operate. The decision to boycott the 1997 national elections was most certainly a setback for the Jordanian branch of the Muslim Brotherhood. The decision had also irked the regime.

In 1999 the Muslim Brotherhood leadership tried to persuade the authority not to close the Hamas offices in Amman and expel senior Hamas leaders. Early in King Abdullah's rule, the regime's policy toward the Muslim Brotherhood had not altered. The regime had no interest in confrontation, and the Brotherhood was careful not to stray too far from the red lines the regime designated.

The Palestinian Element within the Muslim Brotherhood

The relationship between the Palestinians who dwell in Jordan and the Hashemite government is complex. Therefore the Palestinian element within the Muslim Brotherhood, the principal opposition group, merits a separate discussion. Two main factors prompted the Palestinians in Jordan to join the Muslim Brotherhood. First, the movement's Islamic ideology was without a national–territorial–ethnic dimension, rendering it the only political framework in the kingdom that granted legitimacy to the Palestinians' political activity. Second, the movement expanded its activity into the refugee camps in the early 1970s.

The Palestinians had significant representation in the Brotherhood's leadership and institutions. In three election campaigns in the 1990s, between two and three out of seven members (30–40 percent) on the Muslim Brotherhood executive committee were Palestinians. The same held true in the IAF, where fifty Palestinians (40 percent) were elected to the 120-member Shura Council in December 1997, and four Palestinians out of thirteen (30 percent) to the Front's executive committee. This was similar to the proportion following the 1992 elections.

Palestinian representation in the parliament through the IAF was significant in proportion to the East Bank Jordanian representation. Seven Palestinians out of twenty-two delegates (32 percent) entered parliament in the first national elections in Jordan in 1989; in the 1993 elections eight Palestinians out of seventeen (50 percent) were voted in. In the parliamentary elections of November 1997 low voter turnout was conspicuous because of the boycott, especially from the Palestinian refugee camps in Amman and Zarqa, proof of the weight of the Palestinian sector within the Brotherhood. Many of the veteran members of the Brotherhood from the East Bank displayed greater tolerance toward the regime. On the other hand, the younger, more militant generation consisted of many Palestinians. The overlap of the generation gap and Palestinian factor in the Muslim Brotherhood was evident in the 1997 elections boycott. At the same time, there was no correspondence between ethnic background (Jordanian or Palestinian) and political positions, dovish–pragmatic or hawkish–radical. Some senior figures of Palestinian background belonged to the hawkish wing in the movement (Mohammad Abu Zant, Hamam

Sayyid, and Mohammad Abu Faris); other leaders, also of Palestinian background, sat in the dovish–pragmatic camp (including Ishak Farchan, Hamza Mansour, Mohammad Awayda, and Mohammad al-Haj).

Muslim Brotherhood leaders – both East Bank Jordanians and Palestinians – recognized the strength and importance of the Palestinian element. The leadership offered protection and support to the Hamas movement in Jordan, comprised entirely of Palestinians. Despite the regime's sensitivity to all forms of Palestinian involvement in the political arena, its general political attitude toward the Muslim Brotherhood did not differentiate between the ethnic backgrounds of its members. At the same time, although Palestinians formed a major element in the Muslim Brotherhood, including the senior leadership (30–40 percent), this factor had little influence on the movement's policy toward the regime. The Palestinians' influence was expressed mainly in the movement's general Islamic activity and on special issues such as the peace process and normalization with Israel.[23]

The Challenge of the Peace Process with Israel

The position of Jordan's Muslim Brotherhood on the Arab–Israeli conflict and the peace process was similar to that of its Egyptian counterpart: hostility and hatred of Israel and the Jews. The 1989 election platform stated: "The Islamic movement believes that the liberation of all of Palestine is the most important and sacred duty . . . The soil of Palestine is Islamic and belongs to the Muslims for eternity. It is forbidden to surrender even one inch of land."[24] In other words, the Brotherhood categorically rejected Israel's existence, and consequently, any peace treaty. It urged a jihad for liberating Palestine, and over the years it reiterated its anti-Israel credo. In June 1991 King Hussein dispersed the government he had appointed that year. He called on Taher al-Masri, a Palestinian supporter of peace negotiations with Israel, to replace Mudar Badran as the head of government. The Muslim Brotherhood responded by quitting the government.[25]

When King Hussein decided to join the peace process and participate in the Madrid peace conference, the Brotherhood declared its refusal to negotiate with Israel. It termed the opening session in Madrid (October 29, 1991) a day of mourning. It also subsequently inveighed against Israeli–PLO mutual recognition, the Oslo Accords, and the signing of the Declaration of Principles in Washington on September 13, 1993.[26] On the Israeli–Jordanian track, the Brotherhood denounced the signing of the common agenda by the two sides in Washington on September 14, 1993. When Hussein declared his readiness to meet with the Israeli prime

THE MUSLIM BROTHERHOOD IN JORDAN

minister in July 1994 and proceed with negotiations, the IAF condemned the announcement, referring to the meeting as a "dark day." Hussein, however, carefully prepared his countrymen for his peace moves and conveyed the message that the fruits of peace would improve the nation's economic situation and international standing. An experienced ruler, he correctly read Jordan's Islamic map. During the Gulf War, when he realized that the Islamists were likely to cause unrest and subversion, he came out in support of Iraq and even permitted pro-Saddam demonstrations; but in 1994 he estimated that a signed peace agreement with Israel, if presented as a fait accompli, would pass without a major Islamic backlash, with little more than inconsequential protests and remonstrations.[27]

Wednesday, October 26, 1994 – the signing of the Israeli–Jordanian peace treaty – was difficult for the Muslim Brotherhood. It continued its policy of protest and condemnation, and submitted a vote of no-confidence in Majali's government. The IAF spokesman harshly criticized the peace treaty, especially the paragraph relating to the leasing of Jordanian lands to Israel along the Israeli–Jordanian border in the south. After the signing of the agreement, the Brotherhood realized that the king's swift and determined action had transformed the treaty with Israel into an established fact. In the aftermath, the Muslim Brotherhood could only fight against the implementation of the agreement and normalization process, and this it proceeded to do through posters and preaching in the mosques.[28]

While the Brotherhood struggled against normalization with Israel, its ingrained hatred of the Jews rose to the surface; it issued a religious edict forbidding commerce or cooperation with the Jews in tourism, industry, and agriculture. Whoever violated this guideline, the edict warned, would be betraying Allah, his prophet, and the one faith. At the same time, the Brotherhood was keenly aware of its limitations to derail the peace process, and despite the gravity of the issue, it had no intention of clashing with the regime. It realized that the government was committed to peace. As was generally the case when momentous political issues headed the agenda, opinion was divided between the hawks who favored leaving parliament in order to avoid the stain of partnership with official recognition of the peace agreement, and the doves who believed that remaining in parliament was more advantageous for strategic reasons. Differences also cropped up between the younger, militant generation that demanded aggressive action against the agreement, and the older generation that favored a moderate stance. In the end, the pragmatic approach was victorious. The movement's veteran leadership remembered how much its strength had fallen by 1995, compared to 1991 when Jordan first entered the peace process. The Brotherhood's position against peace with Israel was mainly in the form of lip-service, voiced for the protocol. Still, its tough anti-peace stance stemmed from deep ideological wellsprings, with little likelihood of change or moderation.[29]

The two issues of political democracy and the peace process were crucial for the Hashemite kingdom's future, as well as for the Muslim Brotherhood's development. The Brotherhood apparently made the correct decision regarding its own strategic strength in integrating into the democratic process. It became a legal party and power bloc in the parliament and full-time participant in government. This venue provided it with important channels for expounding and preaching its Islamic-based positions, which bolstered its influence in Jordanian society. Therefore, the boycott of the 1997 elections, which reflected the strengthening of the hawks' camp, was a mistake.

The peace process with Israel afforded the Brotherhood an important informational-propaganda tool, especially against the background of popular discontent with the fruits of peace. But the anti-peace policy misfired, and the more the Brotherhood was absorbed with it, the wider the internecine dove–hawk rift grew. The Muslim Brotherhood's automatic opposition, which was a product of its Islamic ideology, worked against it. One of the movement's prominent moderate leaders, MP Dr. Abdullah al-Aka'ila, noted in early 1997 that the Brotherhood simply failed to perceive that it would be impossible to annul the peace treaty in parliament because the treaty had been enshrined in Jordanian law and was an international agreement. The Muslim Brotherhood had based its strategy on the outdated principle of "all or nothing." Aka'ila also criticized the Shura Council's decision to abstain from government lest it be castigated for supporting the peace agreement. Aka'ila claimed that the abstention would only benefit the Zionists since the refusal to join the government excluded the Brotherhood from the hub of political decision-making and left the stage free for the Jews' influence.[30]

Aka'ila was one of the MPs who had disobeyed the boycott and had run in the 1997 elections. Although ousted from the movement, he was elected to parliament as an independent. He reflected the growing apprehension of Muslim Brotherhood moderates over the ascending power of the hawks. The decision to spurn the elections, a turnaround in the Brotherhood's traditional approach, was linked not only to friction with the regime over the Publications Law, for example, that had enervated the Islamic press. The boycott was also linked to internal problems in the movement, such as the young generation's scorn of the veteran leaders who had joined the movement in the seventies and eighties. This veteran leadership maintained a conciliatory policy toward the regime and was often identified as part of it. The young activists were influenced by the increased tensions with the regime during the last decade. In contrast to level-headed veteran leaders, such as General Controller Dunaybat and Secretary General

Farchan, the younger generation tried to lay down new game rules, and therefore supported the election boycott.

The disputes in the Muslim Brotherhood suggested a possible restructuring and change of leadership. Despite the deep schism, however, the movement was unlikely to split apart. The regime also had no interest in the movement's break-up, a development that could radicalize the various groups. Therefore, the mutual dependency of the factions could be expected to continue.

8

JORDAN AGAINST THE MUSLIM BROTHERHOOD

From Ally to Opponent

For most of his reign King Hussein adopted a conciliatory policy toward the Muslim Brotherhood, just as his grandfather, King Abdullah, had done. In the 1950s and 1960s the Hashemite regime needed the Brotherhood to serve as a counterweight to the Communists, the Ba'ath Party, and Nasser's pan-Arabism. Relations between the regime and the Muslim Brotherhood were based on mutual interests as well as an awareness of the unbridgeable gulf that separated one from the other. The Muslim Brotherhood sought to Islamize Jordanian society and establish an Islamic theocratic state; the Hashemite Kingdom wished to remain a nation state with strong, life-supporting ties to the West. The Brotherhood wanted to advance the Islamization process, an agenda it was willing to pay for by supporting the regime; the regime adopted a policy of accommodation with the Brotherhood in order to survive.

Indications of ideological changes in the Arab world began to appear in the late 1960s. Jordan's loss of the West Bank to Israel in the 1967 Six Day War coincided with the decline, and even disappearance of secular ideology in the Arab world. Messianic pan-Arabism, whether under the leadership of Nasser or the Ba'ath Party, waned as a dominant ideology, and Arab socialism, having failed to amend social grievances, was entirely discredited. Two inherently antithetical processes emerged from the ashes of the burnt out ideologies: the rise of Islamic fundamentalism, with its drive to establish an Islamic theocratic state, as an alternative to pan-Arabism and Arab socialism, and the strengtheneing of the nation state that pan-Arabism had threatened to eliminate. Indeed, the growth of support for the territorial state strengthened the Hashemite regime, particularly in its struggle with Nasser's pan-Arabist intrigues in the 1950s and 1960s.

Nonetheless, tranquility and security continued to elude the regime. During the 1960s and early 1970s Jordan was engaged in a struggle for survival against the Palestinian national movement. The turning point came in 1970–71 when the Jordanian army moved into action and crushed the Palestinian uprising. During this difficult period the Muslim Brotherhood remained in close support of the king. But beginning in the late 1970s, and especially from the mid-1980s on, religious Islam, chiefly represented by the Muslim Brotherhood, emerged as the regime's main opponent.[1]

The 1979 Islamic Revolution in Iran enhanced the ascent of Islamic fundamentalism in the Middle East. The shah's ouster, the rise of Khomeini, and the anti-Western, anti-royalty atmosphere pervasive in Iran threatened Jordan and caused deep concern in Amman not only because Hussein was identified as a long-time ally of the West and friend of the shah, but also because the Islamic movement in Jordan, like its counterparts in the region, derived inspiration from the triumph of Iran's Islamic Revolution.[2]

At the same time, Jordan's socio-economic plight hastened the Islamic movement's transformation into the regime's main opposition, particularly in the 1980s. The primary cause of the crisis was Jordan's economic dependency on Arab oil in light of the major changes in the Arab oil economy. In the 1970s and early 1980s the kingdom enjoyed prosperity that paralleled the economic boom in the neighboring Arab oil-producing states, but with the decline in oil prices in the early 1980s, Jordan's revenues plummeted, its economic growth was stunted, and the kingdom suffered from a severe economic crisis throughout the decade. Against the background of the economic slump, the disappointment of pan-Arabism and socialist movements in the Arab world and elsewhere (for example, the Soviet Union and Eastern Europe), and the lack of ideological alternatives, the Islamic movement's popularity increased rapidly. The Muslim Brotherhood's slogan "Islam is the solution" was favored over any foreign ideology proffered by the infidels.

In an attempt to limit the socio-economic crisis, the Hashemite regime embarked upon a policy of political liberalization, hoping that efforts to alleviate the distress would be channeled to a political and parliamentary track. The king tried and failed to undermine the Muslim Brotherhood's support base by allowing a surge of political parties. The Islamic movement's impressive victory in the 1989 general elections, winning 40 percent of the seats in parliament, had far-reaching implications for the regime.[3] The Brotherhood became the regime's main opposition both inside and outside parliament, and the decades-long Islamic–Hashemite alliance that had overcome ideological rifts and assisted the regime in its struggles with domestic and foreign elements came to an end.[4]

Forming the Response

In the 1970s the regime did not regard the Muslim Brotherhood as a threat to stability; it was still perceived, although less so than in the 1950s and 1960s, as a counterbalance to leftist elements and radical nationalists. In fact, the regime was not particularly occupied with the Brotherhood during the 1970s. However, political developments in the Middle East, such as the revolution in Iran, the rise of radical Islam in neighboring countries, and Jordan's ongoing economic crisis, forced the authorities to begin crystallizing a new Muslim Brotherhood policy. The driving influence behind the regime's policy was the activist nature of Muslim Brotherhood operations: its social program, the implementation of its work plan, its public involvement, recruitment drives, modus operandi, organizational strength, and popularity. In the late 1970s the Brotherhood adopted a methodical plan for reaching its strategic goal of establishing an Islamic theocracy. The movement operated according to a detailed four-year plan with activities performed by obedient, highly disciplined members, as would be expected in a disciplined centralized movement. The work plan consisted of well-defined tasks such as the recruitment of new members, preaching, increased power in the trade unions, and Islamic educational activity. Sworn to secrecy, the Brotherhood was careful not to publicize its strategic tasks and intentions. The program was essentially identical to that of the parent movement in Egypt.[5]

By the early 1980s the Muslim Brotherhood understood that its establishment period was over and the time was ripe for the next stage, which entailed the movement's penetration into public sectors. According to the four-year plan, the tasks of this next stage called for involvement in the social and public arenas in order to gain influence in the kingdom's principal institutions: local councils, trade unions, universities, student unions, and health and educational institutions. The successful implementation of the plan increased the movement's growth rate and realized the leadership's expectations. The implementation of its Islamic program in defined stages, however, troubled the regime's agencies responsible for dealing with Muslim Brotherhood activity, especially since the next and final stage was *marhalat al-tamkin* – the ability to seize control of the state – and thus the *al-tamkin* plan meant the overthrow of the secular government and its replacement with an Islamic theocracy. Nevertheless, Jordan's security services estimated that the Muslim Brotherhood would not be prepared to launch the *al-tamkin* stage in the foreseeable future.[6]

In the mid-1980s the mosques became the stage for the Brotherhood's open incitement against government policy. Brotherhood preachers harangued against state officials, ministries, the military, and security and intelligence agencies. The movement demanded the immediate implementation of *shari'a* in the kingdom. Voices in the government increasingly referred to the Muslim Brotherhood as a serious threat and called for a campaign of containment. Although the Brotherhood did not publicly disclaim the regime's legitimacy or employ illegal means for toppling it, the authorities were concerned over its involvement in clandestine activity and the organization of a secret operational body. These fears were based on Muslim Brotherhood activity in other Arab countries where it generally operated anonymously through front organizations it had established but with whom it denied any connection. In Tunisia, al-Nahada was such an organization, in Syria – al-Katala, and in Israel's occupied territories – Hamas. The careful maintenance of secrecy and compartmentalization characterized not only the closed *usras*, but also all levels of the movement. The doctrine of secrecy and compartmentalization is based on a slogan coined by movement founder Hassan al-Banna: "open preaching – secret organization." In other words, the Islamic preaching and education system is public, but the rest of the movement's systems and activities are clandestine, and discussion about them with non-members is forbidden.[7]

The Jordanian authorities worried over the Muslim Brotherhood's education programs that inculcated secrecy, which were perceived as stratagems and deception. Open preaching of the Islamic message to the masses allowed the Brotherhood to gain influence and control of various institutions and organizations. The preaching campaign brought growing numbers of new members into the movement where they were taught the principle that preaching alone is public and other forms of activity are secret. Thus, the movement effectively expanded its ranks through the open preaching system at the same time that it increased in strength and prepared for the day of reckoning through the doctrine of secrecy and compartmentalization.

By 1985 the authorities harbored much more concern over the rise of Islamic fundamentalism in the kingdom, and believed that the Brotherhood posed a future strategic threat to the regime because of its systematic program, the shift to open incitement in the mosques, and its adherence to the secrecy principle. It was then that the regime adopted a policy of containment against the Muslim Brotherhood,[8] and indeed, the king's policy toward the Muslim Brotherhood underwent a major transformation that year. In a television broadcast in January 1985 the king warned of the dangers of radical Islam, which was gaining strength because of its success in Iran, and feared it could precipitate a greater tragedy than what happened in Lebanon. The government of Zaid Rifa'i took steps to limit Muslim Brotherhood activity through legislative measures. In March 1985 parliament passed a law restricting Islamic activists' participation in elections. The law stated that candidates would have to pay a 500 dinar registration fee. The lawmakers assumed that Islamic activists, who generally came from the lower classes, would be hard put to meet this financial demand. The parliament ratified a new election law that redistributed voting districts in order to guarantee the extension of tribal representation, thus impinging on the Brotherhood's power bases. Other measures, designed to limit Brotherhood influence in the mosques, followed.

The regime launched its harshest strike against the movement in late 1985 in measures unassociated with parliamentary legislation. The blow was intended to send a warning to the movement that it had that grown too powerful too fast and that the regime looked unfavorably upon its political involvement. The move was also linked to King Hussein's effort at renewing ties with Syria. After President Assad's massacre of the Muslim Brotherhood in Hama, Syria in 1982, the king had frequently granted political refuge to the survivors. However, developments in the region prompted Hussein to seek rapprochement with Syria, and improved relations with Damascus required the suppression of the Muslim Brotherhood. After the king publicly charged Syrian Muslim Brotherhood members who had found shelter in Jordan of subversive acts against the Syrian regime, Jordanian security forces arrested hundreds of Syrian Islamists and handed them over to the Syrian authorities.

The Jordanian Muslim Brotherhood sensed the intensity of the government's new containment policy. Jordanian intelligence officers heightened their surveillance of the Brotherhood's preachers in the mosques and tightened the reins in the universities. The Muslim Brotherhood was forbidden to hold public rallies, and its freedom of expression was curtailed. Events came to a climax at the Yarmouk University in Irbid in May 1986. Against the background of increased tuition fees and a deteriorating economy, students clashed with security forces. The rioting escalated into a general, state-wide, Islamic political protest that lasted two weeks. At least three students were killed and hundreds wounded. Following these disturbances the regime decided to increase its surveillance at the universities further, and the parliament amended the law to give the authorities near-total freedom to retain control at the campuses. The events of 1986 on top of the ongoing severe economic conditions in the second half of the 1980s amplified the tension between the regime and Muslim Brotherhood, and at the same time demonstrated the movement's ability to organize mass political protests.[9]

Two major events of 1989 were particularly influential in the regime's decision to implement strictly its containment policy against the Muslim

Brotherhood: the violent food riots and the Brotherhood's victory in the national elections.

Over the days April 19–22, 1989 riots erupted in southern Jordan, the worst of their kind since the 1970–71 civil war. The rioting took place in the wake of the government's adoption of economic measures demanded by the International Monetary Fund. The new economic policy caused a dramatic rise in the price of basic food stuffs, gasoline, and cigarettes. The southern region – homeland of the Bedouin tribes loyal to the king – was especially hurt by the price increases. Unlike the Amman area, the south had not benefited from the prosperity of the 1970s, and poverty still prevailed in the cities of Ma'an, Karak, and Toufayla, where, after the price rises, thousands of people took to the streets demolishing stores, banks, and government buildings. Eleven people were killed and over one hundred wounded, including security troops. More than an economic protest, however, the anti-government demonstrations were also an expression of the popular anger toward the king. Significantly, Islamic activists played a prominent role in organizing the riots. On April 21, 1989 at the end of the prayer services in the mosques, Islamists enflamed the crowds with religious tirades. The regime was hard pressed to calm the rioting. This was a loud and clear message to the king that his support base had been damaged even among his loyal subjects. He responded by announcing the first parliamentary elections since 1967.[10]

The second event that prompted the containment policy was the Muslim Brotherhood's impressive results in the 1989 elections. The Brotherhood won twenty-two seats and, with an additional twelve seats from Islamic independents, formed the largest bloc in the eighty-seat Parliament. The election victory came as a complete surprise to many people in the government establishment.[11] Some attributed the gains to the faulty election system, which allowed voters to choose a number of candidates in their constituencies, a method that the well-organized Muslim Brotherhood effectively exploited by instructing its supporters whom to vote for. However, other people in the government recognized the regime's mistaken assumption that the integration of the Muslim Brotherhood and other parties into the competitive democratic process would lead to the movement's decline. In fact the exact opposite occurred, and on the basis of its election victory the Muslim Brotherhood was impelled to believe that the street was ripe for realizing the movement's Islamic program.

The election results, coming on the heels of the severe food riots, threw the regime into a high state of alert. Government leaders realized that the Brotherhood had attained enormous power both as a smoothly organized political force with a large support base, and as a broad, dynamic, legitimate opposition in parliament. The regime was aware that poverty and economic misery had triggered the food riots and were working to the

Muslim Brotherhood's advantage while weakening the Hashemite regime's traditional bastions of support.

Looking back on the previous two decades, the Jordanian authorities concluded that the Muslim Brotherhood had devoted the 1970s to setting up and implanting its infrastructure, and the 1980s to advancing and capturing additional positions in society. To the regime, the future appeared ominous. It saw the Muslim Brotherhood as a shrewd, scheming organization capable of exploiting prevalent socio-economic ills and the shortcomings in the army and internal security agencies. Its members were understood to possess the requisite patience to wait for the right moment for the creation of an Islamic theocracy. The regime estimated that the Muslim Brotherhood was a powerful, highly organized movement that had to be taken seriously and handled with firm and decisive action.[12]

The Regime's Containment Policy

Preventive Measures and Counteraction

The policy of containment was designed to halt the spread of Islamic influence, restrict Muslim Brotherhood activity within clearly-defined parameters, and counter any activity that crossed these red lines. It was neither the liquidation strategy that Assad had applied against the Muslim Brotherhood in Syria in 1982 nor the strategy of all-out confrontation that Mubarak implemented against the movement in the 1990s. Jordan's strategy was based on the premise that the Muslim Brotherhood movement would continue to operate legally in the kingdom and that the regime might even maintain viable relations with it. The following prohibitions defined the threshold of the regime's tolerance:

- No incitement and subversion against the regime
- No incitement exhorting the public to large anti-government demonstrations
- No possession of weapons, establishment of armed groups, or military training and activities for such groups
- No violence or terrorist acts against a Jordanian or other party by exploiting Jordanian soil for this purpose
- No coordination or cooperation with terrorist and subversive organizations in Jordan or abroad; no contact with foreign bodies or acceptance of money from them
- No activity within the security forces or security agencies

All of the prohibitions appear in Jordan's criminal code and the national charter.

The Muslim Brotherhood generally abided by these rules, since it understood that this would allow it to continue to operate, advance, and expand. The authorities too were not eager to clash with the Brotherhood because they were aware of the fate of other regimes in such struggles, and thus a modus vivendi was reached. However, when there were growing indications that Muslim Brotherhood activity was reaching the limit, the regime responded decisively to deter it.[13] Since the movement's approach was clandestine and camouflaged in the framework of "open preaching – secret organization," the government believed that subversive Brotherhood activity that lay outside formal preaching preaching and Islamic education programs could be uncovered mainly through secret intelligence measures. Therefore, the regime deployed a large network of agents to supply a constant flow of accurate information on the movement and its planned responses to political events in the kingdom and region. This information enabled the government to devise countermeasures and take preventive steps when necessary.[14]

Preventive measures were designed to obstruct hostile activity against the regime, such as incitement in the mosques and political demonstrations in the streets, and to foil illegal attempts by individuals or groups to attain political objectives. Members of the Muslim Brotherhood were routinely called in for interrogation if incriminated by suspicious evidence. Members not suspected of illegal activity were warned of the consequences of hostile acts against the regime. The regime also took special measures with political events or sensitive religious incidents that had the potential of adversely influencing internal security. The security establishment held talks with Islamic leaders to convince them to steer clear of hostile activity. The authorities occasionally carried out the preemptive arrest of Islamic activists in order to thwart hostile activity or send a deterrent message to the Muslim Brotherhood. The 1992 arrest of MPs Laith Shbailat and Yaqub Karrash on charges of plotting to overthrow the regime was one prominent example.

In May 1990 violent riots broke out in Jordan after the murder of Palestinian workers in Rishon LeZion, Israel by a Jewish Israeli. Scores of people were killed and wounded in bloody clashes with Jordan's security forces in the main cities and in the Palestinian refugee camps. Police and intelligence officials responded firmly and threatened to move against Islamic leaders unless they acted with responsibility to restore quiet in the kingdom. The Muslim Brotherhood was persuaded that the regime was serious, and thus assisted in pacifying the popular mood and calming the storm in parliament.[15]

The Muslim Brotherhood's intense hatred of Israel and Zionism heightened tensions with the regime when Jordan entered the peace process. Incitement in the mosques against the king's decision to take part in the

Madrid Peace Conference increased. The Jordanian police and intelligence services implemented a series of countermeasures that included warnings, threats, and preemptive arrests; demonstrations and mass rallies were forbidden, and preachers were instructed to shun political issues. These measures stayed in effect and allowed the regime to weather the various sensitive phases of the peace process: from Madrid in 1991 to the common agenda signed by the Israeli and Jordanian delegations in Washington (September 1993); the Washington Declaration issued by King Hussein and Prime Minister Rabin (July 1994); the signing of the peace agreement between Israel and Jordan (October 1994); and the opening of the Israeli embassy in Amman. Each event was a further step toward bilateral normalization.[16]

The regime took decisive preemptive measures against the Islamic Action Front and Muslim Brotherhood prior to the food riots of August 1996. The government had learned some of the lessons from the violent food riots of 1989, and this time was prepared to counter mass demonstrations that could easily erupt over the rise in bread prices. Security officials held talks with Palestinian and Islamic activists to dissuade them from inciting riots and violence. The king himself warned that he would react severely against any attempt to undermine the kingdom's stability. The Muslim Brotherhood realized that the regime fully intended to prevent disorder and that the movement's participation in rioting would give the authorities an excuse to lash out at it. Therefore, the Brotherhood leadership instructed members to avoid anti-government activity despite popular opposition to the soaring price of bread. On Friday noon, as thousands of worshippers exited the mosques, riots erupted in Jordan's southern desert cities but the Brotherhood remained on the sidelines. The Palestinians too avoided the violent demonstrations, recalling their staggering defeat at the hands of the Jordanian army in September 1970.[17]

Despite the decision to eschew the riots and refrain from anti-government activity, the Islamic Action Front and Muslim Brotherhood leaderships could not ignore a social issue as volatile as the price hike of bread and other staples. They requested permission from the authorities to hold a large demonstration in Amman on Friday, August 23, 1996, at the conclusion of prayer services, to be called the "march of the starving million." It was to begin at the large Husseini Mosque in downtown Amman and proceed to Hashemite Square. But the regime decided to cancel the demonstration. Leaders of the Islamic Action Front and the Muslim Brotherhood were brought in for talks with senior intelligence officers and ordered to call off the protest. Despite the Islamic leaders' pleas that their request was legal, permission was denied. Finally, the Islamic Action Front published an announcement concerning the regime's revocation of the rally: "We are shocked by the government's conduct that forbids peaceful, democratic marches in support of the people's rightful demands. We declare that the march is canceled until further notice."[18]

The regime's preemptive measures sometimes managed to tarnish the Muslim Brotherhood's image in the public and heighten differences of opinion within the movement, which was precisely the authorities' intention. It happened, for example, after the Muslim Brotherhood's exclusion from the protests against the price rises, when the movement appeared directionless. The decision to accede to government demands in this case was not only perceived by the public as an expression of weakness, but it also intensified the gap between the movement's pragmatic and radical trends. In a press interview, movement sources admitted that the Islamic opposition had missed an opportunity to topple the government by not exploiting the public's anger over increased bread prices. In the end, the same sources noted, the government had scored a victory and the Muslim Brotherhood was left empty-handed.[19]

"The War of the Mosques"

The local mosque was an ideal locale for the Muslim Brotherhood to transmit the Islamic message to the masses. Thousands of preachers disseminated the message via organized sermons in the mosques. Pupils studied the Qur'an in the mosques, and Islamic *usras* held regular meetings there. The mosque was also the stage used by the Muslim Brotherhood for expounding on political issues, and the Friday sermon (*khoutbat al-jumha*) often served this purpose. Friday's preaching was frequently channeled, directly or indirectly, into anti-regime agitation, and on many occasions the Muslim Brotherhood instigated political protests through its preachers in the mosques.

The Hashemite regime was fully aware of the exploitation of the mosques by the Muslim Brotherhood and other Islamic circles for political goals. Therefore for many years it kept close watch over the mosques and took steps to curb Islamic preachers when they strayed from the government guidelines. In special circumstances, such as the signing of the Israeli–Jordanian peace treaty or the food riots, the regime employed preventive measures to block the Islamists' exploitation of the mosques for anti-government agitation. It also enacted laws and issued regulations for supervising the mosques and obstructing hostile activity that emanated from them.

By the mid-1980s the Muslim Brotherhood engaged in open incitement in the mosques. In a speech delivered at the opening session of parliament in the autumn of 1985, the king attacked the Muslim Brotherhood's militant preachers and urged parliament to pass legislation forbidding unsupervised sermons. The cabinet quickly passed the Preachers Law, which was then ratified in the parliament. This law prohibited preachers from referring to political issues in their sermons and required them to submit a draft of the sermon to the authorities before they delivered it. The law also granted state officials the right to appoint and dismiss mosque preachers. The Muslim Brotherhood representatives in the parliament stated they would vote for the law on condition that the Ministry of Religious Endowments admonished those preachers it judged had crossed the red lines before excluding them from serving in the mosques.

In practice, however, the arrangement was inconsistent. The regime implemented the law to prohibit Muslim Brotherhood clergy from public preaching, and many preachers were summarily dismissed because they introduced political topics into their sermons. In 1988, for example, Sheikh Sayyid Hamam, a Brotherhood activist, was banned from preaching in the mosques without receiving an early warning after he had criticized Jordan's ceding of the West Bank. In contrast, the Mudar Badran government, with its Muslim Brotherhood coalition partner, implemented the Preachers Law in a highly selective manner, especially since the minister of religious endowments, Ali Fakir, was a member of the Muslim Brotherhood. During this period preachers who had been dismissed returned to their positions in the mosques.[20]

The major political events in the 1990s, such as the Gulf War, Jordan's entry into the peace process at the Madrid Conference, the Israeli–Jordanian peace treaty, and the normalization of Israeli–Jordanian relations sparked angry responses in the Muslim Brotherhood. An official report by the minister of the interior in February 1995 stated that as part of the Muslim Brotherhood's program to intensify its criticism of the government, the Brotherhood's representatives in parliament instructed those preachers who were banned by law from delivering sermons to escalate the struggle against the ban. At the same time, Muslim Brotherhood preachers in the mosques began to employ scathing language, and fliers agitating against Jews and the peace process were handed out to the worshippers. The regime tightened its surveillance, took broader counter-measures, and on one occasion applied force. This occurred on October 28, 1994, two days after the signing of the peace treaty with Israel, when at the end of Friday prayers near a mosque in Amman state security troops attacked a senior member of the Islamic Action Front, Abdel Moneim Abu Zant, for violating the prohibition against preaching in public against the peace treaty with Israel. Islamic Action Front leaders blamed the regime for the attack.[21]

The Jordanian minister of religious endowments, Abdel Salam al-Abadi, was forced to deal with the tensions that mounted over the peace treaty with Israel and process of normalization. In a statement to the media on June 9, 1995, Abadi said that his ministry would distribute written sermons for the preachers to read in the mosques on Fridays, which, he claimed, was a step designed to encourage preaching and instruction with spiritual content. He mentioned that a new cadre of preachers would be appointed that included pensioners who had served in the religious directorate in the army and civil servants with religious training. They would be required to deliver the prepared sermons and propagate the message of the regime. This step would prevent veteran preachers and Muslim Brotherhood preachers who were also members of parliament from incorporating in their sermons attacks on the peace treaty.[22]

The media, and especially Islamic circles, criticized the government's decision to distribute written sermons to the preachers as an excessively controlling measure. A senior figure in the Ministry of Religious Endowments tried to calm the uproar by publishing a denial of the accusations. He pointed out that the Ministry of Religious Endowments had granted and would continue to grant preachers complete freedom to choose suitable topics for their congregations. He also noted that the ministry had established a special department for dealing with Friday sermons, whose main task was to assist preachers in preparing sermons that required information on modern subjects and data on social, family, military, and fighting crime.[23]

Nonetheless, the issue remained on the public agenda, and Abadi labored exhaustively to justify it publicly. He repeated what the senior source in his ministry had said: the sermons were not dictated to the preachers, but were distributed because of the contents' relevance to the daily lives of citizens. The minister made it clear that he would persist in obstructing the use of the mosques as political arenas. Members of the Muslim Brotherhood and the Islamic Action Front who continued to weave political themes into their sermons would, as civil servants under his jurisdiction, be counseled – without pressure – to abide by regulations. He denied that infractions of the ministry's instructions would result in the preachers' dismissal. According to Abadi, "There are many subjects of vital concern. Why not deal with the issue of road accidents from a religious point of view; isn't this preferable to leveling accusations against the government?"[24] He reiterated that the Ministry of Religious Endowments was the only government body with the authority to supervise all of Jordan's mosques, and added that Section 3 of the Preachers Law stated that preachers were required to sermonize judiciously and were forbidden to use defamatory, aggressive, or instigating language against individuals and institutions.

To thwart the members of parliament who also preached in mosques and whose parliamentary immunity protected them from the ministry's investigation, cleric-legislators from all parties were ordered to cease preaching activity. Some of the representatives appealed the ruling before the High Court of Justice,[25] and the judges rescinded the decision in a limited number of cases and allowed eight Islamic Action Front parliamentarians to resume preaching. The minister declared he would continue to block representatives and candidates from the IAF from serving as preachers, excluding the eight delegates who had won their appeal.[26]

The struggle, termed by the Jordanian press the "war of the mosques," intensified toward the end of 1995. Three parties were involved in this "war": the Ministry of Religious Endowments – officially responsible for administering the mosques; the Islamic Action Front – represented by delegates in the Parliament and preachers in the mosques; and the al-Ahbash movement – a newly formed religious group that despised the Muslim Brotherhood.[27] The Islamic faction accused the regime of systematically destroying their institutions and diminishing their popular influence by allowing members of al-Ahbash to serve in the mosques as imams and preachers, when they themselves were banned. The Muslim Brotherhood argued that it had been given the right to preach in the mosques since the founding of the movement in the kingdom. The Brotherhood repeatedly accused the regime of patronizing al-Ahbash in order to weaken the Muslim Brotherhood, and bloody clashes broke out between the Brotherhood and al-Ahbash. In late 1995, after al-Ahbash received official permission to hold a general conference, its membership expanded at a daily rate. The group supported the peace process and the peace treaty with Israel. Islamists soon realized that the state viewed al-Ahbash as the alternative to the Muslim Brotherhood and Islamic Action Front in the streets and mosques.[28]

Substantiating its claims of persecution, the Muslim Brotherhood publicly announced that the Ministry of Religious Endowments had replaced almost 200 of the movement's clerics with al-Ahbash members. The Brotherhood also declared that it regarded al-Ahbash members as infidels whose views were antithetical to the spirit of Islam, and who were supported by foreign bodies that sought to oust the Muslim Brotherhood from the mosques. It accused the Ministry of Religious Endowments of shutting down schools where the Qur'an was taught, schools that had been under the Muslim Brotherhood's control since the establishment of the Hashemite Kingdom.[29]

Given Jordan's history of internal conflict, regime leaders and the leaders of the Islamic movement had experience in pacifying growing tensions and calming suspicions. Both sides were interested in preserving viable bilateral relations, and neither wished to reach a head-on confrontation. One of the means of achieving the necessary compromise was through meetings between Islamic and government leaders. Thus, a number of leaders, including members of parliament from the Islamic movement, and the head of Jordan's General Intelligence, General Samih al-Batihi, met in April 1996 to guarantee an ongoing working relationship. The Islamic leaders congratulated Batihi on his appointment as chief of intelligence and assured him that the Islamic movement pledged to preserve the country's security and stability at all costs. They demanded the release of some of the movement's prisoners. Batihi spoke candidly of the numerous legal infringements that the Brotherhod, the IAF, and members of the Islamic bloc in parliament had committed. He rebuked them for the political incitement of their sermons, and warned them that under no circumstances would Jordan compromise on its security. The Islamic delegation stated that the meeting helped them alleviate the destructive atmosphere that had descended on their relationship following the recent visit to Jordan of a senior figure – whose name was not mentioned – who had tried to plant divisions between the Islamic movement and the Kabriti government. Some leaders were favorably surprised by the new intelligence head's ability to persuade, analyze, and reason with them. In return they promised to cooperate with the regime for the good of the country. But other Islamic leaders harbored reservations, and were even angry at their colleagues' glowing description of the man.[30]

With the general public's response to breaking political and economic events, the "war of the mosques" intensified. The regime, drawing on its experience, gave early warning to the preachers, and intervened during the events to take control of the mosques in order to curb incitement and mobilization for demonstrations before matters got out of hand. When the government decided to raise bread prices, the Ministry of the Interior instructed district governors to meet with the imams and counsel them against preaching on the issue, and forbid its discussion in the mosques. Some of the imams were unhappy with what they regarded as the district governors' military style. In response, the governors began to make threats. Clerics who disobeyed the governors' orders received official letters with stiff warnings.[31] Despite these preemptive measures, food riots erupted in Karak on Friday noon immediately after thousands of worshippers left the mosques. The minister of religious endowments denied that the sermons had triggered the riots in the south and claimed that in fact in many cases the sermons had helped temper passions and pleaded with the public to refrain from violence.[32]

Overall, the government maintained effective control over the mosques and made certain that the Muslim Brotherhood did not gain absolute autonomy in their administration. Thus, for example, the Ministry of Religious Endowments was careful to appoint some non-Brotherhood members to the charity committees that managed large sums of money. In sensitive periods ministry authorities also decided which clerics would preach the Friday sermon. The law dealt harshly with preachers who infused their speeches with inflammatory passages, and it prohibited citing verses in the Qur'an that refer to the Jews as sons of death. Punishment was exacted on violators of these rules. The Islamists generally abided by the rules, and during the 1996 food riots the king even commended them for their responsible conduct.

The Regime's Approach to Social Islam

Like its counterparts in other countries, the Muslim Brotherhood in Jordan set up a network of social and welfare institutions. It took advantage of its status as the only legal political body in the country after the 1970 civil war in order to build health clinics, schools, professional associations, and community centers, all of which provided it with direct contact with the public. This social network and the Brotherhood's extended involvement in the mosques were its two key areas of activity. It also made skillful use of its influential position in the Ministry of Education to reach new audiences, although the regime attempted to block the Brotherhood's control of government educational institutions lest the movement benefit from services financed by the regime. Members and supporters of the Muslim Brotherhood received teaching jobs, scholarships for study abroad, and appointments to administrative positions in the universities.[33] The Brotherhood, however, strove not only to infuse its ideological principles into the Jordanian education system but also to administer its own large, independent education network.

The Muslim Brotherhood's welfare activities included having voluntary organizations distribute warm clothes during the winter and gift packages to the public during the Ramadan season, although it often created the impression that it had enlisted the money for certain projects which in reality were state-financed. For example, the Brotherhood's distribution of gift packages at Ramadan was sometimes carried out in parallel to the state's project. Thus, government officials had to assure that the entire distribution project was carried out in the name of the district governors. The regime set up government-run clinics alongside those of the Brotherhood.

Overall, the welfare activity posed a challenge to the regime, which was struggling to overcome misery and economic difficulties in the kingdom but was unable to compete with the extent and quality of Muslim Brotherhood welfare services. In addition, state agencies failed to reach all the areas where the Muslim Brotherhood volunteers were active. There were instances where the regime held an advantage: for example, in the Muslim Brotherhood hospital in Amman – the third largest health center in Jordan – hospitalization was more expensive than in state-run facilities. But the regime found it more difficult to compete with the Muslim Brotherhood in the field of education. The Brotherhood made an outstanding effort to provide the younger generation with Islamic education, and it was unrealistic for the regime to construct a school building next to every Muslim Brotherhood facility. The regime also recognized the benefit the public derived from Muslim Brotherhood voluntary associations and therefore did not try to suppress them. Nevertheless it prohibited civil servants from participating in this area of Muslim Brotherhood activity.[34] In summary, the regime's containment policy in the realm of social Islam was carefully measured.

Sanctioning the World Organization Connection

The Muslim Brotherhood in Jordan was subordinate to the Cairo-based world organization, in accordance with the organization's general regulations. The general guide was both the head of the world leadership and the head of the Muslim Brotherhood in Egypt. Regulations required state leaderships to consult with the general guide and gain his approval on strategic issues and organizational principles.[35] For example, the Muslim Brotherhood in Jordan had to obtain the general guide's approval before it could participate in Jordan's parliamentary elections in 1989 and 1993. Similarly, in 1991 it requested permission to join the government for the first time. To this end, members in the executive committee traveled to Egypt and secured the general guide's approval.[36]

In addition to direct contact with the world leadership for approval on major issues, the Jordanian Brotherhood also consulted and exchanged ideas with colleagues by telephone. Brotherhood leaders in Jordan and Egypt held talks, for example, on the ramifications of the Gulf War on the Islamic movement.[37] In the world organization's geographical division, the Muslim Brotherhood in Jordan is part of the political division of the Syria region, with headquarters in Jordan and led by Jordan's general controller. This bloc included the Muslim Brotherhoods of Syria, Lebanon, Jordan, and Palestine (and Palestinians residing in other countries). As leader of the regional headquarters, Dunaybat headed a delegation to the Arab and Islamic People's Conference in Khartoum in 1995 that discussed current Muslim-related issues, such as the Muslim problem in Bosnia, Chechnya, and the Philippines. Dunaybat returned to Sudan as the head of the Syrian region delegation in early 1997 to express support for the Sudanese people when violence broke out with Eritrea, Ethiopia, and Uganda.[38]

According to Jordan's national charter (1990) and the Political Parties Law (1992), it was illegal for the Muslim Brotherhood to maintain ties with a foreign entity. The charter stated, "[A political] party's leadership and members are forbidden to have connections of an organizational or financial nature with any non-Jordanian element, nor may any political party or organizational activity be guided or directed by a foreign state or element."[39] Traveling to Egypt to obtain permission from the general guide was thus an infraction of the regime's rules, but the authorities neverthe-less allowed the delegations' departures in the three cases because they were not seen as a security risk and the regime was interested in facilitating the Brotherhood's integration into the democratic process.

Another factor that induced the regime to approve the trips to Egypt was the world leadership's special policy toward the Muslim Brotherhood in Jordan. The world leadership recognized Jordan's unique circumstances whereby the Hashemite regime dealt tolerantly with the Brotherhood, as opposed to the often violent treatment it received in other Arab countries. The world organization adopted this conciliatory line out of respect to King Hussein, a devout Muslim and scion of the Prophet. Until 1999 it saw no need for instructing the Jordanian Brotherhood to embark upon clandestine or military activity or break the rules of the game established with the regime.[40]

Unlike the Egyptian Muslim Brotherhood that categorically denied contact with the world organization, the Jordanian Muslim Brotherhood mentioned its ties, albeit on rare occasions and with due circumspection. At a press interview held in honor of the Jordanian movement's jubilee, then leader of the Muslim Brotherhood in Jordan, General Controller Abdel Majid Dunaybat, referred to this link. Answering the charge that the Muslim Brotherhood was a foreign movement because its source of authority dwelt outside of Jordan, Dunaybat claimed that this accusation emanated from political rivals who wished to sully the Brotherhood's image. He added that the Muslim Brotherhood in Jordan was an ideolog-ical, spiritual movement affiliated with the world movement of the Muslim Brotherhood, but its modus operandi, policies, and decisions were based on the Qur'an and Muslim tradition, and its authority for preaching and political involvement lay with the movement's legal leadership in Jordan.[41]

In another interview in early 1997, Dunaybat was asked about his move-ment's ties with the world organization. Weighing his words carefully, he reconfirmed that the Muslim Brotherhood world organization was an ideo-logical association that sought to unite Islamic preaching in all Muslim countries. As for conventional organizational matters and relations with local regimes, each Muslim Brotherhood branch coordinated its policies according to local conditions. To illustrate, Dunaybat noted that the Jordanian's Brotherhood's decision not to join the government was made without consulting the world organization.[42]

Psychological Warfare

The Jordanian government employed psychological warfare in order to weaken the Muslim Brotherhood and the Islamic Action Front. The goal was to enervate the movement, but not split it into smaller groups. The regime understood that internal division would radicalize the movement since the smaller groups would be more extremist and irresponsible. In addition, the authorities would have a harder time tracking them.

After the Brotherhood joined the government for the first time (1991), popular opinion felt that the Islamic ministers floundered in their roles by reneging on commitments they had made before entering the government and failing to relieve poverty and shortcomings in education. Islamic ministers were criticized for enjoying plush offices, government cars, and the amenities of bureaucratic power instead of acting in the public interest. The Brotherhood's failures while it was in power damaged its prestige and public support. Interestingly, the Muslim Brotherhood was convinced that its representatives in the Badran government, especially the minister of education, had served remarkably well. The movement's spokesmen pointed to the thousands of letters – whose publication was banned by the government – sent to the media in support of the education minister's policy, and the fact that regime-backed newspapers relentlessly excoriated the Islamic ministers. Senior officials in the regime claimed they had foreseen that the Islamic ministers would prove inadequate in government and the Brotherhood's public image would be marred as a result. Riding on the wave of public disappointment, political officers in the regime presented the Islamic Action Front as a movement gone amiss, a movement whose strength lay in brandishing slogans but in reality was impotent.[43]

Generally, internal debate within the Muslim Brotherhood has benefited the regime. Between 1996 and 1997 the bitter dispute over the issue of participation in the Kabriti government played naturally into the regime's hands.

Amnesty as a Political Tool

On November 16, 1992, on the occasion of his fifty-eighth birthday two days before, King Hussein declared a general amnesty and freed Jordan's political prisoners. The amnesty did not extend to those charged with first-degree murder, rape, or drug dealing, but over a thousand inmates were set free, including one hundred and fifty security prisoners. Among the pardoned were members of the Army of Mohammad terrorist group, who had been sentenced to long jail terms for conspiring to overthrow the government, Hamas leaders, commanders of various Islamic Jihad factions, and members of the Muslim Brotherhood. Perhaps the main beneficiaries of the amnesty were two Islamic members of parliament, Laith Shbailat and Yaqub Karrash, whose arrest was widely considered a warning by the government to the Brotherhood and other Islamic groups not to overstep the bounds of legal activity.[44]

Hussein proclaimed the amnesty after concluding that Islamic circles had received the regime's message: it was in their interest to adhere to the rules as defined by the regime, and the regime alone determined changes in state politics. The amnesty, however, especially of the parliamentarians, raised a number of questions. Was it granted because the king had come under heavy pressure and thus should be seen as an indication of weakness, inconsistency, and insecurity? Was it an act of unqualified royal generosity, or merely a clever tactic, or perhaps the manifestation of the king's self-assurance in dealing with radical Islam? Would amnesty be a regular recourse in dealing with the fundamentalists? And specifically, was the exoneration of Shbailat and Karrash an unprecedented event or were there similar pardons in the past?

In fact, Jordan had witnessed far more unlikely pardons in its history. In 1957, the chief-of-staff of the Jordanian army, Ali Abu Nawar, led a failed revolt against Hussein. Not only was he not executed: he was granted a pardon and allowed to return to Jordan from exile in Egypt. General Ali Khiari, Abu Nawar's deputy and fellow conspirator, was also permitted to return to Jordan. Similarly, Nadir Rashid, a Free Officer who had conspired to fell the regime, was granted royal amnesty, and was later put in charge of internal security.[45] The king also pardoned other high-ranking Jordanians who had plotted against the regime, including Colonel Abdullah Tal, the governor of Jerusalem in 1948–49, who was sentenced to death in absentia for involvement in the murder of King Abdullah, but was allowed to return to Jordan in the 1960s and was even appointed senator.[46]

Clearly, then, the pardon of Shbailat and Krarash was not an isolated case of amnesty. Moreover, Shbailat was arrested again in early 1996 and sentenced to three years in prison for disparaging the king and his family. Once more, however, Shbailat won a pardon on the occasion of the king's birthday. In a surprise gesture on Friday, November 8, 1996, Hussein drove to Sowaka prison eighty kilometers south of Amman, picked up Shbailat in his car, and drove him to Shbailat's mother's house in Amman. An hour and a half later, Jordanian citizens watched the episode on national television.[47] In the following days, as part of a general amnesty on November 14, the king released all of the citizens arrested during the recent food riots (though security prisoners remained imprisoned).

Amnesty thus appeared as a proven recourse for dealing with radical Islam and other opponents of the regime. The king made wise use of the royal pardon both as a deterrent message and as a means of alleviating political tension.

The Regime and the Hamas Infrastructure in Jordan

In December 1987, immediately after the Hamas movement was founded in Israel's territories, it began developing its infrastructure abroad. The movement established itself in several Arab capitals, and by the mid-1990s it had offices in Amman, Damascus, Beirut, Tehran, Khartoum, Yemen, and a number of the Gulf states. Egypt refused Hamas representation on its soil since the Mubarak regime regarded the movement as an outgrowth of the Muslim Brotherhood and therefore a strategic threat to Egyptian stability.

Hamas was keen on developing an organizational infrastructure in Jordan: Jordan's proximity to Israel and the territories rendered it a strategic staging ground for operations against Israel, and the large concentration of Palestinians and the presence of the parent movement in Jordan, the Muslim Brotherhood, afforded Hamas a strong support base. Indeed, the Jordanian Muslim Brotherhood regarded itself as Hamas' patron in Jordan, helping it financially and in negotiations with the authorities. In some cases Muslim Brotherhood activists in Jordan joined Hamas, and the Brotherhood in Jordan was quick to voice its support of the movement when Hamas staged attacks in the territories or Israel.

Intense Israeli pressure on Hamas in the territories, in response to murderous attacks by the movement in the late 1980s and early 1990s, forced many Hamas members to seek refuge in Jordan. Israel expelled many Hamas activists from the territories and arrested hundreds of others, including senior commanders. The leader of Hamas, Ahmed Yassin, was arrested in May 1989 and sentenced to life imprisonment. These developments depleted the Hamas reservoir of activists and leaders in the territories and contributed to the establishment of the senior leadership abroad, especially in Jordan. Within the kingdom a complete, self-contained, rear-guard, organizational network flourished that absorbed activists and coordinated Hamas activity in the territories during and after the intifada of 1987–93.

Hamas' highest unit in Jordan was the political bureau (*al-maktab al-siyasi*), chaired by Dr. Musa Abu Marzouk since early 1989, which directed all aspects of Hamas activity in the territories. Abu Marzouk was born in Rafah on the Egyptian–Gaza border, joined the Muslim Brotherhood in his twenties, and became an associate of Ahmed Yassin. Another important body established in Jordan was the Internal Committee, chaired at the time by Gazan-born Emad al-Alami. This committee coordinated Hamas' operational–military activity in the territories. The director of Hamas offices and the movement's official representative in Jordan was Mohammad Nazal, a native of Kabatia in Samaria. The movement's spokesman was Ibrahim Ghosha, an engineer originally from Jerusalem.

Alongside these bodies, a secret military unit (*gihaz askari*) was set up to recruit new members and handle training and instruction in Jordan. The connection between the headquarters in Jordan and the Hamas cells in the territories was maintained mostly by go-betweens who relayed messages, cash, and instructions for attacks. During the 1990s the Jordanian headquarters smuggled money and fighting matériel into the territories despite Jordan's surveillance of the border and the army's efforts to intercept such activity.

The regime permitted Hamas offices to operate in Amman legally and publicly, provided they did not overstep the red lines delineated by the authorities. The movement was explicitly warned not to use the Israeli–Jordanian border for activity in the territories or Israel, and not to exploit Jordanian soil for covert military activity. The regime also stipulated that only holders of a Jordanian passport could join Hamas. Although Hamas pledged to honor the conditions, the organization readily conducted training exercises on Jordanian soil, transferred money and matériel, and directed attacks from across the border.

In 1991, after the Gulf War, the Jordanians apprehended a large Hamas group – the Jihad Action Committee (Lajnat al-'Amal al-Jihadi) – in which the head of the Hamas Political Bureau, Abu Marzouk, was involved. In the same operation, four large weapons caches were uncovered in Amman, which included 130 Kalashnikov assault rifles and hundreds of hand grenades. Although Jordanian intelligence officers initially believed that the caches were intended for use against the regime, they later accepted the Hamas version that the weapons were planned for use against Israel in the territories. As a result, all of the detained suspects were released during the general amnesty, whereupon many fled to Syria. This large Hamas ring in Jordan thus disbanded, and no similar groups were subsequently uncovered.

The signing of the Israeli–Jordanian peace treaty in October 1994 was a turning point in the regime's relations with Hamas. The treaty committed Jordan to combating terrorism and terrorism's infrastructure on its soil, while given the agreements between Israel, the PLO, and the PA, any Hamas operations against Israel were wont to hurt the Palestinian cause. Jordan also feared the international arena would accuse it of providing a safe haven for a terrorist organization, and punish it with economic sanctions. Thus surveillance of Hamas was tightened, and following complaints by Israel and the PA about Hamas' freedom of action, Jordanian authorities began calling in official Hamas representatives for warnings. Hamas lowered its profile for a while, but after the Hamas attacks on the Gaza Strip Israeli settlements of Kfar Darom and Netzarim in April 1995, Jordan authorities, responding to pressure from Israel and from Arafat, arrested Hamas activists and expelled two senior Hamas figures, Abu Marzouk and

Emad al-Alami, neither of whom had Jordanian citizenship. Other Hamas activists were likewise arrested. The king, in deference to Arafat at a meeting with the PA chairman on May 24, declared, "There is no leadership other than Arafat's, and no organization other than the PLO. We will not cooperate with nor allow any organization to operate on Jordanian soil that runs counter to this view."[48] Yet while Hamas activists lowered their profile in light of the regime's actions, unidentified Hamas sources expressed outrage at Jordan's violation of its agreement with the movement, though they acknowledged that it was not Hamas' intention to clash with the regime.

After the murderous suicide attacks in Jerusalem and Tel Aviv in late February–early March 1996, the Muslim Brotherhood in Jordan publicly affirmed its support of the strikes by Hamas and other groups in the struggle for Palestine. The announcement stated that the entire Islamic nation stood behind the attacks, and Muslim religious leaders and Islamic political activists issued a religious edict condoning acts of suicide against Israel. In March 1996 one such edict was signed by twenty-seven leading religious figures, including eleven members of parliament representing the Islamic bloc. The edict appeared in its entirety in the Islamic newspaper *Al-Sabil*, and proclaimed:

> Regarding the warmongering Jews, it is a religious decree . . . and an obligation to fight and banish them from Palestine . . . Islam permits resistance to the invader and aggressor even if it leads to the death of soldiers or civilians . . . Regarding acts of sacrifice [istish'had], this is a legitimate act and forms the holy war [jihad] . . . Islamic religious thought encourages acts of sacrifice like these on Palestinian soil.[49]

The religious edict was, in effect, the Muslim Brotherhood's challenge to the regime and as such, it crossed well-defined red lines.

Following the wave of suicide attacks inside Israel in February-March 1996 and the summit against terrorism convened in their aftermath in Sharm el-Sheikh, the regime came under heavy pressure from Israel, the United States, moderate Arab states, and the PA. All of the participants urged the Jordanians to move forcibly against Hamas and other Islamic terrorist organizations. The regime responded with scores of arrests, searches, and interrogations. Activists of Hamas, the Muslim Brotherhood, and Islamic Jihad, former members of the Jordanian Afghanis and the Islamic Liberation Party, were rounded up.[50]

The frequent arrests of Hamas activists led to bitter disputes between the Muslim Brotherhood and the government. The Brotherhood defended Hamas and denounced the regime. In a press conference in Amman, Muslim Brotherhood General Controller Dunaybat declared that Hamas operated legally in Jordan in the information and political arenas, and every attack against the organization detracted from the unity of the Jordanian people and amounted to an attack against the Muslim Brotherhood. He also demanded the release of Hamas detainees.[51] Hamza Mansour, an Islamic parliamentary delegate, said that Hamas was part of the Palestinian agenda and that its presence in Jordan served political and propaganda purposes. Suggesting that the regime had been pressured by Israel into moving against Hamas, he also admitted that the Hamas-Islamic Action Front shared a common goal since Hamas sought to liberate Palestine while emphasizing the Palestinian people's Islamic identity. He called on the Jordanian government to reconsider its relations with Israel and Hamas.[52]

Abu Marzouk's role as head of the bureau was assumed by Khaled Mash'al in late 1995. Mash'al was born in 1955 in the village of Silwad near Ramallah. As a youngster he immigrated with his family to Kuwait where he entered the Muslim Brotherhood. He joined Hamas when the movement was founded in late 1987, and was expelled from Kuwait after the 1991 Gulf War along with hundreds of thousands of Palestinians. Mash'al became a member of Hamas' Political Bureau on his arrival in Jordan, and as chairman, he was one of the movement's senior figures. In September 1997 Mash'al found himself at the center of an international incident with political ramifications for Hamas, Jordan, Israel, and the PA, and the interrelations between these parties. On the morning of September 25 two Israeli Mossad agents tried to assassinate Mash'al near his office in Amman. The would-be killers used a lethal chemical weapon and fled the scene. Mash'al's bodyguard pursued the assailants and with the help of passers-by captured them and handed them over to the Jordanian police. Four additional Israeli agents involved in the operation reached the safety of the Israeli embassy in Amman. The following day Mash'al's condition worsened and Hussein demanded that Israel administer an antidote. An Israeli doctor was flown to Jordan to inject Mash'al with a serum, and thereby saved his life.

In the politically delicate aftermath, Israel acceded to Hussein's demand to release Sheikh Ahmed Yassin from jail. Yassin was transferred to Amman for a brief period of hospitalization, and then returned to his home in Gaza where he was greeted by cheering crowds. Israel also freed scores of Palestinian and Jordanian prisoners. In exchange, Israel received its two agents who were held by the Jordanian police and the four agents who had found refuge in the embassy. The incident precipitated a severe crisis in Israeli–Jordanian relations and King Hussein's solid distrust of then Prime Minister Netanyahu. Israeli–Canadian relations also suffered a serious blow as the two assailants were holding false Canadian passports. In the territories Hamas gained widespread public support and rose in credibility, while Arafat's position weakened because it was the king who had freed Yassin from prison. Hatred toward Israel increased in the Arab world.

For his part, Hussein had acted shrewdly in demanding Yassin's release rather than exacting a political concession from Israel. The leader and symbol of Islamic resistance, Sheikh Yassin, was treated by Jordanian doctors in a military hospital reserved for senior government officials after being freed from an Israeli prison thanks to the intervention of the Jordanian monarch. Yassin's arrival in Jordan thus conferred upon his host, King Hussein, national-religious validation, a step that aroused much consternation in the Islamic opposition. And indeed, Hussein displayed impressive diplomacy and tactical flexibility in response to Islamic fundamentalism in other instances as well. After the passage of the Publications Law, for example, which in effect limited the publication of Islamic newspapers, the king agreed to Abu Marzouk's return to Jordan.

But there was also a flip side to the coin. After the assassination attempt, Hamas became a prominent element in Jordanian politics in the November 1997 national elections. Its independent style of operations had made it a model for imitation, even if only briefly, for the Muslim Brotherhood, which traditionally had been submissive to the king and adhered to the regime's rules of the game. After the attempt on Mash'al's life, the Brotherhood stood at the forefront of the Mash'al, Yassin, and Abu Marzouk supporters and the Hamas struggle. The surge in sympathy for Hamas after the botched assassination forced Hussein to come out in open support of movement. The Mash'al affair bestowed on Hamas a degree of immunity in Jordan, if only temporary, as the regime's basic policy toward Hamas did not change. Yet the growing cooperation between Hamas and the Muslim Brotherhood strengthened the Islamic opposition and increased its bargaining position with the regime.[53]

In mid-1998 relations between the Hashemite regime and Hamas began to deteriorate, and the regime took steps to limit the movement's activity. In November, Mash'al, still head of the political bureau, announced that the authorities had begun restricting the movement of Hamas political leaders, who were warned that if they left the kingdom they would not be allowed to return. "This harassment is the result of pressure exerted on Jordan," he stated.[54] Nor did the change in Jordanian leadership with the rise of King Abdullah in February 1999 imply better relations. In September 1999 a senior government official declared that a police raid on Hamas offices the previous month had uncovered dangerous evidence of activity that threatened the stability of the kingdom. Speaking to a reporter of the French News Agency, the official charged that, "Hamas had infiltrated radical elements into the ranks of the Islamists in Jordan and had started directing them and opposition groups in a way reminiscent of the tragic events of Black September in 1970–72." Hamas was also accused of taking control of Muslim Brotherhood institutions and the movement's mouthpiece, *Al-Sabil*. The official further noted that the authorities had thousands of Hamas documents and voice and video recordings testifying to this activity. The Hamas movement, he added, "has violated a gentleman's agreement with us."[55] In the following months, former head of the political bureau, Musa Abu Marzouk, was once again expelled from Jordan and Khaled Mash'al, Ibrahim Ghousha, and two other Hamas leaders were deported to Qatar.

Many people were surprised by the king's move. Hamas leaders had been certain that their strength and the Brotherhood's backing would offset any attempt by the regime to terminate their activity. But King Abdullah had reached the end of his tolerance, and all the pleas of the Muslim Brotherhood to arrive at a compromise with Hamas were of no avail. The king had a few principal reasons for shutting down Hamas activity in Amman and moving forcefully against its leadership. One was an intelligence report that warned of Hamas' intentions of launching an armed coup, to be carried out by people it had trained on Jordanian soil. The second was Arafat's request for the king's help in limiting Hamas influence in Jordan, which incited Hamas leaders inside the PA to escalate violence and terrorism. Furthermore, the United States and Israel were also demanding a halt to Hamas activity in Jordan. The king, however, emphasized that the closing of Hamas offices and the arrest of Hamas activists stemmed only from Jordanian interests and not from external pressure of any kind.[56]

King Abdullah II's Hamas policy was different from his father's. King Hussein arrested and interrogated Hamas members but never went so far as to expel the political leadership and close its offices. Abdullah's moves against Hamas may be seen as a demonstration of self-assurance and the priority extended to what he believed were Jordan's security and political interests.

Deterrent and Stabilizing Factors

Despite the Muslim Brotherhood's agreement to abide by the regime's rules, which allowed it to function legally in the kingdom, the movement regularly assessed the regime's strong and weak points. An evaluation of the balance of power led it to the conclusion that a head-on confrontation with the regime or the recourse to violence would be self-defeating, and perhaps even suicidal. This assessment, long accepted by the Muslim Brotherhood, stemmed from essential deterrent and stabilizing factors: the monarchy – especially King's Hussein's status, personality, and authority; Jordan's geopolitical position; the strength of the Hashemite kingdom and its army; and the operational methods employed by the state's security and intelligence services. These factors have also deterred terrorist groups and other adversaries of the regime.

The Monarchy and Jordanian Society

King Hussein was admired in the kingdom as a man, an Arab nationalist, a Muslim, and a ruler. His personality, background, status, authority, and style offered a broad common denominator to his subjects, including Muslim Brotherhood members, and won his reign popular legitimacy.

According to the Jordanian constitution, the monarchy has both uncontested dominance over the internal balance of forces and priority over parliament. The king is authorized to appoint and dismiss governments and to disperse parliament. He is the supreme commander of the army. Nonetheless, King Hussein acted cautiously in applying the constitution and exerted his authority prudently.[57] He frequently met with his fellow countrymen, talked with them, and demonstrated that he was of their fabric. His bestowal of pardons, even to conspirators against the throne, demonstrated compassion and self-assurance, and he was perceived as courageous, wise, generous, and just. Hussein conducted himself as a devout Muslim, showing reverence for Islam, and as a Hashemite was considered a descendant of Mohammad. Consequently, the power struggle between the regime and the Muslim Brotherhood was less intense than in other countries.

In addition, Islamic activity in Jordan was always recognized by the regime, and the Islamic factor was a key stabilizing element in the country. The Muslim Brotherhood habitually termed the secular government in Arab states a "perverted regime" (*nizam fasik*), but (excluding extremist circles) refrained from applying this expression when referring to the Hashemites.[58] An Islamic Action Front member of parliament, Dib Abdullah, was asked in a press interview about his party's relations with the regime after the signing of the peace treaty with Israel. His reply:

> Regarding the Front's relations with the palace, his Royal Highness derives his legitimacy from the fact that he is an offspring of the [holy] family [*min ahel al bayt*] and a Hashemite Muslim . . . The Islamic movement, both before the peace treaty and afterwards, has no interest in clashing with the regime. First, because this is not a regime [that seeks to spill] blood; and second, because Jordan is the only safe haven for those interested in acting on behalf of Islam in an organized or independent manner. This [freedom] is absent in other countries; therefore a confrontation is not in the interest of the party or the homeland. [59]

On another occasion Abdullah remarked, "We are incapable of establishing an Islamic theocratic state in Jordan, but we can live lives here filled with Islamic content."[60] Overall, the regime succeeded in reaching a working understanding with the Brotherhood even though the movement had been established as a protest against the present order and a vehicle for radical change. Unlike other countries, therefore, Jordan was spared a violent conflict with the Islamic fundamentalists.[61]

Family–Tribal Structure and the Army

The family–tribal structure had a moderating influence in Jordanian politics and society and contributed to the regime's stability. Any individual was very much dependent on the family or tribe. Loyalty to the family–tribal system was not limited to the Bedouin, and was also found in other sectors of society. The Bedouin tribes and long-established, extended Jordanian families formed a strong and determined elite whose destiny was tied to the Hashemite regime. They saw Jordan as their homeland and strove to bolster the regime and defend it.[62] For his part, King Hussein recognized his main sources of support. In his speeches and at meetings with various groups, he enhanced the sense of family and tribal affinity, as well as the common bond to the Arab nation and Islam. At the same time he endeavored to create a uniform, collective national identity, stressing Islamic, tribal, Arab, and Jordanian (or Palestinian) affiliation.[63]

The army's loyalty to the Hashemite regime was a major contribution to Jordan's security and stability throughout its history. Large for a kingdom of Jordan's size, the army's strength and loyalty served to a degree as a deterrent against hostile Islamic groups and other elements that conspired against the state. The armed forces have come to the regime's defense in times of extreme crisis and have quashed domestic and foreign existential threats. In April 1957, for example, when Suleiman al-Nabulsi's government was in power, the chief-of-staff, Ali Abu Nawar, dispatched a Bedouin battalion to the palace to force the king to accept Nabulsi's appointees to government. The Bedouin, who have traditionally been loyal to the king and assumed an important role in the army – with chiefs-of-staff, division commanders, brigade officers, and other senior level officers appointed from their ranks[64] – responded furiously and tried to lynch Abu Nawar, who fled to Syria.[65]

The king appointed a new chief-of-staff, Habes al-Majali, who hailed from the southern tribes. Majali declared martial law for a nineteen-month period, purged the army of hostile elements, and reinstated Bedouin commanders dismissed by Nawar. He also outlawed political parties. Immediately after Majali's appointment more than fifty officers were arrested for plotting against the regime. Only two were Bedouin. Since then Jordanian army officers and enlistees have been carefully screened; distinct priority was given to the recruitment and advancement of native Jordanians and Bedouin, while Palestinian candidates were looked upon with suspicion. Figures from the 1960s indicate that while the Palestinians made up 40–45 percent of the inductees, most of them were posted to technical units, a situation that continued in the following decades. The second and most critical test occurred in 1970–71 when the Jordanian army was ordered to crush the Palestinian organizations' uprising in what many viewed as a civil war struggle between the legitimate government and elements that sought to overthrow it. The army ruthlessly quashed the insurrection.[66]

In the last decades of the twentieth century the armed forces and security and intelligence services were not called upon to intervene in political events but rather served as a psychological buffer that forced the regime's enemies to think twice before undertaking acts of incitement or subversion.[67] With the government's implementation of the containment policy, the Muslim Brotherhood came to respect the skill and effectiveness of Jordan's intelligence services in preventing or frustrating the movement's plans. Also, the king's mustering of the army to crush Palestinian subversion in the early 1970s clearly served as a permanent reminder and ongoing deterrent to the Muslim Brotherhood and other radical Islamic groups.

Concern over Foreign Intervention

Lying at a key geopolitical crossroads, Israel considered Jordan important for its obstruction of a hostile eastern front. Therefore Israel regarded Jordan's stability as a strategic interest and would intervene to save the Hashemite regime. Regional instability could have a disastrous effect on the international flow of oil and the Western economy, and the United States and the West were likewise motivated to avert any overthrow of the Hashemite regime.[68]

King Abdullah I and King Hussein understood – as has King Abdullah II – that of all their neighbors, only Israel could be relied on for immediate assistance in an emergency. One of the main reasons that Hussein maintained ties with Israel, in periods of more or less warmth between the two countries, was Israel's guarantee to preserve Jordanian sovereignty against a foreign or domestic-initiated military coup. Thus, the Hashemite kings were in secret contact with Israeli leaders for decades, and the one rupture between Jerusalem and Amman occurred with the Six Day War and lasted for only three weeks. Although Jordan suffered a devastating defeat in the war, with its borders irreparably altered, it did not change Amman's longtime understanding of Jordan's high priority in Israel's security doctrine. This basic understanding stood the test in 1970 when Hussein needed Israel's help to deter Syria from invading the kingdom. The Israeli–Jordanian peace treaty that was signed on October 26,

1994 transformed the strategic arrangement into an open and official alliance.[69]

The Muslim Brotherhood Policy – Avoiding Violence

The Muslim Brotherhood's decision to avoid a clash with the regime was influenced not only by Jordan's deterrent and stabilizing factors but also by the fate of the movement's counterparts in other Arab states. The recollection of what had befallen its members elsewhere in the previous decades strengthened the view that violence was self-defeating. General Controller Abdel Majid Dunaybat declared in October 1995:

> We have always desired a dialogue [with the government] . . . Our opposition is legitimate and based on our Islamic values and traditions . . . The Muslim Brotherhood has no strategy or policy calling for the destruction of the regime.

Dunaybat went on to state that the Islamic movement in Jordan has had a unique history, different from that of Islamic movements in other Arab states. He reiterated that, "we have been spared the fate of our brothers in Egypt and Algeria. The Islamic experience in Jordan has been . . . a model of Islamic activity."[70]

Jordan's peace treaty with Israel belied the Brotherhood's basic ideological outlook and hampered the movement's promotion of a pragmatic approach toward the regime. But even in this area the Muslim Brotherhood strove to retain proper working relations with the regime. During April–May 1996, the London-based *Al-Hayat* and the Jordan-based *Al-Mushriq* published a series on the Islamic movement in Jordan in light of the peace treaty and democratic process in the kingdom. The articles criticized the Islamic Action Front and Muslim Brotherhood for their internal weakness that had stymied their pursuit of the Islamic movement's goals in various areas. Islamic Action Front member Ibrahim Gharayiba, one of the leading writers of the series, claimed that the party lacked serious leadership and that the Muslim Brotherhood had been overtaken by elitism when certain wealthy individuals had infiltrated the movement in order to advance their own interests.

Alongside this scathing criticism, Gharayiba gave wholehearted support to the continuation of traditional relations between the Islamic movement and the regime. He stressed that the movement's leadership had to remain a non-violent opposition force in the kingdom not only because this corresponded with Islamic tolerance, but also because of the negative repercussions that violent activity against the regime could have on the movement, as in Egypt and Syria. Regarding the Islamic movement's struggle against the peace process with Israel, Gharayiba advocated the pragmatic approach. He reminded his readers how the Brotherhood in

Egypt had accepted the Camp David Accords. Furthermore, thirty-six Islamic members of parliament supported Mubarak's bid for a second six-year term in office in 1987, and Egypt's peace treaty with Israel had not proven an obstacle to their voting. According to Gharayiba, the Islamic movement in Israel went even further and participated in the 1996 Knesset elections. Some observers felt that Hamas might negotiate a ceasefire with Israel and participate in PA elections. Given these examples, Gharayiba said the Islamic movement in Jordan would probably act in similar fashion.

Gharayiba noted that no religious edict in Islam stated that political activity had to follow a particular line. According to Islamic theology, each individual was free to decide on the basis of *ijtihad* (an independent effort at interpretation of the Qur'an and traditions related to the Prophet). To strengthen his claims Gharayiba recalled that even the Islamic movement found nothing amiss with Saladin's agreements with the Crusaders. As for Jordan's democratic process, Gharayiba pointed out that the Islamic movement supported its continuation of the process and had itself benefited from it.[71]

Dr. Abdullah al-Aka'ila, an Islamist member of parliament who represented his movement's moderate camp, expressed a manifestly pragmatic view. He supported the Islamists' participation in government as a means of influencing from within, and claimed that while the goal of the Islamic movement – the establishment of a theocratic state and renewal of the Islamic caliphate – was unattainable, Jordan already had, in effect, the characteristics of an Islamic state. In his view, although the Hashemite regime implemented a containment policy against the Muslim Brotherhood, it was a far milder one than in other Arab countries where the Islamic movement had been suppressed. Aka'ila argued for a rational approach toward the peace agreement with Israel and pointed out that Jordan could not legally abrogate the treaty since it had become enshrined in Jordanian law and international agreement.[72]

In a newspaper interview in late 1996, Jamil Abu Baker, in charge of the Brotherhood's information portfolio, was asked if his movement had not clashed with the regime because it had been a partner in Jordan's political system for the last four years. Abu Baker replied, "The absence of violent clashes and the moderation in [our] activity and positions do not imply that we are part of the establishment. The Muslim Brotherhood, more than any other movement, suffered from persecution during the last two decades." When asked at which point the movement would resort to violence in order to obtain its goal, he answered, "We have not employed violence, and we reject this line [of activity] in the advancement of our goals."[73]

It is common in the world of politics to regard political leaders' declarations skeptically, especially when they refer to relations between government and the opposition. In the case of the Muslim Brotherhood, however, statements made by its leaders and spokesmen repudiating violence and confrontation should be taken seriously. The Muslim Brotherhood in Jordan absorbed the lessons of its brethren in Syria, Egypt, and Algeria who clashed with the regime and paid dearly for it. The Brotherhood was thus reconciled to the fact that the use of violence in Jordan would be counterproductive to its own interests.

Summary

In the 1960s and 1970s the deterrent factors contributing to Jordan's stability proved their ability to restrain and suppress the regime's domestic and foreign enemies, which included Nasserite, pan-Arab subversives, and the Palestinian organizations. When radical Islam emerged as Jordan's main threat in the 1980s, the Hashemite regime again managed to thwart terrorist groups and the Muslim Brotherhood thanks to its deterrent factors and strategy of opposition.

The regime determined the guidelines of the national discourse and the rules of the game according to which the Muslim Brotherhood was permitted to operate. Clearly, the state controlled the Islamists, and not the opposite as in Iran, Sudan, and Algeria. But the Islamists in Jordan were not always a passive element, and the regime often had to take counter-measures, as part of its containment strategy against the Muslim Brotherhood,[74] which was implemented shrewdly and effectively with full coordination between the king and government branches. Using a "carrot and stick" policy in solid proportions, it acted decisively to neutralize hostile activity perpetrated by the Brotherhood and at the same time afforded the movement a number of channels to release pressure when necessary. The regime possessed the required resources and prudence to continue its co-existence with the movement; and the Muslim Brotherhood, in order to survive, generally adhered to the rules of the game.

9 JORDANIAN RESISTANCE TO FUNDAMENTALISM

Throughout King Hussein's reign, many diplomats, political commentators, Middle East experts, and academics predicted that his regime would not survive. This was especially true during domestic or regional crises, as in the 1950s and 1960s when Nasserism sought to undermine the Hashemite regime and the Arab world perceived Jordan as an artificial, illegitimate state. Similar assessments were heard after Jordan's defeat in the Six Day War; during the 1970–71 civil war with the PLO; and in the 1991 Gulf War. A bleak report on the regime's chances of surviving was published following the 1989 and 1996 food riots, as well as when Islamic fundamentalism was on the rise in the 1989 national elections or when it rode the wave of popular enthusiasm for Saddam Hussein during the 1990–91 Gulf crisis.

Three major political assassinations marked Jordan's history, those that targeted King Abdullah and two prime ministers, Haza al-Majali and Wasfi al-Tal. Although Tal's death in 1971 was the last political murder in the Hashemite kingdom, there were many attempts on King Hussein's life and challenges to the regime. At public appearances Hussein would recall his age and the years of his reign, as if to emphasize his endurance. Speaking in Aqaba in 1997, he said: "I thank you for your good wishes today – the forty-fifth anniversary of my coronation. Because of your love, these have been forty-five wonderful years."[1] Jordan proved its survivability despite the misgivings of its enemies, past and present, domestic and foreign.[2]

In the 1980s Jordan's traditional foes – pan-Arabists, Palestinians, and leftists – were replaced by a new rival: Islamic groups, some violent, others non-violent. The Islamists encountered a toughened, experienced regime, no longer the easy prey that Nasser and the Palestinian organizations had assumed in previous decades. Jordan's security and intelligence services used the experience earned from the 1950s through the 1970s of suppressing the subversion that had threatened the kingdom. By penetrating terrorist groups and Islamic organizations and thwarting most of their planned attacks, Jordanian intelligence thus gained effective control over them.

The Muslim Brotherhood's leadership recognized the legitimacy of the Hashemite regime, primarily because of King Hussein's status as a descendant of the Prophet Mohammad, his devotion to Islam, and his outstanding personality. The Hashemite regime, however, was an autocratic, non-religious government, with the primary authority vested in the monarchy that oversees the government's branches. The regime aspired for Jordan to remain a pluralistic nation state with strong links to the West and a commitment to the peace treaty and normalization with Israel. On the other hand, the Muslim Brotherhood has always aimed to Islamize society by subordinating all state institutions, including the monarchy, to Islamic religious doctrine and its ambassadors.[3] In other words, the Brotherhood's goal has been the establishment of an Islamic theocracy in place of the Hashemite regime. Both sides have realized that the gap between them is unbridgeable.

Despite the ideological divide and its political vision, the Muslim Brotherhood avoided violent confrontations with the regime and was likely to continue to do so. The Brotherhood considered the futility of violent confrontation with the Hashemite regime, in part because of its inherent stability and the competency of the Jordanian army and intelligence services, and in part because of the fate of its fellow organizations in Syria, Egypt, and Algeria, which were hit hard by the regimes in those countries. In effect, the Muslim Brotherhood had little choice other than to pursue its activities in the Hashemite kingdom in a relatively restrained manner. Therefore in its work toward Islamization of society and the economy, the Brotherhood chose the path of moderation and used the democratic process to its advantage insofar as was possible.

At the same time, it did not abandon its ultimate vision, and it prepared for the optimal moment to achieve its strategic goal. It was not in a hurry, and patience (*sabr*) was an ingrained value in the movement. Since the regime was aware of this long-term threat, it defined the game rules and red lines that the Muslim Brotherhood was forbidden to cross. Thus, every time the movement deviated from these guidelines, state security and intelligence agencies intervened quickly with strong countermeasures. The regime too wished to avoid a confrontation that could have serious repercussions on Jordanian society. The two sides therefore achieved a political co-existence whose resiliency was tried and proven since the Islamic wave swept through the Middle East beginning in the late 1970s.

Notwithstanding its stability, Jordan wrestled with several weak points that influenced its economic, political, and social development. The economic plight continued to dominate. In 1997, the birthrate stood at 3.5 percent and inflation came to 6.5 percent – figures that indicated a marked reduction in the standard of living, along with the rampant unemployment. The Jordanian public grew embittered over every price rise in basic food stuffs, and was disappointed by the few benefits from the peace agreement with Israel. The country's southern region, traditionally most loyal to the king, was especially hard hit by poverty. The regime's failure to transform the south into a development zone generated a continuous migration to Amman. Moreover, Bedouin and East Bank Jordanians begrudged the economic success of the Palestinians who dominated the kingdom's private sector. If and when the fruits of peace with Israel ripen, they stand to be enjoyed more by the Palestinians in the private sector than by non-Palestinian Jordanians employed in the public sector and security establishment. Because of the Palestinians' superior economic situation and the lessons they internalized from their defeat in the civil war in 1970–71, they were conspicuously absent from the food riots.[4]

Another of Jordan's weak spots related to the prolonged crisis in the Israeli–Palestinian peace process. The regime's interest in peace was not only regional or strategic, like Mubarak's, but also existential. The derailing of the peace process could generate frustration and despair in the occupied territories, which could trigger the migration of tens of thousands of Palestinians eastward to Jordan. The Jordanian economy and the regime's stability could not weather such a shock. The longer the situation was not resolved, the greater the regime's fear that the idea of an "alternative homeland" (alwatan al-badil), that is, a Palestinian state on the East Bank, was likely to garner support among Palestinians and in Israel.[5] The Jordanians were concerned over Israel's expansionist settlement policy in the West Bank and Jerusalem's declared intentions to remain in portions of Judea and Samaria, even in a permanent status agreement. The Jordanians worried that violence in the occupied territories might precipitate the flight of hundreds of thousands of Palestinians into Jordan or that Palestinians would be compelled to move to Jordan because of Israel's discriminatory policy.

The Muslim Brotherhood and other Islamic circles were able to take Jordan's weak spots into account in their regular assessment of the balance of power. In this light, the kingdom's Achilles' heels – economic hardship, unemployment, the lack of major development projects, and the crisis in the peace process – advanced the Islamic movement. When Israel and Jordan signed the peace treaty, expectations soared at the prospective benefits and support for the Muslim Brotherhood declined. But as time passed and the Israeli–Palestinian peace process drew to a standstill, the Brotherhood re-emerged to attack the Jordan's treaty with Israel and the kingdom's leaders who sought normalization with the Zionist entity. An improvement in the economy and reduction in unemployment thus remained the crucial factors in countering Islamic opposition.[6]

Jordan's most unsettling problem in recent years was the loss of its immensely admired king, who lost his seven-year battle with cancer. Although his illness highlighted the question of inheritance and the kingdom's future and witnessed the deposition of the longstanding crown prince, the transfer of power following his death occurred smoothly. King Hussein died in the Royal Hospital in Amman on February 7, 1999. Several hours after his demise, Abdullah was sworn in before parliament as the king of Jordan.

From the moment that Abdullah became king the Hashemite establishment consolidated around him: the army, the security and intelligence services, tribal heads, the multi-branched, established families, party leaders, and the leaders of the Islamic movement.[7] Furthermore, he signaled that he would continue in his father's footsteps by supporting democratization, improving the economy, fighting subversion and terror, and advancing the peace process. He also adopted his father's Muslim Brotherhood policy, which would reflect acceptance of the Islamic factions but within the boundaries set by the Hashemite regime. Abdullah, a career officer who assumed the monarchy with a lack of experience in running the affairs of state, succeeded in stabilizing the regime thanks to the backing of the country's elite.[8] This elite that supported his father and stubbornly overcame the perilous crises the kingdom faced after the murder of King Abdullah I would likely do all that it could to ensure that the rule of his great-grandson, Abdullah II, will remain stable and secure.

RADICAL ISLAM IN EGYPT AND JORDAN: AN INTEGRATIVE CONCLUSION

A summary of the Islamic wave of the 1990s requires a comparison of Islamic radicalism in Egypt and Jordan and the strategies each regime adopted for dealing with it. However, by definition such a comparison is difficult. Islamic radicalism arose mainly in nation states such as Egypt, Jordan, and Algeria in the last two decades of the twentieth century. Predictably, local conditions heavily influenced the movement's development, operations, and relations with the government. It is, for example, difficult to compare Islamic radicalism in Egypt with its counterpart in Jordan because of basic differences between the two states: population, size, land area, regime type, historical legacy, and the nature of each country's domestic problems. A comparison highlights the differences more than the similarities, and thus the story of Islamic fundamentalism in each state is its own narrative.

Islamic radicalism promotes the strategic goal of the seizure of government and establishment of an Islamic theocratic state. It is manifested in two principal modes of operation: the widespread non-violent trend, represented mainly by the Muslim Brotherhood; and the violent trend, represented by terrorist groups. The regimes of both countries viewed Islamic radicalism as a long-term, strategic danger, but the diverse conditions between the states meant that there were differences, often salient ones, in almost every aspect of Islamic radicalism and their responses to the threat it posed (see the tables: "The Muslim Brotherhood in Egypt and Jordan," on the opposite page; "Islamic Violence and Terrorism in Jordan," p. 241).

Islamic radicalism embarked upon three paths to attain its strategic goal: *da'wa* (Islamic education and preaching for the Islamization of the society); violence and terrorism; and integration into the democratic process (participation in elections to the Egyptian People's Assembly and Jordanian parliament, and joining the government). Since Islamic fervor began to spread through the Middle East from the end of the 1970s, Islamic radicalism succeeded in the social–cultural arena but failed to attain its primary goal – control of government. At the close of the twentieth century and after a decade of particularly intense activity, Islamic radicalism was in decline.

The Muslim Brotherhood in Egypt and Jordan

	Egypt	Jordan
Historical background	The movement was established in Egypt in 1929 to counter the growing penetration of Western culture and against the background of a severe economic crisis	The movement was established in Jordan in 1945 under the auspices of the Hashemite regime as a counterweight to nationalists, Communists, and left-wing groups.
Relations with the regime	Strong rivals of Nasser, Sadat, and Mubarak. In the 1950s it resorted to violence and terror.	Rivals to the Hashemite regime beginning in the mid-1980s. This was a limited form of rivalry, based on a controlled dynamic of "confrontational coexistence."
Goal	Gradual takeover of the government through the Islamization of society; establishment of an Islamic theocratic state.	
Perception of the regime	Secular	The Hashemite king won legitimacy and admiration in the eyes of the Muslim Brotherhood because of his lineage to the Prophet Mohammad and his image as a devout Muslim.
Legal status	Illegal	Legal
Integration into the political process	Participated in the 1984 and 1987 elections to the People's Assembly. Forced to remain outside the political arena in the 1990 elections, and since then did not participate in elections.	Participated in all the election campaigns in Jordan, excluding its boycott of the November 1997 elections. Joined the government of Mudar Badran in 1991.
Attitude of the regime	Long-term, strategic threat in both countries	
Regime's strategy	"All-out confrontation" designed to emphasize its	A containment strategy intended to prevent the

	illegitimacy. Members of the movement were regularly arrested, interrogated, and tried in military courts.	movement's deviations from the regime's rules of the game. Preventive arrests, interrogations, warnings, but mainly surveillance and supervision.
Outome	As a result of the regime's pressure, the Muslim Brotherhood experienced a serious crisis that its leadership was hard-pressed to overcome. The government rejected the Brotherhood's proposal for a dialogue.	The Muslim Brotherhood operated within the rules of the game; deviation would jeopardize its continued existence under the kingdom's favorable conditions.

Although the regimes adopted a policy of containment, the Islamic movement still wielded much influence on the public in social and cultural matters. The Egyptian regime's policy on family planning, for example, made little headway because Islamic preachers condemned it in the mosques. Occasionally the regime was forced to make concessions on issues such as women's veils, alcohol sales, and the censoring of films, plays, and video cassettes. The Islamic movement in Egypt launched a legal campaign against anti-Islamic behavior, and incited a witch-hunt in the media and mosques against intellectuals associated with religious heresy or deviation. Despite the legal system's opposition to female circumcision, radical activists fomented a public debate in favor of the operation. Islamic fundamentalism regarded all of these issues as a battlefield for society's ethical–normative image. Radical groups, especially the Muslim Brotherhood, had an advantage in this area over Egypt's religious establishment (al-Azhar and the Ministry of Religious Endowments) because of their broad, efficient, well-organized infrastructure in the mosques, preachers associations, and health, education, and welfare institutions.

Social Islam was extremely successful mainly due to the strength and energy of thousands of voluntary Islamic associations spread across Egypt (and to a lesser extent in Jordan). These associations remained powerful and influential in Egypt despite their administrative scandals, the bankruptcy of Islamic financial institutions, and the regime's repressive measures against the Muslim Brotherhood. The Islamic movement's religious message was conveyed through the associations to a vast public, and in this way it recruited many supporters. Conditions in Egypt facilitated the associations' activities, enabling them to assume the state's role in providing educational, welfare, and aid services to hundreds of poverty-stricken neighborhoods. The associations assisted young people and university graduates in finding jobs and housing, thus amassing a large reservoir of new members to Islamic radicalism.

The success of social Islam might have served as a springboard for gaining political power, but this did not happen. The movement, with all its branches, was suppressed and weakened. It failed to reap the political dividends that could have advanced its seizure of government. Another factor impeding the radicals was the public's desire for quiet, stability, and the continued pursuit of Western lifestyles. The radicals tried to Islamize society in order to halt the public tilt toward modernity and secularism, but at the same time they acknowledged the popular opposition to the draping of women in chadors, and the youth's tendency to purchase modern products, view Western films, and listen to rock music. Budget permitting, a television was standard in almost every home. All of these trends stirred up doubts among Islamic activists over their ability to convince the masses that Islam is the solution.

Islamic Violence and Terrorism in Egypt and Jordan

	Egypt	Jordan
Organizational framework	Local terrorists organizations, some large, arose in Egypt. The dominant organization, al-Jama'a al-Islamiyya, gained support and sympathy in Upper Egypt.	No large local terror organizations in Jordan. During the 1990s terror groups emerged at the rate of one a year, but the regimme suppressed them. Islamic Jihad and Palestinian groups operated in limited fashion, crossing into Jordan from Syria.
Image of the regime	The government of the infidel	
Goal	Seizing control of the government by force and establishing an Islamic theocratic state	
Extent of violence	Islamic violence and terrorism existed in Egypt during the regimes of Nasser and Sadat, and peaked during Mubarak's regime. In the terrorism wave of 1990–99, 3,457 people were killed or wounded.	Very limited Islamic terrorism, and almost no casualties in the 1990s
Public view of terrorist groups	Disgust and condemnation, except in the south	Disgust and condemnation
Regime's strategy	All-out war	All-out war
Outcome	By 1999 the regime succeeded in suppressing the terror wave of the '90s.	No violence or terrorism

The second means the radicals employed to seize control of government was through violence and terrorism. Radical movements and terrorist groups in Egypt and Jordan believed in the efficacy of violence. They attempted to gain control of the government from top to bottom, that is, from the political superstructure to the social infrastructure. By the late 1990s this path had failed in both Egypt and Jordan. The terrorism wave was suppressed in Egypt, and no attacks occurred in Jordan in the latter years of the 1990s. The main reason for the failure of violence and terrorism was the large-scale, aggressive counteraction taken by the two regimes, based on extensive intelligence gathering, operational cooperation with Arab, Muslim, and Western states, iron-handed tactics, collective punishment, and the mobilization of the legal system (for example, Egypt's declaration of a state of emergency and the terrorist trials in military courts). The Egyptian regime isolated the militants, ousted them from the Cairo and Delta regions, forced them to flee to Upper Egypt, and aggravated divisions among their leaders. The willingness of al-Jama'a al-Islamiyya leaders to announce a ceasefire (*hudna*) stemmed from their setbacks and weakened condition. Apparently many Islamic radicals no longer believed in their ability to usurp the government, and the regime derived encouragement in its campaign against Islamic radicalism from the public's disgust with acts of terror.

The third way the radicals tried to capture the government was by integrating into the democratic process. This was not an easy route for the Muslim Brotherhood since democracy, whose source of authority is human, stands in total opposition to Islamic doctrine, whose source of authority and sovereignty is God. Once the Muslim Brotherhood recognized the advantages of participating in the People's Assembly or government, however, it overcame the ideological hurdle and adopted a pragmatic approach. It took part in the 1984 and 1987 elections to the Egyptian People's Assembly after forming an alliance with other parties, and used the parliamentary podium for transmitting the Islamic message. But its attempts to advance Islamic legislation were rejected by a large majority of the government party. The regime eventually forced the Muslim Brotherhood to leave the People's Assembly, and the Brotherhood stayed outside of the 1990 and 1995 elections, convinced that its participation in the legislative body had been a mistake.

In Jordan the Muslim Brotherhood won a stunning victory in the 1989 elections and later, for the first time in its history, joined the government. The Brotherhood's strength declined in the 1993 elections because of a change in the voting system but it remained a substantial opposition. Despite its influence in the Hashemite kingdom, however, it failed to block a peace treaty and the normalization of relations between Jordan and Israel. Like its Egyptian counterpart, the Muslim Brotherhood in Jordan was unable to enact Islamic legislation because of the monarchy's over-whelming strength in parliament. Under pressure from its hawkish wing, the Brotherhood boycotted the 1997 parliamentary elections even though the Hashemite regime, in contrast to the Egyptian regime, permitted it to participate in the democratic process.

Regime pressure naturally contributed to the radicals' failure to inte-grate into the democratic process in Egypt, and to a lesser degree in Jordan, but other factors were also at play. The supporters of democracy in Egypt (intellectuals, liberals, and establishment figures) distrusted the Islamic radicals because of the inherent anti-democratic nature of Islam. They feared that if the Islamic movement developed into a powerful, influential opposition it would exploit the democratic process for establishing an Islamic theocratic regime, like in Sudan or Iran. Islamic activists proclaimed that Islam is democratic and that they would accept a majority decision: this is what Muslim Brotherhood leaders avowed when they decided to take part in the elections to the Egyptian People's Assembly and the Jordanian parliament. But such pronouncements did not dispel public concern. The regime and state security services did not trust the radicals and their rhetoric, while liberal circles hoped for the end of violence and terrorism, or at least for indications of this trend. The key question remained whether Islamic radicalism could genuinely adhere to the polit-ical process' rules of the game.

An article by Professor Emmanuel Sivan published in *Middle East Quarterly* in 1997 noted that independent thinkers in radical circles began discussing this complex situation.[1] Munir Shafik, originally a Christian from northern Jordan who converted to Islam and moved to Lebanon, presented a clearly-stated position. According to Shafik, if radical Islam in fact desired to become part of the political process, it must alleviate fears in the regime and the public by accepting the principles of pluralism and tolerance. Shafik rejected the claim that Islam was equal to democracy because it is loyal to the Shura principle (seeking counsel before the elec-tion of the caliph), as even in the Golden Age of Islam the principle was not applied. Therefore, until the Brotherhood altered its approach, the apprehension of the regimes, their security services, and the liberal middle class would remain intact, especially in light of the Iranian, Sudanese, and Afghani experiences, and the violence and terrorism perpetrated by the radical groups.

Shafik's voice, however, was a cry in the wilderness. Radical groups that chose the parliamentary option were satisfied with declarations such as "Shura equals democracy," but such sloganeering fell short of convincing the regime and liberals of the radicals' credibility. State officials and the general public in Egypt remembered that the Muslim Brotherhood resorted to violence and terror in the 1950s, and that Hassan Tourabi, who often equated Shura with democracy in the 1980s, was the bloodstained leader of the Islamic regime in Sudan. This history did not help the radicals generate credibility. Egyptian liberal circles were divided over the question of trusting Muslim Brotherhood offshoots, for example, groups that founded the Wasat party and declared their commitment to democracy. Islamic radicalism failed to advance its goals in Egypt even when it integrated into the democratic process, and its anti-democratic views aided the regime in expelling it from the People's Assembly. The Hashemite regime permitted the Muslim Brotherhood to participate in the democratic process by "respecting it but suspecting it," while it constantly checked that the game rules were observed.

Overall, the radicals made great strides in social and cultural projects but failed in the political arena. Their successes in establishing Islamic regimes in Iran, Sudan, and Afghanistan (until the toppling of the Taliban regime in December 2001) hardly served as inspiring examples for the Muslim Brotherhood in Egypt and Jordan. The promise "Islam is the solution" remained unrealized and the problems they vowed to solve continued to fester. The Islamic revolution in fact exacerbated economic distress, and in two cases (Sudan and Afghanistan) it precipitated bloody civil wars. These failures could not be concealed from the public.

Thus, the Islamic wave of the 1990s was characterized by two conflicting phenomena. On the one hand, the Muslim Brotherhood won massive support after it set up thousands of voluntary associations that extended assistance to a populace mired in socio-economic indigence. This activity attracted thousands of new members, mostly young people, into the movement's depleted ranks following the regime's crackdowns. On the other hand, acts of violence and terrorism lessened the quality of life, aggravated the national economy, and generated public hostility toward the entire Islamic movement. The situation allowed the regime to isolate the Islamic movement, and cast both trends – the violent and non-violent ones – as a single entity, and justify its hard-handed tactics. This cycle promised to continue unless Islamic radicalism learned to adapt to the rules of the democratic game, and if the regime showed its willingness to integrate the radicals into the political process. An improvement in the economy and rise in the standard of living would increase the chances of this process. However, ongoing economic distress, continued pressure by the regimes on the radicals, and the inherent difficulty of essential change in a fundamentalist movement suggested little imminent change. This is a critical conclusion of the present study.

In the twentieth century Egypt and Jordan successfully dealt with the challenge of Islamic fundamentalism in its violent form and non-violent form (mainly the Muslim Brotherhood). Each regime implemented measures suited to the particular conditions and norms of its country.

Egypt employed a strategy of *à la guerre comme à la guerre* against ruthless Islamic terror that threatened to paralyze life in the state. By the end of the decade the regime had managed to curb the wave of terrorism, but it had no illusions that Islamic violence would not resurface. Terrorism in Egypt was not only political violence but also an expression of socio-economic destitution. The Hashemite regime, on the other hand, had to face small, tightly-organized Islamic terrorist groups for the first time in the 1990s. For three decades, from the 1950s through the 1970s, the regime succeeded in quelling subversion and terrorism stemming from Arab revolutionary regimes and Palestinian organizations. It countered Islamic terror by calling on its highly skilled, confident, and experienced intelligence services.

In both countries the Muslim Brotherhood formed an important social stratum that could not be uprooted. The two regimes defined the Brotherhood as a long-term, strategic threat, and each applied a different strategy in combating it. The Egyptians saw it as a breeding ground for terrorist leaders; therefore they outlawed the movement and adopted an aggressive policy of all-out confrontation. In contrast, the Muslim Brotherhood in Jordan enjoyed a legal status and freedom of movement as long as it kept to the game rules the regime set.

By the end of the 1990s, the Muslim Brotherhood and terror groups did not pose an existential threat to the Egyptian and Jordanian regimes, since there was little chance of their seizing the government in the foreseeable future. They may succeed in toppling a head of state, but not in establishing an Islamic regime. At the same time, both regimes realized that poverty and socio-economic distress were important factors in the future of Islamic radicalism. They were also aware that a solution to these problems was not in sight. Likewise, they acknowledged that it was beyond their power to eradicate Islamic radicalism, and they would face its challenge for a long time ahead.

NOTES

Introduction

1   Moshe Sharon, "The Islamic Factor in the Politics of the Middle East," in *Islamic Fundamentalism* (Tel Aviv: IDF, Combat-Corps Headquarters Intelligence, 1994) [Hebrew].

2   David Menashri, "Introduction," in *Islamic Fundamentalism* (IDF, Combat-Corps Headquarters Intelligence, Tel Aviv, 1994), p. 9 [Hebrew]; Aylon-Shinar, *Arabic–Hebrew Dictionary* (Hebrew University, Jerusalem, 1952), p. 7.

3   Author's conversation with Sheikh Ahmed Yassin in his cell at Ashmoret Prison, Israel, March 6, 1995. The sheikh scornfully rejected the term *usuliya*, claiming that like other terms it was coined by infidels or interested parties.

4   As'ad Abu Khalil, "The Incoherence of Islamic Fundamentalism: Arab Islamic Thought at the End of the 20th Century," *Middle East Journal* 48, no. 4 (1994), pp. 677–8.

5   Ibid.

6   Anwar al-Harawi, "Patriotism, Regionalism, and Internationalism: Two Trends in Fundamentalist Thought," in *The Arab Strategic Report 1994* (Cairo: *Al-Ahram* Center for Political and Strategic Studies, Cairo, 1995), pp. 299–300.

7   "The General Regulations of the Muslim Brotherhood," in Abdullah Fahad al-Nafisi (ed.), *The Islamic Movement: A Look to the Future, Pages of Self-Criticism* (Cairo: Makhtabat Madbouli, 1989), pp. 402–3 [Arabic] [hereafter: "Muslim Brotherhood Regulations"]; Beni Kalvari and Haim Orpaz (eds.), *Hamas, The Islamic Resistance Movement, and the Manifesto* (Jerusalem: Ministry of Education and Culture, Information Center, 1990), p.1 [Hebrew]; the sources emphasize the responsibility of every group in the fundamentalist movement to bring about the Islamization of society and government in its country.

8   Emmanuel Sivan, *Islamic Radicals* (Tel Aviv: Ofakim/Am Oved, 1994), pp. 93–100 [Hebrew]. The term "radical Islam," which I also use in this work, relates (according to Sivan) to the same trend in the Islamic revival movement that claims that Islam has declined and now faces an existential danger because

of the secular–materialist culture of the West, whether directly or because of secular political regimes that have taken control of Islamic countries. According to the radicals, the regimes and political elites that cooperate with the West, including the state's official religious establishment, are the factors responsible for the moral, political, economic, and military decline of the Islamic world. The radical view holds that the secular regimes must be ousted and an Islamic theocracy established in their place. This goal is agreed upon by all the radical organizations but opinion varies regarding the means of attaining the goal: some propose gradual change carried out legally through Islamic education and the winning of people's hearts, and others call for the path of violence and terror.

9   Ibid., pp. 12, 13.
10 Rashid al-Ghanoushi, "Again, We and the West," in Ghanoushi (ed.), *Articles: The Islamic Movement in Tunis* (Paris: Dar al-Karwan, 1984), pp. 59–61 [Arabic].
11 The *mahdi* means the "one rightly guided," that is, by Allah. According to Shiite belief, the *mahdi* is the imam who will appear at the end of days. See: Henri Lammens, *Islam: Beliefs and Institutions* (Jerusalem: Masada Publications, Hebrew University, 1954), p. 14 [Hebrew, translated from the French].
12 Mohammad Hussein Fadlallah, "In Light of the Present Reality in the Islamic World," in Fuad al-Zayn (ed.), *Al-Orfan* (Beirut, 1985), pp. 4–9 [Arabic].
13 Ghanoushi, "Again, We and the West," pp. 59–61.
14 *Time*, November 30, 1992.
15 Matti Steinberg, "When the Lights Go Out," *Davar*, March 25, 1994.
16 Sivan, *Islamic Radicals*, pp. 14, 24, 26.
17 Ibid., p. 37.
18 Ibid., pp. 37–8.

1   Egypt and Islamic Fundamentalism

1   Arnon Sofer, "Egypt: A Traditional Agricultural Society in the Process of Change," in *Egypt: An Anthology of Articles* (Tel Aviv: IDF, Combat-Corps Headquarters Intelligence, 1994), pp. 14–15, 20–8 [Hebrew]; Sever Plotzker, "The Economy in a Burning Condition," *Yediot Ahronot*, September 25, 1994; Eli Podeh, "The Islamic Revival in the Land of the Pharaohs," in *Egypt: An Anthology of Articles*, p. 188; *Ha'aretz*, October 6, 1997; Ami Ayalon, "Egypt," in Ami Ayalon and Bruce Maddy-Weitzman, eds., *Middle East Contemporary Survey (MECS) 1994* (Boulder, CO: Westview Press, 1996), pp. 273–5; *Al-Ahram Weekly*, July 24–30, 1997; "Egypt – Country Report," 3rd Quarter 1997, Economist Intelligence Unit Limited, 1997, 1999, 2000, 2002; Zvi Barel, "President Mubarak's Immunity Depends on the Economy," *Ha'aretz*, December 7, 1999; Zvi Barel, "The So-Called Privatization of the Economy," *Ha'aretz*, October 15, 1999.
2   *October*, May 23, 1993; "Assiut: The Home of Revenge," *Newsweek*, August 2, 1993; conversation with Prof. Saad Eddin Ibrahim at the Ibn Khaldoun Center in Cairo, January 16, 1996.
3   Mamoun Fandy, "Egypt's Islamic Group: Regional Revenge?" *Middle East Journal* 48, no. 4 (1994), pp. 607–12.

4 Gregory R. Copley, *Defense and Foreign Affairs Handbook on Egypt 1995* (International Media Corporation, 1995), p. 132.
5 *International Defense Review* 12 (1993), p. 943.
6 *Ha'aretz*, May 13, 1996.
7 Copley, *Defense and Foreign Affairs Handbook on Egypt 1995*, p. 133.
8 *Ha'aretz*, September 19, 1997; *Yediot Ahronot*, November 19, 20, 1997.
9 Yaakov Baham, "The Muslim Brotherhood Movement in Egypt," in Yaakov Shimoni (ed.), *The New East*, Vol. III, Book 4 (12) (Jerusalem: Hebrew University, 1952), p. 333 [Hebrew].
10 Ibid, p. 334; Yaakov Shimoni and Evyatar Levin, *A Political Lexicon of the Middle East in the 20th Century* (Jerusalem: Dvir, 1971), p. 71 [Hebrew].
11 "Muslim Brotherhood Regulations," pp. 405, 408, 410, 412–15; Boehm, "Muslim Brotherhood Movement in Egypt," pp. 334, 335. Figure 1.1 illustrates the structure of the Muslim Brotherhood in Egypt. A number of secondary functions were added or rescinded in different periods according to the leadership's decision or pressure from the regime.
12 "Muslim Brotherhood Regulations," pp. 405, 408, 412–15; *Al-Musawwar*, May 27, 1994; June 3, 1994; June 10, 1994.
13 *Al-Musawwar*, May 27, 1994; June 3, 1994; June 10, 1994; "Muslim Brotherhood Regulations," pp. 401, 402; Boehm, "Muslim Brotherhood Movement in Egypt," pp. 334, 335; Hala Mustafa, *The Political Reform in Egypt, from the Reform Movement to Violent Groups* (Cairo: *Al-Ahram* Center for Political and Strategic Studies, 1992), pp. 107–30 [Arabic]; Richard P. Mitchell, *The Society of the Muslim Brothers* (London: Oxford University Press, 1969), pp. 161–78.
14 Mitchell, *Society of the Muslim Brothers*, pp. 232, 244, 246; Boehm, "Muslim Brotherhood Movement in Egypt," p. 338; "Muslim Brotherhood Regulations," p. 402.
15 "Muslim Brotherhood Regulations," pp. 403, 404.
16 Boehm, "Muslim Brotherhood Movement in Egypt," pp. 338, 339.
17 Ibid., p. 304.
18 P.G. Vatikiotis, *Egypt, From Mohammad Ali to Sadat* (Jerusalem: Magnes Press, Hebrew University of Jerusalem, 1983), p. 321 [Hebrew].
19 Shimoni and Levin, *Political Lexicon*, p. 18; Boehm, "Muslim Brotherhood Movement in Egypt," pp. 344, 347.
20 Boehm, "Muslim Brotherhood Movement in Egypt," pp. 350–2.
21 *Akhar Sa'ah*, July 14, 1993.
22 *Sabah al-Khier*, April 22, 1993.
23 *The Arab Strategic Report 1993*, (Cairo: *Al-Ahram* Center for Political and Strategic Studies, 1994), pp. 342–3.
24 *Sabah al-Khier*, April 22, 1993.
25 Ibid; Podeh, "Islamic Revival in the Land of the Pharaohs," p. 183.
26 *October*, April 25, 1993.
27 *Davar*, March 12, 1993; *October*, April 25, 1993; Sheikh Omar Abdel Rahman was born in 1938 in the Daqahleya district in the Delta, and received ordination as a sheikh and preacher from al-Azhar University. In this capacity he served as the spiritual leader of al-Jihad in Upper Egypt, and later of al-Jama'a

al-Islamiyya. The sheikh issued many *fatwas*, among them the murder of President Sadat, the assassination of state ministers and senior officials in the government and security establishment, attacks on tourists, and the robbery of jewelry stores for financing the movement's operations.

28 Gehad Auda, "The Normalization of the Islamic Movement in Egypt from the 1970s to the Early 1990s," in N. E. Mary and R. S. Appleby (eds.), *Accounting for Fundamentalism* (Chicago: University of Chicago Press, 1994), pp. 400–1.
29 Yonah Alexander, *Middle East Terrorism: Selected Group Profiles* (Washington D.C.: The Jewish Institute for National Security Affairs, 1994), pp. 48–50.
30 Fandy, "Egypt's Islamic Group: Regional Revenge?" pp. 607, 608.
31 *Al-Ahram*, August 14, 1995; Jeffrey Bartholet, "The Sudan Connection," *Newsweek*, July 10, 1995, pp. 27–8.
32 Alexander, *Middle East Terrorism: Selected Group Profiles*, p. 50.
33 *Sabah al-Khier*, April 22, 1993.
34 *Al-Akhbar*, August 22, 1993; *Roz al-Yussef*, August 30, 1993; *Patterns of Global Terrorism* (US State Department, 1993), pp. 47–8.
35 *Al-Akhbar*, August 17, 1993.
36 Israel Altman, "Islamic Opposition Groups in Sadat's Regime," in *Egypt: An Anthology of Articles*, pp. 141–49; *Sabah al-Khier*, April 22, 1993.
37 *Sabah al-Khier*, April 22, 1993; *Al-Ahram*, September 2, 1987.
38 *Sabah al-Khier*, April 22, 1993; Auda, pp. 401–2.
39 *Al-Akhbar*, May 22, 1993; Auda, pp. 399–400.

2 Egypt's Struggle against the Muslim Brotherhood

1 Ami Ayalon, "The Political Order in Egypt: Continuity and Challenges," in *Egypt: An Anthology of Articles*, pp. 174–75; Hala Mustafa, "The Egyptian Regime and the Opposition in 1994: Challenges and Responses," in *The Arab Strategic Report 1994* (Cairo: Al-Ahram Center for Political and Strategic Studies, 1995), pp. 94, 104, 105, 107.
2 Mustafa, "The Egyptian Regime and the Opposition in 1994."
3 Ayalon, "The Political Order in Egypt," p. 176.
4 David Sagiv, *Davar*, March 12, 1993.
5 Conversation in Cairo with Hussein Ahmed Amin, former Egyptian ambassador to Algeria (1987–90), January 17, 1996.
6 Israel Altman, *Trends in Radicalization in the Positions of the Egyptian Muslim Brotherhood* (Tel Aviv: Shiloach Institute, Tel Aviv University, 1979), pp. 4–10.
7 Saad Eddin Ibrahim, "The Changing Face of Islamic Activism," *Civil Society*, 1995, p. 5.
8 Mustafa, "The Egyptian Regime and the Opposition in 1994," pp. 108–9.
9 R. Springborg, *Mubarak's Egypt: Fragmentation of the Political Order* (London: Westview Press, 1989), pp. 240–1.
10 Auda, "The Normalization of the Islamic Movement," pp. 389–90; and a conversation with Gehad Auda in Cairo on January 16, 1996.
11 Khalil, "The Incoherence of Islamic Fundamentalism," p. 678.
12 Auda, "The Normalization of the Islamic Movement," pp. 389–90.

13   Podeh, "Islamic Revical in the Land of the Pharaohs," p. 187.

14   Auda, "The Normalization of the Islamic Movement," pp. 390–1.

15   *Al-Wafd*, April 29, 1993.

16   *Al-Gumhuriya*, May 7, 1993.

17   *Al-Musawwar*, January 29, 1993, p. 22; Podeh, p. 187.

18   *Al-Sha'ab*, January 8, 1993; *Al-Sha'ab*, February 2, 1993; *The Arab Strategic Report 1992*, pp. 274–5; *Akhar Sa'ah*, December 2, 1993.

19   *Al-Hayat*, January 25, 1997; Guy Bechor, "The Battle for the Mosques," *Ha'aretz*, March 4, 1997.

20   From a conversation by a staff member of the Israeli embassy in Cairo with Abdel Hamid Sa'id, head of the office of the Egyptian minister of religious endowments, February 4, 1997. Different statistics are offered for the number of mosques in Egypt, both those under government control and those under Muslim Brotherhood control. It is thus difficult to assess precisely the extent of the government's success in the struggle for control of the mosques.

21   Guy Bechor, "The Battle of the Mosques," *Ha'aretz*, March 4, 1997.

22   Nemat Guenena, "Islamic Activism in Egypt," *Civil Society*, June 1995, pp. 5–8; and a conversation with Saad Eddin Ibrahim in Cairo, January 16, 1996.

23   *Roz al-Yussef*, May 10, 1993.

24   *Al-Musawwar*, December 18, 1992.

25   Ibrahim, "The Changing Face of Islamic Activism," p. 5.

26   Guenena, pp. 5–8; a conversation with Saad Eddin Ibrahim in Cairo, January 16, 1996; Hala Mustafa, "The Political Regime and the Islamic Opposition in Egypt," in *The State and the Islamic Opposition Movement: Between Ceasefire and Confrontation* (Cairo: Al-Mahroussa Center, 1995), pp. 335–6, 338, 340–2 [Arabic].

27   Rivka Yadlin, "Two Converged by Chance: Democracy and Islam in Egypt," in Meir Litvak (ed.), *Islam and Democracy in the Arab World* (Tel Aviv: HaKibbutz HaMeuhad, 1997), pp. 72–3, 76, 78 [Hebrew].

28   Mustafa, "The Political Regime and the Islamic Opposition in Egypt," p. 316; Mustafa, "The Egyptian Regime and the Opposition in 1994," pp. 108–9.

29   Mustafa, "The Political Regime and the Islamic Opposition in Egypt," pp. 303–6, 317.

30   Mustafa, "The Political Regime and the Islamic Opposition in Egypt," pp. 317, 319.

31   Mustafa, "The Political Regime and the Islamic Opposition in Egypt," pp. 320–1.

32   Mustafa, "The Egyptian Regime and the Opposition in 1994," pp. 109–10.

33   Mustafa, "The Egyptian Regime and the Opposition in 1994," pp. 111–12.

34   Mustafa, "The Egyptian Regime and the Opposition in 1994," pp. 113–14; Auda, "The Normalization of the Islamic Movement," p. 387.

35   Mustafa, "The Egyptian Regime and the Opposition in 1994," pp. 114–15.

36   *Al-Ahram Weekly*, February 5–9, 1995.

37   "Lawyers' Fury," *Civil Society*, June 1994, pp. 4–5. The article is based on newspaper reports, including: *Al-Hayat*, May 15, 1994; *Al-Ahram*, May 18, 1994; *Al-Hayat*, May 19, 1994; *Akhbar al-Yawm*, May 21, 1994.

38   Ayalon, "Egypt," *MECS 1994*, p. 266. For additional details on the continu-

ation of the struggle against the Muslim Brotherhood through the trade unions see the section that follows.

39 *Al-Musawwar*, May 27, 1994, June 3, 1994, June 10, 1994; Makram Mohammad Ahmed, the editor of the weekly, wrote on May 27, 1994 that already for half a year he had been in possession of authentic documents of the Muslim Brotherhood that he considered publishing following a careful examination. But the incidents that the Muslim Brotherhood initiated in reaction to the arrest of Madani on May 17, 1994, brought him to the decision to publish the documents earlier in order to expose the Muslim Brotherhood's plan to seize control of the state, as reflected in the documents.

40 Mustafa, "The Egyptian Regime and the Opposition in 1994," p. 114.

41 Ayalon, "Egypt," *MECS 1994*, p. 266.

42 Conversation in Cairo with Gehad Auda, January 16, 1996.

43 Conversation in Cairo with Saad Eddin Ibrahim, January 16, 1996. See also Ibrahim, "The Changing Face of Islamic Activism," p. 5.

44 Conversation in Cairo with Abdel Moneim Said, January 16, 1996; conversation with an Arab academic on July 14, 1997.

45 Mustafa, "The Egyptian Regime and the Opposition in 1994," p. 115.

46 Ibid.

47 *Al-Ahram Weekly*, February 5–9, 1995.

48 Ibid.

49 Ayalon, "Egypt," *MECS 1994*, p. 267.

50 Ayalon, "Egypt," *MECS 1994*, p. 266. See also note 39.

51 Mustafa, "The Egyptian Regime and the Opposition in 1994," pp. 115–17; Ayalon, "Egypt," *MECS 1994*, pp. 267–70.

52 Guy Bechor, *Ha'aretz*, February 12, 1995.

53 "Military Court in Egypt Sentences 54 Leaders of the Muslim Brotherhood Movement to Jail," *Ha'aretz*, November 24, 1995.

54 Guy Bechor, "Egyptian Terror takes the Initiative," *Ha'aretz*, January 4, 1995.

55 *Al-Hayat*, February 2, 1995. The Egyptian legislative body is comprised of two houses: the parliament and the advisory council (Shura). The latter is an insignificant advisory forum, consisting of former politicians, public figures, academics, and artists. Some are elected and some are appointed by the president. See Ayalon, "The Political Order in Egypt," p.169.

56 Guy Bechor, *Ha'aretz*, September 13, 1995.

57 *Al-Majala*, September 17, 1995.

58 *Roz al-Yussef*, July 24, 1995.

59 *Al-Hayat*, October 9, 1995.

60 *Al-Hayat*, July 26, 1995; *Roz al-Yussef*, October 2, 1995, *Filastin al-Muslima*, October 1995, p. 27.

61 "Egyptian Authorities Disperse 11 Election Rallies of Muslim Groups, Arrest 400 Supporters," *Ha'aretz*, November 28, 1995.

62 Saad Eddin Ibrahim, "Civil Society and Electoral Politics in Egypt," *Civil Society*, December 1995, p. 4.

63 Guy Bechor, *Ha'aretz*, December 1, 1995.

64 Hamad Rizek, "The Secrets of the World Organization of the 'Muslim Brotherhood,'" *Al-Musawwar*, February 17, 1995; the document was appar-

ently published with the direction of the regime. I point out many details from its content since it gives important background for understanding the trend of the regime to attack the Muslim Brotherhood because of its link to the world organization. I use both the terms "world organization" and "international organization" because they appear in different sources.

65 *Al-Usbu al-Arabi*, February 6, 1995.
66 *Al-Ahram*, August 28, 1995.
67 *Al-Sharq al-Awsat*, August 29, 1995.
68 "The Secrets of the Muslim Brotherhood World Organization," *Al-Musawwar*, February 17, 1995; and a conversation with an Arab academic, July 14, 1997.
69 A conversation in Cairo with Abdel Moneim Said, January 16, 1996.
70 *Al-Ahram*, November 7, 1995; *Al-Gumhuriya*, November 28, 1995; French news agency from Cairo, October 30, 1995.
71 Cairo Mena, April 2, 1996, in *FBIS NES*, April 3, 1996.
72 *Ha'aretz*, November 28, 1995; see also below, chapter 4, "Cooperation with Western Countries."
73 *Al-Sharq al-Awsat*, March 5, 1996, in *FBIS NES*, March 6, 1996.
74 Hamed Abu Nasser was the fourth general guide of the Muslim Brotherhood. Before him were the founder, Hassan al-Banna, who was murdered in February 1945; the second was Ismail al-Houdeibi; the third, Omar al-Talmasani; Abu Nasser was appointed to his office in 1986. Mustafa Mashour became the fifth general guide.
75 Guy Bechor, "The General Guide: Militant Turned Peacemaker," *Ha'aretz*, February 6, 1996.
76 *Al-Hayat*, February 13, 1996.
77 *Al-Ahali*, February 2, 1996.
78 *Al-Hayat*, October 10, 1996.
79 *Al-Hayat*, May 18, 1996, in *FBIS NES*, May 21, 1996.
80 *Al-Ahali*, February 7, 1996.
81 Guy Bechor, "Muslim Underground Planned to Topple Egyptian Regime and Establish Islamic State," *Ha'aretz*, December 30, 1996.
82 Radio Tehran, March 22, 1998; Egyptian News Agency Mena, March 22, 1998.
83 Egyptian News Agency Mena, November 1, 3, 9, 1998.
84 *Al-Masa*, January 15, 1999.
85 *Al-Hayat*, January 5, 1999.
86 Middle East News Agency, October 16, 1999; Egyptian News Agency Mena, October 16, 1999.
87 *Al-Arabi*, October 19, 1999.
88 *Al-Sharq al-Awsat*, November 4, 1999.
89 *Al-Sha'ab*, November 30, 1999.
90 *Civil Society*, April 2000, p. 26.
91 *Al-Hayat*, August 15, 2000.
92 Cairo Mena, November 19, 2000.
93 *Civil Society*, September 1999, p. 4.
94 *Al-Hayat*, July 14, 1998.

95 *Al-Hayat*, July 29, 1998.
96 *Al-Hayat*, September 28, 1999.
97 *Al-Hayat*, July 29, 2000 and August 30, 2000.
98 *Al-Hayat*, November 16–18, 2000.

3 Islamic Terrorism in Egypt

1 Saad Eddin Ibrahim, "The Changing Face of Islamic Activism," pp. 4–6. Ibrahim explained in a study conducted by the Ibn Khaldoun Center and in a personal conversation I had with him in his Cairo office on June 16, 1996 that of the various descriptions being used in academia and the media, such as "the revival of Islam," "Islamic extremists," "Islamic fundamentalism," and "political Islam," he decided to use the least connotational expression, "Islamic activism." I use the term "Islamic terrorism" when terrorism is the issue. See also Ibrahim, "Arab Modernity and the Challenge of Islam: The Case of Egypt's Islamic Activism – How Much of a Threat?" (Cairo: Ibn Khaldoun Center for Development Studies, July 1994), pp. 6, 7, 9.
2 Saad Eddin Ibrahim, "Arab Modernity and the Challenge of Islam," pp. 6, 7, 9; and *The Arab Strategic Report 1998* [Arabic], p. 343, and *The Arab Strategic Report 1999* [Arabic], pp. 324–5, both published by the *Al-Ahram* Center in Cairo.
3 Ami Ayalon, "Egypt," in Ami Ayalon (ed.), *Middle East Contemporary Survey 1992* (Tel Aviv: The Moshe Dayan Center, Tel Aviv University, and San Francisco: Westview Press, 1995), p. 364.
4 Ibrahim, "The Changing Face of Islamic Activism," pp. 5–6; *Civil Society*, January 1997, p. 14; *Al-Musawwar*, February 5, 1993, p. 18; *Al-Ahram Weekly*, January 22–28, 1998.
5 Nemat Guenena, "Islamic Activism in Egypt," *Civil Society*, June 1995, pp. 5–8.
6 Ibrahim, "The Changing Face of Islamic Activism," p. 6.
7 Guenena, "Islamic Activism in Egypt," pp. 5–8.
8 Fandy, "Egypt's Islamic Group: Regional Revenge?" pp. 607–12.
9 *October*, May 23, 1993.
10 Fandy, "Egypt's Islamic Group: Regional Revenge?" p. 625.
11 *October*, May 23, 1993.
12 Nemat Guenena and Saad Eddin Ibrahim, *The Changing Face of Egypt's Islamic Activism*, 2nd Draft (Cairo: Ibn Khaldoun Center for Development Studies, 1997), p. 57.
13 *The Arab Strategic Report 1993*, pp. 437–8.
14 *Roz al-Yussef*, May 17, 1993; *Intelligence Newsletter*, April 21, 1994.
15 *Roz al-Yussef*, January 11, 1993.
16 Conversation with Abdel Moneim Said at *Al-Ahram* Center for Political and Strategic Studies in Cairo, January 16, 1996.
17 *Roz al-Yussef*, July 19, 1993.
18 *Al-Sha'ab*, June 15, 1993.
19 *Roz al-Yussef*, June 14, 1993, p. 42. During the 1970s, Bedouin traders from the Sinai also used to transfer weapons and mines left in the desert to Palestinian terrorist organizations acting against the Israeli authorities in Gaza.

NOTES TO PP. 92–99

In order to deal with this phenomenon, the Israeli military administration in Gaza and Sinai hired Bedouin collaborators to collect mines and other weapons from the desert, paying them a fixed sum for each item handed over. Phenomenal numbers of mines and other weapons were collected in the framework of this operation, which continued through the remaining years of Israeli administration of these areas. They were brought to fixed places in the desert and destroyed by IDF (Israel Defense Forces) sappers. Source: author's extensive period of security service in Gaza and Sinai.

20   *Akher Sa'ah*, April 28, 1993.

21   *Al-Wafd*, April 10, 1993.

22   *October*, June 27, 1993.

23   *Akher Sa'ah*, March 31, 1993.

24   Emmanuel Sivan, *Ma'ariv*, June 27, 1995.

25   *Ma'ariv*, May 6, 1987; *Davar*, August 30, 1987.

26   *Yediot Ahronot*, August 16, 1987.

27   *Ha'aretz*, December 17, 1989.

28   Guy Bechor, "Egyptian Minister of Interior Injured by Ambush Shooting in Heart of Cairo. Egypt will intensify its steps against the extremists," *Ha'aretz*, August 19, 1993.

29   *Roz al-Yussef*, August 23, 1993, September 2, 1993.

30   *October*, August 22, 1993.

31   *The Arab Strategic Report 1993*, p. 361; *Jerusalem Post*, October 14, 1990.

32   Shai Gabai, *Ma'ariv*, April 21, 1993.

33   Shai Gabai, *Ma'ariv*, November 26. 1993.

34   "Senior Police Officer Murdered by Egyptian Extremists in Upper Egypt," *Ha'aretz*, August 9, 1993.

35   *The Arab Strategic Report 1994*, pp. 474–5.

36   "Islamic Extremists in Egypt Shot to Death Eight Policemen and Three Civilians," *Ha'aretz*, January 3, 1995.

37   *Hadashot*, June 5, 1987; Podeh, "Islamic Revival in the Land of the Pharaohs," p. 185.

38   Ayalon, "Egypt," *MECS 1992*, pp. 368–9.

39   "Death Sentence for Two Perpetrators of Attempt on Life of Egyptian Writer Naguib Mahfouz," *Ha'aretz*, January 11, 1995; *The Arab Strategic Report 1994*, pp. 476–7.

40   *Newsweek*, June 19, 1995; Guy Bechor, "Foreign Reports in Cairo: Attempt by Islamic Extremists to Murder Mubarak Thwarted," *Ha'aretz*, January 6, 1997.

41   Podeh, "Islamic Revival in the Land of the Pharaohs," p. 185.

42   Guy Bechor, *Ha'aretz*, March 31, 1993.

43   Ayalon, "Egypt," *MECS 1992*, p. 370.

44   *Al-Ahram*, April 29, 1993.

45   Ayalon, "Egypt," *MECS 1992*, pp. 370–1; Guy Bechor, *Ha'aretz*, March 31, 1993.

46   Ayalon, "Egypt," *MECS 1992*, p. 370.

47   *International Herald Tribune*, March 17, 1993.

48   Guy Bechor, "Fundamentalistic Organization Calls on Business People to

Liquidate their Investments in Egypt," *Ha'aretz*, March 7, 1993.

49   *Newsweek*, August 2, 1993, p. 25.
50   Guy Bechor, "Bomb Explodes in One of the Pyramids at Giza," *Ha'aretz*, March 31, 1993; *Ma'ariv*, March 31, 1993.
51   Ibrahim, "The Changing Face of Islamic Activism," p. 6.
52   *Al-Musawwar*, April 9, 1993.
53   *Al-Wafd*, February 12, 1993.
54   *Al-Ahram*, June 18, 1993.
55   Podeh, "Islamic Revival in the Land of the Pharaohs," p. 185.
56   "Eight Austrian Tourists Injured in Shooting Attack on Bus in Cairo," *Ha'aretz*, December 28, 1993.
57   *Ha'aretz*, February 20, 1994.
58   *International Herald Tribune*, February 24, 1994.
59   *Patterns of Global Terrorism* (US State Department, 1995), p. 15; *Ma'ariv*, September 18, 1994.
60   *Ma'ariv*, October 24, 1994.
61   *Ha'aretz*, November 10, 1995.
62   *Jerusalem Post*, April 21, 1996.
63   *Ha'aretz*, September 19, 1997; *Yediot Ahronot*, September 19, 1997.
64   *Ha'aretz*, November 18 and 19, 1997; *Yediot Ahronot*, November 18, 19, and 20, 1997; *Al-Ahram*, November 19 and 20, 1997.
65   *The Arab Strategic Report 1993*, p. 363; Fandy, "Egypt's Islamic Group: Regional Revenge?" p. 623; *Akher Sa'ah*, December 16, 1992.
66   *Jerusalem Post*, August 30, 1988.
67   *Risk*, September 30, 1988.
68   *The Arab Strategic Report 1992*, p. 279. The slogan "the Copts are under our protection" expresses the traditional attitude in Islam toward non-Islamic religious minorities.
69   Ayalon, "Egypt," *MECS 1992*, p. 367.
70   D. Vardi, *Ha'aretz*, August 29, 1994.
71   Guy Bechor, *Ha'aretz*, February 27, 1996.
72   *Jerusalem Post*, February 16, 1997; *Al-Ahram Weekly*, December 26, 1996–January 1, 1997; Guy Bechor, "When the Cross Embraces the Crescent," *Ha'aretz*, March 9, 1997; *Civil Society*, April 1997, pp. 4, 6, 7.
73   Smadar Perry, *Yediot Ahronot*, November 20, 1995; Oded Granot, *Ma'ariv*, November 20, 1995.
74   "At Least 30 Dead and 100 Injured in Car-Bomb Explosion in Northern Pakistan," *Ha'aretz*, December 22, 1995.
75   Tzadok Yehezkeli, "Sheikh Rahman – Guilty of Terrorism," *Yediot Ahronot*, October 2, 1995; Shlomo Shamir, "Sheikh Abdel Rahman and Nine Cohorts Convicted of Conspiracy to Carry Out Terrorist Attacks in US," *Ha'aretz*, October 2, 1995.
76   "Defense Officials in Italy: Muslim Extremists Planned to Assassinate Mubarak in Rome in 1994," *Ha'aretz*, June 27, 1995.
77   "Three Egyptians Arrested on Suspicion of Planning Terrorist Actions against Jewish Targets in Copenhagen," *Ha'aretz*, July 23, 1995.
78   "The Sudan Connection," *Newsweek*, July 10, 1995.

79 "Egyptian Organization, al-Jama'a al-Islamiyya, Claimed Responsibility for the Assassination Attempt," *Ha'aretz*, June 26, 1995; "Egyptian President: Attackers very Likely Reached Ethiopia via Sudan," *Ha'aretz*, June 27, 1995; *Ha'aretz*, June 29, 1995.

80 *Ha'aretz*, June 27, 1995.

81 "Iraq Praised Assassination Attempt against Mubarak; Iran Denies Connection to the Act," *Ha'aretz*, June 28, 1995.

82 Guy Bechor, "Attempt to Paralyze the Egyptian System," *Ha'aretz*, June 27, 1995.

83 Oded Granot, "With the Back against the Wall," *Ma'ariv*, June 27, 1995.

84 *Al-Ahram*, August 14, 1995.

85 Ibid.; *Newsweek*, July 10, 1995, pp. 27–8.

4 Egypt Battles Islamic Terrorism

1 *The Arab Strategic Report 1992*, p. 280.

2 Ahmed Galal Ezzeddin, "The Phenomenon of Terrorism and Fundamentalist Violence in 1994," in *The Arab Strategic Report 1994* (Cairo: *Al-Ahram* Center for Political and Strategic Studies, 1995), p. 478.

3 *Akhbar al-Yawm*, May 8, 1993.

4 *The Arab Strategic Report 1994*, pp. 477–8.

5 *International Defense Review*, No. 12, 1993, pp. 943–4.

6 Ayalon, "Egypt," *MECS 1992*, p. 368.

7 Ayalon, "Egypt," *MECS 1992*, pp. 368, 371; Shefi Gabai, *Ma'ariv*, December 13, 1992; Oded Granot, *Ma'ariv*, December 15, 1992, Guy Bechor, "Hollywood of the East has Turned into Little Tehran," *Ha'aretz*, December 14, 1992; "Moslem Extremists Threaten Tourists, Embassies in Cairo," *Jerusalem Post*, December 15, 1992; *Akher Sa'ah*, December 16, 1992; *Roz al-Yussef*, December 14, 1992. During my visit to Cairo in January 1996, I learned of the significance of Imbaba from researchers, government sources, and personal observation. Among the Islamic radicals, Imbaba is a symbol of the legacy of war and opposition to the regime. In the eyes of the government, Imbaba symbolizes the complexity of the problem. This is much of the rationale for giving the incident so much attention in these pages.

8 Guy Bechor, *Ha'aretz*, March 11, 1993.

9 Shefi Gabai, *Ma'ariv*, March 19, 1993.

10 *International Defense Review*, No. 12, 1993, pp. 943–4.

11 Ayalon, "Egypt," *MECS 1992*, p. 371.

12 Guy Bechor, "New Game Rules in Egypt," *Ha'aretz*, March 11, 1993.

13 *Al-Ahram*, September 6, 1993.

14 Guy Bechor, "A Prison the Size of a City," *Ha'aretz*, December 28, 1992.

15 *Roz al-Yussef*, September 6, 1993.

16 *Al-Ahram*, September 6, 1993.

17 *Al-Ahram*, September 8, 1993.

18 *Roz al-Yussef*, April 19, 1993, *Al-Wafd*, April, 22, 1993.

19 *Al-Musawwar*, April 23, 1993.

20 Podeh, "Islamic Revival in the Land of the Pharaohs," p. 187.

21 *October*, April 25, 1993.

22 Ezzeddin, "The Phenomenon of Terrorism and Fundamentalist Violence in 1994," pp. 479–80.
23 Podeh, "Islamic Revival in the Land of the Pharaohs," p. 187.
24 Ezzeddin, "The Phenomenon of Terrorism and Fundamentalist Violence in 1994," pp. 479–80.
25 *Roz al-Yussef*, June 14, 1993; *Akher Sa'ah*, March 31, 1993.
26 *International Defense Review*, No. 12, 1993, p. 944.
27 *Ha'aretz*, July 16, 1993.
28 Podeh, "Islamic Revival in the Land of the Pharaohs," p. 186.
29 *International Herald Tribune*, May 16, 1994.
30 Ezzeddin, "The Phenomenon of Terrorism and Fundamentalist Violence in 1994," pp. 480, 482.
31 *Jerusalem Post*, January 10, 1995; *Civil Society*, May, 1995, p. 6.
32 *International Herald Tribune*, January 17, 1995; Guy Bechor, *Ha'aretz*, September 16, 1997.
33 *Ha'aretz*, February 1, 1995.
34 Cairo Mena, March 17, 1996, in *FBIS NES*, March 18, 1996.
35 Guy Bechor, "No to Violence, No to Dialogue," *Ha'aretz*, September 16, 1997; *Ha'aretz*, November 21, 1997; Khaled Daoud, "Ceasefire in the Balance," *Al-Ahram Weekly*, Aug. 28–Sep. 3, 1997; *Al-Ahram Weekly*, July 10–16, 1997, July 17–23, 1997, July 24–30, 1997. For further information on *hudna* see Lammens, *Islam: Beliefs and Institutions*, pp. 24–26; Bernard Lewis, *The Arabs in History* (Tel Aviv: Tushia Publishing, 1995, translation from English), pp. 43–44; conversation with Hamas leader Sheik Ahmed Yassin on March 5, 1995 in his jail cell in Israel; *Al-Sabil*, March 22, 1995, on the issuance of a *fatwa* (Islamic religious edict) regarding a *hudna* by Mohammad Suliman al-Ashkar.
36 *The Arab Strategic Report 1998*, pp. 337–9; *Al-Hayat*, August 13, 2000; *Patterns of Global Terrorism* (US State Department, 1998).
37 *The Arab Strategic Report 1998*, pp. 340–2.
38 *The Arab Strategic Report 1999*, pp. 324–5; *Patterns of Global Terrorism* (US State Department, 1999), p. 27–8; *Ha'aretz*, September 27, 2000.
39 Ayalon, "Egypt," *MECS 1992*, pp. 369, 370.
40 Podeh, "Islamic Revival in the Land of the Pharaohs," p. 186.
41 *The Arab Strategic Report 1994*, p. 380.
42 Amr Hashem Rabie, *The Arab Strategic Report 1994*, pp. 422–3.
43 Ayalon, "Egypt," *MECS 1992*, p. 372.
44 *The Arab Strategic Report 1994*, p. 380.
45 "The Military Courts – Disregard for Democracy," *Al-Wafd*, September 5, 1995.
46 Podeh, "Islamic Revival in the Land of the Pharaohs," p. 186; *Ma'ariv*, August 17, 1993 and December 21, 1993; "The Terrorism and Bilateral Escalation – 1993," *1993 Misr al-Mahroussa Report* (Cairo: Al-Mahroussa Center for Newspaper Distribution, Services, and Information, 1995), p. 409 [Arabic].
47 Shefi Gabai, "Five Islamic Extremists Who Tried to Murder Egyptian Minister Hanged," *Ma'ariv*, August 23, 1994.

48 "Six Islamic Extremist Executed in Egypt for Incursions from Sudanese Territory," *Ha'aretz*, June 4, 1996.
49 Conversation with an Arab academic on July 14, 1997 and June 16, 2000.
50 Podeh, "Islamic Revival in the Land of the Pharaohs," p. 186.
51 Ayalon, "The Political Order in Egypt," p. 176.
52 D. Vardi, *Ha'aretz*, August 29, 1994; conversation with an Arab academic on July 14, 1997; the concept of *mutha*, accepted among the Shiites, is a marriage for a limited period of time. In reference to *mutha*, see also Lammens, *Islam: Beliefs and Institutions*, p. 117. Lammens elucidates that *mutha* is one of the most outstanding theological disagreements between the Shia and Sunni Islam. Observant Sunnis regard *mutha* as adultery, and thus null and void.
53 Conversation with Abdel Moneim Said, head of *Al-Ahram* Center, at his office in Cairo, January 16, 1996; *Al-Gumhuriya*, June 30, 1993; *Roz al-Yussef*, July 19, 1993.
54 Ehud Ya'ari, "The Afghanis are Coming," *Ma'ariv*, July 5, 1996. Because it was never properly documented, estimates vary as to how many volunteers belonged to the Arab Brigade in Afghanistan. One commonly cited estimate put the number of volunteers from the Middle East at some 5,000. See Abdel Salam Sidahmed and Anoushiravan Ehteshami (eds.), *Islamic Fundamentalism* (Boulder, CO: Westview Press, 1996), p. 127.
55 Ya'ari, "The Afghanis are Coming."
56 Nagwa El-Gamal et al., "The Issue of Terrorism," *The Arab Strategic Report 1993*, p. 436.
57 Guy Bechor, "Religious Fundamentalists in Egypt Intensify Their Struggle: Threaten to Attack Foreign Embassies," *Ha'aretz*, December 15, 1992. Among the names of the wanted men listed in the extradition request were: Mohammad Shouki Islambouli, brother of the man who assassinated President Sadat; Mustafa Hassan Hamza, head of the military arm of al-Jama'a al-Islamiyya; Rifa'i Ahmed Taha; Othman Khaled Ibrahim Salman; Ahmed Mustafa Nawara; Tal'at Mohammad Yassin Hamam; Tal'at Fuad Qassem; all members of al-Jama'a al-Islamiyya who had been sentenced to death in Egypt and had managed to flee the country.
58 El-Gamal et al., "The Issue of Terrorism," p. 441.
59 *Ha'aretz*, May 7, 1993.
60 El-Gamal et al., "The Issue of Terrorism," pp. 436, 441.
61 *Ha'aretz*, June 27, 1996; Zvi Barel, "School for Roadside Bombs," *Ha'aretz*, June 28, 1996.
62 Nitzan Horowitz, "Regime without a Country" and other articles on Afghanistan, *Ha'aretz*, September 29, 1996.
63 *Al-Ahram*, December 31, 1993.
64 *Al-Musawwar*, March 19, 1993.
65 *Sabah al-Khier*, February 4, 1993.
66 *Al-Ahram*, May 7, 1993. Mustafa Hamza planned the attempted assassination of Mubarak in Addis Ababa in June 1995.
67 *Al-Musawwar*, March 13, 1996, in *FBIS NES*, April 2, 1996.
68 Conversation with Arab academic on October 8, 1996.
69 *Al-Musawwar*, April 9, 1993.

70 "Sunday Telegraph: Iran Established System of Training Camps for Terrorists," *Ha'aretz*, July 8, 1996.
71 Conversation with Arab academic on July 14, 1997.
72 *The Arab Strategic Report 1993*, pp. 436–37; *Al-Ahram*, May 7, 1993, June 19, 1993.
73 *The Arab Strategic Report 1993*, p. 442.
74 Podeh, "Islamic Revival in the Land of the Pharaohs," p. 188.
75 *The Arab Strategic Report 1993*, p. 442.
76 *The Arab Strategic Report 1994*, p. 442.
77 Cairo Mena, April 12, 1996; *FBIS NES*.
78 *Ha'aretz*, May 13, 1996.
79 *Ma'ariv*, January 26, 1995.
80 Zvi Barel, "The Independent Life of Terrorism," *Ha'aretz*, January 27, 1995.
81 "Representatives of Industrialized Countries Meet Today to Discuss the Global Struggle with Terrorism," *Ha'aretz*, July 30, 1996.
82 Guy Bechor, *Ha'aretz*, January 6, 1997.
83 *Al-Ahram Weekly*, June 3–9, 1993, April 27–May 3, 1995.
84 *Al-Ahram Weekly*, May 4–10, 1995; El-Gamal et al., "The Issue of Terrorism," p. 443; Podeh, "Islamic Revival in the Land of the Pharaohs," p. 188.
85 *Roz al-Yussef*, March 29, 1993.
86 *Al-Sharq al-Awsat*, July 18, 1995.
87 Zvi Barel, "The Independent Life of Terrorism," *Ha'aretz*, January 27, 1995.
88 Guy Bechor, "Anwar Circling the Globe," *Ha'aretz*, January 6, 1997.
89 *Ha'aretz*, July 31, 1996.
90 *Al-Ahram Weekly*, September 12–18, 1996.
91 Guy Bechor, "The Islamic Problem on the West's Threshold," *Ha'aretz*, August 1, 1996.
92 Guy Bechor, "A War Circling the World," *Ha'aretz*, January 6, 1997.

5 *Egyptian Resistance to Fundamentalism*

1 Jailan Halawi, "Terrorism Down But Not Out," *Al-Ahram Weekly*, December 26, 1996–January 1, 1997.
2 Ezzeddin, "The Phenomenon of Terrorism and Fundamentalist Violence in 1994," pp. 469, 470.
3 A conversation with Abdel Moneim Sa'id in Cairo, January 16, 1996.
4 Conversations with Egyptian civilians in Cairo and on the boardwalk of the Nile, January 16–17, 1996.
5 Ezzeddin, "The Phenomenon of Terrorism and Fundamentalist Violence in 1994," 470, 471.
6 Conversation with an Arab academic, October 1, 1997.
7 Ezzeddin, "The Phenomenon of Terrorism and Fundamentalist Violence in 1994," pp. 480, 481, and conversation with an Arab academic, June 16, 2000.
8 Uri Nir, "Patience and a Number of Intermediary Pleasures," *Ha'aretz*, January 5, 1995; conversation with Matti Steinberg, November 27, 1996.
9 Emmanuel Sivan, "Why Radical Muslims aren't Taking over Governments," *Middle East Quarterly* 12, no. 4 (1997), p. 9; a conversation with Hussein Ahmed Amin in Cairo, January 17, 1996.

10   Conversations in Cairo, January 16, 17, 1996 with Abdel Moneim Said, Saad Eddin Ibrahim, and Hussein Ahmed Amin; a conversation with Shimon Shamir, August 28, 1997.

6   Jordan's Struggle with Subversion and Terrorism

1   N. Sofer, "Jordan," *The Hebrew Encyclopedia* (Jerusalem, 1957) Vol. VI, p. 615 [Hebrew]; Yaakov Shimoni, The *Arab States* (Tel Aviv: Am Oved, 1977), p. 503 [Hebrew]; Asher Susser, "Political Murder in Jordan: The Influence of Violence on Domestic and Foreign Affairs," lecture at the cornerstone laying ceremony of the Yitzhak Rabin House, Tel Aviv University, March 2, 1997.

2   Helen Chapin Metz (ed.), *Jordan: A Country Study* (Washington, D.C.: Federal Research Division, Library of Congress, 1991), p. 36.

3   Ibid, pp. 38–44; Susser, "Political Murder in Jordan."

4   Metz, *Jordan: A Country Study*, p. 229.

5   Conversations with Arab academics, July 23, 1995 and August 20, 1995.

6   Beverly Milton-Edwards, "Climate of Change in Jordan's Islamist Movement," in Sidahmed and Ehteshami (eds.), *Islamic Fundamentalism*, pp. 127–30; *Ha'aretz*, August 17, 1991; *Ha'aretz*, August 18, 1995; Ben Wedeman, "The King's Loyal Opposition?" *Middle East Insight* 11 (January–February 1995), p. 18; Lawrence Tal, "Dealing with Radical Islam: The Case of Jordan," *Survival* 37, no. 3 (1995), p. 140.

7   *Davar*, October 2, 1992.

8   Ibid.; Asher Susser, "Jordan," in *MECS 1992*, pp. 545–7.

9   Guy Bechor, "The Subversive in the Delegate's Suit," *Ha'aretz*, September 9, 1992.

10   Susser, "Jordan," in *MECS 1992*, pp. 545–7.

11   Wedeman, "The King's Loyal Opposition?" p. 16.

12   Susser, "Jordan," in Ami Ayalon (ed.), *Middle East Contemporary Survey 1993* (Boulder, CO: Westview Press, 1995), p. 458; Wedeman, "The King's Loyal Opposition?" p. 18; Beverly Milton-Edwards, "A Temporary Alliance with the Crown: The Islamic Response in Jordan," in James Piscatori (ed.), *Islamic Fundamentalisms and the Gulf Crisis* (Chicago: 1991), p. 95.

13   Susser, "Jordan," in *MECS 1993*, pp. 458–9; Wedeman, "The King's Loyal Opposition?" p. 18; *Sawat al-Sha'ab*, November 19, 1990.

14   Hamed al-Dabbas, *The Islamic Political Movements in Jordan* (Amman: al-Urdun al-Jedid Laldirasat Center, 1995), pp. 56–8 [Arabic].

15   *Khilafa Magazine*, March 1996; conversation with an Arab academic, July 23, 1995.

16   Wedeman, "The King's Loyal Opposition?" p. 18.

17   Susser, "Jordan," in *MECS 1993*, pp. 458–9; Wedeman, "The King's Loyal Opposition?" p. 18.

18   Conversation with an Arab academic, July 23, 1995.

19   "The Youth are Active despite the Arrests – The Liberation Party Circulates an Outline of the Caliphate State in Amman," *Al-Mushriq*, May 30, 1997.

20   Conversation with Matti Steinberg, October 8, 1996.

21   Conversation with an Arab academic, July 23, 1995.

22 "Islamic Fanatics Suspected of Planning to Murder Husseini and Ashrawi," *Ha'aretz*, March 31, 1994; "The Military Court in Jordan Hands Down the Death Penalty to Eleven Islamic Extremists," *Ha'aretz*, December 22, 1994; *Jordan Times*, July 19, 1994; *AFP*, Paris, March 30, 1994; conversation with an Arab academic, July 23, 1995; Dabbas, *The Islamic Political Movements in Jordan*, p. 12.

23 *Ha'aretz*, March 31, 1996; conversation with an Arab academic, July 23, 1995.

24 *Al-Ra'y*, June 13, 1996.

25 *Al-Shurouk*, September 1995; *Al-Bilad*, September 1995; *Yediot Ahronot*, August 18, 1997; *Ha'aretz*, August 18, 1997; "Four Islamists in Jordan Receive Long Jail Terms for Planning Attacks against Israel," *Ha'aretz*, December 31, 1997.

26 *Ha'aretz*, September 19, 2000; Jordanian News Agency "Petra," September 19, 2000; *Yediot Ahronot*, July 17, 2000; *Al-Hadeth*, January 17, 2000; *Al-Dustur*, March 28, 2000.

27 Anat Kurz and David Tal, "Palestinian Islamic Jihad," in Anat Kurz (ed.), *Islamic Terror and Israel* (Tel Aviv: Papyrus and Jaffee Center for Strategic Studies, 1993), p. 119 [Hebrew]; conversation with an Arab academic, July 23, 1995.

28 Conversations with an Arab academic, July 23, 1995; *Al-Khadeth*, October 28, 1996; "Fighting against Israel – but the Jordanian Royal Palace is also in Danger," *Ma'ariv*, June 1, 1992; Milton-Edwards, "A Temporary Alliance with the Crown," p. 94.

29 Conversations with Arab academics, July 23, 1995 and September 1, 1996; Kurz and Tal, "Palestinian Islamic Jihad," p. 129.

30 Conversations with Arab academics, July 23, 1995 and September 1, 1996.

31 Voice of Israel radio, August 1, 1996.

32 "Syria Apprehends a Terrorist Gang on its Way to Attack Israeli Tourists in Jordan," *Ha'aretz*, August 19, 1996.

33 Conversation with an Arab academic, July 23, 1995.

34 Tal, "Dealing with Radical Islam: The Case of Jordan," p. 140.

35 *Foreign Report*, February 17, 1994.

7 The Muslim Brotherhood in Jordan

1 Sabah El-Said, *Between Pragmatism and Ideology: The Muslim Brotherhood in Jordan, 1989–1994* (The Washington Institute for Near East Policy, Washington D.C., 1995), p. 1.

2 Asher Susser, "The Islamic Challenge in Jordan – A Case of Limited Rivalry," in *Islamic Fundamentalism* (Tel Aviv: IDF, Combat-Corps Headquarters Intelligence, 1994), p. 174. [Hebrew].

3 Dabbas, "The Islamic Political Movements in Jordan," pp. 18–21; *Al-Nada*, April 19, 1995; Ibrahim Ghara'iba, *Al-Mushriq*, May 16, 1996.

4 Radio Monte Carlo, July 14, 1995; Jordan Television in English, July 13, 1995, in *FBIS NES*, 95–135, July 14, 1995.

5 "Muslim Brotherhood Regulations," pp. 401–16; Guy Bechor, "The Next Shura," *Ha'aretz*, June 16, 1994; conversation with an Arab academic on July 23, 1995.

6   El-Said, *Between Pragmatism and Ideology*, pp. 1, 6–8.
7   Susser, "The Islamic Challenge in Jordan," p. 174; Wedeman, "The King's Loyal Opposition?" pp. 15–16.
8   Milton-Edwards, "A Temporary Alliance with the Crown," pp. 93–100.
9   Ibid.
10 El-Said, *Between Pragmatism and Ideology*, p. 10.
11 Dabbas, "The Islamic Political Movements in Jordan," pp. 24–6.
12 *Al-Rabat*, January 20, 1993.
13 El-Said, *Between Pragmatism and Ideology*, pp. 12–13; Asher Susser, "The Muslim Brotherhood in Jordan: Coexistence and Controlled Confrontation," in *Islam and Democracy in the Arab World*, p. 133 [Hebrew].
14 Dabbas, "The Islamic Political Movements in Jordan," p. 28.
15 El-Said, *Between Pragmatism and Ideology*, pp. 11–12.
16 *Al-Ra'y*, July 9, 1997; Radio Tehran, July 10, 1997; Rami Khouri, "Jordan – A Country of All its Citizens," *Ha'aretz*, March 11, 1997; *Ha'aretz*, October 5, 1997.
17 *Ha'aretz*, November 4, 6, 1997; *Yediot Ahronot*, November 4, 6, 1997; *Al-Ra'y*, October 13, 1997; *Al-Dustur*, October 14, 1997.
18 *Jordan Times*, August 25, 1998; Jordan Television, August 23, 1998.
19 Radio Amman, November 24, 1998.
20 *Al-Arab al-Yawm*, February 8, 1999.
21 *Petra* (Jordan News Agency), March 18, 1999; *Jordan Times*, March 20, 1999.
22 *Jordan Times*, July 1, 1999, July 24, 25, 1999; *Al-Majd*, July 19, 1999.
23 Conversation with Asher Susser, November 19, 1998; Dabbas, "The Islamic Political Movements in Jordan," pp. 59, 63–4.
24 El-Said, *Between Pragmatism and Ideology*, p. 15.
25 Milton-Edwards, "A Temporary Alliance with the Crown," p. 106.
26 El-Said, *Between Pragmatism and Ideology*, pp. 16–17.
27 Guy Bechor, *Ha'aretz*, July 17, 1994.
28 "The Muslim Brotherhood will Propose a No-Confidence Vote in the Majali Government Because of the Agreement," *Ha'aretz*, October 26, 1994.
29 El-Said, *Between Pragmatism and Ideology*, pp. 17–19.
30 *Al-Wasat*, February 13, 1997.

8   *Jordan against the Muslim Brotherhood*

1   Susser, "The Islamic Challenge in Jordan," p. 174.
2   Metz, *Jordan: A Country Study*, p. 55.
3   Susser, "The Islamic Challenge in Jordan," pp. 174–5.
4   "Maneuvers in the Name of Democracy," *Ha'aretz*, January 27, 1993.
5   "Muslim Brotherhood Regulations," pp. 401–16; Guy Bechor, "To the Next Shura," *Ha'aretz*, June 16, 1994; conversation with an Arab academic, July 23, 1995.
6   Conversation with an Arab academic, July 23, 1995. For details on the Muslim Brotherhood's *al-tamkin* plan, see *Al-Musawwar*, May 27, 1994, June 10, 1994, and the discussion in Chapter 2.
7   Training for secrecy is a well-established principle in the Muslim Brotherhood. In 1995 a Muslim Brotherhood booklet was found in the West

Bank (without date or place of publication) that dealt with the rules of preaching. One of the chapters was called "The Theory of the Brotherhood's Activity," and it contained the sub-chapter, "Secrecy in the Organization." This section stated, *inter alia,* "The Muslim Brotherhood organization [*al-Tanzim al-Akhwani*] must be so secretive that even members of the *da'wa* will not recognize it." This sentence is identical to the slogan "open preaching [*da'wa*] – secret organization."

8 A conversation with an Arab academic on July 23, 1995; the term "containment" accurately describes Jordan's policy toward the Muslim Brotherhood that operates legally but within boundaries determined by the regime; conversations with Gehad Auda and Saad Eddin Ibrahim in Cairo on the Muslim Brotherhood policy of Arab regimes, January 16, 1996.

9 Metz, *Jordan: A Country Study*, p. 230; Tal, "Dealing with Radical Islam: The Case of Jordan," p. 143; Rami Keidar, "From a Social Protest Movement to a Political Party," in *Jordan: An Anthology of Articles* (Tel Aviv: IDF, Combat-Corps Headquarters Intelligence, 1995), pp. 120–1 [Hebrew].

10 "Jordan's Relative Stability," in *Contemporary Middle East Backgrounder*, no. 256, Media Analysis Center, Jerusalem, May 1989, pp. 1–2; Tal, "Dealing with Radical Islam: The Case of Jordan," p. 143; Metz, *Jordan: A Country Study*, p. 231.

11 Israel Landres, "The Religious Threat," *Davar*, November 24, 1989.

12 Talks with Arab academics, July 23, 1995 and August 20, 1995.

13 Ibid.

14 Ibid; Tal, "Dealing with Radical Islam: The Case of Jordan," p. 140.

15 *Ma'ariv*, May 23, 1990; *Ha'aretz*, May 25, 1990; *Ha'aretz*, June 12, 1990. On Shbailat and Karrash, see pp. 174–5.

16 *Al-Sabil*, December 8, 1994; *Al-Ra'y*, February 13, 1995; Wedeman, "The King's Loyal Opposition?" pp. 17–18.

17 *Ma'ariv*, August 18 and 19, 1996; *Yediot Ahronot*, August 18, 1996.

18 *French News Agency*, Amman, August 22, 1996.

19 *Al-Hayat*, September 12, 1996.

20 Keidar, "From a Social Movement to a Political Party," p. 121; *Jordan Times*, January 30, 1990.

21 *Al-Sabil*, February 28, 1995; *Al-Hayat*, October 30, 1994.

22 *Al-Quds*, July 10, 1995.

23 Reuters, Amman, July 11, 1995.

24 *Al-Bilad*, July 26, 1995.

25 *Al-Ra'y*, September 23, 1995.

26 *Al-Sabil*, November 7, 1995; *Al-Ra'y*, September 15, 1995; *Al-Sabil*, September 19, 1995.

27 The Muslim Brotherhood claimed that the al-Ahbash group was established by the regime in order to suppress Muslim Brotherhood activity in the mosques. The group's name derived from its founder, Abdullah al-Habashi.

28 *Al-Quds al-Arabi*, November 11, 1995.

29 *Shihan*, November 11, 1995.

30 *Al-Urdun*, April 29, 1996.

31 *Sawt al-Mara*, July 31, 1996.

32 *Al-Dustur*, August 27, 1996.
33 Tal, "Dealing with Radical Islam: The Case of Jordan," p. 141.
34 Conversation with an Arab academic, July 23, 1995.
35 "Muslim Brotherhood Regulations," pp. 401–2, 415; for additional details on the structure of the world organization, see Chapter 2.
36 Conversation with a member of the Shura Council of the headquarters of the Syria region, World Organization of the Muslim Brotherhood, September 24, 1997.
37 *Rabat*, Jordan-Nicosia, April 9, 1991, p. 54.
38 Conversation with member of the Shura Council, September 24, 1997.
39 "The Principles of the Organization of Parties and their Frameworks of Action," in "The National Manifest of Jordan," published in *Al-Dustur*, September 30, 1990.
40 Conversations with a member of the Shura Council, September 24, 1997 and November 20, 1999.
41 *Al-Ra'y*, November 13, 1996.
42 *Al-Urdan*, February 17, 1997.
43 *Jerusalem Post*, March 25, 1991; Tal, "Dealing with Radical Islam: The Case of Jordan," p. 148; *Filastin al-Muslima*, March 1993.
44 *Ha'aretz*, November 17, 1992; *Jerusalem Post*, November 13, 1992. For more details on the trial, see pp. 193–5.
45 Hazem Saghaya, "Jordan Succeeded in Overcoming the Difficulties of Peace and Relations with Iraq," *Al-Aswak*, January 28, 1996.
46 Conversation with Asher Susser, September 2, 1997.
47 *Al-Nahar*, November 10, 1996.
48 Aviva Shaabi and Roni Shaked, *Hamas, From Faith in Allah to the Path of Terror* (Jerusalem: Keter, 1994), pp. 150–51, 155, 239; Khaled al-Haroub, *Al-Hayat*, May 21, 1995; *Al-Diar*, May 23, 1995; *Al-Bilad*, May 27, 1995; Guy Bechor, *Ha'aretz*, July 30, 1995; *Jerusalem Post*, June 2, 1995.
49 *Al-Sabil*, March 18 and 26, 1996.
50 Reuters, March 19, 1996; Radio Tehran in Arabic, March 30, 1996.
51 Radio Tehran in Arabic, October 21, 1996.
52 *Al-Bilad*, October 23, 1996.
53 *Yediot Ahronot*, October 6–7, 1997; Zvi Barel, "When Hamas Dictates Conditions," *Ha'aretz*, October 5, 1997; Guy Bechor, "A Month before Elections in Jordan Hamas Becomes the Most Influential Political Factor," *Ha'aretz*, October 8, 1997.
54 Yossi Melman, *Ha'aretz*, November 19, 1998.
55 Daniel Sobleman, *Ha'aretz*, September 24, 1999.
56 Zvi Barel, *Ha'aretz*, November 22, 1999.
57 Susser, "The Islamic Challenge in Jordan," p. 175; and a conversation with Asher Susser, September 2, 1997.
58 Conversation with Asher Susser, September 2, 1997.
59 *Al-Bilad*, April 3, 1996.
60 *Akhbar al-Usbue*, March 28, 1996.
61 Musa Zayd al-Kilani, *The Islamic Movements in Jordan and Palestine* (Amman, 1994), pp. 45, 116–17 [Arabic].

62 Conversation with Asher Susser, September 2, 1997.
63 Schirin H. Fathi, *Jordan – An Invented Nation?* (Hamburg: Deutsches Orient Institut, 1994), pp. 201, 237.
64 Fathi, *Jordan – An Invented Nation?* pp. 133–7.
65 Uriel Dan, "The Regime in Jordan and its Opponents, 1949–1970," in *Jordan: An Anthology of Articles,* pp. 54, 57, 58 [Hebrew].
66 Fathi, *Jordan – An Invented Nation?* pp. 137–8, 140.
67 Fathi, *Jordan – An Invented Nation?* p. 141.
68 Susser, "Political Murder in Jordan"; conversation with Asher Susser, September 2, 1997.
69 Moshe Zak, *Hussein the Peacemaker* (Ramat Gan: Bar Ilan University, 1996), pp. 7, 26, 320, 321 [Hebrew].
70 *Jordan Times,* October 12–13, 1995.
71 Ibrahim Gharayiba, "The Position of the Islamic Movement Fluctuates between Naïveté and Romance – the Future of the Islamists Depends on the Positive or Negative Interaction in the Movement," *Al-Mushriq,* May 16, 1996, pp. 14, 15; *ijtihad* is the right to derive an entirely new interpretation based on the Qur'an and the traditions attributed to the Prophet Mohammad, and to express this view without recourse to traditional commentaries. Its function is a creative one, designed to draw conclusions on practical and religious matters. See Lammens, *Islam: Beliefs and Institutions,* p. 76.
72 *Al-Wasat,* February 13, 1997.
73 *Saut al-Murua,* December 4, 1996.
74 Tal, "Dealing with Radical Islam: The Case of Jordan," pp. 142–3.

9 Jordanian Resistance to Fundamentalism

1 From King Hussein's speech in Aqaba, Radio Amman, August 14, 1997.
2 Susser, "Political Assassination in Jordan."
3 Susser, "The Islamic Challenge in Jordan."
4 A conversation with Asher Susser, September 15, 1997.
5 Guy Bechor, "The King's Nightmare," *Ha'aretz,* March 12, 1997.
6 Conversation with an Arab academic, September 1, 1996.
7 Daniel Sobelman, "Abdullah Seeks to Establish his Government in Jordan," *Ha'aretz,* January 27, 1999; "The United States, Britain, and France Promise Economic Aid to Jordan to Guarantee a Quiet Transition of Government," *Ha'aretz,* February 9, 1999.
8 Conversations with Asher Susser, May 19, 2003; August 28, 2003; Zvi Barel, "The King Runs Forward, The State Drags Behind," *Ha'aretz,* June 25, 2003.

Radical Islam in Egypt and Jordan: An Integrative Conclusion

1 Sivan, "Why Radical Muslims aren't Taking over Governments," pp. 3–9.

BIBLIOGRAPHY

Note: In addition to the sources listed below, Middle East newspapers and other journalistic publications were used extensively in preparation for this book. References to these publications appear in the chapter endnotes. Select additional documents and personal interviews comprise the remaining source material.

Alexander, Yonah. *Middle East Terrorism Selected Group Profiles*. Washington, D.C.: Jewish Institure for National Security Affairs, 1994.

Altman, Israel. *Trends in Radicalization in the Positions of the Egyptian Muslim Brotherhood*. Tel Aviv: Tel Aviv University, Shiloach Institute for Middle East and Africa Studies, 1979 [Hebrew].

Altman, Israel. "Islamic Opposition Groups in Sadat's Regime," in *Egypt: An Anthology of Articles*. Tel Aviv: IDF, Combat-Corps Headquarters Intelligence, 1994, 134-56 [Hebrew].

Arab Strategic Report 1992. Cairo: *Al-Ahram* Center for Political and Strategic Studies, 1993.

Arab Strategic Report 1993. Cairo: *Al-Ahram* Center for Political and Strategic Studies, 1994.

Arab Strategic Report 1994. Cairo: *Al-Ahram* Center for Political and Strategic Studies, 1995.

Arab Strategic Report 1997. Cairo: *Al-Ahram* Center for Political and Strategic Studies, 1998 [Arabic].

Arab Strategic Report 1998. Cairo: *Al-Ahram* Center for Political and Strategic Studies, 1999 [Arabic].

Arab Strategic Report 1999. Cairo: *Al-Ahram* Center for Political and Strategic Studies, 2000 [Arabic].

Auda, Gehad. "The Normalization of the Islamic Movement in Egypt from the 1970s to the Early 1990s," in N. E. Mary and R. S. Appleby (eds.), *Accounting for Fundamentalism*. Chicago: University of Chicago Press, 1994, 374-412.

Ayalon, Ami (ed.). *Middle East Contemporary Survey 1992*. Boulder, CO: Westview Press, 1994.

Ayalon, Ami (ed.). *Middle East Contemporary Survey 1993*. Boulder, CO: Westview Press, 1995.

Ayalon, Ami and Maddy-Weitzman, Bruce (eds.). Middle *East Contemporary Survey 1994*. Boulder, CO: Westview Press, 1996.

Ayalon, Ami. "The Political Order in Egypt: Continuity and Challenges," in *Egypt: An Anthology of Articles*. Tel Aviv: IDF, Combat-Corps Headquarters Intelligence, 1994, 163–81 [Hebrew].

Baham, Yaakov. "The Muslim Brotherhood Movement in Egypt," in Yaakov Shimoni (ed.), *The New East*, Vol. III, Book 4 (12). Jerusalem: The Hebrew University, 1952, 335–52 [Hebrew].

Brawer, Moshe. *Carta Atlas – Middle East*. Jerusalem: Carta, 1990.

Copley, Gregory R. *Defense and Foreign Affairs Handbook on Egypt 1995*. London: International Media Corporation, 1995.

Al-Dabbas, Hamed. *The Islamic Political Movements in Jordan*. Amman: 1995 [Arabic].

Dan, Uriel. "The Regime in Jordan and its Opponents, 1949-1970," in *Jordan: An Anthology of Articles*. Tel Aviv: IDF, Combat-Corps Headquarters Intelligence, 1995, 56–61 [Hebrew].

Fadlallah, Mohammad Hussein. "In Light of the Present Reality in the Islamic World," in Fuad al-Zayn (ed.), *Al-Orfan*. Beirut: 1985, 4–16 [Arabic].

Fandy, Mamoun. "Egypt's Islamic Group: Regeional Revenge?" *Middle East Journal* 48, no. 4, 1994: 607–25.

Fathi, Schirin H. *Jordan – An Invented Nation?* Hamburg: Deutsches Orient Institut, 1994.

Al-Ghanoushi, Rashid (ed.). *Articles: The Islamic Movement in Tunis*. Paris: Dar al-Kouran, 1984 [Arabic].

Guenana, Nemat. "Islamic Activism in Egypt." *Civil Society*, June 1995: 5–8.

Guenena, Nemat and Ibrahim, Saad Eddin. *The Changing Face of Egypt's Islamic Activism*, 2nd Draft, Cairo: Ibn Khaldoun Center for Development Studies, 1997.

Ibrahim, Saad Eddin. "Arab Modernity and the Challenge of Islam: The Case of Egypt's Islamic Activism – How Much of a Threat?" Cairo: Ibn Khaldoun Center for Development Studies, 1994, 1–20.

Ibrahim, Saad Eddin. "The Changing Face of Islamic Activism." *Civil Society*, May 1995: 4–8.

Ibrahim, Saad Eddin. "Civil Society and Electoral Politics in Egypt." *Civil Society*, December 1995: 4–6.

Kalvari, Beni and Orpaz, Haim (eds.). *Hamas, the Islamic Resistance Movement, and the Manifesto*. Jerusalem: Ministry of Education and Culture Information Center, 1990.

Kam, Ephraim (ed.). The *Middle East Military Balance 1994–1995*. Boulder, CO.: Westview Press and Tel Aviv: Jaffee Center for Strategic Studies, 1996.

Keidar, Rami. "From a Social Protest Movement to a Political Party," in *Jordan: An Anthology of Articles*. Tel Aviv: IDF, Combat-Corps Headquarters Intelligence, 1995, 108–26 [Hebrew].

Abu Khalil, As'ad. "The Incoherence of Islamic Fundamentalism: Arab Islamic Thought at the End of the 20th Century." *Middle East Journal* 48, no. 4 (1994): 677–94.

Al-Kilani, Musa Zayd. *The Islamic Movements in Jordan and Palestine*. Amman: 1994 [Arabic].

Kurz, Anat (ed.). *Islamic Terror and Israel.* Tel Aviv: Papyrus and Jaffee Center for Strategic Studies, 1993 [Hebrew].

Lammens, Henri. *Islam: Beliefs and Institutions.* Jerusalem: Masada Publications, Hebrew University, 1954 [Hebrew, translated from the French].

Lazarus-Yaffe, Chava. "More on the Islamic Religion," in *Islamic Fundamentalism.* Tel Aviv: IDF, Combat-Corps Headquarters Intelligence, 1994, 27–8 [Hebrew].

Lev Zion, Nehemiah. "Islam as a Factor in International Relations," *Monthly Survey* 12 (1987): 3–9 [Hebrew].

Lewis, Bernard. *The Arabs in History.* Tel Aviv: Tushia Publishing, 1995 (translation from English).

Litvak, Meir (ed.). *Islam and Democracy in the Arab World.* Tel Aviv: HaKibbutz HaMeuhad, 1997 [Hebrew].

Menashri, David. "Introduction," in *Islamic Fundamentalism.* Tel Aviv: IDF, Combat-Corps Headquarters Intelligence, 1994 [Hebrew].

Metz, Helen Chapin (ed.). *Jordan: A Country Study.* Washignton, D.C.: Federal Research Division, Library of Congress, 1991.

Milton-Edwards, Beverly. "A Temporary Alliance with the Crown: The Islamic Response in Jordan," in James Piscatori (ed.), *Islamic Fundamentalisms and the Gulf Crisis* (Chicago, 1991), 88–108.

Milton-Edwards, Beverly. "Climate of Change in Jordan's Islamist Movement," in Abdel Salam Sidahmed and Anoushiravan Ehteshami (eds.), *Islamic Fundamentalism.* Boulder, CO: Westview Press, 1996, 127–30.

Mitchell, Richard P. The Society of the Muslim Brothers. London: Oxford University Press, 1969.

Mustafa, Hala. *The Political Reform in Egypt, from the Reform Movement to Violent Groups.* Cairo: *Al-Ahram* Center for Strategic Studies, 1992 [Arabic].

Mustafa, Hala. "The Political Regime and the Islamic Opposition in Egypt," in *The State and the Islamic Opposition Movement: Between Ceasefire and Confrontation.* Cairo: Al-Mahroussa Center, 1995 [Arabic].

Al-Nafisi, Abdullah Fahad (ed.). "The General Regulations of the Muslim Brotherhood," in *The Islamic Movement: A Look to the Future, Pages of Self-Criticism.* Cairo: 1989 [Arabic].

Patterns of Global Terrorism, US State Department, 1993.

Patterns of Global Terrorism, US State Department, 1995.

Patterns of Global Terrorism, US State Department, 1998.

Patterns of Global Terrorism, US State Department, 1999.

Podeh, Eli. "The Islamic Revival in the Land of the Pharaohs," in *Egypt: An Anthology of Articles.* Tel Aviv: IDF, Combat-Corps Headquarters Intelligence, 1994, 182–9 [Hebrew].

El-Said, Sabah. *Between Pragmatism and Ideology: The Muslim Brotherhood in Jordan, 1989–1994.* Washington, D.C.: 1995.

Shabi, Aviva and Shaked, Roni. *Hamas: From Belief in Allah to the Path of Terror.* Jerusalem: Keter, 1994 [Hebrew].

Sharon, Moshe. "The Islamic Factor in the Politics of the Middle East," in *Islamic Fundamentalism.* Tel Aviv: IDF, Combat-Corps Headquarters Intelligence, 1994, 29–33 [Hebrew].

Shimoni, Yaakov. *The Arab States.* Tel Aviv: Am Oved, 1977 [Hebrew].

Shimoni, Yaakov and Levin, Evyatar. *A Political Lexicon of the Middle East in the 20th Century.* Jerusalem: Jerusalem Publishing House, 1971 [Hebrew].

Sivan, Emmanuel. *Islamic Radicals.* Tel-Aviv: Ofakim/Am Oved, 1994 [Hebrew].

Sivan, Emmanuel. "Why Radical Muslims aren't Taking over Governments," *Middle East Quarterly* 4, no. 4 (1997): 3–9.

Sofer, Arnon. *Changes in the Geography of the Middle East.* Tel Aviv: Am Oved, 1987 [Hebrew].

Sofer, Arnon. "Egypt: A Traditional Agricultural Society in the Process of Change," in *Egypt: An Anthology of Articles.* Tel Aviv: IDF, Combat-Corps Headquarters Intelligence, 1994, 14–28 [Hebrew].

Sofer, Arnon. "Jordan Apporaching the Nineties: Location, Metropolis, and Water," in *Jordan: An Anthology of Articles.* Tel Aviv: IDF, Combat-Corps Headquarters Intelligence, 1995, 25–32 [Hebrew].

Sofer, N. "Jordan," *The Hebrew Encyclopedia.* Jerusalem, 1967, Vol. VI [Hebrew].

Springborg, R. Mubarak's *Egypt: Fragmentation of the Political Order.* London: 1989.

Susser, Asher. "The Islamic Challenge in Jordan – A Case of Limited Rivalry," in *Islamic Fundamentalism.* Tel Aviv: IDF, Combat-Corps Headquarters Intelligence, 1994, 174–5 [Hebrew].

Tal, Lawrence. "Dealing with Radical Islam: The Case of Jordan," *Survival* 37, no. 3 (1995): 139–56.

Vatikiotis, P. G. *Egypt, From Mohammad Ali to Sadat.* Jerusalem: Magnes Press, Hebrew University of Jerusalem, 1983 [Hebrew].

Wedeman, Ben. "The King's Loyal Opposition?" *Middle East Insight* 11, no. 2 (1995): 3–19.

Zak, Moshe. *Hussein the Peacemaker.* Ramat Gan: Bar Ilan University, 1996 [Hebrew].

INDEX

al-Abadi, Abdel Salam, 213–14
Abd al-Wahab, Mohammad, 6
Abdullah, Dib, 228
Abdullah I, King of Jordan, 168, 187,
    203, 221, 230, 234, 237
Abdullah II, King of Jordan, 197–8, 226,
    227, 230, 237
Abu Baker, Jamil, 232
Abu Basha, Hassan, 32, 61, 94
Abu Faris, Mohammad, 199
Abu Halima, Mohammad, 147
Abu Hoshar, Khader, 181, 182
Abu Khanifa approach, 44
Abu Marzouk, Musa, 222, 223, 224,
    225, 226, 227
Abu Mualik, Abdel Muati Abdel Aziz,
    183, 184, 185
Abu Nasser, Mohammad Hamad, 55,
    63, 72, 252n
Abu Nawar, Ali, 169, 221, 229
Abu Rishta, Ata, 176
Abu Za'abal prison, 116, 117
Abu Zant, Abdel Moneim, 191, 193,
    213
Abu Zant, Mohammad, 198
Abu Zubeida, Mohammad, 181
Abul-Ala al-Mahdoudi, 6
Abul Fatah Abdel Hadi, Abdel Moneim,
    66
al-Adli, Habib, 103, 131
Afghan alumni, 1, 137–40, 141, 148
    Army of Mohammad, 172–3
    see also Jordanian Afghanis
al-Afghani, Jamal al-Din, 6
Afghanistan, 5, 121, 132, 148, 244
    cooperation on fighting terrorism,
        140
    drug smuggling to finance terrorism,
        89

Islamic regime in, 2, 69, 160
Islamic terrorism 108, 137, 143, 181,
    182
mujahidin–Soviet conflict, 1, 28–9,
    82, 85, 86, 107, 137–9, 141, 142,
    151, 172, 185, 258n
al-Ahali, 73
al-Ahbash movement, 215, 263n
Ahmed, Ibrahim Mohammad Sayyid,
    117
Ahmed, Makram Mohammad, 32, 63,
    96–7, 251n
al-Ahram, 65, 74, 100, 110
Al-Ahram Center for Political and
    Strategic Studies, 59, 70
al-Ahrar party (Egyptian Liberal Party),
    50, 53, 67, 68
al-Aka'ila, Abdullah, 201, 232
Akef, Mohammad Mahdi Othman, 71
Akhbar al-Yawm, 57
al-Alami, Emad, 222, 224
al-Alfi, Hassan
    attempted assassination of, 94–5, 133
    domestic anti-terrorism strategies,
        124, 127, 135
    and international Muslim
        Brotherhood, 69–70
    interstate cooperation on terrorism,
        144, 146
    and Madani's death, 57–8
    resignation of, 103
    stance on terrorism, 61, 116, 119,
        121, 124
    terrorism abroad, 141, 148
Algeria
    inter-Arab cooperation against
        terrorism, 144, 145
    Islamic movement in, 160, 233, 235,
        238

Islamic terrorism in, 108, 140, 141, 142
threat of Islamic fundamentalism in, 1, 8, 9, 69
Ali, Gaber Ahmed, 114
Allam, Fu'ad, 61
Allegiance to the Imam Movement (*Harakat Bay'at al-Imam*), 172, 174, 180
al-'amal (implementation, according to Muslim Brotherhood), 22
al-Amal party (Egyptian Labor Party), 50, 53, 64–5, 66, 67, 77
Arab Afghanis *see* Afghan alumni
Arabiyyat, Abdel Latif, 175, 192
Arafat, Yasir, 73, 144
  agreements with Jordanian regime, 170
  and Hamas in Jordan, 223–4, 226, 227
  and Jordanian fundamentalist groups, 177, 179
al-Arian, Essam, 63, 65
Army of Mohammad (*Jaysh Mohammad*), 172–4, 178, 180, 181, 220
Ashrawi, Hanan, 179
ashwa'ayiat (shantytowns), 87
Askar, Sheikh Sa'id, 66
al-Assad, Hafez, 7, 8, 109, 146, 160, 207, 209
Assiut
  illegal weapons in, 89–92
  security operations in, 115, 116
Auda, Gehad, 59
Awayda, Mohammad, 199
Azam, Abdullah, 172
al-Azhar (religious establishment in Egypt), 34, 40, 41, 42, 43–5
al-Azzazi, Hilmi Issa Ibrahim, 71

Ba'ath ideology, 3, 203
Badawi, Khaled, 75
Bader, Zaki, 41, 94, 135
Badran, Mudar, 171, 192, 199, 213, 220
al-Bahi, Mohammad, 5
Bakri, Omar, 151
al-Banna, Hassan Ahmed Abdel Rahman, 6, 17, 78
  assassination of, 17, 23, 252*n*
  foundation of Muslim Brotherhood, 16, 20, 37, 187

and importance of Muslim education, 22
and Islamic caliphate, 3, 22
and political systems, 49
and secrecy doctrine, 206
and Secret Organization, 19, 20
and Western ideologies, 20, 21
al-Banna, Sa'if, 78
Baraka, Sayyid, 172, 185
al-Barawi, Ahmed, 33
Bashir, Omar, 8, 142
al-Batihi, Samih, 144, 181, 215–16
al-Baz, Osama, 141
Bedouin, 121
  and Egyptian terrorism armament 92, 120, 253–54*n*
  loyalty to Hashemite regime, 168, 169, 170, 208, 229, 236
Bhutto, Benazir, 29, 139, 140
al-Biltagi, Mamdouh, 102
Bin Laden, Osama, 151
  funding of terrorist organizations, 88, 178
  al-Qaeda, 1, 30, 132, 181, 182
Bisher, Mohammad Ali, 75
Black September group, 171
bolshevism, 21
Bosnia, 88, 218
  Afghan alumni in, 138
Boutrous-Ghali, Boutrous, 28, 107, 108
Britain, 22, 99
  Islamic rally (1996), 150–1
  support for Jordan, 168
  terrorist extraditions, 71, 147

Cairo
  and Muslim Brotherhood, 17, 20, 62, 69, 71, 72, 159, 218
  socio-economic background, 13, 14, 87
  terrorist activity in, 26, 30, 31, 33, 87–8, 103, 107, 121, 124, 152, 154
  see also Imbaba neighborhood
capitalism, 6, 21
Central Intelligence Agency (CIA), 138, 181
Chad, weapons smuggling, 92
Christians, 103, 173
  see also Coptic community
Communism, 6, 114
Coptic community, 13, 87
  civil rights of, 23
  and political activity, 74, 78, 97

Coptic community *(continued)*
    "taxes" in Imbaba quarter, 114
    terrorist attacks on, 27, 28, 60, 82,
        86, 98, 103–7, 111, 127, 128, 152,
        154
Croatia, terrorist attacks in, 107, 148

al-Dahabi, Sheikh Hassan, 32
Dahlan, Mohammad, 144
al-Dardiri, Atef, 92–3
da'wa
    in Jordan, 178, 182, 263*n*
    Muslim Brotherhood in Egypt, 5, 17,
        19, 22, 40, 49
al-Da'wa, (Muslim Brotherhood publi-
        cation), 72
democracy, 6
    and Muslim Brotherhood in Egypt,
        49, 161, 242, 243–4
    and Muslim Brotherhood in Jordan,
        191, 201, 242–3, 244
Democratic Front for the Liberation of
        Palestine, 169, 170
Denmark
    cooperation with Egypt against
        terrorism, 146–7
    terrorist attacks, 109
Disciples of Victory (*al-Wathikoun min
        al-Naser*), 28
Dunaybat, Abdel Majid
    on democracy and violence, 191, 231
    on Jordan election boycott, 195, 202
    and Jordanian Hamas, 224–5
    and Muslim Brotherhood world
        organization, 218, 219
    paper on Muslim Brotherhood
        positions, 197

Egypt
    arrest of intellectuals in Muslim
        Brotherhood, 64–6
    confrontation policy with Muslim
        Brotherhood, 58–79, 159–60, 209
    containment policy with Muslim
        Brotherhood, 39–58, 159
    cooperation with West against
        terrorism, 146–51
    elections (1984), 50, 51, 53, 242
    elections (1987), 50, 52, 53, 242
    elections (1995), 66–68, 72, 242
    elections (2000), 78, 159–60, 242
    Free Officers coup (1952), 25,
        37
    inter-Arab cooperation against
        terrorism, 143–6, 150, 157
    Mubarak's regime, 39–79, 81,
        159–60, 209
    Muslim Brotherhood, 16–25, 35–79
    Nasser's regime, 20, 25, 37, 81, 158
    national dialogue, 63–4
    peace treaty with Israel, 38, 231–2
    prisons and terrorism, 113, 116–18
    public anxiety over terrorism, 155–6
    regime concessions to fundamentalist
        demands, 53, 240
    resistance to Islamic fundamentalism,
        153–63
    Sadat's regime, 20, 37–9, 81, 158–9
    security and intelligence services,
        15–16, 112–16, 117–24, 155–7
    social Islam in, 46–9, 78, 160, 240–1
    socio-economic background of,
        13–16
    strategy against terrorism, 112–52
    struggle on religious issues with
        Muslim Brotherhood, 40–6, 250*n*
    suppression of Muslim Brotherhood
        (1998–99), 74–8
    threat of Islamic fundamentalism, 8, 9
    tourism and terrorism, 98–103, 104,
        128, 154, 157
    trade unions and Muslim
        Brotherhood, 36, 54–8, 60, 62–3,
        75–6, 78
    see also Coptic community; Islamic
        terrorist organizations (Egypt)
Egyptian Central Security (*al-Amn al-
        Markazi*), 15, 113, 114
Egyptian Directorate of State Security
        Investigations, 15, 16, 43, 70
Egyptian General Intelligence (*al-
        Mukhabarat al-Aama*), 15–16
Egyptian Military Intelligence, 15
Egyptian Ministry of Religious
        Endowments, 40, 41, 42, 43, 44–5
Elbab, Ali Sayyid Fath, 74
Eritrea, 144
Ethiopia
    assassination attempt on Mubarak,
        29, 107, 109–11, 125, 154
    Muslim minorities in, 5
    security cooperation with Egypt, 144
ethnic minorities *see* Coptic community
Ezzat, Sa'id Mahmoud, 66
Ezzeddin, Ahmed Galal, 25, 155, 156

Fadlallah, Sheikh Hussein, 6
Fakir, Ali, 213
Farag, Mohammad Abdel Salam, 27
al-Farchan, Ishak, 188, 193, 194, 199, 202
Farouk, King of Egypt, 20, 22
Fatah, 169, 171, 179
Fath Elbab, Ali Sayyid, 74
al-Fauri, Yussef, 173
Federal Bureau of Investigation (FBI), 181
Foda, Farag, 59, 82, 93, 97, 117
France, 107, 146
Freij, Elias, 103

Galil, Ahmed Hassan Abdel, 121
Gebara, Mohammad Abdel Hammid, 96
Germany, 88, 108, 147, 175
Ghali, Boutrous, 80
al-Ghanoushi, Rashid, 5–7
Gharayiba, Ibrahim, 231–2
Ghosha, Ibrahim, 222, 227
Group for International Justice, 107, 148
Gulf States, 143–4, 222
Gulf War, 167, 192–3, 200, 213, 218, 223, 225, 234
    and Jordanian terrorist organizations, 175, 176,179, 184

Habalah, Omar Abdel Hamid, 30–1
Habash, George, 169, 170
Habib, Mohammad, 66
al-Hadeth, 182
al-Haj, Mohammad, 199
al-Halbawi, Kamel, 71
Halim, Mohammad Amin Abdel, 125–7
Hama, Islamic revolt in, 1, 69, 146, 207
Hamam, Sheikh Sayyid, 199, 213
Hamam, Tal'at Mohammad Yassin, 29, 121, 258n
Hamas, 144
    on grand Islamic theocracy, 3–4
    and Israel, 1, 206, 222, 223–4, 232
    in Jordan, 198, 199, 220, 222–7
Hamza, Mustafa, 29, 110, 142, 258n
Harakat Bay'at al-Imam see Allegiance to the Imam Movement (Harakat Bay'at al-Imam)
Harakat al-Jihad al-Islami Bayt al-Maqdas see Islamic Jihad Movement – Bayt al-Maqdas

Harakat al-Jihad al-Islami fi Filastin see Islamic Jihad Movement in Palestine – Shqaqi Faction
Harakat al-Tajdid al-Islami see Movement of Islamic Renewal (Harakat al-Tajdid al-Islami)
al-Harakiyoun, 28
Hariri, Rafiq, 138
Hashemite kingdom, see Jordan
Hassan, Aziz Sha'aban, 128
Hassan bin Talal, Crown Prince of Jordan, 197
Hawatma, Naif, 169
al-Hayat, 77, 231
Hazem, Mohammad, 33
Hejazi, Ra'id, 181
Hekmatyar, Golbodin, 139, 140
Higher Council for Islamic Affairs, 41
hijra (religious flight or emigration), 31–2
al-Hindi, Amin, 182
Hizb al-Tahrir al-Islami see Islamic Liberation Party (Hizb al-Tahrir al-Islami)
Hizbollah, 1, 183, 185
Hizbollah Palestine, 172, 184
al-Houdeibi, Hassan Ismail, 20, 23, 37, 252n
al-Houdeibi, Ma'amoun
    elections (1995), 66, 67
    Mashour's appointment as general guide, 72
    Muslim Brotherhood arrests by security forces, 74, 75
    Muslim Brotherhood international organization, 69, 70
    political demands, 77
Hudaibiya Agreement, 125
hudna (ceasefire), 125, 242
Hussein, Adel, 64–5
Hussein bin Talal, King of Jordan, 144, 167, 168–9, 228, 229
    apprehension over Islamic fundamentalism, 7
    assassination attempt on Mash'al, 225
    as assassination target, 234
    death of, 197, 237
    government efficiency and competency, 195
    and Hamas, 220, 225–6, 227
    and Islamic terrorist organizations, 173, 175, 177, 183, 185

Hussein bin Talal, King of Jordan
   (*continued*)
   Israeli–Jordanian relations, 199, 200,
      210–11, 230
   Muslim Brotherhood in Jordan,
      203–7, 228–9, 235–6
   Muslim Brotherhood world organiza-
      tion, 219
   Palestinian uprising (1970–71),
      169–71
   political shrewdness, 186, 208, 220–1
   rapprochement with Syria, 207
   release of Yassin, 225–6
   support for Iraq in Gulf War, 193,
      200
Hussein, Saddam, 160, 179, 193, 234
al-Husseini, Faisal, 179
al-Husseini, Haj Amin, 168

Ibrahim, Saad Eddin, 60
ijtihad, 232, 265*n*
Imbaba neighborhood
   anti-government animosity, 112
   attacks on Copts, 103–5
   Muslim Brotherhood schools in, 47
   security operations in, 113, 114–15,
      117
   significance of, 256*n*
imperialism, 6, 21, 168
infitah policy, 38
Interpol, 139
Iran, 160, 206, 233, 243
   and Afghan alumni, 138, 141
   and attack on Mubarak in Ethiopia,
      109
   and Egyptian terrorist groups, 88,
      107, 137, 139, 140, 141–2, 143,
      144
   Islamic Revolution (1979), 1, 2, 3,
      85, 133, 204, 205, 244
   and Jordanian terrorist groups, 172,
      174, 175, 183, 184, 186
   religious persecution in, 103
Iranian Revolutionary Guards (IRG),
   141, 183, 185
Iraq, 141
   anti-terrorism policies, 146
   attack on Mubarak in Ethiopia, 109
   Gulf War, *see* Gulf War
   inter-Arab cooperation against
      terrorism, 145
   and Jordanian terrorist groups, 175,
      176–7

Muslim Brotherhood in Jordan,
      192–3
   opposition to Jordan, 168–9, 170
al-Islambouli, Khaled, 27, 28, 87
al-Islambouli, Mohammad, 29, 110, 148,
      258*n*
Islamic Action Front (IAF)
   elections (1993), 194
   elections (1997), 196
   food riots (1996), 211–12
   foundation and ideology of, 193
   Israeli-Jordanian peace treaty, 194,
      200, 213, 225, 228
   local elections (1995), 188
   Palestinian element in, 198
   political themes in sermons, 214, 215
   press criticism of, 231
   psychological warfare against, 219–20
Islamic Army – Abdel Muati Abu
      Mualik Group, 172, 185
Islamic Front in Sudan, 69–70
Islamic fundamentalism, 1–9, 238–45
   crisis of Islam, 5–7
   Egyptian resistance to, 153–63
   essence of, 2–5
   Jordanian resistance to, 234–47
   threat to current regimes, 7–9
   use of mosques in Egypt, 42–3
   see also Islamic organizations (Jordan);
      Islamic terrorist organizations
      (Egypt); Muslim Brotherhood in
      Egypt; Muslim Brotherhood in
      Jordan
Islamic Group *see* al-Jama'a al-Islamiyya
Islamic investment companies, 46, 47,
   48
Islamic Jihad Battalions, 179
Islamic Jihad Movement – Bayt al-
      Maqdas, 172, 183–4
Islamic Jihad Movement in Palestine –
      Shqaqi Faction,
      172, 179, 182–3, 186
Islamic Liberation Front, 175
Islamic Liberation Party (Hizb al-Tahrir
      al-Islami),
      172, 176–8, 224
Islamic Revolutionary Army, 172, 185
Islamic terrorist organizations (Egypt),
      25–34, 59, 60–1,
      153–8, 162–3, 241–2, 245
   early efforts against, 112–19, 149
   Egyptian government response,
      112–52

ethnic minorities as targets, 103–7
funding and armament of, 88–93
government negotiations with leaders,
118–19
government officials and public
figures as targets of, 93–8
government strategy against, 119–25,
132–6
inter-Arab cooperation against,
143–6, 150, 157
international arena and cooperation
against, 137–51
legislation and courts to combat,
132–5, 150
prisons as schools for, 113, 116–18
propaganda and psychological
warfare against, 135–6, 150
proposed ceasefire of, 125–32, 152,
154, 157
surge of activity in the 1990s, 80–8
terrorism abroad, 107–9
tourists and foreigners as targets of,
98–103, 104, 128, 154, 157
see also individual organizations
Islamic terrorist organizations (Jordan),
171–86, 241–2, 245
Islamic voluntary associations, 46–9,
240, 244
Islamic Welfare Party (Turkey), 1
Israel, 174
Hamas, 1, 206, 222, 223–5, 232
Islamic movement in, 232
release of Yassin, 225–6
support for Jordan, 168, 170, 230
and terrorist attacks, 148, 170, 172,
183, 185
Israeli–Egyptian peace treaty, 38, 231–2
Israeli–Jordanian peace treaty, 230
and Hamas, 223–24
and Muslim Brotherhood in Jordan,
194–5, 199–202, 210–11, 213–14,
231, 232, 236–7
and terrorist organizations, 177, 185
Israeli–Palestinian peace process, 199,
236
istib'ad (non-recognition), 60
Italy, terrorist attacks, 108, 110

al-Jama'a al-Islamiyya, 4, 25–6, 28–30,
60
Adel Hussein's arrest, 65
and Allegiance to the Imam
Movement, 180

attacks on Copts, 106, 152
attacks on Mubarak, 94, 98, 109–10
attacks on security, government, and
public figures, 93–8, 127
attacks on tourists, 98–103, 128, 152
ceasefire, 125, 127–31, 152, 154, 157
elimination of commanders by
government, 156
establishment of, 28, 86–7
funding of, 88
links to Muslim Brotherhood, 71
members executed, 133, 134
negotiations with Egyptian government, 118
overseas activities, 107, 109, 110,
137, 138, 141, 142, 144
pact with al-Jihad, 27
presence in Imbaba quarter, 114
prison activities, 117
proposed ceasefire, 125, 127–32,
152, 154, 157, 242
Sadat's assassination, 87
Jama'at al-Takfir wal Hijra, 25, 26, 31–2,
144, 180
Jaysh Mohammad see Army of
Mohammad (Jaysh Mohammad)
jihad, 4, 22, 25, 26, 69
Islamic Jihad factions, 172, 182–5
Islamic Liberation Party, 176, 178
see also al-Jama'a al-Islamiyya; al-Jihad
(Holy War) organization; Tala'ie el-
Fath (Vanguard of Conquest)
al-Jihad al-Jadid see al-Shawkiyoun
al-Jihad (Holy War) organization, 4, 25,
26–8, 30, 57, 60
attacks on Copts, 105
attacks on Mubarak, 98
attacks on public figures, 94, 96
attacks on tourists, 101
forerunners of, 80
funding of, 88
links to Muslim Brotherhood, 70, 71
members executed, 133, 134
overseas activities, 107, 108, 137,
138, 141, 142, 143, 144
pact with al-Jama'a al-Islamiyya, 27
prison activities, 117
proposed ceasefire, 125, 127, 131,
132
Sadat's assassination, 39, 93
Jordan
amnesty used as a political tool,
220–1

Jordan *(continued)*
Christian minority, 173
containment policy toward Muslim
Brotherhood, 206–27, 233
economic dependence on oil, 191–2,
204
elections (1989), 1, 192, 198, 204–5,
208, 242
elections (1993), 1, 194, 198, 242
elections (1997), 195–96, 197, 198,
201–2, 243
food riots (1989), 208
food riots (1996), 211
Hamas in, 198, 199, 220, 222–7
Hashemite dynasty, 167
and Iraq, 168–9, 170
mosques, 206, 212–17
Muslim Brotherhood in, 187–202
national charter (1990), 218–19
non-fundamentalist opposition,
168–71
Palestinian population, 167, 169, 236
Palestinian uprising (1970–71),
170–1, 204, 230
preaching restrictions, 212–13, 214
Publications Law (1997), 195, 201,
226
rapprochement with Syria, 207
resistance to Islamic fundamentalism,
234–7
security cooperation with Egypt, 144
security and intelligence services,
167–8, 210, 235
social fabric of, 229–30
social Islam in, 217–18
struggle with subversion and
terrorism, 167–86, 245
threat of Islamic fundamentalism, 8, 9
see also Islamic organizations (Jordan);
Israeli-Jordanian peace treaty
Jordanian Afghanis, 172, 174, 178–9,
224
Jordanian General Intelligence (*al-
Mukhabarat al-Aama*), 167–8
Jordanian General Security (*al-Amn al-
Aam*), 167
Jordanian Military Intelligence (*al-
Istikhbarat al-Askariya*), 167
Jordanian Military Security, 167, 168
Jordanian Ministry of Religious
Endowments, 213–14, 215, 216
Jordanian National Constitutional Party,
195, 196

Kadamani, Farid, 131
Kahane, Rabbi Meir, 108
Karrash, Yaqub, 174–5, 210, 220–1
Khajawi, Sa'id, 196
Khalawa, Rami, 182
Khalifa, Mohammad Abdel Rahman,
194
Khalifa, Mohammad Jamal, 178–9
Khazindar, Ahmed, 25
Khiari, Ali, 169, 221
Khirat, Ra'uf, 96
Khomeini, Ayatollah Ruhallah, 1, 3, 143,
204

Lebanon
establishment of Hizbollah, 1
and Jordanian fundamentalist organizations, 176–7, 183, 185
Muslim Brotherhood, 218
terrorists in 138, 139
Libya, 145, 146, 184
armament of terrorists from, 92, 120
Luxor
attack at Hashepsut Temple (1997),
30, 102–3, 127, 128, 154
terrorism against tourism, 98, 99,
101, 102–3, 154

Madani, Abassi, 127
Madani, Abdel Kharit, 57–8, 59, 251*n*
Madrid peace conference, 199, 210–11
mahdi (messiah), 6, 31, 247*n*
Mahdi, Abu Ala, 63
Maher, Ahmed, 80
Mahfouz, Naguib, 59, 97, 136, 156
Mahgoub, Mohammad Ali, 42
Mahgoub, Rif'at, 28, 95
Mahmoud, Mustafa, 98
al-Majali, Abdel Hadi, 195
al-Majali, Abdel Salam, 179, 195, 200
al-Majali, Habes, 170, 229
al-Majali, Haza, 169, 234
Mansour, Annis, 100
Mansour, Hamza, 199, 225
al-Maqdasi, Abu Mohammad, 180
Mash'al, Khaled, 225, 226, 227
Mashour, Mustafa
appointment as general guide, 72–3,
252*n*
and arrests of senior members of
Muslim Brotherhood, 76
document on Muslim Brotherhood
world organization, 69

elections (1995), 67–8
internal rift in Muslim Brotherhood, 159, 160
parliamentary arena, 49–50
political office resignations, 77
al-Wasat party, 74
al-Masri, Taher, 199
Mohammad the Prophet, 2, 5, 31, 125, 176
Hashemites as descendants of, 167, 228, 235
mosques
in Egypt, 42–6, 78, 250n
in Jordan, 206, 212–17
Mount al-Matarid, 89–92
Movement of Islamic Renewal (Harakat al-Tajdid al-Islami), 172, 179
Mubarak, Husni, 15, 81, 82
and Adel Hussein's arrest, 65
and Afghan alumni, 138
anti-terrorism laws, 132–33
attempted assassination of, 28, 29, 30, 60, 94, 97–8, 107, 108, 109–11, 125, 131, 154
authorization of executions, 134
confrontation policy to Muslim Brotherhood, 58–79, 159–60, 209
containment policy to Muslim Brotherhood, 39–58, 159
differentiation of Islam and terrorism, 135
and economic reform and ties to the West, 14, 35
and inter-Arab cooperation on terrorism, 143, 144
Luxor, visit to and terrorism in, 102–3
and Muslim Brotherhood, 20, 36, 161
and overseas terrorist activities, 141, 142, 144, 146, 147, 151
and security closure in Imbaba, 114–15
threat of Islamic fundamentalism to, 7, 8, 33–34
al-Mughrabi, Abdel Azzim Abdel Majid, 71
Muhana, Ahmed, 172, 183, 184
mujahidin
and rise of Islamic fundamentalism 1, 85, 172
training of Islamic terrorists, 28–9, 31, 82, 137–9, 141, 142, 185

al-Mukbil, Sheikh Saber, 179
Muneim, Yousri Abdel, 33
al-Musawwar, 32, 63, 69, 96
al-Mushriq, 231
Muslim Brotherhood
founding and goals of, 3–4
on grand Islamic theocracy, 3–4
principal trend in Islamic movement, 3–5
secrecy doctrine of, 206, 263n
threat to current regimes, 7
world organization, 68–71, 218–19
Muslim Brotherhood in Egypt, 16–25, 35–79, 153, 239–40, 242–5
condemnation of Mubarak assassination attempt in Ethiopia, 109
connection to funding of terrorist organizations, 88–9
and Copt community, 105
da'wa, 5, 17, 19, 22, 40, 49
elections (1984), 50, 51, 53, 242
elections (1987), 50, 52, 53, 242
elections (1995), 66–8, 72, 242
elections (2000), 78, 159–60, 242
ideology and implementation, 20–3
and Mubarak regime policy of confrontation, 58–79, 159–62, 209
and Mubarak regime policy of containment, 39–58, 159
under Nasser's regime, 20, 25, 37, 158
and parliamentary activity, 36, 49–54, 60, 78, 242
religious struggle of, 40–6
under Sadat's regime, 20, 37–39, 158–9
Secret Organization, 19–20
and social Islam, 46–9, 78, 160, 240–1
structure of, 17–20
trade unions activity, 36, 54–8, 60, 62–3, 75–6, 78
Muslim Brotherhood in Jordan, 187–233, 239–40, 245
avoidance of violence, 173, 231–3, 235
and democracy, 191, 201, 242–3, 244
elections (1989), 192, 198, 204–5, 208, 242
elections (1993), 194, 198, 242
elections (1997), 195–6, 197, 198, 201–2, 243
goals of, 187–9, 235

Muslim Brotherhood in Jordan
  (continued)
  and Hamas, 222, 224–5, 226–7
  mosque activity, 206, 212–17
  Palestinian element in, 198–9
  on peace process with Israel, 194–5,
    199–202, 210–11, 213–14, 231–2,
    236–7
  political involvement of, 189–98
  psychological warfare against, 219–20
  regime policy of containment,
    206–27, 233
  and social Islam, 187–8, 217–18
  structure of, 188–9, 190
  and support for Iraq in Gulf War,
    192–3
  and Youth of the Islamic Trumpet,
    175
Muslim Brotherhood in Lebanon, 218
Muslim Brotherhood in Palestine, 218
Muslim Brotherhood in Sudan, 1, 69
Muslim Brotherhood in Syria, 191, 207,
  209, 218
Mussa, Abdel Halim, 118–19
Mustafa, Shukri Ahmed, 31–2, 33
mutha (temporary marriage), 136, 258*n*

al-Nabahani, Sheikh Taki Eddin, 176
Nabawi, Ismail, 32, 94
al-Nabulsi, Suleiman, 169, 229
Nadi, Abdel Karim, 110
Nafa, Ibrahim, 65
al-Nagoun min al-Nar (Survivors of
  Hellfire), 28, 32, 94, 127
Najibullah, Mohammad, 140
Nasser, Gamal Abdel,
  assassination attempt (1954), 37, 73,
    158
  Higher Council for Islamic Affairs,
    41
  Imbaba quarter, 114
  and Muslim Brotherhood, 20, 25, 37,
    158
  opposition to Hashemite regime,
    168–9, 234
  pan-Arabism of, 14, 37, 168, 187,
    203, 204
nationalism, in Muslim Brotherhood
  ideology, 3–4, 5, 21, 22
Nawara, Ahmed Mustafa, 258*n*
Nazal, Mohammad, 222
Nazmi, A'ala Eddin, 148
Netanyahu, Benjamin, 225

New Jihad *see* al-Shawkiyoun; Tala'ie el-
  Fath (Vanguard of Conquest)
Nofal, Ahmed, 191
North Yemen, 32
Nouh, Mukhtar, 75
al-Numeiri, Ja'afar, 142
al-Nuqrashi, Mahmoud Fahmi, 17, 23,
  25, 80

occupied territories,
  growth of Hamas in, 1, 206, 222
Oslo Accords, 176, 199

Pakistan
  cooperation with Egypt against
    terrorism, 132, 139–40
  and Egyptian terrorist groups, 28–30,
    107, 137, 138–9, 141
  terrorist attacks in, 107–8, 125, 156
Palestine
  Hamas goal to Islamize, 3, 225
  Islamic Liberation Party, 176–7
  and Muslim Brotherhood, 38, 193,
    199, 224
Palestine Liberation Organization
  (PLO), 169, 170, 171, 176–7, 199,
  224
Palestinian Authority, 103, 180, 184,
  223. 224, 227, 232
Palestinian fundamentalist organizations,
  172, 182–5, 186
Palestinian Liberation Army (PLA), 170
Palestinian terrorist organizations, 168
Palestinians
  Israeli–Palestinian peace process, 236
  in Jordan, 167, 169, 170–1, 204, 236,
    236
  in Jordanian army, 229–30
  in Movement of Islamic Renewal,
    179
  and Muslim Brotherhood in Jordan,
    198–99
pan-Arabism, 3, 14, 37, 168–9, 187,
  203–4
patriotism, in Muslim Brotherhood
  ideology, 3–4, 22
Popular Front for the Liberation of
  Palestine (PFLP), 169, 170
prisons, as breeding ground for Egyptian
  terrorists, 113, 116–18

Qaddafi, Muammar, 160
al-Qaeda, 1, 30, 132, 172, 181–2

al-Qasawna, Ma'amoun, 181
Qassem, Tal'at Fuad, 29, 147, 148, 258*n*
Qur'an, 2, 21, 17, 19, 47, 114, 176, 189,
    212, 215, 217, 219, 232, 265*n*
Qutb, Sayyid, 4, 6, 25
    execution of, 37, 38
    Milestones, 9, 27, 37
al-Qutbian group, 25, 61, 62, 74

Rabbani, Burhanuddin, 140
Rabin, Yitzhak, 211
radical Islam, 2, 246–7*n*
    see also Islamic fundamentalism
Rahman, Sheikh Omar Abdel, 26, 27,
    30, 31, 33, 146, 151, 248–9*n*
    Diaspora Council, 29
    Egyptian extradition request, 147
    fatwa on tourist activities, 98–9, 108
    life imprisonment, 102, 108
    murder of Foda, 97
    proposed ceasefire, 127, 128–31
    terrorist activity in US, 108
Ramadan, Yassin, 175
Rashid, Nadir, 221
al-Rifa'i, Zaid, 174, 207

Saad, Adel Hussein, 93
al-Sabil, 224, 227
sabr (patience), concept of, 79, 161,
    235
Sadat, Anwar
    and Afghan alumni, 138
    assassination, 1, 26, 27, 28, 29, 30,
    39, 80, 87, 93–4, 127, 133
    and Muslim Brotherhood, 20, 37–9,
    79, 158–9
    and terrorist activity trend, 81
Sa'id, Abdel Hamid, 250*n*
Sa'id, Abdel Moneim, 70, 155–6
sa'id population (southerners), 14–15,
    26, 28, 87, 92
al-salafi (fundamentalist) trend, 25
Salim, Sheikh Mohammad Sayyid, 95
Salman, Othman Khaled Ibrahim, 258*n*
Salsabil computer company, 58, 59,
    63
al-Samawi, Abdullah Ahmed, 33–4
al-Samawiya, 33–4
Sarag, Mohammad, 110
Sari, Yasir Taufik Ali, 70–1
Saudi Arabia, 88, 168, 192
    cooperation with Egypt against
    terrorism

Egyptian terrorist groups, 28, 138–40
    terrorist attacks, 138, 148
al-Sha'ab, 64, 77
Sha'aban, Anwar, 108, 148
Shabab al-Nafir al-Islami *see* Youth of
    the Islamic Trumpet (Shabab al-
    Nafir al-Islami)
Shafik, Munir, 243
Shalach, Ramadan Abdullah, 172, 183,
    186
Sharf Eddin, Abdel Wahab, 70, 71
shari'a (Islamic law), 2, 8
    as Muslim Brotherhood demand, 4,
    23, 35, 38, 50, 64, 158, 161, 187,
    193, 206
    as terrorist organization demand, 28,
    118, 140
Sharif, Nawaz, 139
al-Sharif, Safwat, 87, 95, 136
al-Shawkiyoun, 28, 33
Shbailat, Laith, 174–5, 210, 220, 221
al-Sheikh, Ahmed Ismail, 98
al-Sheikh, Shawki, 33
al-Shiami, Mohammad, 95
Shqaqi, Fathi, 172, 179, 182, 183
Shukri, Ali, 175
Shukri, Ibrahim, 67
Shura Council (Egyptian legislative
    body), 66, 67, 251*n*
Shura Council (Muslim Brotherhood in
    Egypt), 17–18, 21
Shura Council (Muslim Brotherhood in
    Jordan), 188, 194, 195, 196, 197,
    198, 201
Sidki, Atef, 71, 95, 118, 132, 133, 143
Siriya, Salah, 177
Sivan, Emmanuel, 243
Six Day War, 92, 169, 176, 183, 203,
    230, 234
Siyam, Adel, 121
Siyam, Nabil, 116
social Islam
    in Egypt, 46–9, 78, 160, 240–1
    in Jordan, 187–8, 217–18
socialism, 3, 6, 21, 37, 203
Sudan, 73, 103, 121, 160, 218
    attempt on Mubarak in Ethiopia,
    109–10
    drug and weapons smuggling from,
    89, 92, 112, 120, 134, 157
    Egyptian terrorist groups in, 29, 107,
    109, 110, 137, 139, 140, 141–2,
    143

Sudan *(continued)*
    fundamentalist regime in, 1, 2, 8,
        69–70, 143, 160, 233, 243, 244
    and inter-Arab cooperation against
        terrorism, 144, 145
    Muslim Brotherhood in, 1, 69
Sufism, 4, 5
Suleiman, Omar, 144
Survivors of Hellfire *see* al-Nagoun min
    al-Nar (Survivors of Hellfire)
Switzerland 30, 89, 180
    cooperation with Egypt against
        terrorism, 146
    terrorist attacks, 107, 148
Syria, 31, 109, 171, 223, 229, 230
    Afghan alumni, 138
    inter-Arab cooperation against
        terrorism, 145, 182
    Islamic revolt in Hama, 1, 69, 146,
        158, 207
    and Jordanian fundamentalist organi-
        zations, 172, 177, 183, 184, 185,
        186
    Muslim Brotherhood in, 191, 206,
        207, 209, 218, 231, 232, 235
    opposition to Jordan, 168–9, 170
    rapprochement with Jordan, 207
    threat of Islamic fundamentalism, 7,
        8, 9, 145

Taha, Rifa'i, 29, 131, 258n
Taher, Essam Mohammad, 180
al-takfir trend, 4, 25, 26
    see also Jama'at al-Takfir wal Hijra; al-
        Samawiya; al-Shawkiyoun;
        al-Tawakuf wal Tabyeen
al-Tal, Abdullah, 168, 221
al-Tal, Wasfi, 170–1, 234
Tala'ie el-Fath (Vanguard of Conquest),
    28, 30–1, 127
Talal bin Abdullah, King of Jordan, 168
Taliat al-Muqatelin (Warrior Pioneers),
    31
Taliban, 140, 244
Talmasani, Omar, 55, 252n
al-Tamimi, Sheikh As'ad Bayud,
    183–4
al-tamkin (capability, to overthrow
    secular government), 58, 205
Tantawi, Mohammad Sayyid, 102, 106,
    134
Tarawnah, Fa'iz, 197

al-tarbiyya (education, according to
    Muslim Brotherhood), 22
al-Tawakuf wal Tabyeen, 32–3
Tirawi, Tawfiq, 182
Tora prison, 64, 116, 125
al-toujiyya (observance, according to the
    Muslim Brotherhood), 22
Tourabi, Hassan, 1, 8, 69, 70, 141,
    243–4
trade unions
    in Egypt, 36, 54–8, 60, 62–3, 75–8
    in Jordan, 188
Tunisia, 144, 177
Turkey, 1, 5, 177

Uda, Sheikh Abdel Aziz, 182
United Nations, 146, 151
United States, 88
    Afghan alumni, 138
    economic aid and ties to Egypt, 14,
        35
    support for Jordan, 168, 169, 170
    target of terrorism, 1–2, 107, 108
Upper Egypt, 14–15, 28
    illegal weapons, 89–92
    private mosques, 43
    terrorist organizations, 29, 86–7, 88,
        128
al-Usra al-Arabiya, 41
usra (Muslim Brotherhood "family"
    unit), 19, 189, 206, 212
usuliya (fundamentalism), 2, 246n

Vanguard of Conquest *see* Tala'ie el-
    Fath (Vanguard of Conquest)

al-Wa'ee, 176
al-Wafd, 42, 100, 133
Wafd party, 50, 53, 54
Warrior Pioneers (Taliat al-Muqatelin),
    31
Warriors for God *see* Army of
    Mohammad (Jaysh Mohammad)
al-Wasat party, 73–4, 159, 244
Wasel, Nasser Farid, 44
al-Watan al-Arabi, 180
al-Wathikoun min al-Naser, 28
al-Watidi, Akid Abdullah, 89
West
    and Egyptian terrorist groups, 137
    ties with Egypt, 35, 146–51
    see also United States

World Trade Center, 108, 109, 147

Yassin, Sheikh Ahmed, 2, 222, 225–6, 246*n*
Yemen, 5, 143
Youth of the Islamic Trumpet (Shabab al-Nafir al-Islami), 172, 174–5

Zaghlul, Sa'ad, 75
Zaki, Ahmed, 115
Zakzuk, Mohammad Hamdi, 44–5
al-Zawahiri, Ayman, 30, 132, 146, 148, 180
Zeidan, Samih, 172–3, 174
Zumur, Abud, 30, 31, 118